THE
Barbecue
COLLECTION

TRANSCONTINENTAL BOOKS
1100 René-Lévesque Boulevard West
24th floor
Montreal, Que. H3B 4X9
Tel: (514) 340-3587
Toll-free: 1-866-800-2500
www.canadianliving.com

Bibliothèque et Archives nationales du Québec
and Library and Archives Canada cataloguing
in publication

Chase, Andrew
The barbecue collection
"Canadian living".
Includes index.
ISBN 978-0-9809924-9-6
1. Barbecue cookery. I. Canadian living. II. Title.

TX840.B3C42 2010   641.5'784   C2010-940296-0
Project editor: Christina Anson Mine
Copy editor: Rehana Begg
Indexer: Gillian Watts
Art direction: Michael Erb
Design: Chris Bond
Production coordinator: Erin Poetschke

Printed in Canada
© Transcontinental Books, 2010
Legal deposit – 2nd quarter 2010
National Library of Quebec
National Library of Canada
ISBN 978-0-9809924-9-6

We acknowledge the financial support of our
publishing activity by the Government of
Canada through the BPDIP program of the
Department of Canadian Heritage.

For information on special rates for
corporate libraries and wholesale purchases,
please call 1-866-800-2500.

Canadian Living

THE Barbecue COLLECTION

The Best Barbecue Recipes from Our Kitchen to Your Backyard

Andrew Chase & The Canadian Living Test Kitchen

Transcontinental Books

Thrill of the Grill

Charcoal or Gas?

Grilling is enormously popular in Canada. Many dedicated cooks even grill throughout the winter bundled in parkas and tuques. Perhaps because of our relatively cold climate, we prefer gas grilling by a large margin (compared to Americans, who are almost evenly split).

While nothing can quite compare to open-fire wood grilling, charcoal gives a natural smoky flavour and intense heat. Lump charcoal burns hot and quickly, but many cooks prefer charcoal briquettes because they maintain a more even, longer-burning heat.

Gas burns clean, so you don't get a natural smoky flavour from it. But a handful of soaked wood chips can do the trick, adding a taste of natural smoke to your grilled dishes. Follow the manufacturer's instructions for using wood chips, as gas grills come in all shapes and sizes and have different specifications.

Cooking Temperatures

Grilling isn't an exact science. Because it's done outdoors, the temperature and wind – even humidity – can change cooking conditions, which affects timing and even appropriate grilling heat. So take the recommended times and temperatures in this cookbook as guidelines, not as scripture, and use common sense. If, for example, a recipe doesn't call for a covered grill but the weather is inclement, then close the lid anyway. Just remember that it's heat that cooks food, and anything that takes heat away from the grill will change the grilling results.

Always preheat your grill to the right temperature. Many come with temperature gauges attached to the lid, which makes preheating easy. You can set an ovenproof thermometer inside the grill (try to keep it slightly above the grates) or use the easy and surprisingly accurate hand test to gauge (right).

Heat Hand Test

Hold your hand, palm down, 2 to 3 inches/5 to 7.5 cm above the hot grill. Count how many seconds you can keep it there comfortably to determine the heat level.

5 seconds	Low
4 seconds	Medium
3 seconds	Medium-High
2 seconds	High

Grilling Temperatures

Low	325 to 350°F/ 160 to 180°C
Medium	350 to 375°F/ 180 to 190°C
Medium-High	375 to 400°F/ 190 to 200°C
High	425 to 450°F/ 220 to 230°C

Essential Barbecue Tools

- If you have a charcoal grill, a **chimney charcoal starter** is indispensable. You just crumble up a few sheets of newspaper on the bottom of the starter, pile charcoal over them, light the paper and, in 15 to 20 minutes, you have perfect glowing coals.

- Heat-resistant **grilling gloves** are a must for safety.

- Short **tongs** are much easier to use, but long tongs keep your hands away from the heat, so both are nice to have.

- A **long-handled fork** is useful, especially for large cuts of meat or poultry.

- A couple of **wide spatulas** make turning fish an easy task.

- A solid **wire brush** keeps the grates clean.

- An **instant-read thermometer** takes the guesswork out of determining the doneness of grilled meats and poultry. It helps you avoid cutting into the food and wasting delicious juices.

- **Grill pans and baskets** are useful for vegetables and small pieces of meat or poultry, and for grilling whole fish.

- If you're a rib lover, you might want to invest in a simple **rib rack**, which holds multiple racks of ribs at one time over indirect heat.

- **Silicone brushes** don't burn and let you baste foods easily without leaving nasty bristles behind.

Avoid Flare-Ups

Minimize barbecue flare-ups, which can scorch and char food, by keeping a clean grill. Turn heat to high after each use or when preheating until grease and residue have burned off, then scrub with a wire brush. Always keep a squirt bottle of water handy to douse flames. An even more effective way of putting out flare-ups is to use baking soda instead of water, but you must be extremely careful not to get it on your food – it tastes terrible. Most people prefer the water method.

Brochettes & Kabobs

Beef Satay

In Indonesia and Malaysia, beef, mutton and, occasionally, pork (for non-Muslims) satays are usually served with a sauce made from kecap manis, a sweet soy sauce. You can buy kecap manis at Chinese or Southeast Asian grocers and large grocery stores with Asian sections. Serve the satays with sliced cucumber and red onion.

1 tsp / 5 mL finely grated or minced **fresh ginger**

1 clove **garlic**, pressed or minced

1 tsp / 5 mL **salt**

½ tsp / 2 mL **black pepper**

½ tsp / 2 mL **ground coriander**

½ tsp / 2 mL **turmeric**

¼ tsp / 1 mL **cayenne pepper**

¼ tsp / 1 mL **ground cumin**

1 lb / 500 g **beef sirloin** or other **grilling steak**, or lamb or pork loin, cut into 3- x 1- x ¼-inch/8 x 2.5 x 0.5 cm strips

SWEET SOY SATAY SAUCE:

¼ cup / 60 mL **peanut** or vegetable **oil**

¼ cup / 60 mL thinly sliced **shallots**

3 cloves **garlic**, thinly sliced

1 tbsp / 30 mL chopped **Thai (bird-eye) chilies** or other hot peppers

⅓ cup / 75 mL **kecap manis**

¼ cup / 60 mL **lime juice**

3 tbsp / 45 mL finely chopped **roasted peanuts**

● **Sweet Soy Satay Sauce:** In small saucepan, heat oil over medium-high heat; fry shallots until golden. Remove with slotted spoon. Add garlic to pan; fry until golden. Remove with slotted spoon, reserving oil. In mortar with pestle, pound chilies to paste; add shallots and garlic and pound until almost smooth (or finely mince chilies, then add shallots and garlic and mince until almost smooth). Mix in kecap manis, lime juice and peanuts.

● Mix together 1 tbsp/15 mL of the reserved oil (save remainder for another use), ginger, garlic, salt, pepper, coriander, turmeric, cayenne and cumin; toss with beef until coated. Marinate for 30 minutes or, refrigerated, up to 8 hours.

● Thread onto skewers. Grill on greased grill over high heat, turning once, until desired doneness, about 4 minutes for medium. Serve with Sweet Soy Satay Sauce.

Makes 4 to 6 main-course servings.

TIP

If you can't find kecap manis for this recipe, boil together ⅓ cup/75 mL granulated sugar, ¼ cup/ 60 mL soy sauce and 1½ tbsp/22 mL fancy molasses until sugar is dissolved.

PER EACH OF 6 SERVINGS: about 224 cal, 17 g pro, 9 g total fat (2 g sat. fat), 20 g carb, 1 g fibre, 35 mg chol, 1,036 mg sodium, 370 mg potassium. % RDI: 3% calcium, 17% iron, 1% vit A, 5% vit C, 6% folate.

Citrus Steak Kabobs

If you wish, add other vegetables to these simple, brightly flavoured beef brochettes.

1 tsp / 5 mL grated **lime** or lemon **rind**

2 tbsp / 30 mL **lime** or lemon **juice**

1 tbsp / 15 mL **olive** or vegetable **oil**

2 cloves **garlic**, pressed or minced

Half to 1 **jalapeño pepper**, seeded and minced

1 tsp / 5 mL **chili powder**

½ tsp / 2 mL **ground cumin**

¼ tsp / 1 mL each **salt** and **black pepper**

1 lb / 500 g **grilling steak**, cut into 1-inch/2.5 cm cubes

1 each **sweet red** and **green pepper**, cut into 1-inch/2.5 cm pieces

● Mix together lime rind and juice, oil, garlic, jalapeño, chili powder, cumin, salt and pepper; toss with beef until coated. Let stand for 10 minutes.

● Alternately thread beef and peppers onto skewers. For rare, grill on greased grill over high heat, turning once, for about 6 minutes; for medium-rare to well-done, grill over medium-high heat until desired doneness, 10 to 12 minutes for medium.

Makes 4 main-course servings.

Soak wooden or bamboo skewers in water for about 30 minutes before using to keep them from charring.

PER SERVING: about 221 cal, 27 g pro, 10 g total fat (3 g sat. fat), 6 g carb, 1 g fibre, 65 mg chol, 202 mg sodium. % RDI: 3% calcium, 24% iron, 21% vit A, 163% vit C, 9% folate.

Steak Shish Kabobs

Middle Eastern spices add interest to a fine cut of steak.

Half **onion**, grated

2 tbsp / 30 mL **extra-virgin olive oil**

4 tsp / 20 mL **lemon juice**

2 cloves **garlic**, pressed or minced

½ tsp / 2 mL **ground allspice**

½ tsp / 2 mL **ground cumin**

¼ tsp / 1 mL **black pepper**

Generous pinch **cinnamon**

Generous pinch **cayenne pepper**

1½ lb / 750 g **rib eye** or strip loin **grilling steak**, cut into 1-inch/2.5 cm cubes

1 lb / 500 g **cherry tomatoes**

½ tsp / 2 mL **salt**

● Mix together onion, oil, lemon juice, garlic, allspice, cumin, pepper, cinnamon and cayenne; toss with beef until coated. Marinate for 20 minutes or, refrigerated, up to 4 hours.

● Alternately thread beef and tomatoes onto skewers; sprinkle with salt. For rare, grill on greased grill over high heat, turning once, for about 6 minutes; for medium-rare to well-done, grill over medium-high heat until desired doneness, 10 to 12 minutes for medium.

Makes 4 to 6 main-course servings.

Photo, page 32

When threading meat onto skewers, don't cram the pieces up against one another. Leave a little space for even cooking.

PER EACH OF 6 SERVINGS: about 252 cal, 20 g pro, 17 g total fat (6 g sat. fat), 4 g carb, 1 g fibre, 48 mg chol, 234 mg sodium. % RDI: 2% calcium, 19% iron, 6% vit A, 17% vit C, 6% folate.

Deli-Spiced Steak Kabobs with Pearl Onions

Grilling the onions on separate skewers ensures both the steak kabobs and onions are cooked perfectly.

1½ lb / 750 g **beef** or bison **grilling steak**, cut into 1-inch/2.5 cm cubes

1 tbsp / 15 mL **Deli-Style Steak Spice Mix** (below)

1 tbsp / 15 mL **vegetable oil**

PEARL ONION SKEWERS:

2 cups / 500 mL **pearl onions** (10 oz/300 g)

1 tbsp / 15 mL **vegetable oil**

2 tsp / 10 mL **Deli-Style Steak Spice Mix** (below)

● **Pearl Onion Skewers:** In saucepan of boiling water, boil unpeeled onions for 2 minutes; drain. Slip off skins; toss onions with oil. Thread onto skewers; sprinkle with spice mix.

● Toss together beef, spice mix and oil; thread onto skewers. For rare, grill beef on greased grill over high heat, turning once, for about 6 minutes; for medium-rare to well-done, grill over medium-high heat until desired doneness, 10 to 12 minutes for medium. Meanwhile, grill onions on greased grill over high or medium-high heat until lightly charred and tender, 3 to 5 minutes.

Makes 6 main-course servings.

Deli-Style Steak Spice Mix

● Coarsely grind together 1 tbsp/15 mL lightly toasted **coriander seeds**, 1 tbsp/15 mL **black peppercorns**; and 1 tsp/5 mL **dill seeds**. Mix in 4 tsp/20 mL **coarse sea salt** or kosher salt, 2 tsp/10 mL each **paprika** and **hot pepper flakes**; and 1½ tsp/7 mL **granulated garlic** (or 1 tsp/5 mL garlic powder). (Store in airtight container.)

Makes about 5 tbsp/75 mL.

PER SERVING (WITHOUT ONIONS): about 186 cal, 26 g pro, 8 g total fat (2 g sat. fat), 1 g carb, 1 g fibre, 56 mg chol, 252 mg sodium, 264 mg potassium. % RDI: 18% iron, 2% vit A, 2% folate.

Beef & Green Onion Kabobs

3 cloves **garlic**, minced

2 tbsp / 30 mL grated **fresh ginger**
(or 1 tsp/5 mL ground ginger)

2 tbsp / 30 mL **soy sauce**

2 tsp / 10 mL **rice vinegar** or cider
vinegar

2 tsp / 10 mL **sesame oil**

½ tsp / 2 mL **granulated sugar**

1 lb / 500 g **grilling steak**, cut into
1-inch/2.5 cm cubes

10 **green onions** (white and light
green parts only), cut into 2-inch/
5 cm lengths

● Mix together garlic, ginger, soy sauce, vinegar, sesame oil and sugar; toss with beef until coated. Let stand for 10 minutes.

● Reserving any remaining marinade, alternately thread beef and onions onto skewers; brush with marinade. For rare, grill on greased grill over high heat, turning once, for about 6 minutes; for medium-rare to well-done, grill over medium-high heat until desired doneness, 10 to 12 minutes for medium.

Makes 4 main-course servings.

Two categories of boneless beefsteaks work for kabobs.
The first is grilling steak. For un- or briefly marinated kabobs,
the most luxurious choices are rib-eye (well-marbled, tender and
tasty) and strip loin, or New York steaks (leaner and denser);
tenderloin is ultra-tender but can lack flavour unless well-aged.
Top sirloin, tri-tip and wing grilling steaks are lean and flavourful
but not as tender, and are suited to longer marinating. The second
type is marinating grilling steak, which needs long marinating.
We recommend inside or outside round or sirloin tip for kabobs.

PER SERVING: about 179 cal, 22 g pro, 7 g total fat (2 g sat. fat), 6 g carb, 1 g fibre, 51 mg chol, 563 mg sodium. % RDI: 4% calcium, 21% iron, 1% vit A, 8% vit C, 11% folate.

Beef Koftas with Pitas & Minted Yogurt

Koftas are Middle Eastern kabobs made from ground meat.

1 cup / 250 mL lightly packed **fresh parsley leaves**

3 **green onions**, coarsely chopped

1 tsp / 5 mL **dried mint**

¾ tsp / 4 mL **salt**

½ tsp / 2 mL **ground cumin**

½ tsp / 2 mL **paprika**

¼ tsp / 1 mL **black pepper**

1 **egg**

1 lb / 500 g **lean ground beef**

4 **whole wheat pitas**

MINTED YOGURT:

½ cup / 125 mL **plain yogurt**

2 tbsp / 30 mL minced **fresh parsley**

1 tsp / 5 mL **dried mint**

Pinch **salt**

1 tbsp / 15 mL **extra-virgin olive oil** (optional)

● In food processor, purée together parsley, onions, mint, salt, cumin, paprika and pepper. Transfer to large bowl; stir in egg and 2 tbsp/30 mL water. Mix in beef.

● Using generous 2 tbsp/30 mL each, shape into small sausages; thread lengthwise onto skewers. Grill, covered, on greased grill over medium heat, turning once, until no longer pink inside, about 12 minutes.

● Meanwhile, grill pitas, turning once, until crisp, about 4 minutes; cut into quarters.

● **Minted Yogurt:** Mix together yogurt, parsley, mint and salt; drizzle with oil (if using). Serve with koftas and pitas.

Makes 4 main-course servings.

PER SERVING: about 393 cal, 31 g pro, 14 g total fat (5 g sat. fat), 37 g carb, 5 g fibre, 109 mg chol, 862 mg sodium. % RDI: 10% calcium, 41% iron, 14% vit A, 42% vit C, 36% folate.

Lebanese Sweetbread Kabobs

Sweetbreads are delectable morsels indeed, the bulk of which are bought by high-end restaurants. Look for them at butchers that sell veal. Sweetbreads are not difficult to make, though they do require a little extra preparation before cooking.

1½ lb / 750 g **veal sweetbreads**

2 tbsp / 30 mL **dry sherry** or white wine, or 2 tsp/10 mL white wine vinegar

½ tsp / 2 mL **salt**

1½ tbsp / 22 mL **extra-virgin olive oil**

MARINADE:

½ cup / 125 mL **fresh parsley leaves**

½ cup / 125 mL **fresh mint leaves**

½ cup / 125 mL chopped **onion**

1 clove **garlic**, smashed

2 tbsp / 30 mL **lemon juice**

1 tsp / 5 mL **caraway seeds**, lightly crushed

¾ tsp / 4 mL **salt**

Generous ¼ tsp / 1.5 mL each **black pepper** and **ground allspice**

¼ tsp / 1 mL **granulated sugar**

Pinch **cayenne pepper**

MUSHROOMS:

8 oz / 250 g **white** or cremini **mushrooms**

1½ tbsp / 22 mL **extra-virgin olive oil**

1 tbsp / 15 mL **lemon juice**

¼ tsp / 1 mL **salt**

● Soak sweetbreads in a few changes of cold water for 1 hour; drain. Place in saucepan with enough water to cover, sherry and salt. Bring to boil; reduce heat and simmer just until no longer pink in centre, about 12 minutes. Let cool in pan; drain. Place sweetbreads on plate or in shallow pan; cover with plastic wrap and weigh down lightly. Refrigerate for at least 4 hours or overnight.

● **Marinade:** In food processor, pulse together parsley, mint, onion, garlic and lemon juice until very finely minced but not puréed; mix in caraway, salt, pepper, allspice, sugar and cayenne.

● Drain off any juices from sweetbreads; trim off thin outer membranes and any tough connective tissues. Cut into 1½-inch/4 cm chunks. Mix with olive oil and all but 2 tbsp/30 mL of the marinade. Marinate for 1 hour or, refrigerated, up to 8 hours.

● **Mushrooms:** Meanwhile, trim mushroom stems flush with caps; toss together mushrooms, remaining marinade, oil, lemon juice and salt until coated. Marinate for at least 1 or up to 8 hours.

● Reserving remaining marinade, alternately thread sweetbreads and mushrooms onto skewers. Grill over medium heat, turning often and basting with marinade for the first 5 minutes, until golden and tender, about 15 minutes.

Makes 4 to 6 main-course servings.

PER EACH OF 6 SERVINGS: about 202 cal, 18 g pro, 13 g total fat (3 g sat. fat), 4 g carb, 1 g fibre, 167 mg chol, 430 mg sodium, 378 mg potassium. % RDI: 3% calcium, 17% iron, 5% vit A, 38% vit C, 10% folate.

Souvlaki

These skewers of fragrant pork or lamb (or, in Canada, chicken) are a favourite in Greektowns and Greek restaurants. Souvlaki are usually served casually on pocketless pitas with the yogurt sauce tzatziki, tomatoes and fresh or pickled cucumbers. But you can enjoy them as a dinner with Greek Village Salad (page 505) and rice or potatoes.

2 lb / 1 kg **boneless pork** or lamb **shoulder** (or boneless chicken), cut into 1¼-inch/3 cm cubes

⅓ cup / 75 mL **extra-virgin olive oil**

3 tbsp / 45 mL **lemon juice**

3 tbsp / 45 mL **red wine**

2 tsp / 10 mL **coriander seeds**, coarsely ground

2 tsp / 10 mL **dried Greek oregano**, crumbled

1¼ tsp / 6 mL **salt**

½ tsp / 2 mL **black pepper**

Tzatziki (right)

● Toss together pork, oil, lemon juice, wine, coriander, 1½ tsp/7 mL of the oregano, ¼ tsp/1 mL of the salt and the pepper. Marinate, refrigerated, for 1 day.

● Thread onto skewers; sprinkle with remaining oregano. Grill over medium heat, turning often, until no longer pink in centre for pork or chicken, 12 to 15 minutes, or until desired doneness for lamb. Sprinkle with remaining salt; serve with Tzatziki.

Makes 6 to 8 main-course servings.

Tzatziki

● Mix 2 cups/500 mL shredded **cucumber** with 1 tsp/5 mL **salt**; let stand for 10 minutes. Squeeze out as much moisture from cucumbers as possible. Mix together cucumber; 1½ cups/375 mL full-fat **Balkan-style plain yogurt**; 3 cloves **garlic**, minced; and 2 tbsp/30 mL each **lemon juice** and **extra-virgin olive oil**. If desired, flavour with 3 tbsp/45 mL chopped **fresh dill**, 2 tbsp/30 mL chopped fresh parsley or 2 tsp/10 mL dried mint.

Makes 2¼ cups/560 mL.

PER EACH OF 8 SERVINGS: about 328 cal, 25 g pro, 22 g total fat (7 g sat. fat), 6 g carb, 1 g fibre, 81 mg chol, 583 mg sodium, 442 mg potassium. % RDI: 8% calcium, 11% iron, 3% vit A, 7% vit C, 6% folate.

Italian Pork Tenderloin Brochettes

This Italian method of grilling meat with bread (spiedini) results in perfectly cooked pork tenderloin and crispy seasoned bread.

1½ lb / 750 g **pork tenderloin**, cut into ¾-inch/2 cm slices

8 slices **pancetta**, halved

Half **baguette**, cut into ¾-inch/2 cm slices

8 fresh **bay** or sage **leaves**

¼ tsp / 1 mL each **salt** and **black pepper**

3 tbsp / 45 mL **extra-virgin olive oil**

● Wrap each pork slice in pancetta. Onto skewers, thread in order: bread, pork, bay leaf, pork, bread, pork, bay leaf, pork, bread. Sprinkle with salt and pepper; drizzle with oil.

● Grill, covered, over medium-high heat, turning once, until just a hint of pink remains inside pork, about 12 minutes.

Makes 4 main-course servings.

PER SERVING: about 406 cal, 45 g pro, 15 g total fat (5 g sat. fat), 19 g carb, 1 g fibre, 108 mg chol, 512 mg sodium. % RDI: 4% calcium, 24% iron, 1% vit A, 2% vit C, 15% folate.

Honey-Mustard Pork Kabobs

2 tbsp / 30 mL **hot** or Dijon **mustard**

2 tbsp / 30 mL **liquid honey**

1 tbsp / 15 mL **vegetable oil**

3 cloves **garlic**, pressed or minced

½ tsp / 2 mL **ground ginger**

¼ tsp / 1 mL each **salt** and **black pepper**

1 lb / 500 g **pork loin** or tenderloin, cut into 1-inch/2.5 cm cubes

● Mix together mustard, honey, oil, garlic, ginger, salt and pepper; toss with pork until coated. Let stand for 10 minutes.

● Reserving remaining marinade, thread onto skewers; brush with marinade. Grill, covered, on greased grill over medium-high heat, turning once, until just a hint of pink remains inside, about 12 minutes.

Makes 4 main-course servings.

When choosing pork to marinate, check the label and choose pork that hasn't been "seasoned," an unfortunate brining method now common in supermarket pork. So much fat has been bred out of modern pigs that the meat is dry when even slightly overcooked, so it is injected with a saline solution and labelled "seasoned." In our experience, this procedure prevents the pork from absorbing marinades and results in moist but flabby meat.

PER SERVING: about 199 cal, 22 g pro, 8 g total fat (2 g sat. fat), 8 g carb, 0 g fibre, 60 mg chol, 247 mg sodium. % RDI: 3% calcium, 7% iron, 2% vit C, 1% folate.

Jerk Pork Kabobs

Hot and spicy jerk seasoning has become the emblem of Jamaican cuisine. Usually whole pork shoulders are jerked and spit-barbecued; kabobs are easier to prepare and serve.

6 **green onions**, chopped

4 **Scotch bonnet (habanero) peppers**, seeded and chopped

4 cloves **garlic**, smashed

¼ cup / 60 mL **lime juice**

1 tbsp / 15 mL chopped **fresh ginger**

1 tsp / 5 mL **fresh thyme leaves**

2 tbsp / 30 mL **soy sauce**

½ tsp / 2 mL **ground allspice**

½ tsp / 2 mL **ground coriander**

¼ tsp / 1 mL **black pepper**

¼ tsp / 1 mL **nutmeg**

Pinch **cinnamon**

3 lb / 1.5 kg **pork loin** or shoulder, cut into 1½-inch/4 cm cubes

2 tbsp / 30 mL **vegetable oil**

● In food processor, purée together green onions, hot peppers, garlic, lime juice, ginger and thyme. Stir in soy sauce, allspice, coriander, pepper, nutmeg and cinnamon; set aside 2 tbsp/30 mL. In bowl, toss pork with remainder until coated. Marinate, refrigerated, for at least 3 hours or up to 1 day.

● Bring pork to room temperature; thread onto skewers. Mix reserved seasoning with oil. Grill skewers, covered, on greased grill over indirect medium heat (see Tip, below), basting occasionally with oil mixture, until just a hint of pink remains inside for loin or until no longer pink inside for fattier shoulder, 30 to 40 minutes.

Makes 8 main-course servings.

Photo, page 294

To grill over indirect heat on gas grill, set foil drip pan under 1 rack of 2-burner barbecue or under centre of 3-burner barbecue. Heat remaining burner(s) to temperature indicated (see Grilling Temperatures, page 10). For charcoal grill, place drip pan in centre and arrange hot charcoal on either side. Set meat on greased grill over drip pan. Grill as directed.

PER SERVING: about 321 cal, 37 g pro, 17 g total fat (5 g sat. fat), 3 g carb, 1 g fibre, 109 mg chol, 371 mg sodium. % RDI: 4% calcium, 17% iron, 1% vit A, 10% vit C, 9% folate.

Island Pork Loin & Pineapple Brochettes

The citrus marinade, laced with hot peppers, offsets the sweet fresh pineapple in this West Indian–inspired grill.

2 or 3 **Scotch bonnet (habanero) peppers**, halved and seeded

4 cloves **garlic**, smashed

⅓ cup / 75 mL chopped **onion**

2 tbsp / 30 mL each **lime juice** and **orange juice**

1 tbsp / 15 mL **tomato paste**

2 tsp / 10 mL chopped **fresh ginger**

¾ tsp / 4 mL **ground cumin**

¾ tsp / 4 mL **dried oregano**, crumbled

¾ tsp / 4 mL **salt**

½ tsp / 2 mL **ground allspice**

¼ tsp / 1 mL **black pepper**

1¼ lb / 625 g **pork loin** or shoulder, cut into 1-inch/2.5 cm cubes

3 cups / 750 mL cubed (1 inch/2.5 cm) **fresh pineapple**

1 tbsp / 15 mL **vegetable oil**

Fresh coriander sprigs

Lime wedges

● In blender or food processor, purée together hot peppers, garlic, onion, lime and orange juices, tomato paste and ginger; transfer to bowl. Stir in cumin, oregano, ½ tsp/2 mL of the salt, allspice and pepper; toss with pork until coated. Marinate, refrigerated, for at least 3 or up to 8 hours.

● Toss pineapple with remaining salt. Reserving any remaining marinade, alternately thread pork and pineapple onto skewers. Stir oil into marinade; brush over skewers. Grill over medium-high heat, turning once, until just a hint of pink remains inside for loin or until no longer pink inside for fattier shoulder, 12 to 15 minutes. Garnish with coriander; serve with lime wedges.

Makes 4 to 6 main-course servings.

PER EACH OF 6 SERVINGS (WITHOUT LIME WEDGES): about 198 cal, 24 g pro, 5 g total fat (1 g sat. fat), 15 g carb, 2 g fibre, 47 mg chol, 333 mg sodium. % RDI: 3% calcium, 10% iron, 16% vit A, 93% vit C, 7% folate.

Top to bottom: Pork & Poblano Kabobs
(opposite), Steak Shish Kabobs (page 18),
Sweet & Sour Shrimp Kabobs (page 74)

Pork & Poblano Kabobs

Poblano peppers have just a hint of heat and a full, dark flavour.

2 cloves **garlic**, pressed or minced

3 tbsp / 45 mL **tomato-based chili sauce** or ketchup

2 tbsp + 2 tsp / 30 mL + 10 mL **olive** or vegetable **oil**

2 tsp / 10 mL **lime juice**

1½ tsp / 7 mL **chipotle chili powder**

¾ tsp / 4 mL **salt**

½ tsp / 2 mL crumbled **dried marjoram**

1½ lb / 750 g **pork loin** or shoulder, cut into 1-inch/2.5 cm cubes

2 **poblano peppers** or 1 sweet green pepper, cut into 1-inch/2.5 cm pieces

Half **red onion**, cut into 1-inch/ 2.5 cm pieces

Lime wedges

● Mix together garlic, chili sauce, 2 tbsp/30 mL of the oil, lime juice, chipotle chili powder, ½ tsp/2 mL of the salt and marjoram; toss with pork until coated. Marinate for 20 minutes or, refrigerated, up to 8 hours.

● Stir together peppers, onion and remaining oil and salt until coated. Alternately thread pork, peppers and onion onto skewers. Grill over medium heat, turning once, until just a hint of pink remains inside for loin or until no longer pink inside for fattier shoulder, about 15 minutes. Serve with lime wedges.

Makes 4 to 6 main-course servings.

PER EACH OF 6 SERVINGS: about 226 cal, 23 g pro, 12 g total fat (3 g sat. fat), 6 g carb, 1 g fibre, 60 mg chol, 394 mg sodium. % RDI: 2% calcium, 9% iron, 3% vit A, 27% vit C, 4% folate.

Philippine Pork Kabobs

Garlic, bay leaf, black pepper and cloves is such a popular combination of seasonings in the Philippines that they are sold packaged together at every corner store.

¼ cup / 60 mL **soy sauce**

2 tbsp / 30 mL minced **fresh coriander**

2 tbsp / 30 mL **rice vinegar**

2 cloves **garlic**, pressed or minced

1 tbsp / 15 mL minced **fresh ginger**

1 **bay leaf**

½ tsp / 2 mL **black pepper**

Generous pinch **ground cloves**

Generous pinch **cayenne pepper**

1½ lb / 750 g **boneless pork shoulder** or loin, cut into 1½-inch/4 cm cubes

BASTING SAUCE:

3 tbsp / 45 mL **ketchup**

2 tbsp / 30 mL **lime juice**

1 tbsp / 15 mL **granulated sugar**

1 tbsp / 15 mL **vegetable oil**

● Mix together soy sauce, coriander, vinegar, garlic, ginger, bay leaf, pepper, cloves and cayenne; toss with pork until coated. Marinate, refrigerated, for at least 2 hours or up to 1 day. Thread onto skewers.

● **Basting Sauce:** Mix together ketchup, lime juice, sugar and oil. Grill skewers, covered, on greased grill over medium-high heat, turning often and brushing with sauce, until no longer pink inside for fattier shoulder or until just a hint of pink remains inside for loin, 12 to 15 minutes.

Makes 4 main-course servings.

PER SERVING: about 270 cal, 28 g pro, 13 g total fat (4 g sat. fat), 9 g carb, trace fibre, 80 mg chol, 877 mg sodium. % RDI: 3% calcium, 13% iron, 2% vit A, 5% vit C, 5% folate.

Thai Minced Pork Kabobs

2 **shallots** (or 1 green onion), minced

2 cloves **garlic**, pressed or minced

4 **Thai (bird-eye) chilies** (optional), minced

½ cup / 125 mL minced **fresh coriander**

¼ cup / 60 mL ground **roasted peanuts**

1 **egg**

4 tsp / 20 mL **fish sauce** or soy sauce

2 tsp / 10 mL minced **lemongrass**

2 tsp / 10 mL packed **brown sugar**

2 tsp / 10 mL **lime juice**

2 to 4 tsp / 10 to 20 mL **Thai red curry paste**

1 lb / 500 g lean **ground pork**

Fresh coriander sprigs

Lime wedges

● Stir together shallots, garlic, chilies (if using), coriander, 3 tbsp/45 mL of the peanuts, egg, fish sauce, lemongrass, sugar, lime juice and curry paste; mix in pork.

● Using heaping 1 tbsp/15 mL each, shape into small sausages; thread lengthwise onto skewers. Refrigerate for at least 1 or up to 12 hours.

● Grill, covered, on greased grill over medium heat, turning once, until no longer pink inside, about 12 minutes. Sprinkle with remaining peanuts; garnish with coriander sprigs. Serve with lime wedges.

Makes 4 to 6 main-course servings.

PER EACH OF 6 SERVINGS (WITHOUT LIME WEDGES): about 195 cal, 17 g pro, 12 g total fat (4 g sat. fat), 4 g carb, 1 g fibre, 80 mg chol, 360 mg sodium. % RDI: 3% calcium, 7% iron, 3% vit A, 9% folate.

Grilled Sausage Spiedini

*Serve these brochettes with mustard, Balsamic Grilled Peppers (below)
and a juicy tomato salad. Grill the peppers first so that they cool down enough
to allow peeling.*

1 lb / 500 g **Hot Italian Sausages** (page 139) or other Italian sausages

1 piece (8 inches/20 cm) **baguette**, cut into 1-inch/2.5 cm cubes

Half **red onion**, cut into 1-inch/ 2.5 cm pieces

2 tbsp / 30 mL **extra-virgin olive oil**

1 clove **garlic**, pressed or minced

Pinch each **salt** and **black pepper**

● Prick sausages with fork. Microwave, covered, at high until no longer pink, about 5 minutes. Cut into 1½-inch/4 cm pieces.

● Alternately thread sausage, bread and onion onto skewers. Mix together oil, garlic, salt and pepper; brush over bread. Grill, covered, over medium heat, turning often, until browned and onion is tender, about 10 minutes.

Makes 4 main-course servings.

Balsamic Grilled Peppers

● Seed, core and cut 3 **sweet peppers** into eighths. Grill, covered, on greased grill over medium-high heat, turning once, until tender, about 10 minutes. Peel if desired. Toss together peppers, 2 tbsp/30 mL **balsamic vinegar**, 1 tbsp/15 mL each chopped **fresh basil** and **extra-virgin olive oil**, and pinch each **granulated sugar**, **salt** and **black pepper**.

Makes 4 servings.

PER SERVING (WITHOUT PEPPERS): about 354 cal, 19 g pro, 23 g total fat (7 g sat. fat), 17 g carb, 1 g fibre, 48 mg chol, 854 mg sodium. % RDI: 4% calcium, 14% iron, 5% vit C, 11% folate.

Herbed Lamb Kabobs

2 cloves **garlic**, smashed

2 **anchovy fillets**

1 **green hot pepper**, seeded and chopped

½ cup / 125 mL chopped **fresh coriander**

⅓ cup / 75 mL packed **fresh mint leaves**

¼ cup / 60 mL chopped **onion**

3 tbsp / 45 mL **extra-virgin olive oil**

2 tbsp / 30 mL **lemon** or lime **juice**

1 tbsp / 15 mL chopped **fresh ginger**

2 tsp / 10 mL **fennel seeds**

1 tsp / 5 mL **salt**

½ tsp / 2 mL **ground cumin**

¼ tsp / 1 mL **black pepper**

Pinch **ground cloves**

12 **mushrooms**

1½ lb / 750 g **boneless lamb leg** or shoulder, cut into 1-inch/2.5 cm cubes

● In food processor, purée together garlic, anchovies, hot pepper, coriander, mint, onion, half of the oil, the lemon juice, ginger, fennel seeds, salt, cumin, pepper and cloves. Transfer 1 tbsp/15 mL to bowl; toss with mushrooms and remaining oil. In separate bowl, toss lamb with remainder. Marinate for 20 minutes or, refrigerated, up to 8 hours.

● Alternately thread lamb and mushrooms onto skewers. Grill over medium-high heat, turning often, until lamb is medium-rare, 8 to 10 minutes.

Makes 4 to 6 main-course servings.

PER EACH OF 6 SERVINGS: about 213 cal, 22 g pro, 12 g total fat (3 g sat. fat), 4 g carb, 1 g fibre, 76 mg chol, 452 mg sodium. % RDI: 3% calcium, 20% iron, 2% vit A, 7% vit C, 4% folate.

Indian Minced Lamb Kabobs

These authentically spiced North Indian lamb kabobs give any barbecue international flair. Serve them with Indian-Spiced Coleslaw (page 478).

½ cup / 125 mL **raw cashews** or blanched almonds

6 green **hot peppers**, seeded and chopped

Half **onion**, chopped

2 tbsp / 30 mL chopped **fresh ginger**

2 tbsp / 30 mL **butter**, melted

1 **egg**

1 **egg yolk**

1¾ tsp / 9 mL **salt**

1 tsp / 5 mL **turmeric**

½ tsp / 2 mL **white pepper**

¼ tsp / 1 mL **cayenne pepper**

¼ tsp / 1 mL each **ground cardamom**, **cinnamon**, **cloves**, **cumin**, **nutmeg** and **black pepper** (or 1½ tsp/7 mL garam masala)

1½ lb / 750 g **ground lamb**

⅓ cup / 75 mL finely chopped **fresh coriander**

● In food processor, purée together cashews, hot peppers, onion, ginger and butter. Whisk egg with egg yolk; whisk in cashew paste, salt, turmeric, white pepper, cayenne, cardamom, cinnamon, cloves, cumin, nutmeg and black pepper. Mix in lamb and coriander. Refrigerate for at least 2 hours or up to 1 day.

● With moistened hands, using ¼ cup/60 mL each, shape into small sausages; thread each lengthwise onto skewer. Grill, covered, on greased grill over medium heat, turning once, until no longer pink inside, about 12 minutes.

Makes 6 to 8 main-course servings.

Photo, page 479

PER EACH OF 8 SERVINGS: about 266 cal, 18 g pro, 20 g total fat (8 g sat. fat), 4 g carb, 1 g fibre, 114 mg chol, 580 mg sodium. % RDI: 3% calcium, 16% iron, 6% vit A, 7% vit C, 12% folate.

Sage Lamb Kabobs

Tiny cubes of lamb really soak up the simple Italian seasonings.

2 tbsp / 30 mL **olive oil**

2 tbsp / 30 mL thinly sliced **fresh sage leaves**

1 tsp / 5 mL minced **garlic**

½ tsp / 2 mL **salt**

½ tsp / 2 mL **black pepper**

1 lb / 500 g **lamb shoulder**, cut into ½-inch/1 cm cubes

● Mix together oil, sage, garlic, salt and pepper; toss with lamb until coated. Marinate, refrigerated, for at least 4 hours or overnight.

● Thread onto skewers. Grill over medium-high heat, turning often, until medium-rare, 8 to 10 minutes.

Makes 4 main-course servings.

PER SERVING: about 244 cal, 22 g pro, 17 g total fat (4 g sat. fat), 1 g carb, trace fibre, 78 mg chol, 362 mg sodium, 327 mg potassium. % RDI: 3% calcium, 12% iron, 8% folate.

Spiced Lamb Kabobs

If you like, thread vegetables, such as sweet or hot peppers, onions and cherry tomatoes, onto the skewers.

1 tsp / 5 mL **curry powder**

1 tsp / 5 mL **coriander seeds**

¾ tsp / 4 mL **paprika**

¾ tsp / 4 mL **cumin seeds**

½ tsp / 2 mL **dried thyme**

½ tsp / 2 mL **hot pepper flakes**

¼ cup / 60 mL minced **fresh parsley**

¼ cup / 60 mL **olive oil**

2 cloves **garlic**, minced

1 tbsp / 15 mL **lemon juice**

¾ tsp / 4 mL each **salt** and **black pepper**

1 lb / 500 g lean **boneless lamb leg** or shoulder, cut into 1-inch/2.5 cm cubes

● In skillet over medium-low heat, toast curry powder, coriander seeds, paprika, cumin seeds, thyme and hot pepper flakes until fragrant, 30 to 60 seconds. Let cool slightly. Grind to fine powder.

● Mix together spices, parsley, oil, garlic, lemon juice, salt and pepper; toss with lamb until coated. Marinate, refrigerated, for at least 2 or up to 8 hours, stirring occasionally.

● Reserving remaining marinade, thread lamb onto skewers; brush with marinade. Grill, covered, on greased grill over medium-high heat, turning often, until medium-rare, about 12 minutes.

Makes 4 main-course servings.

41

PER SERVING: about 283 cal, 23 g pro, 20 g total fat (4 g sat. fat), 2 g carb, 1 g fibre, 74 mg chol, 496 mg sodium. % RDI: 3% calcium, 22% iron, 6% vit A, 7% vit C, 11% folate.

Lamb Kabobs with Kachumber Salad

An uncomplicated Indian marinade flavours and tenderizes these lamb kabobs.

1 cup / 250 mL **Balkan-style plain yogurt**

1 tbsp / 15 mL **vegetable oil**

2 cloves **garlic**, minced

1 tbsp / 15 mL grated **fresh ginger**

1 tsp / 5 mL **ground cumin**

1 tsp / 5 mL **ground coriander**

1 tsp / 5 mL **turmeric**

1 tsp / 5 mL **lime juice**

½ tsp / 2 mL **salt**

2½ lb / 1.25 kg **boneless lamb leg** or shoulder, cut into 1½-inch/4 cm cubes

KACHUMBER SALAD:

1 cup / 250 mL coarsely chopped **cucumber**

1 cup / 250 mL coarsely chopped **red onion**

1 cup / 250 mL coarsely chopped **tomato**

2 tbsp / 30 mL coarsely chopped **fresh coriander**

1 **green hot pepper**, chopped

2 tbsp / 30 mL **lime juice**

¼ tsp / 1 mL **granulated sugar**

¼ tsp / 1 mL **salt**

¼ tsp / 1 mL **cayenne pepper**

● Drain yogurt in cheesecloth-lined sieve set over bowl for 30 minutes. Transfer yogurt to clean bowl, discarding whey. Stir in oil, garlic, ginger, cumin, coriander, turmeric, lime juice and salt; toss with lamb until coated. Marinate, refrigerated, for at least 15 minutes or up to 8 hours.

● **Kachumber Salad:** Toss together cucumber, onion, tomato, coriander, hot pepper, lime juice, sugar, salt and cayenne.

● Thread lamb onto skewers. Grill, covered, on greased grill over medium-high heat, turning once, until medium-rare, about 10 minutes. Serve with Kachumber Salad.

Makes 6 to 8 main-course servings.

PER EACH OF 8 SERVINGS: about 227 cal, 27 g pro, 10 g total fat (4 g sat. fat), 6 g carb, 1 g fibre, 97 mg chol, 269 mg sodium, 335 mg potassium. % RDI: 6% calcium, 18% iron, 4% vit A, 10% vit C, 5% folate.

Adana Lamb Kabobs

These beautifully spiced kabobs, from the Turkish city of Adana, are grilled on long metal skewers and served with Turkish Onion Salad (below) and sliced or chopped cucumber and tomatoes drizzled with extra-virgin olive oil.

1 lb / 500 g **ground lamb**

1 small **onion**, minced

1 large clove **garlic**, pressed or minced

½ cup / 125 mL finely chopped **fresh parsley**

⅓ cup / 75 mL puréed **roasted red pepper**

1½ tsp / 7 mL **ground coriander**

1 tsp / 5 mL **ground cumin**

1 tsp / 5 mL **salt**

1 tsp / 5 mL **hot paprika**, or ¾ tsp/ 4 mL sweet paprika and ¼ tsp/1 mL cayenne pepper

¼ tsp / 1 mL **black pepper**

1 tbsp / 15 mL (approx) **olive oil**

● Mix together lamb, onion, garlic, parsley, red pepper purée, coriander, cumin, salt, paprika and pepper until smooth. Refrigerate for at least 2 hours or, preferably, overnight.

● With hands, knead meat and shape into tight 1-inch/ 2.5 cm diameter cylinders around long metal skewers, each about two-thirds length of skewer. Brush with oil to coat lightly. Grill on greased grill over medium heat, turning occasionally, until no longer pink inside, about 10 minutes.

Makes 4 to 6 main-course servings.

Turkish Onion Salad

3 cups / 750 mL thinly sliced **Spanish**, sweet or white **onion**

½ tsp + pinch / 2 mL + pinch **salt**

1 tbsp / 15 mL **lemon juice**

1½ tsp / 7 mL **sumac**

3 tbsp / 45 mL chopped **fresh parsley** or dill

1 tsp / 5 mL **extra-virgin olive oil**

● Mix onion with ½ tsp/2 mL of the salt, using hands to rub in; let stand for 30 minutes. Rinse and drain onion well, lightly squeezing out excess moisture. Toss together onion, lemon juice, sumac and pinch salt until coated; toss in parsley and oil. Let stand for at least 5 minutes before serving.

Makes 4 to 6 servings.

PER EACH OF 6 SERVINGS WITH ONION SALAD: about 208 cal, 14 g pro, 14 g total fat (5 g sat. fat), 8 g carb, 2 g fibre, 51 mg chol, 626 mg sodium, 348 mg potassium. % RDI: 4% calcium, 14% iron, 12% vit A, 58% vit C, 17% folate.

Devilled Kidney Kabobs

If you have never had the pleasure of eating lamb kidneys before, you will be delighted by their mild flavour and lovely texture. They are prized and expensive in many parts of the world but remain an economical treat in Canada.

8 **lamb kidneys** or 1 lb/500 g cubed veal kidneys

1 tsp / 5 mL **salt**

16 **mushrooms**, halved

MARINADE:

3 tbsp / 45 mL **olive oil**

2 tbsp / 30 mL **lemon juice**

2 cloves **garlic**, minced

1 tbsp / 15 mL **Worcestershire sauce**

½ tsp / 2 mL **black pepper**

¼ tsp / 1 mL **salt**

BASTING SAUCE:

¼ cup / 60 mL **butter**, melted

2 tbsp / 30 mL chopped **fresh parsley**

1 tbsp / 15 mL **hot** or Dijon **mustard**

● Combine kidneys, 4 cups/1 L cold water and salt; soak for 30 minutes. Drain and rinse; drain well. Cut each kidney in half horizontally; cut out white centre.

● **Marinade:** Mix together oil, lemon juice, garlic, Worcestershire sauce, pepper and salt; toss with kidneys until coated. Marinate, refrigerated, for 30 minutes. Alternately thread kidneys and 2 mushroom halves onto skewers.

● **Basting Sauce:** Mix together butter, parsley and mustard. Grill skewers, covered, on greased grill over medium-high heat, turning and basting often with sauce, until kidneys are crisp but still pink inside, about 10 minutes.

Makes 4 main-course servings.

VARIATION

Devilled Liver Kabobs

Instead of kidneys, use halved chicken livers or cubed calves' or baby beef liver. Do not soak.

PER SERVING: about 231 cal, 17 g pro, 17 g total fat (8 g sat. fat), 4 g carb, 1 g fibre, 391 mg chol, 458 mg sodium. % RDI: 2% calcium, 64% iron, 20% vit A, 18% vit C, 29% folate.

Lemon Chicken Kabobs

2 tbsp / 30 mL **olive oil**

2 tbsp / 30 mL **lemon juice**

3 cloves **garlic**, pressed or minced

½ tsp / 2 mL **dried thyme**

½ tsp / 2 mL **salt**

¼ tsp / 1 mL **black pepper**

1 lb / 500 g **boneless skinless chicken breasts**, cut into 1-inch/2.5 cm cubes

1 **sweet green** or 2 banana **peppers**, cut into 1-inch/2.5 cm pieces

● Mix together oil, lemon juice, garlic, thyme, salt and pepper; toss with chicken until coated. Marinate for 15 minutes or, refrigerated, up to 1 day.

● Alternately thread chicken and pepper onto skewers. Grill over medium-high heat, turning occasionally, until chicken is browned and no longer pink inside, about 12 minutes.

Makes 4 main-course servings.

PER SERVING: about 189 cal, 26 g pro, 8 g total fat (1 g sat. fat), 3 g carb, 1 g fibre, 66 mg chol, 303 mg sodium. % RDI: 1% calcium, 6% iron, 2% vit A, 40% vit C, 4% folate.

Southwest Chicken & Okra Skewers

A favourite of the American South, okra is a fabulous crispy vegetable when grilled.

1½ lb / 750 g **boneless skinless chicken breasts** or thighs, cut into 1-inch/ 2.5 cm cubes

1 bunch **green onions**, cut into 1½-inch/4 cm lengths

12 **okra pods**, halved crosswise

12 large or 24 small **cherry tomatoes**

1 tbsp / 15 mL **peanut** or vegetable **oil**

CHIPOTLE GLAZE:

2 cloves **garlic**, pressed or minced

1 tbsp / 15 mL **peanut** or vegetable **oil**

⅓ cup / 75 mL **bottled strained** or crushed **tomatoes**

2 tbsp / 30 mL packed **brown sugar**

2 tbsp / 30 mL **dark soy sauce**

1 tbsp / 15 mL **cider vinegar**

2 or 3 **canned** or soaked dried **chipotle peppers**, minced

½ tsp / 2 mL **dried oregano**, crumbled

¼ tsp / 1 mL **ground cumin**

2 tbsp / 30 mL **lime juice**

● **Chipotle Glaze:** In small saucepan over medium-low heat, heat garlic with oil until fragrant, 1 to 2 minutes; stir in tomatoes, sugar, soy sauce, vinegar, chipotles, oregano and cumin. Bring to boil; reduce heat and simmer, stirring occasionally, until thickened, 10 to 12 minutes. Stir in lime juice. Press through fine sieve over bowl; discard pepper seeds and skins.

● Alternately thread chicken, onions, okra and tomatoes onto skewers; brush with oil. Grill over medium-high heat, turning often, until just a hint of pink remains inside chicken, about 10 minutes. Brush with Chipotle Glaze; grill, turning once and basting again with glaze, until chicken is no longer pink inside, about 2 minutes.

Makes 6 main-course servings.

PER SERVING: about 212 cal, 28 g pro, 6 g total fat (1 g sat. fat), 12 g carb, 2 g fibre, 66 mg chol, 458 mg sodium. % RDI: 5% calcium, 11% iron, 9% vit A, 23% vit C, 15% folate.

Chicken & Prosciutto Brochettes

Fresh basil complements the salty prosciutto and livens up simple chicken kabobs.

1 cup / 250 mL lightly packed **fresh basil leaves**

¼ cup / 60 mL **extra-virgin olive oil**

3 cloves **garlic**

½ tsp / 2 mL **salt**

4 **boneless skinless chicken breasts**

8 slices **prosciutto**

8 slices (½ inch/1 cm thick) **yellow** or green **zucchini**, halved

● In food processor, pulse basil, half of the oil, the garlic and salt to rough paste. Cut chicken horizontally in half; between waxed paper, pound each to ¼-inch/ 5 mm thickness.

● Place each slice prosciutto on work surface; top with chicken. Spread with generous 1 tsp/5 mL of the basil mixture; roll up and cut in half crosswise.

● Alternately thread 2 chicken rolls and 2 zucchini halves onto skewers; brush with remaining oil. Grill, covered, over medium-high heat, turning once, until chicken is no longer pink inside, about 10 minutes.

Makes 4 main-course servings.

SUBSTITUTION

These kabobs are also wonderful with baby artichokes instead of zucchini. To prepare baby artichokes, pull off any tough outer leaves; trim off tops and remove prickly inner leaves and choke. Boil with 2 slices lemon in salted water until almost tender, about 10 minutes. Slice thickly.

PER SERVING: about 342 cal, 38 g pro, 18 g total fat (4 g sat. fat), 4 g carb, 2 g fibre, 100 mg chol, 778 mg sodium. % RDI: 4% calcium, 8% iron, 6% vit A, 6% vit C, 8% folate.

Chicken Bacon Brochettes

Traditional English flavourings give a boost to mild chicken breast.

2 tbsp / 30 mL **vegetable oil**

2 tsp / 10 mL **Worcestershire sauce**

2 tsp / 10 mL **soy sauce**

½ tsp / 2 mL **malt** or other **vinegar**

¼ tsp / 1 mL **black pepper**

1 lb / 500 g **boneless skinless chicken breasts**, cut into twelve 1½-inch/ 4 cm cubes

12 large **mushrooms**

2 tsp / 10 mL **lemon juice**

¼ tsp / 1 mL **salt**

4 slices **bacon**, cut into thirds

4 **green onions**, cut into thirds

● Mix together half of the oil, the Worcestershire sauce, soy sauce, vinegar and pepper; toss with chicken until coated. Let stand for 20 minutes.

● Meanwhile, toss together mushrooms, remaining oil, lemon juice and salt; let stand for 20 minutes. Reserving remaining marinade, wrap each chicken cube in bacon; thread onto skewers alternately with mushrooms and onions.

● Grill, covered, on greased grill over medium-high heat, for 5 minutes. Turn and brush with marinade. Grill until chicken is no longer pink inside, 5 to 7 minutes.

Makes 4 main-course servings.

PER SERVING: about 245 cal, 29 g pro, 12 g total fat (3 g sat. fat), 5 g carb, 1 g fibre, 72 mg chol, 509 mg sodium. % RDI: 2% calcium, 13% iron, 1% vit A, 7% vit C, 9% folate.

Chicken & Mango Kabobs

These pretty tropical kabobs are slightly sweet, mildly tart and just a little bit spicy.

1 tsp / 5 mL grated **lime rind**

¼ cup / 60 mL **lime juice**

2 tbsp / 30 mL **peanut** or vegetable **oil**

3 cloves **garlic**, minced

2 tsp / 10 mL **chili powder**

½ tsp / 2 mL **salt**

¼ tsp / 1 mL **cayenne pepper**

1 lb / 500 g **boneless skinless chicken breasts**, cut into 1-inch/2.5 cm cubes

2 tsp / 10 mL **liquid honey**

2 **mangoes**, cut into ¾-inch/2 cm cubes

1 **sweet red pepper**, cut into ¾-inch/ 2 cm pieces

12 red or white **pearl onions**, or 1 small red or sweet onion, cut into 1-inch/ 2.5 cm pieces

● Mix together lime rind and juice, oil, garlic, chili powder, salt and cayenne; toss half with chicken until coated. Stir honey into remainder; set aside. Marinate for 20 minutes or, refrigerated, up to 4 hours.

● Alternately thread mango and red pepper onto skewers; brush with half of the reserved honey marinade. Alternately thread chicken and onions onto separate skewers. Grill, covered, on greased grill over medium-high heat, turning once and basting with remaining honey marinade, until fruit is softened and chicken is no longer pink inside, about 8 minutes.

Makes 4 main-course servings.

53

PER SERVING: about 291 cal, 26 g pro, 8 g total fat (1 g sat. fat), 31 g carb, 4 g fibre, 63 mg chol, 308 mg sodium. % RDI: 4% calcium, 7% iron, 45% vit A, 128% vit C, 12% folate.

Chicken Tikka

Compete with the best Indian restaurants with these authentic, ever-popular kabobs. The ingredient list might seem long, but the method is simple and straightforward.

¼ cup / 60 mL **lemon juice**

¼ cup / 60 mL **full-fat plain yogurt**

¼ cup / 60 mL chopped **fresh coriander**

¼ cup / 60 mL chopped **fresh mint**

3 tbsp / 45 mL chopped **fresh ginger**

2 tbsp / 30 mL **chickpea flour** (optional)

8 cloves **garlic**, smashed

1½ tsp / 7 mL **salt**

1 tsp / 5 mL **ground coriander**

½ tsp / 2 mL each **ground cardamom, cayenne pepper, cumin, turmeric**, and **white** or **black pepper**

½ tsp / 2 mL each **ground mace** and **nutmeg** (or ¾ tsp/4 mL nutmeg)

3 tbsp / 45 mL **peanut** or vegetable **oil**

4 **boneless skinless chicken breasts**, cut into 8 cubes each, or 12 boneless skinless thighs, cut into 3 pieces each

GARNISH:

1 small **red onion**, thinly sliced

½ tsp / 2 mL **salt**

¼ cup / 60 mL **lemon juice**

Fresh coriander sprigs

● In blender or food processor, purée together lemon juice, yogurt, fresh coriander, mint, ginger, chickpea flour (if using), garlic, salt, ground coriander, cardamom, cayenne, cumin, turmeric, pepper, mace and nutmeg; mix in oil. Toss with chicken until coated. Marinate, refrigerated, for 3 to 4 hours.

● **Garnish:** Meanwhile, mix onion with salt; pour lemon juice over top. Let stand for 30 minutes; drain.

● Thread chicken onto skewers, leaving about ½ inch/ 1 cm between pieces. Grill, covered, over medium-high heat, turning once, until no longer pink in centre, 8 to 10 minutes.

● Drain onion. Garnish chicken with onion and coriander.

Makes 4 main-course servings.

PER SERVING: about 288 cal, 32 g pro, 13 g total fat (3 g sat. fat), 10 g carb, 2 g fibre, 82 mg chol, 924 mg sodium. % RDI: 6% calcium, 11% iron, 3% vit A, 20% vit C, 7% folate.

Ginger Soy Chicken Skewers

¼ cup / 60 mL **sodium-reduced soy sauce**

4 tsp / 20 mL **granulated sugar**

4 tsp / 20 mL **sesame oil**

2 cloves **garlic**, pressed or minced

1 tbsp / 15 mL minced **fresh ginger**

¼ tsp / 1 mL **hot pepper flakes**

8 **boneless skinless chicken thighs**, quartered

1 **sweet onion**, quartered

8 **green onions**, cut into 1½-inch/ 4 cm pieces

● Mix together soy sauce, sugar, sesame oil, garlic, ginger and hot pepper flakes until sugar is dissolved; toss with chicken until coated. Let stand for 20 minutes.

● Separate onion quarters into pieces 3 layers thick; toss together onion, green onions, chicken and marinade until coated. Alternately thread chicken, onion and green onions onto skewers.

● Grill, covered, on greased grill over medium heat, turning once, until juices run clear when chicken is pierced, 12 to 15 minutes.

Makes 4 main-course servings.

PER SERVING: about 236 cal, 24 g pro, 11 g total fat (2 g sat. fat), 11 g carb, 1 g fibre, 95 mg chol, 636 mg sodium. % RDI: 4% calcium, 15% iron, 5% vit A, 13% vit C, 13% folate.

Chinese Seasoned Chicken Kabobs

A base of seasoned oil in the marinade gives this grilled chicken a rich yet subtle flavour.

1½ lb / 750 g **boneless skinless chicken breasts** or thighs, cut into 1-inch/ 2.5 cm cubes

2 **Cubanelle peppers**, cut into 1½-inch/4 cm pieces

Half **sweet onion**, cut into 1½-inch/ 4 cm pieces

MARINADE:

3 tbsp / 45 mL **peanut** or vegetable **oil**

4 tsp / 20 mL **coriander seeds**

4 tsp / 20 mL **black peppercorns**

4 **dried hot peppers**

3 cloves **garlic**, smashed

8 slices **fresh ginger**

1 tbsp / 15 mL **soy sauce**

2 tsp / 10 mL **Chinese black vinegar** or balsamic vinegar

2 tsp / 10 mL **sesame oil**

● **Marinade:** In small skillet, heat oil over medium-low heat; fry coriander seeds, peppercorns and hot peppers until hot peppers darken. Add garlic and ginger; fry until garlic turns golden. Into large heatproof bowl, strain oil through fine sieve, discarding solids; let cool until warm. Whisk in soy sauce, vinegar and sesame oil; toss with chicken, peppers and onion until coated. Marinate for 30 minutes or, refrigerated, up to 12 hours.

● Alternately thread chicken, peppers and onion onto skewers. Grill, covered, over medium-high heat until chicken is no longer pink inside, about 12 minutes.

Makes 4 to 6 main-course servings.

PER EACH OF 6 SERVINGS: about 208 cal, 26 g pro, 10 g total fat (2 g sat. fat), 3 g carb, trace fibre, 67 mg chol, 211 mg sodium. % RDI: 1% calcium, 4% iron, 1% vit A, 5% vit C, 5% folate.

Peanut & Coconut Chicken Skewers

Sliced cucumber, jicama and red onions tossed with lime juice and a touch of sugar and salt is an excellent accompaniment to these tropical skewers.

1½ lb / 750 g **boneless skinless chicken breasts**, cut into 1-inch/2.5 cm cubes

¼ cup / 60 mL shredded **coconut**

6 long **hot peppers**, cut into 1-inch/ 2.5 cm lengths

1 **lime**, cut into wedges

PEANUT SAUCE:

1½ tsp / 7 mL **peanut** or vegetable **oil**

4 cloves **garlic**, minced

½ cup / 125 mL chopped **shallots** or onion

2 tsp / 10 mL **ground coriander**

1 tsp / 5 mL **ground cumin**

¾ tsp / 4 mL **salt**

½ tsp / 2 mL each **ground ginger**, **turmeric** and **paprika**

¼ tsp / 1 mL **cayenne pepper**

¾ cup / 175 mL **coconut milk**

2 tsp / 10 mL packed **brown sugar**

½ tsp / 2 mL grated **lime** or lemon **rind**

3 tbsp / 45 mL **crunchy natural peanut butter**

1 tbsp / 15 mL **lime** or lemon **juice**

● **Peanut Sauce:** In small saucepan, heat oil over medium heat; fry garlic and shallots until softened, about 2 minutes. Stir in coriander, cumin, salt, ginger, turmeric, paprika and cayenne; cook, stirring, until fragrant, about 2 minutes. Stir in coconut milk, sugar and lime rind; cook, stirring, just until boiling. Reduce heat and simmer for 2 minutes. Stir in peanut butter and lime juice; let cool.

● Toss chicken with ⅓ cup/75 mL of the peanut sauce until coated. In skillet, toast coconut over medium-low heat until golden, about 6 minutes.

● Alternately thread chicken and hot peppers onto skewers. Grill on greased grill over medium-high heat, turning often, until no longer pink inside, about 10 minutes.

● Transfer skewers to serving platter along with lime wedges. Brush with ¼ cup/60 mL of the remaining peanut sauce; sprinkle with some of the toasted coconut. In serving bowl, sprinkle remaining coconut over remaining peanut sauce; serve with chicken.

Makes 6 main-course servings.

PER SERVING: about 281 cal, 29 g pro, 14 g total fat (8 g sat. fat), 10 g carb, 1 g fibre, 67 mg chol, 401 mg sodium. % RDI: 3% calcium, 16% iron, 3% vit A, 8% vit C, 9% folate.

Thai Chicken or Shrimp Satay

Thai cooks have put their special flavour signature on originally Malay satays, resulting in one of the most popular dishes worldwide.

60

1 lb / 500 g **boneless skinless chicken breast**, cut into 3- x 1- x ½-inch/8 x 2.5 x 1 cm strips, or **large shrimp**, peeled and deveined

1 tbsp / 15 mL minced **fresh coriander**

1 tbsp / 15 mL **peanut** or vegetable **oil**

2 tsp / 10 mL **fish sauce**

1 tsp / 5 mL **palm sugar**, or light brown or granulated sugar

1 clove **garlic**, pressed or minced

¾ tsp / 4 mL finely grated **fresh ginger**

¾ tsp / 4 mL **turmeric**

½ tsp / 2 mL finely minced **kaffir lime leaves**, or finely grated kaffir or regular lime rind

¼ tsp / 1 mL **cayenne pepper**

Pinch **black pepper**

Lime wedges

Thai Peanut Coconut Sauce (opposite)

● Toss together chicken or shrimp, coriander, oil, fish sauce, sugar, garlic, ginger, turmeric, lime leaves, cayenne and pepper. Marinate for 30 minutes or, refrigerated, up to 8 hours.

● Thread onto skewers. Grill on greased grill over medium-high heat, turning once, until chicken is no longer pink in centre or shrimp is opaque, 5 to 8 minutes. Serve with lime wedges and Thai Peanut Coconut Sauce.

Makes 4 main-course servings.

PER SERVING (WITH PEANUT SAUCE): about 164 cal, 26 g pro, 5 g total fat (1 g sat. fat), 2 g carb, trace fibre, 67 mg chol, 291 mg sodium, 349 mg potassium. % RDI: 1% calcium, 5% iron, 1% vit A, 2% vit C, 2% folate.

Thai Peanut Coconut Sauce

Rich, luscious tropical flavours commingle in this classic Thai accompaniment to satays. It's also a lovely dipping sauce for vegetable crudités and shrimp chips.

1 cup / 250 mL **raw** or roasted **peanuts**

¼ cup / 60 mL chopped **sweet red pepper**

1 tbsp / 15 mL **Thai red curry paste**

1 tbsp / 15 mL **peanut** or vegetable **oil**

2 tsp / 10 mL **Thai shrimp paste**, Malaysian blachan or Chinese fermented shrimp paste

2 tsp / 10 mL minced **Thai (bird-eye) chilies**, or 1 tsp/5 mL Thai chili powder or cayenne pepper

2 cloves **garlic**, smashed

¼ tsp / 1 mL **white pepper**

4 tsp / 20 mL **palm sugar** or light brown sugar

1 can (14 oz/400 mL) **coconut milk**

2 tbsp / 30 mL **palm vinegar**, rice vinegar or lime juice

1 tbsp / 15 mL **fish sauce**

● In dry skillet over medium heat, toast raw peanuts until golden (omit this step if using roasted peanuts); let cool. In food processor, pulse peanuts until fine powder (do not process into paste); set aside. In food processor, purée together red pepper, curry paste, oil, shrimp paste, chilies, garlic and white pepper; transfer to saucepan. Cook over medium heat, stirring constantly, until fragrant and dark, 4 to 5 minutes.

● Stir in sugar; cook until dissolved. Stir in peanuts; slowly stir in coconut milk. Bring to simmer. Stir in vinegar and fish sauce; simmer, stirring often, until thickened, 10 to 15 minutes. Let cool to room temperature. (Refrigerate for up to 2 days; bring to room temperature or warm over low heat before serving.)

Makes about 2 cups/500 mL.

PER 1 TBSP/15 mL: about 59 cal, 2 g pro, 5 g total fat (3 g sat. fat), 2 g carb, 1 g fibre, 1 mg chol, 47 mg sodium, 67 mg potassium. % RDI: 1% calcium, 4% iron, 1% vit A, 3% vit C, 6% folate.

Chicken Liver Brochettes

Chicken livers are a "cheap and cheerful" — never mind tasty — addition to any barbecue, and these brochettes are a breeze to make. The best livers come from naturally or organically raised chickens. Discard any that aren't firm and bright.

12 oz / 375 g **chicken livers**

2 tsp / 10 mL **balsamic vinegar**

½ tsp / 2 mL **salt**

1 tbsp / 15 mL minced **fresh sage leaves** (or ¾ tsp/4 mL crumbled dried sage)

1 large clove **garlic**, minced

¾ tsp / 4 mL **fennel seeds**

¼ tsp / 1 mL **black pepper**

¼ tsp / 1 mL **hot pepper flakes** (optional)

½ cup / 125 mL **red onion pieces** (1½ inches/4 cm)

2 tbsp / 30 mL **olive oil**

2 tsp / 10 mL minced **fresh parsley**

● Separate 2 lobes of each liver, removing any connective tissue; cut larger lobe in half. Mix together livers, vinegar and salt; let stand for 5 minutes. Drain; mix in sage, garlic, fennel seeds, pepper and hot pepper flakes (if using). Let stand for 20 to 30 minutes.

● Alternately thread livers and onion onto skewers; brush with oil. Grill over medium-high heat, turning often, until liver is well browned but still pink in centre, 8 to 9 minutes. Sprinkle with parsley.

Makes 4 main-course servings.

PER SERVING: about 170 cal, 16 g pro, 10 g total fat (2 g sat. fat), 3 g carb, 1 g fibre, 397 mg chol, 48 mg sodium, 134 mg potassium. % RDI: 2% calcium, 40% iron, 310% vit A, 20% vit C, 222% folate.

Ancho Turkey Waves

Sweet and moderately hot ancho chilies add good flavour to mild turkey breast.

1 lb / 500 g **boneless skinless turkey breast**

2 tbsp / 30 mL **vegetable oil**

2 tbsp / 30 mL **red wine vinegar**

2 cloves **garlic**, minced

2 tsp / 10 mL **ancho chili powder**

½ tsp / 2 mL **dried oregano**

½ tsp / 2 mL **salt**

Pinch **granulated sugar**

● Slice turkey crosswise into ¼-inch/5 mm thick strips. Mix together oil, vinegar, garlic, ancho chili powder, oregano, salt and sugar; toss with turkey until coated. Marinate, refrigerated, for at least 2 or up to 6 hours.

● Thread into wave shapes on skewers. Grill, covered, on greased grill over medium-high heat, turning once, until no longer pink inside, about 6 minutes.

Makes 4 main-course servings.

VARIATION

Chipotle Turkey Waves
Substitute 1½ tsp/7 mL chipotle chili powder for the ancho chili powder.

PER SERVING: about 170 cal, 27 g pro, 6 g total fat (1 g sat. fat), 1 g carb, trace fibre, 74 mg chol, 269 mg sodium. % RDI: 1% calcium, 11% iron, 3% vit A, 2% vit C, 3% folate.

Top to bottom: Mojito Rack of
Lamb (page 225), Caesar
Turkey Brochettes (opposite)

Caesar Turkey Brochettes

The clam and tomato juices of one of Canada's favourite drinks are mimicked in this marinated turkey basted with an oyster sauce–scented barbecue sauce.

2 tbsp / 30 mL **lime juice**

2 tbsp / 30 mL **vodka**

1 tbsp / 15 mL **sesame oil**

¾ tsp / 4 mL **celery salt**

¼ tsp / 1 mL **black pepper**

1 **boneless turkey breast**, skinned, or 4 turkey thighs, skinned and boned, cut into 1½-inch/4 cm cubes

2 stalks **celery** or banana peppers, cut into 1½-inch/4 cm chunks

1 **red onion**, cut into 1½-inch/4 cm chunks

BASTING SAUCE:

⅓ cup / 75 mL **ketchup**

3 tbsp / 45 mL **oyster sauce**

1 tsp / 5 mL **Worcestershire sauce**

½ tsp / 2 mL **hot pepper sauce**

● Mix together lime juice, vodka, sesame oil, celery salt and pepper; toss with turkey until coated. Marinate for 30 minutes or, refrigerated, up to 8 hours.

● Alternately thread turkey, celery and red onion onto skewers.

● **Basting Sauce:** Mix together ketchup and oyster, Worcestershire and hot pepper sauces.

● Grill skewers over medium heat, turning often and brushing with Basting Sauce during last 5 minutes, until glazed and turkey is no longer pink inside, about 18 minutes.

Makes 6 to 8 main-course servings.

PER EACH OF 8 SERVINGS: about 186 cal, 30 g pro, 3 g total fat (1 g sat. fat), 9 g carb, 1 g fibre, 79 mg chol, 489 mg sodium. % RDI: 3% calcium, 14% iron, 3% vit A, 42% vit C, 8% folate.

Pickerel with Charmoula

Charmoula is a green sauce from Morocco that's often used to flavour fish. Its fresh herbal notes and spicy undertones are a good match for sweet Canadian pickerel.

1½ lb / 750 g **skin-on pickerel**, perch or other freshwater fish **fillets**

¼ tsp / 1 mL each **salt** and **black pepper**

CHARMOULA:

½ cup / 125 mL finely chopped **fresh parsley**

½ cup / 125 mL finely chopped **fresh coriander**

2 **green onions**, finely chopped

¼ cup / 60 mL **extra-virgin olive oil**

3 tbsp / 45 mL **lemon juice**

2 cloves **garlic**, minced

1 tsp / 5 mL **ground cumin**

1 tsp / 5 mL **paprika**

¼ tsp / 1 mL **cayenne pepper**

¼ tsp / 1 mL each **salt** and **black pepper**

● **Charmoula:** Mix together parsley, coriander, green onions, oil, lemon juice, garlic, cumin, paprika, cayenne pepper, salt and pepper; set aside.

● Divide fish into 4 servings. Thread each crosswise onto 2 skewers; sprinkle with salt and pepper.

● Grill, covered and skin side down, on greased grill over medium-high heat, turning once, until fish flakes easily, about 5 minutes per ½ inch/1 cm thickness. Top with some of the Charmoula; serve remainder on side.

Makes 4 main-course servings.

PER SERVING: about 274 cal, 30 g pro, 16 g total fat (2 g sat. fat), 3 g carb, 1 g fibre, 129 mg chol, 374 mg sodium. % RDI: 18% calcium, 24% iron, 15% vit A, 27% vit C, 18% folate.

Tamarind-Glazed Salmon Kabobs

Rich Canadian salmon takes as naturally to a tasty sweet-and-sour Southeast Asian-style glaze as a hot dog does to mustard.

1 lb / 500 g **skinless salmon fillet**, cut into 1½-inch/4 cm cubes

1 clove **garlic**, pressed or minced

1 tbsp / 15 mL minced **fresh coriander**

1 tbsp / 15 mL **peanut** or vegetable **oil**

¼ tsp / 1 mL each **salt** and **black pepper**

4 **green onions**, cut into 1½-inch/ 4 cm lengths

Fresh coriander sprigs

TAMARIND GLAZE:

1 tbsp / 15 mL **peanut** or vegetable **oil**

3 tbsp / 45 mL **seedless tamarind paste**

2 tbsp / 30 mL **palm sugar** or brown sugar

1 tbsp / 15 mL **soy sauce**

1 tsp / 5 mL finely grated **fresh ginger**

¾ tsp / 4 mL **chili-garlic sauce** (sambal oelek)

2 tsp / 10 mL **lemon juice**

● Toss together salmon, garlic, coriander, oil, salt and pepper until coated. Let stand for 15 minutes.

● **Tamarind Glaze:** In small saucepan, heat oil over medium heat; add tamarind, sugar, soy sauce and ginger. Bring to boil, stirring until sugar is dissolved; reduce heat to low and simmer, stirring, for 3 minutes. Remove from heat; stir in chili-garlic sauce. Let cool; stir in lemon juice.

● Alternately thread salmon and onions onto skewers. Grill on greased grill over medium-high heat, turning occasionally, until just a hint of pink remains in centre of salmon, about 3 minutes. Turn, brushing both sides with glaze; grill for 1 minute. Turn, brushing both sides again with glaze; grill for 1 minute. Garnish with coriander sprigs.

Makes 4 main-course servings.

PER SERVING: about 291 cal, 20 g pro, 18 g total fat (3 g sat. fat), 12 g carb, 1 g fibre, 56 mg chol, 431 mg sodium, 463 mg potassium. % RDI: 3% calcium, 7% iron, 3% vit A, 10% vit C, 18% folate.

Soy-Glazed Halibut Kabobs

Whether Pacific or Atlantic, halibut is one of our finest fishes. Because it has such a rich yet subtle flavour, you don't need to do much to it. A simple glaze is all you need.

5 tsp / 25 mL **peanut** or vegetable **oil**

1 clove **garlic**, minced

1 tsp / 5 mL minced **fresh ginger**

1 **bay leaf** (preferably fresh)

¼ cup / 60 mL **soy sauce**

1 tbsp / 15 mL **liquid honey**

1 tbsp / 15 mL **lemon juice**

1 tsp / 5 mL **cornstarch**

1 lb / 500 g **skinless halibut fillet**, cut into 1-inch/2.5 cm cubes

1 **Asian (long) eggplant**, cut into 1-inch/2.5 cm slices

⅓ cup / 75 mL **sweet onion** pieces (1 inch/2.5 cm)

½ tsp / 2 mL each **five-spice powder** and **salt**

1 tbsp / 15 mL toasted **sesame seeds**

1 tbsp / 15 mL thinly sliced **green onion**

● In small saucepan, heat 2 tsp/10 mL of the oil over medium heat; fry garlic, ginger and bay leaf until fragrant, about 1 minute. Stir in 3 tbsp/45 mL water, soy sauce, honey and lemon juice; simmer for 3 minutes. Mix cornstarch with 2 tsp/10 mL water; stir into sauce. Simmer for 2 minutes. Let cool.

● Toss together halibut, eggplant, sweet onion, five-spice powder, salt and remaining oil until coated; thread onto skewers. Grill over medium-high heat, turning occasionally, until fish flakes easily and eggplant is tender, 6 to 7 minutes. Brush with glaze; grill, brushing and turning often, until well-glazed, about 3 minutes. Garnish with sesame seeds and green onion.

Makes 4 main-course servings.

PER SERVING: about 234 cal, 26 g pro, 10 g total fat (2 g sat. fat), 11 g carb, 2 g fibre, 36 mg chol, 1,251 mg sodium, 630 mg potassium. % RDI: 6% calcium, 12% iron, 5% vit A, 3% vit C, 11% folate.

Glazes

Ginger Teriyaki Glaze

¼ cup / 60 mL **chicken** or vegetable **stock**

2 tbsp / 30 mL **soy sauce**

2 tbsp / 30 mL **sake**, dry sherry or apple juice

2 tbsp / 30 mL **corn syrup**

1 tbsp / 15 mL minced **fresh ginger**

2 tsp / 10 mL **cornstarch**

• In small saucepan, bring stock, soy sauce, sake, corn syrup and ginger to boil; reduce heat and simmer for 5 minutes. Mix cornstarch with 2 tsp/10 mL water; stir into sauce. Cook until thickened, about 30 seconds.

Makes about ⅓ cup/75 mL.

Curry Glaze

2 tsp / 10 mL **vegetable oil**

2 tbsp / 30 mL minced **onion**

1 clove **garlic**, minced

2 tbsp / 30 mL minced **fresh coriander**

2 tbsp / 30 mL **tomato paste**

4 tsp / 20 mL **curry paste**

1 tsp / 5 mL packed **brown sugar**

¼ cup / 60 mL **chicken** or vegetable **stock**

1 tbsp / 15 mL **cider vinegar**

2 tsp / 10 mL **cornstarch**

• In small saucepan, heat oil over medium heat; fry onion, garlic and coriander, stirring, until fragrant, about 1 minute. Stir in tomato paste, curry paste and sugar; cook for 1 minute. Stir in stock and vinegar; bring to boil. Reduce heat and simmer for 5 minutes. Mix cornstarch with 2 tsp/10 mL water; stir into sauce. Cook until thickened, about 30 seconds.

Makes ½ cup/125 mL.

Glazed Fish Kabobs

Use saltwater fish, such as monkfish, swordfish, marlin, halibut, kingfish or salmon, for these kabobs, glazed with either of the flavourful glazes opposite.

1 lb / 500 g **thick fish fillets**, cut into 1½-inch/4 cm cubes

½ tsp / 2 mL **salt**

¼ tsp / 1 mL **black pepper**

Half **onion**, cut into bite-size pieces

1 **sweet red**, green or yellow **pepper**, cut into bite-size pieces

1 tbsp / 15 mL **vegetable oil**

Ginger Teriyaki Glaze or **Curry Glaze** (opposite)

Lemon wedges

● Sprinkle fish with salt and pepper. Alternately thread fish, onion and red pepper onto skewers; brush with oil.

● Grill, covered, on greased grill over medium-high heat, turning once, until fish is firm but starting to flake, about 7 minutes. Brush with glaze; cook for 2 minutes. Turn and brush with glaze; cook until fish flakes easily, about 1 minute. Serve with lemon wedges.

Makes 4 main-course servings.

PER SERVING WITH GINGER TERIYAKI GLAZE: about 180 cal, 18 g pro, 5 g total fat (trace sat. fat), 14 g carb, 1 g fibre, 28 mg chol, 887 mg sodium. % RDI: 2% calcium, 6% iron, 12% vit A, 85% vit C, 7% folate.
PER SERVING WITH CURRY GLAZE: about 195 cal, 18 g pro, 19 g total fat (1 g sat. fat), 9 g carb, 1 g fibre, 29 mg chol, 364 mg sodium. % RDI: 2% calcium, 8% iron, 15% vit A, 92% vit C, 7% folate.

Greek-Style Seafood Kabobs

¼ cup / 60 mL **extra-virgin olive oil**

2 cloves **garlic**, minced

2 tsp / 10 mL minced **fresh thyme**

¼ tsp / 1 mL each **salt** and **black pepper**

¼ tsp / 1 mL **dried marjoram** or oregano

6 oz / 175 g **skinless centre-cut salmon fillets**, cut into 1-inch/2.5 cm cubes

Half **sweet green pepper**, cut into 1-inch/2.5 cm pieces

8 **jumbo shrimp**, peeled and deveined

6 oz / 175 g **sea scallops**

Lemon wedges

● Mix together oil, garlic, thyme, salt, pepper and marjoram; toss with salmon, green pepper, shrimp and scallops until coated. Let stand for 15 minutes.

● Reserving any remaining marinade, alternately thread seafood and pepper loosely onto skewers; brush with marinade. Grill, covered, on greased grill over medium heat, turning once, until fish flakes easily, 6 to 8 minutes. Serve with lemon wedges.

Makes 4 main-course servings.

PER SERVING: about 323 cal, 26 g pro, 22 g total fat (4 g sat. fat), 3 g carb, trace fibre, 88 mg chol, 414 mg sodium. % RDI: 4% calcium, 10% iron, 3% vit A, 25% vit C, 14% folate.

Sweet & Sour Shrimp Kabobs

A Malay-style tamarind glaze makes these shrimp-and-pineapple kabobs simply irresistible. Tamarind concentrate is seeded tamarind pulp mixed with a little water to make a thin paste. It's available in jars in the Asian-food section of some grocery stores and at most Southeast Asian and Chinese grocers.

1½ lb / 750 g **jumbo** or large **shrimp**, peeled and deveined

Half **pineapple**, cut into 1-inch/ 2.5 cm cubes

4 **green onions**, cut into 1½-inch/ 4 cm lengths

2 tbsp / 30 mL ground **roasted peanuts**

GLAZE:

2 tbsp / 30 mL packed **brown sugar**

2 tbsp / 30 mL **tamarind concentrate**

2 tsp / 10 mL **Thai red curry paste**

2 tsp / 10 mL **peanut** or vegetable **oil**

2 tsp / 10 mL **fish sauce**

1½ tsp / 7 mL **curry powder**

● **Glaze:** Mix together sugar, tamarind, curry paste, oil, fish sauce and curry powder until smooth.

● Alternately thread shrimp, pineapple and onions onto skewers; brush with Glaze. Grill over high heat, turning once and brushing with remaining glaze, until shrimp are pink and opaque in centre, about 5 minutes. Sprinkle with peanuts.

Makes 4 to 6 main-course servings.

Photo, page 32

TIP

If you can't find tamarind concentrate, you can make your own for this recipe. Soak 2 tbsp/30 mL seedless tamarind pulp in 2 tbsp/30 mL boiling water until softened, then press through fine sieve, discarding solids.

PER EACH OF 6 SERVINGS: about 173 cal, 19 g pro, 5 g total fat (1 g sat. fat), 13 g carb, 1 g fibre, 129 mg chol, 287 mg sodium. % RDI: 6% calcium, 19% iron, 5% vit A, 22% vit C, 8% folate.

Shrimp Skewers with Coriander & Almond Relish

Both the colour and flavour of these simply seasoned shrimp balance the lovely green relish.

1 lb / 500 g **jumbo shrimp**, peeled and deveined

1½ cloves **garlic**, pressed

1 tbsp / 15 mL **extra-virgin olive oil**

¼ tsp / 1 mL **salt**

¼ tsp / 1 mL **smoked paprika**

CORIANDER & ALMOND RELISH:

1 cup / 250 mL lightly packed chopped **fresh coriander**

⅓ cup / 75 mL toasted **almonds**

¼ cup / 60 mL chopped **sweet onion**

½ tsp / 2 mL **salt**

Pinch **ground cumin**

Pinch **cayenne pepper**

¼ cup / 60 mL **extra-virgin olive oil**

2 tbsp / 30 mL **lemon juice**

● Toss together shrimp, garlic, oil, salt and paprika until coated. Tail first, thread shrimp lengthwise through centre onto skewers. Marinate for 10 minutes or, refrigerated, up to 8 hours.

● **Coriander & Almond Relish:** In food processor, pulse together coriander, almonds, onion, salt, cumin and cayenne until finely minced; pulse in oil and lemon juice. Transfer to serving dish.

● Grill shrimp over high heat, turning once, until pink and opaque in centre, about 5 minutes. Serve with Coriander & Almond Relish.

Makes 4 main-course servings.

PER SERVING: about 330 cal, 23 g pro, 25 g total fat (3 g sat. fat), 5 g carb, 2 g fibre, 150 mg chol, 583 mg sodium. % RDI: 8% calcium, 23% iron, 8% vit A, 8% vit C, 8% folate.

Seafood Kabobs with Saffron Aioli

If you make these kabobs with fish, choose a fairly firm-fleshed variety. Salmon is also nice — just cube the fillets with the skin on to help hold the pieces together on the grill.

12 oz / 375 g large **shrimp**, peeled and deveined

12 oz / 375 g **sea scallops** or fish, cut into 1½-inch/4 cm cubes

¼ cup / 60 mL **lemon juice**

½ tsp / 2 mL **salt**

2 tbsp / 30 mL **olive oil**

¼ tsp / 1 mL **black pepper**

2 tbsp / 30 mL finely chopped **fresh parsley** or coriander

SAFFRON AIOLI:

Pinch **saffron threads**

2 tbsp / 30 mL **extra-virgin olive oil**

2 tsp / 10 mL **lemon juice**

1 clove **garlic**, pressed or pounded into paste

Pinch **salt**

½ cup / 125 mL **mayonnaise**

● **Saffron Aioli:** In dry small skillet over medium-low heat, toast saffron until fragrant and dried, 10 to 20 seconds; crumble finely into small bowl. Pour in 1 tsp/5 mL boiling water; let cool. Whisk in oil, lemon juice, garlic and salt. In separate bowl, slowly whisk saffron mixture into mayonnaise.

● Toss together shrimp, scallops, lemon juice and salt; let stand for 15 minutes. Drain; toss with oil and pepper until coated.

● Thread onto skewers. Grill over high heat, turning once, until shrimp and scallops are opaque, about 6 minutes. Garnish with parsley and serve with Saffron Aioli.

Makes 4 to 6 main-course servings.

PER EACH OF 6 SERVINGS: about 304 cal, 20 g pro, 24 g total fat (4 g sat. fat), 2 g carb, trace fibre, 92 mg chol, 359 mg sodium, 306 mg potassium. % RDI: 3% calcium, 12% iron, 6% vit A, 5% vit C, 5% folate.

Shrimp & Mango Brochettes

If you like a little heat with your sweet, dip these simply spiced kabobs into Thai Sweet Chili Sauce (below). It's a perfect match with all kinds of grilled and fried foods.

1 firm **mango**, peeled, pitted and cut into sixteen 1-inch/2.5 cm chunks

1 **sweet red pepper**, cut into 16 triangles

8 **okra pods**, trimmed and halved

8 **red pearl onions**, peeled and halved

16 **large shrimp**, peeled and deveined

2 **limes**, each cut into 8 wedges

¼ cup / 60 mL **extra-virgin olive oil**

1 tsp / 5 mL **ground coriander**

½ tsp / 2 mL **ground cumin**

½ tsp / 2 mL **cayenne pepper**

½ tsp / 2 mL **salt**

● Thread 1 piece each mango, red pepper, okra, onion, shrimp and lime onto each of 16 skewers.

● Mix together oil, coriander, cumin, cayenne and salt; brush over skewers. Grill, covered, on greased grill over medium-high heat, turning once, until shrimp are pink and opaque in centre and vegetables are tender-crisp, about 5 minutes.

Makes 4 to 6 main-course servings.

Thai Sweet Chili Sauce

● In saucepan, stirring constantly, bring ¾ cup/175 mL **rice vinegar**, ½ cup/125 mL **granulated sugar**, ¼ cup/60 mL **water**, 1 tbsp/15 mL **fish sauce** and ¼ tsp/1 mL **salt** to boil; reduce heat to medium and simmer until as thick as maple syrup, 10 to 15 minutes. Stir in 3 **red finger hot peppers** or 10 Thai (bird-eye) chilies, seeded and chopped, and 3 cloves **garlic**, minced; simmer for 3 minutes. Let cool. (Refrigerate for up to 1 month.)

Makes about 1 cup/250 mL.

PER EACH OF 6 SERVINGS (WITHOUT SAUCE): about 151 cal, 7 g pro, 10 g total fat (1 g sat. fat), 11 g carb, 2 g fibre, 43 mg chol, 236 mg sodium. % RDI: 3% calcium, 7% iron, 20% vit A, 78% vit C, 7% folate.

Miso-Orange Grilled Scallops

Japanese miso piqued with orange makes a vibrant glazed coating, contrasting the delicate ivory flesh of the scallops.

¼ cup / 60 mL **red** or white **miso paste**

2 tbsp / 30 mL **granulated sugar**

1 tsp / 5 mL grated **orange rind**

2 tbsp / 30 mL **orange juice**

12 oz / 375 g **sea scallops**

2 **green onions**

- In small saucepan, heat miso, sugar, and orange rind and juice over medium-low heat until smooth and sugar is dissolved, about 2 minutes. Set aside.

- Pat scallops dry. Cut green onions into green and white parts; cut white parts into 8 pieces.

- Alternately thread scallops and white parts of onions onto skewers; brush with miso mixture.

- Grill, covered, on greased grill over medium-high heat, turning once, until miso is caramelized and scallops are opaque, about 6 minutes. Thinly slice green parts of onions; sprinkle over scallops.

Makes 4 main-course servings.

PER SERVING: about 140 cal, 16 g pro, 2 g total fat (trace sat. fat), 14 g carb, 2 g fibre, 28 mg chol, 765 mg sodium. % RDI: 3% calcium, 6% iron, 1% vit A, 5% vit C, 8% folate.

Burgers & Sandwiches

Classic Backyard Burgers

Enjoy this lightly seasoned basic burger with any of the suggested toppings on pages 101 and 102 or top them with cheese for a classic cheeseburger.

1 **egg**

Half small **onion**, grated

1 tbsp / 15 mL **Dijon mustard**

1 tsp / 5 mL **Worcestershire sauce**

1 clove **garlic**, minced

½ tsp / 2 mL each **salt** and **black pepper**

½ tsp / 2 mL **dried oregano**

1 lb / 500 g regular or lean **ground beef**

4 **buns**

● Whisk together egg, 2 tbsp/30 mL water, onion, mustard, Worcestershire sauce, garlic, salt, pepper and oregano; mix in beef. Shape into four ¾-inch/2 cm thick patties.

● Grill on greased grill over medium heat, turning once, until no longer pink inside or digital thermometer registers 160°F/71°C, about 15 minutes. Serve in buns.

Makes 4 burgers.

Keeping a stash of homemade burgers in the freezer makes large-crowd or impromptu barbecues easy. Just layer the uncooked patties between waxed paper in an airtight container and freeze for up to 1 month. Thaw in refrigerator.

PER BURGER: about 392 cal, 28 g pro, 16 g total fat (6 g sat. fat), 32 g carb, 2 g fibre, 107 mg chol, 749 mg sodium. % RDI: 10% calcium, 30% iron, 2% vit A, 2% vit C, 32% folate.

Classy Beef Burgers

The quintessential burger with a touch of extra class, it's especially good topped with Cherry Tomato Salsa (page 521).

2 tbsp / 30 mL **butter**

¾ cup / 175 mL finely chopped **onion**

1 clove **garlic**, minced

¾ tsp / 4 mL chopped **fresh thyme** (or ¼ tsp/1 mL dried)

2 tbsp / 30 mL **brandy**

1 **egg**

1 tbsp / 15 mL **Dijon mustard**

½ tsp / 2 mL each **salt** and **black pepper**

1 lb / 500 g **lean ground beef**

● In skillet, melt butter over medium heat; fry onion, garlic and thyme until golden, about 8 minutes. Add brandy; cook until evaporated, about 1 minute. Scrape into bowl; let cool slightly. Stir in egg, mustard, salt and pepper; mix in beef. Shape into four ¾-inch/2 cm thick patties.

● Grill on greased grill over medium heat, turning once, until no longer pink inside or digital thermometer registers 160°F/71°C, about 15 minutes.

Makes 4 burgers.

PER BURGER (WITHOUT BUN): about 267 cal, 23 g pro, 18 g total fat (8 g sat. fat), 3 g carb, 1 g fibre, 124 mg chol, 472 mg sodium. % RDI: 3% calcium, 18% iron, 8% vit A, 3% vit C, 9% folate.

Steak Burgers

For medium-rare burgers, you should ideally grind your own meat or have your butcher grind a steak. If you're using store-bought ground meat, make sure to cook the burgers until they're no longer pink inside. Use large "stuffing" mushrooms.

1 lb / 500 g **ground sirloin**

2 tsp / 10 mL **Worcestershire sauce**

¾ tsp / 4 mL **salt**

½ tsp / 2 mL **black pepper**

2 thick slices **sweet onion**

4 extra-large **white** or cremini **mushrooms**, cut into ½-inch/1 cm thick slices

1 tbsp / 15 mL **olive oil**

4 **buns**

4 **lettuce leaves**

4 thick slices **tomato**

● Lightly mix together beef, Worcestershire sauce, ½ tsp/2 mL of the salt and ¼ tsp/1 mL of the pepper. Shape into four ¾-inch/2 cm patties, handling meat as little as possible.

● Skewer onions through edges to keep rings intact. Toss together onion slices, mushrooms, oil, and remaining salt and pepper.

● Grill mushrooms (in grill basket if grill rack has wide spaces) and onions over medium-high heat until golden, 4 to 5 minutes. Remove skewers from onions and separate into rings. Grill burgers on greased grill over high heat, turning once, until medium-rare, 3 to 5 minutes.

● Serve in buns with grilled onions and mushrooms, lettuce and tomato.

Makes 4 burgers.

Overworking the meat mixture for burgers can make them shrink during cooking. To prevent this, shape into balls then gently press into ¾-inch/2 cm thick patties.

PER BURGER: about 423 cal, 28 g pro, 18 g total fat (5 g sat. fat), 36 g carb, 3 g fibre, 60 mg chol, 862 mg sodium, 582 mg potassium. % RDI: 10% calcium, 38% iron, 5% vit A, 15% vit C, 36% folate.

Sangria Burgers

The wine, brandy and subtle orange of classic sangria inspired the flavourings of these burgers. For Spanish flair, top with slices of peeled grilled sweet red pepper.

8 oz / 250 g **lean ground beef**

8 oz / 250 g **lean ground pork**

⅓ cup / 75 mL minced **fresh coriander**

3 tbsp / 45 mL **dry red wine**

2 tbsp / 30 mL **brandy**

2 tbsp / 30 mL **extra-virgin olive oil**

2 cloves **garlic**, pressed or minced

1 small **onion**, minced

½ tsp / 2 mL **salt**

¼ tsp / 1 mL **cayenne pepper**

¼ tsp / 1 mL **black pepper**

¼ tsp / 1 mL grated **orange rind**

● Mix together beef, pork, coriander, wine, brandy, oil, garlic, onion, salt, cayenne, pepper and orange rind. Shape into four ¾-inch/2 cm thick patties.

● Grill on greased grill over medium heat, turning once, until no longer pink inside or digital thermometer registers 160°F/71°C, about 15 minutes.

Makes 4 burgers.

87

PER BURGER (WITHOUT BUN): about 268 cal, 21 g pro, 18 g total fat (5 g sat. fat), 2 g carb, 0 g fibre, 66 mg chol, 347 mg sodium. % RDI: 2% calcium, 12% iron, 1% vit A, 3% vit C, 4% folate.

Stuffed Cheddar Burgers

These cheese-stuffed burgers are even more delicious — and indulgent — when topped with crisp bacon.

1 **egg**

¼ cup / 60 mL **dry bread crumbs**

1 small **onion**, grated

2 tsp / 10 mL **Dijon mustard**

½ tsp / 2 mL **dried thyme**

½ tsp / 2 mL **salt**

¼ tsp / 1 mL **black pepper**

1 lb / 500 g **lean ground beef**

½ cup / 125 mL shredded **extra-old Cheddar cheese**

4 **buns**

● Whisk together egg, 2 tbsp/30 mL water, bread crumbs, onion, mustard, thyme, salt and pepper; mix in beef.

● Shape into 4 balls; make well in each. Fill each with one-quarter of the cheese; press meat over to enclose. Shape into four ¾-inch/2 cm thick patties.

● Grill on greased grill over medium heat, turning once, until no longer pink inside or digital thermometer registers 160°F/71°C, about 15 minutes. Serve in buns.

Makes 4 burgers.

VARIATION

Stuffed Feta Burgers

Replace beef with ground pork or lamb, thyme with oregano, and Cheddar with crumbled feta. Top burgers with sliced tomato and cucumber.

PER BURGER: about 464 cal, 32 g pro, 20 g total fat (8 g sat. fat), 37 g carb, 2 g fibre, 121 mg chol, 867 mg sodium. % RDI: 20% calcium, 34% iron, 6% vit A, 2% vit C, 38% folate.

Shiitake Beef Burgers

Chinese flavours infuse these delectable burgers. Serve with hot mustard to spread on the buns.

12 **dried shiitake mushrooms**

1 tbsp / 15 mL **peanut** or vegetable **oil**

2 tbsp / 30 mL **Chinese rice wine** or dry sherry

2 tsp / 10 mL grated **fresh ginger**

¼ tsp / 1 mL **salt**

Pinch **granulated sugar**

1 **egg**

2 tbsp / 30 mL **soy sauce**

2 tsp / 10 mL **sesame oil**

½ tsp / 2 mL **black pepper**

1 lb / 500 g **ground beef**

4 **green onions**, thinly sliced

HOISIN GARLIC SAUCE:

2 tsp / 10 mL **sesame oil**

3 cloves **garlic**, minced

2 tbsp / 30 mL **hoisin sauce**

¼ tsp / 1 mL **granulated sugar**

● Hoisin Garlic Sauce: In small saucepan, heat oil over medium-low heat; fry garlic until soft and fragrant, 2 to 3 minutes. Stir in hoisin sauce, sugar and 1 tbsp/15 mL water; cook, stirring, for 30 seconds. Scrape into bowl; let cool.

● Soak dried shiitake mushrooms in 1½ cups/375 mL warm water until soft, about 30 minutes. Reserving soaking liquid, drain. Remove stems (save for stockpot); dice caps.

● In small nonstick skillet, heat peanut oil over medium-high heat; fry mushrooms until golden, about 4 minutes. Add wine, ginger, salt and sugar; sauté for 30 seconds. Add reserved mushroom liquid; cook until liquid is reduced to about 2 tbsp/30 mL. Scrape into bowl; let cool.

● Whisk in egg, soy sauce, sesame oil and pepper; mix in beef and green onions. Shape into four ¾-inch/2 cm thick patties.

● Grill on greased grill over medium heat, turning once, until no longer pink inside or digital thermometer registers 160°F/71°C, about 15 minutes. Spread one-quarter of the Hoisin Garlic Sauce over top of each burger.

Makes 4 burgers.

PER BURGER (WITHOUT BUN): about 334 cal, 25 g pro, 20 g total fat (6 g sat. fat), 14 g carb, 2 g fibre, 107 mg chol, 868 mg sodium. % RDI: 4% calcium, 21% iron, 3% vit A, 5% vit C, 15% folate.

Argentine Burgers

Argentine flavours of parsley, hot pepper and vinegar give these burgers fresh taste. Top with ripe tomato slices.

1 cup / 250 mL packed **fresh parsley leaves**

¼ cup / 60 mL **dry bread crumbs**

2 tbsp / 30 mL packed **fresh oregano leaves** or 1½ tsp/7 mL dried

2 tbsp / 30 mL **olive oil**

Half to 1 **jalapeño pepper**, seeded and chopped

1 tbsp / 15 mL **red wine vinegar**

¼ tsp / 1 mL each **salt** and **black pepper**

4 cloves **garlic**, minced

1 **egg yolk**

1 lb / 500 g **lean ground beef** or veal

4 **buns**

● In food processor, finely chop together parsley, bread crumbs, oregano, oil, jalapeño, vinegar, 1 tbsp/15 mL water, salt and pepper; pulse in garlic and egg yolk. Scrape into large bowl; mix in beef. Shape into four ¾-inch/2 cm thick patties.

● Grill on greased grill over medium heat, turning once, until no longer pink inside or digital thermometer registers 160°F/71°C, about 15 minutes. Serve in buns.

Makes 4 burgers.

PER BURGER: about 508 cal, 30 g pro, 23 g total fat (7 g sat. fat), 45 g carb, 2 g fibre, 115 mg chol, 652 mg sodium. % RDI: 7% calcium, 36% iron, 11% vit A, 20% vit C, 42% folate.

Clockwise from left: Veal & Gorgonzola Burger with Onions (page 99), Smoky Beef Burger with Chipotle Ketchup (opposite), Lamb Burger with Tzatziki (page 114)

Smoky Beef Burgers with Chipotle Ketchup

For a smoky cheeseburger, melt some aged Cheddar on top — or go overboard and use smoked Cheddar.

1 tbsp / 15 mL **butter**

3 oz / 90 g **double-smoked bacon**, finely chopped

1 **onion**, finely chopped

2 cloves **garlic**, minced

1 **egg**

3 tbsp / 45 mL **dry red wine**

½ tsp / 2 mL each **salt** and **black pepper**

1 lb / 500 g **ground beef** or bison

CHIPOTLE KETCHUP:

⅓ cup / 75 mL **ketchup**

1 **canned chipotle pepper**, minced

1 tbsp / 15 mL **adobo sauce** from canned chipotles

● **Chipotle Ketchup:** Mix together ketchup, chipotle pepper and adobo sauce.

● In small skillet, cook butter with bacon over medium-high heat until bacon fat is rendered; sauté onion and garlic until golden, about 3 minutes. Scrape into bowl; let cool. Whisk in egg, wine, salt and pepper; mix in beef. Shape into four ¾-inch/2 cm thick patties.

● Grill on greased grill over medium heat, turning once, until no longer pink inside or digital thermometer registers 160°F/71°C, about 15 minutes. Serve with Chipotle Ketchup.

Makes 4 burgers.

PER BURGER (WITHOUT BUN): about 371 cal, 26 g pro, 24 g total fat (12 g sat. fat), 11 g carb, 1 g fibre, 130 mg chol, 849 mg sodium. % RDI: 3% calcium, 19% iron, 11% vit A, 10% vit C, 10% folate.

Hamburger Buns

Step aside, store-bought buns – here are the finest hamburger buns you'll ever taste. For a grainier bun, use multigrain flour or substitute up to 2 cups/500 mL of the all-purpose flour with whole wheat or whole spelt flour.

2 tbsp / 30 mL **granulated sugar**

1 cup / 250 mL **warm water**

1 pkg **active dry yeast** (or 2¼ tsp/11 mL)

1 cup / 250 mL **milk**

2 tbsp / 30 mL **butter**

1½ tsp / 7 mL **salt**

5 cups / 1.25 L (approx) **all-purpose flour**

1 **egg yolk**

Sesame seeds (optional)

● In large bowl, dissolve 1 tsp/ 5 mL of the sugar in warm water. Sprinkle in yeast; let stand until frothy, 10 minutes.

● Meanwhile, in saucepan, heat milk, remaining sugar, butter and salt over low heat just until butter is melted; let cool to lukewarm. Add to yeast mixture.

● In stand mixer with paddle attachment or using wooden spoon, beat in 3 cups/750 mL of the flour, 1 cup/250 mL at a time, until smooth. Stir in enough of the remaining flour to make stiff dough.

● Turn out onto lightly floured surface. Knead, adding more flour if necessary to prevent sticking, until smooth and elastic, 10 minutes. Place in greased bowl, turning to grease all over. Cover and let rise in warm draft-free place until doubled in bulk, 1 to 1½ hours.

● Lightly push down dough; turn out onto lightly floured surface. Roll into log and divide into 16 pieces; shape each into ball, stretching and pinching dough underneath to smooth tops. Place, 2 inches/ 5 cm apart, on greased baking sheet; flatten slightly. Cover and let rise in warm draft-free place until doubled in bulk, 30 to 60 minutes.

● Whisk egg yolk with 1 tbsp/ 15 mL water; brush gently over tops; sprinkle with sesame seeds (if using). Bake in centre of 400°F/200°C oven until golden and buns sound hollow when tapped on bottoms, 20 to 25 minutes. Transfer to rack; let cool. (Freeze unused buns in airtight containers for up to 2 months.)

Makes 16 buns.

PER BUN: about 174 cal, 5 g pro, 2 g total fat (1 g sat. fat), 32 g carb, 1 g fibre, 18 mg chol, 239 mg sodium. % RDI: 2% calcium, 12% iron, 3% vit A, 25% folate.

Meat Loaf Burgers

These family-friendly burgers are great topped with sliced Cheddar cheese and served on onion buns.

1 **egg**

¼ cup / 60 mL **dry bread crumbs**

¼ cup / 60 mL chopped **fresh parsley**

1 **onion**, grated

2 cloves **garlic**, minced

2 tbsp / 30 mL **milk** or cream

1 tsp / 5 mL **dried oregano**

½ tsp / 2 mL **dried thyme**

½ tsp / 2 mL each **salt** and **black pepper**

8 oz / 250 g **lean ground pork**

8 oz / 250 g **lean ground beef**

¼ cup / 60 mL **barbecue sauce**

4 **buns**

● Whisk together egg, bread crumbs, parsley, onion, garlic, milk, oregano, thyme, salt and pepper; mix in pork and beef. Shape into four ¾-inch/2 cm thick patties.

● Grill on greased grill over medium heat for 7 minutes; turn and spread with barbecue sauce. Grill until no longer pink inside or digital thermometer registers 160°F/71°C, about 8 minutes. Serve in buns.

Makes 4 burgers.

PER BURGER: about 479 cal, 30 g pro, 19 g total fat (6 g sat. fat), 43 g carb, 3 g fibre, 113 mg chol, 1,008 mg sodium. % RDI: 14% calcium, 34% iron, 6% vit A, 15% vit C, 40% folate.

Left to right: Bocconcini Chicken Burger
(page 117), Feta & Lamb Burger Pita (page 115),
Glazed Cheddar Pork Burger (page 108),
Veal Patty Melt (page 104)

Bison Burgers

Farmers' markets and specialty butchers are good sources for homegrown bison. Try these burgers with grainy mustard on whole wheat buns.

1 tbsp / 15 mL **vegetable oil**

¾ cup / 175 mL finely chopped **onion**

1 **egg**

¼ cup / 60 mL **dry bread crumbs**

2 tbsp / 30 mL **beer** or water

2 tbsp / 30 mL **grainy mustard**

½ tsp / 2 mL crumbled **dried thyme**

½ tsp / 2 mL each **salt** and **black pepper**

1 lb / 500 g **ground bison**

4 **buns**

● In nonstick skillet, heat oil over medium heat; fry onion, stirring often, until softened, about 10 minutes.

● Whisk together egg, bread crumbs, beer, mustard, thyme, salt and pepper; mix in onion then bison. Shape into four ¾-inch/2 cm thick patties.

● Grill on greased grill over medium heat, turning once, until no longer pink inside or digital thermometer registers 160°F/71°C, about 15 minutes. Serve in buns.

Makes 4 burgers.

Photo, page 126

PER BURGER: about 499 cal, 29 g pro, 24 g total fat (8 g sat. fat), 39 g carb, 3 g fibre, 123 mg chol, 859 mg sodium. % RDI: 12% calcium, 40% iron, 2% vit A, 3% vit C, 39% folate.

Veal & Gorgonzola Burgers with Onions

Serve these burgers in focaccia buns or halved focaccia bread.

1 **egg**

1 clove **garlic**, minced

¼ cup / 60 mL minced **fresh parsley**

3 tbsp / 45 mL **ground tomatoes**

½ tsp / 2 mL **salt**

¼ tsp / 1 mL **black pepper**

1 lb / 500 g **ground veal**

4 oz / 125 g **Gorgonzola cheese**

SAUTÉED ONION:

2 tbsp / 30 mL **extra-virgin olive oil**

12 **fresh sage leaves**

1 large **white onion**, sliced into rings

¼ cup / 60 mL **dry white vermouth** or wine

Pinch **salt**

● **Sautéed Onion:** In skillet, heat oil over medium-high heat; fry sage until fragrant, about 20 seconds. Add onion; sauté until golden (lowering heat if browning unevenly), about 20 minutes. Add vermouth and salt; cook until liquid is evaporated, 2 to 3 minutes.

● Whisk together egg, garlic, parsley, tomatoes, salt and pepper; mix in veal. Shape into 4 balls; make well in each. Fill each with one-quarter of the cheese; press meat over to enclose. Shape into four ¾-inch/2 cm thick patties.

● Grill on greased grill over medium heat, turning once, until no longer pink inside or digital thermometer registers 160°F/71°C, about 15 minutes. Serve with Sautéed Onion.

Makes 4 burgers.

Photo, page 92

PER BURGER (WITHOUT BUN): about 389 cal, 31 g pro, 25 g total fat (10 g sat. fat), 9 g carb, 2 g fibre, 168 mg chol, 866 mg sodium. % RDI: 21% calcium, 14% iron, 14% vit A, 15% vit C, 20% folate.

Italian Stuffed Veal Burgers

These mouthwatering burgers are adapted from the meat loaf (polpettone) *recipe of Rosa Paris of Toronto. Rosa is from the small town of Modugno in Puglia, southern Italy, and this burger reflects the rich flavours of her native cuisine.*

Half bunch **spinach**, blanched, or half pkg (300 g pkg) frozen whole-leaf spinach, thawed

2 cloves **garlic**, minced

½ tsp / 2 mL each **salt** and **black pepper**

1 **egg**

¼ cup / 60 mL **dry Italian bread crumbs**

¼ cup / 60 mL grated **Parmesan cheese**

1 tbsp / 15 mL chopped **fresh parsley**

1 lb / 500 g **ground veal**

2 slices **prosciutto cotto** (Italian cooked ham) or Black Forest ham

2 slices **provolone cheese**

● Mix together spinach and half each of the garlic, salt and pepper.

● Whisk together egg, bread crumbs, Parmesan cheese, parsley and remaining garlic, salt and pepper; mix in veal.

● Place prosciutto cotto on cutting board; top each slice with 1 slice cheese, then half of the spinach mixture. Roll up; cut in half. Shape veal mixture into 4 balls; make well in each. Fill each with ham roll-up; press meat over to enclose. Shape into four ¾-inch/2 cm thick patties.

● Grill on greased grill over medium heat, turning once, until no longer pink inside or digital thermometer registers 160°F/71°C, about 15 minutes.

Makes 4 burgers.

PER BURGER (WITHOUT BUN): about 293 cal, 33 g pro, 14 g total fat (7 g sat. fat), 7 g carb, 1 g fibre, 157 mg chol, 856 mg sodium. % RDI: 20% calcium, 14% iron, 25% vit A, 8% vit C, 20% folate.

Quick-Fix Toppings

Tart-Sweet Cucumber Slices

- Toss together 1 cup/250 mL thinly sliced **cucumber**, ⅓ cup/75 mL thinly sliced **red** or sweet **onion**, 2 tbsp/30 mL **white wine vinegar** and 2 tsp/10 mL **granulated sugar**; let stand for 30 minutes. Drain.

Makes about 1⅓ cups/325 mL.

PER 1 TBSP/15 mL: about 3 cal, 0 g pro, 0 g total fat (0 g sat. fat), 6 g carb, 0 g fibre, 0 mg chol, 0 mg sodium.

Grilled Marinated Peppers

- Grill 4 **sweet red peppers**, turning, until charred; let cool. Peel and seed; cut into 1-inch/2.5 cm strips. Whisk 3 tbsp/45 mL **extra-virgin olive oil**, 1 tbsp/15 mL **sherry vinegar**, and ¼ tsp/1 mL each **salt**, **black pepper** and **granulated sugar**; toss with peppers.

Makes about 2 cups/500 mL.

PER 1 TBSP/15 mL: about 15 cal, trace pro, 1 g total fat (trace sat. fat), 1 g carb, trace fibre, 0 mg chol, 18 mg sodium. % RDI: 1% iron, 5% vit A, 40% vit C, 1% folate.

Minty Mayonnaise

- Whisk together ½ cup/125 mL **mayonnaise**; 2 tbsp/30 mL each chopped **fresh mint** and **coriander**; half **jalapeño pepper**, seeded and minced; 2 tsp/10 mL **lemon juice**; and pinch each **salt** and **black pepper**.

Makes about ½ cup/125 mL.

PER 1 TBSP/15 mL: about 100 cal, trace pro, 11 g total fat (2 g sat. fat), 1 g carb, trace fibre, 5 mg chol, 79 mg sodium. % RDI: 1% calcium, 1% iron, 2% vit A, 2% vit C, 1% folate.

Tahini Sauce

- Whisk together ¼ cup/60 mL **Balkan-style plain yogurt**; ¼ cup/60 mL **tahini**; 2 tbsp/30 mL each **extra-virgin olive oil** and **water**; 1 tbsp/15 mL **lemon juice**; 1 clove **garlic**, minced; and ¼ tsp/1 mL each **paprika** and **salt**.

Makes about ¾ cup/175 mL.

PER 1 TBSP/15 mL: about 50 cal, 1 g pro, 5 g total fat (1 g sat. fat), 2 g carb, trace fibre, 1 mg chol, 70 mg sodium. % RDI: 3% calcium, 4% iron, 1% vit A, 3% folate.

Brandied Mushrooms

- In small nonstick skillet, heat 1 tbsp/15 mL **olive oil** or butter over medium heat; fry 1 each **shallot** or small onion and clove **garlic**, minced, until softened, about 2 minutes. Add 2 cups/500 mL **sliced mushrooms**, 2 tbsp/30 mL each minced **fresh parsley** and **brandy**, and ¼ tsp/1 mL each **salt** and **dried thyme**. Fry, stirring occasionally, until mushrooms are lightly browned, about 8 minutes. If desired, stir in ½ tsp/2 mL **truffle oil**.

Makes 1 cup/250 mL.

PER ¼ CUP/60 mL: about 33 cal, 1 g pro, 2 g total fat (trace sat. fat), 1 g carb, trace fibre, 0 mg chol, 73 mg sodium. % RDI: 1% calcium, 2% iron, 1% vit A, 2% vit C, 2% folate.

-->

<--

Golden Onions

- In skillet, heat 2 tbsp/30 mL **olive oil** over medium-low heat; fry 2 **onions**, thinly sliced; 1 clove **garlic**, sliced; and 1 **bay leaf**, stirring occasionally, until golden, about 15 minutes. Stir in ¼ cup/60 mL **dry white wine** (or water and 2 tsp/10 mL wine vinegar), ¼ tsp/1 mL each **salt** and **black pepper**; and pinch **ground allspice** or cloves. Cook until liquid is evaporated; discard bay leaf. Stir in 2 tbsp/30 mL minced **fresh parsley**.

Makes 1 cup/250 mL.

PER ¼ CUP/60 ML: about 30 cal, trace pro, 2 g total fat (trace sat. fat), 3 g carb, trace fibre, 0 mg chol, 74 mg sodium. % RDI: 1% calcium, 1% iron, 1% vit A, 4% vit C, 3% folate.

Blue Cheese and Horseradish Sauce

- Mix together 2 tbsp/30 mL each crumbled **blue cheese** and **light sour cream**; 1 tbsp/ 15 mL each minced **fresh chives**, prepared **horseradish** and **mayonnaise**; ¼ tsp/1 mL **black pepper**; and pinch **salt**.

Makes ⅓ cup/75 mL.

PER 1½ TBSP/22 ML: about 37 cal, 2 g pro, 3 g total fat (1 g sat. fat), 2 g carb, trace fibre, 5 mg chol, 96 mg sodium. % RDI: 4% calcium, 1% iron, 2% vit A, 2% folate.

Fresh Tomato and Onion Relish

- Mix together half each **tomato** and **dill pickle**, finely diced; 1 tbsp/15 mL each minced **red onion**, minced **fresh parsley**, chopped **capers** and **extra-virgin olive oil**; ½ tsp/2 mL **red wine vinegar**; ¼ tsp/1 mL **dried oregano**; and dash **hot pepper sauce**.

Makes ½ cup/125 mL.

PER 2 TBSP/30 ML: about 37 cal, trace pro, 3 g total fat (trace sat. fat), 1 g carb, trace fibre, 0 mg chol, 171 mg sodium. % RDI: 1% iron, 2% vit A, 8% vit C, 2% folate.

Why Do Ground Meats Need to Be Cooked Well?

Bacteria is introduced to meat through its air-exposed surface. Since ground meat has significantly more surface area than a simple cut, it is particularly susceptible to bacterial contamination. Searing a steak kills the surface bacteria, allowing you to serve the meat rare, but burgers must be cooked through to a specific temperature to be safe.

Different ground meats are fully cooked at slightly different temperatures. To test, take one burger off the grill and insert a digital instant-read thermometer horizontally; leave for 30 seconds before reading the temperature.

GROUND MEAT	SAFE INTERNAL TEMPERATURE
Chicken, Turkey	165°F/74°C
Beef, Bison, Veal, Venison	160°F/71°C
Lamb	160°F/71°C
Pork	160°F/71°C
Fish	158°F/70°C

From top: Brandied
Mushrooms, Minty
Mayonnaise, Tart-Sweet
Cucumber Slices,
Golden Onions, Grilled
Marinated Peppers,
Tahini Sauce (pages
101 and 102)

Veal Patty Melts

Patty melts, an old-fashioned diner favourite, get a delicious flavour update with veal.

2 tbsp / 30 mL **vegetable oil**

2 **onions**, sliced

Pinch each **salt** and **black pepper**

2 tsp / 10 mL **Russian** or sweet **mustard**

8 slices **dark rye bread**

4 oz / 125 g **Swiss cheese**, thinly sliced

PATTIES:

1 **egg**

1 clove **garlic**, minced

¼ cup / 60 mL chopped **fresh parsley**

1 tbsp / 15 mL **Dijon mustard**

½ tsp / 2 mL **salt**

¼ tsp / 1 mL **caraway seeds**

¼ tsp / 1 mL **black pepper**

1 lb / 500 g **ground veal**

● In large skillet, heat oil over medium heat; fry onions, salt and pepper, stirring occasionally, until golden, about 10 minutes.

● **Patties:** Whisk together egg, 1 tbsp/15 mL water, garlic, parsley, mustard, salt, caraway seeds and pepper; mix in veal. Shape into four ¾-inch/2 cm thick patties.

● Grill on greased grill over medium heat, turning once, until no longer pink inside or digital thermometer registers 160°F/71°C, about 15 minutes.

● Spread mustard over 4 of the bread slices; top with patties, cheese and fried onions. Sandwich with remaining bread. Grill, covered, on greased grill over medium-low heat, turning once, until bread is toasted and cheese is melted, about 6 minutes.

Makes 4 burgers.

Photo, page 97

PER BURGER: about 513 cal, 38 g pro, 26 g total fat (9 g sat. fat), 31 g carb, 4 g fibre, 171 mg chol, 846 mg sodium, 535 mg potassium. % RDI: 33% calcium, 21% iron, 13% vit A, 12% vit C, 35% folate.

Juicy Pork Burgers

Pork makes for a succulent and flavourful burger. We hope this new recipe will quickly become a classic.

½ cup / 125 mL minced **sweet green pepper**

½ cup / 125 mL minced **sweet onion**

¼ cup / 60 mL **plain yogurt**

1 tbsp / 15 mL minced **fresh sage** or 1 tsp/5 mL crumbled dried

2 tsp / 10 mL **hot mustard**

1 tsp / 5 mL **Worcestershire sauce**

¾ tsp / 4 mL **salt**

¼ tsp / 1 mL **black pepper**

1 lb / 500 g **lean ground pork**

● Mix together green pepper, onion, yogurt, sage, mustard, Worcestershire sauce, salt and pepper; mix in pork. Shape into four ¾-inch/2 cm thick patties.

● Grill on greased grill over medium heat, turning once, until no longer pink inside or digital thermometer registers 160°F/71°C, about 15 minutes.

Makes 4 burgers.

PER BURGER (WITHOUT BUN): about 215 cal, 22 g pro, 12 g total fat (5 g sat. fat), 4 g carb, 1 g fibre, 74 mg chol, 543 mg sodium, 393 mg potassium. % RDI: 5% calcium, 9% iron, 1% vit A, 25% vit C, 6% folate.

Green Onion Pork Burgers

Serve these Chinese-inspired burgers topped with Napa Slaw (below) on sesame buns.

1 **egg**

1 cup / 250 mL finely chopped **green onions**

⅓ cup / 75 mL **dry bread crumbs**

1 **green hot pepper**, seeded and minced (optional)

1 clove **garlic**, minced

1 tbsp / 15 mL **soy sauce**

1 tbsp / 15 mL **fish sauce** or soy sauce

1 tbsp / 15 mL **Chinese rice wine** or dry sherry (or 1 tsp/5 mL balsamic vinegar)

2 tsp / 10 mL grated **fresh ginger**

2 tsp / 10 mL **sesame oil**

½ tsp / 2 mL **white pepper**

¼ tsp / 1 mL **hot pepper sauce**

1 lb / 500 g **lean ground pork**

● Whisk together egg, onions, bread crumbs, hot pepper (if using), garlic, soy sauce, fish sauce, wine, ginger, sesame oil, white pepper and hot pepper sauce; mix in pork. Shape into four ¾-inch/2 cm thick patties.

● Grill on greased grill over medium heat, turning once, until no longer pink inside or digital thermometer registers 160°F/71°C, about 15 minutes.

Makes 4 burgers.

Napa Slaw

● Whisk together 2 tbsp/30 mL **rice vinegar**, 2 tsp/ 10 mL **granulated sugar**, 1 tsp/5 mL **sesame oil**, ½ tsp/ 2 mL **salt**, and pinch **hot pepper flakes**. Toss with 3 cups/750 mL shredded **napa cabbage**; 1 small **carrot**, shredded; and ½ cup/125 mL thinly sliced **sweet red pepper** until coated. Let stand for 15 minutes before serving.

Makes 1½ cups/375 mL, enough for 4 servings.

PER BURGER (WITHOUT BUN OR SLAW): about 309 cal, 25 g pro, 18 g total fat (6 g sat. fat), 10 g carb, 1 g fibre, 116 mg chol, 763 mg sodium. % RDI: 6% calcium, 16% iron, 6% vit A, 15% vit C, 13% folate.

Glazed Cheddar Pork Burgers

Skewering the onions with metal or soaked wooden skewers keeps the slices together while grilling.

2 tbsp / 30 mL **Dijon mustard**

2 tbsp / 30 mL **maple syrup**

1 tsp / 5 mL **cider vinegar**

1 small **red onion**, cut into 4 thick slices

1 tbsp / 15 mL **vegetable oil**

Pinch each **salt** and **black pepper**

4 **buns**

PATTIES:

1 **egg**, beaten

¾ cup / 175 mL shredded **extra-old Cheddar cheese**

¼ cup / 60 mL **dry bread crumbs**

1 clove **garlic**, minced

½ tsp / 2 mL crumbled **dried sage**

½ tsp / 2 mL **salt**

¼ tsp / 1 mL **black pepper**

1 lb / 500 g **lean ground pork**

● **Patties:** Stir together egg, 1 tbsp/15 mL water, cheese, bread crumbs, garlic, sage, salt and pepper; mix in pork. Shape into four ¾-inch/2 cm thick patties.

● Whisk together Dijon mustard, maple syrup and cider vinegar; set aside.

● Skewer onion slices through edges to keep rings intact. Brush both sides with oil; sprinkle with salt and pepper. Grill on greased grill over medium heat, turning once, until tender, about 10 minutes. Remove skewers and separate into rings.

● Meanwhile, grill patties on greased grill over medium heat for 5 minutes. Turn and brush with half of the mustard mixture; grill for 5 minutes. Turn again; brush with remaining mustard mixture. Grill until no longer pink inside or digital thermometer registers 160°F/71°C, about 5 minutes. Serve in buns with onions.

Makes 4 burgers.

Photo, page 97

PER BURGER: about 586 cal, 34 g pro, 28 g total fat (10 g sat. fat), 47 g carb, 3 g fibre, 140 mg chol, 979 mg sodium, 536 mg potassium. % RDI: 27% calcium, 28% iron, 8% vit A, 2% vit C, 39% folate.

Mexican Burgers

The herbs and spices used in Mexican fresh chorizo highlight this piquant patty. Serve in warm tortillas or whole wheat buns with your favourite Mexican hot sauce.

1 **egg**

2 tbsp / 30 mL **red wine vinegar**

4 cloves **garlic**, minced

1 tsp / 5 mL **granulated sugar**

¾ tsp / 4 mL **salt**

½ tsp / 1 mL **black pepper**

½ tsp / 2 mL **cinnamon**

½ tsp / 2 mL **ground cumin**

¼ to 1 tsp / 1 to 5 mL **cayenne pepper**

¼ tsp / 1 mL **dried oregano**

Pinch **ground cloves**

8 oz / 250 g **lean ground beef**

8 oz / 250 g **lean ground pork**

1 **avocado**, peeled, pitted and sliced

● Whisk together egg, vinegar, garlic, sugar, salt, pepper, cinnamon, cumin, cayenne, oregano and cloves; mix in beef and pork. Shape into four ¾-inch/ 2 cm thick patties.

● Grill on greased grill over medium heat, turning once, until no longer pink inside or digital thermometer registers 160°F/71°C, about 15 minutes. Top with avocado slices.

Makes 4 burgers.

PER BURGER (WITHOUT BUN): about 296 cal, 23 g pro, 20 g total fat (6 g sat. fat), 7 g carb, 3 g fibre, 113 mg chol, 517 mg sodium. % RDI: 4% calcium, 19% iron, 6% vit A, 8% vit C, 20% folate.

Lamb Burgers

Serve these basic lamb burgers with Minty Mayonnaise (page 101).

1 **egg**

¼ cup / 60 mL **dry bread crumbs**

1 **onion**, grated

2 tbsp / 30 mL **wine vinegar**

2 tsp / 10 mL **Dijon mustard**

1 tsp / 5 mL **dried marjoram**

1 clove **garlic**, minced

½ tsp / 2 mL each **salt** and **black pepper**

1 lb / 500 g **ground lamb**

4 **buns**

● Whisk together egg, 2 tbsp/30 mL water, bread crumbs, onion, vinegar, mustard, marjoram, garlic, salt and pepper; mix in lamb. Shape into four ¾-inch/2 cm thick patties.

● Grill on greased grill over medium heat, turning once, until no longer pink inside or digital thermometer registers 160°F/71°C, about 15 minutes. Serve in buns.

Makes 4 burgers.

PER BURGER: about 503 cal, 27 g pro, 26 g total fat (10 g sat. fat), 38 g carb, 3 g fibre, 126 mg chol, 786 mg sodium. % RDI: 12% calcium, 30% iron, 2% vit A, 3% vit C, 40% folate.

Herb & Spice Lamb Burgers

Serve these lively and sophisticated burgers topped with sliced tomato and cucumber and Tahini Sauce (page 101), or with Grilled Marinated Peppers (page 101).

1 **egg**

1 small **onion**, finely chopped

⅓ cup / 75 mL minced **fresh mint**

⅓ cup / 75 mL minced **fresh parsley**

2 tbsp / 30 mL **lemon juice**

1 tbsp / 15 mL minced seeded **hot green pepper**

2 cloves **garlic**, minced

2 tsp / 10 mL **ground coriander**

1 tsp / 5 mL **dried marjoram** or oregano

¾ tsp / 4 mL **salt**

½ tsp / 2 mL **ground cumin**

½ tsp / 2 mL **black pepper**

¼ tsp / 1 mL **ground allspice**

1 lb / 500 g **lean ground lamb**

● Whisk together egg, onion, mint, parsley, lemon juice, hot pepper, garlic, coriander, marjoram, salt, cumin, pepper and allspice; mix in lamb. Shape into four ¾-inch/2 cm thick patties.

● Grill on greased grill over medium heat, turning once, until no longer pink inside or digital thermometer registers 160°F/71°C, about 15 minutes.

Makes 4 burgers.

PER BURGER (WITHOUT BUN): about 251 cal, 21 g pro, 16 g total fat (7 g sat. fat), 4 g carb, 1 g fibre, 120 mg chol, 371 mg sodium. % RDI: 5% calcium, 20% iron, 8% vit A, 25% vit C, 15% folate.

Lamb Burgers with Grilled Vegetables

Top these Middle Eastern—spiced burgers with yogurt or hummus and pickled peppers.

1 **egg**

1 cup / 250 mL minced **red onion**

¼ cup / 60 mL **fresh bread crumbs**

¼ cup / 60 mL chopped **fresh dill**

¼ cup / 60 mL chopped **fresh parsley**

4 cloves **garlic**, minced

1 tbsp / 15 mL **pine nuts** (optional)

1 tbsp / 15 mL **ketchup**

½ tsp / 2 mL each **salt** and **black pepper**

¼ tsp / 1 mL **paprika**

¼ tsp / 1 mL **cayenne pepper**

1 lb / 500 g **lean ground lamb** or beef

GRILLED VEGETABLES:

4 thick slices peeled large **eggplant**
or 12 thick slices Asian eggplant
(unpeeled)

4 thick slices **tomato**

2 tbsp / 30 mL **extra-virgin olive oil**

¼ tsp / 1 mL each **salt** and **black pepper**

● Whisk together egg, onion, bread crumbs, dill, parsley, garlic, pine nuts (if using), ketchup, salt, pepper, paprika and cayenne; mix in lamb. Shape into four ¾-inch/2 cm thick patties.

● Grill on greased grill over medium heat, turning once, until no longer pink inside or digital thermometer registers 160°F/71°C, about 15 minutes.

● **Grilled Vegetables:** Meanwhile, brush eggplant and tomato with oil; sprinkle with salt and pepper. Grill, turning once, until tender, about 5 minutes for eggplant and 1 minute for tomato. Serve on burgers.

Makes 4 burgers.

PER BURGER (WITHOUT BUN): about 336 cal, 24 g pro, 21 g total fat (7 g sat. fat), 13 g carb, 3 g fibre, 126 mg chol, 567 mg sodium. % RDI: 4% calcium, 21% iron, 9% vit A, 27% vit C, 19% folate.

Lamb Burgers with Tzatziki

2 tbsp / 30 mL **extra-virgin olive oil**

1 **leek** (white and light green parts only), finely chopped

1 **egg**

⅓ cup / 75 mL minced **fresh parsley**

1 tsp / 5 mL **dried oregano**, crumbled

½ tsp / 2 mL each **salt** and **black pepper**

¼ tsp / 1 mL **cayenne pepper**

¼ tsp / 1 mL **ground cumin**

¼ tsp / 1 mL **ground allspice**

1 lb / 500 g **ground lamb**

Half recipe **Tzatziki** (page 25)

● In skillet, heat oil over medium heat; fry leek, stirring often, until softened, about 4 minutes. Let cool. Whisk together egg, leek, parsley, oregano, salt, pepper, cayenne, cumin and allspice; mix in lamb. Shape into four ¾-inch/2 cm thick patties.

● Grill over medium heat, turning once, until no longer pink inside or digital thermometer registers 160°F/71°C, about 15 minutes. Serve with Tzatziki.

Makes 4 burgers.

Photo, page 92

PER BURGER (WITHOUT BUN): about 342 cal, 25 g pro, 23 g total fat (9 g sat. fat), 8 g carb, 1 g fibre, 134 mg chol, 668 mg sodium. % RDI: 10% calcium, 21% iron, 8% vit A, 17% vit C, 16% folate.

Feta & Lamb Burger Pitas

Serve with leaf lettuce, sliced cucumbers and chopped tomatoes to add to the pita.

¼ cup / 60 mL **plain yogurt**

1 tbsp / 15 mL chopped **fresh mint**

4 **pitas** (with pockets)

½ cup / 125 mL crumbled **feta cheese**

2 tbsp / 30 mL sliced **Kalamata olives**

PATTIES:

1 **egg**

¼ cup / 60 mL **dry bread crumbs**

Half **onion**, grated

2 cloves **garlic**, minced

2 tbsp / 30 mL **wine vinegar**

2 tsp / 10 mL **Dijon mustard**

½ tsp / 2 mL **salt**

½ tsp / 2 mL **dried oregano**

¼ tsp / 1 mL **black pepper**

1 lb / 500 g **ground lamb**

● **Patties:** Whisk together egg, 1 tbsp/15 mL water, bread crumbs, onion, garlic, vinegar, mustard, salt, oregano and pepper; mix in lamb. Shape into four ¾-inch/2 cm thick patties.

● Grill on greased grill over medium heat, turning once, until no longer pink inside or digital thermometer registers 160°F/71°C, about 15 minutes.

● Mix yogurt with mint. Serve burgers in pitas with yogurt mixture, feta cheese and olives.

Makes 4 burgers.

Photo, page 96

115

PER BURGER: about 544 cal, 31 g pro, 27 g total fat (12 g sat. fat), 43 g carb, 2 g fibre, 143 mg chol, 1,129 mg sodium, 454 mg potassium. % RDI: 20% calcium, 30% iron, 5% vit A, 2% vit C, 48% folate.

Venison Burgers with Red Wine Mushrooms

Fabulously tasty but very lean, venison benefits from the addition of a little animal fat, such as lard or butter; egg yolks add extra richness.

3 tbsp / 45 mL **lard** or butter

1 **onion**, finely chopped

¾ tsp / 4 mL **salt**

1 tsp / 5 mL **paprika**

¼ tsp / 1 mL **chipotle chili powder** or pinch cayenne pepper

¼ tsp / 1 mL **ground cumin**

¼ tsp / 1 mL **black pepper**

2 **egg yolks**

1 tsp / 5 mL **Worcestershire sauce**

1 lb / 500 g **ground venison**

RED WINE MUSHROOMS:

8 oz / 250 g **white** or cremini **mushrooms**

2 tbsp / 30 mL **butter**

1 clove **garlic**, minced

⅓ cup / 75 mL **dry red wine**

¼ tsp / 1 mL **salt**

¼ tsp / 1 mL **dried oregano**, crumbled

1 tsp / 5 mL **sherry vinegar** or red wine vinegar

2 tbsp / 30 mL chopped **fresh parsley**

● **Red Wine Mushrooms:** With mandoline or sharp knife, slice mushrooms as thinly as possible. In skillet, melt butter over medium-high heat; sauté mushrooms and garlic until mushrooms are browned, 3 to 5 minutes. Add wine, salt and oregano; cook until wine is evaporated. Stir in vinegar. Remove from heat; stir in parsley. Set aside.

● In skillet, melt lard over medium-high heat; fry onion and ¼ tsp/1 mL of the salt, stirring often, until golden, 6 to 8 minutes. Reduce heat to low; stir in paprika, chipotle chili powder, cumin and pepper. Cook, stirring, for 1 minute. Scrape into bowl; let cool slightly. Whisk in egg yolks, Worcestershire sauce and remaining salt; mix in venison. Shape into four ¾-inch/2 cm thick patties.

● Grill over medium heat, turning once, until no longer pink inside or digital thermometer registers 160°F/71°C, about 15 minutes. Top with Red Wine Mushrooms.

Makes 4 burgers.

PER BURGER (WITHOUT BUN): about 382 cal, 28 g pro, 26 g total fat (12 g sat. fat), 6 g carb, 2 g fibre, 218 mg chol, 710 mg sodium, 598 mg potassium. % RDI: 4% calcium, 34% iron, 14% vit A, 10% vit C, 16% folate.

Bocconcini Chicken Burgers

Grinding chicken thighs in your food processor for this burger, rather than using already-ground chicken, gives the best flavour and texture. A Caprese salad topping of bocconcini cheese, tomatoes and basil adds a fresh kick.

4 **buns**

4 slices **bocconcini cheese** (one 4-oz/125 g ball)

1 **plum tomato**, sliced

4 large **fresh basil leaves**

PATTIES:

1 lb / 500 g **boneless skinless chicken thighs**

1 **egg**

Half **onion**, grated

2 cloves **garlic**, minced

⅓ cup / 75 mL grated **Parmesan cheese**

¼ cup / 60 mL **dry bread crumbs**

2 tbsp / 30 mL chopped **fresh basil**

2 tbsp / 30 mL chopped drained **oil-packed sun-dried tomatoes**

¼ tsp / 1 mL each **salt** and **black pepper**

● **Patties:** In food processor, pulse chicken until coarsely ground; set aside. Whisk together egg, 1 tbsp/ 15 mL water, onion, garlic, cheese, bread crumbs, basil, sun-dried tomatoes, salt and pepper; mix in chicken. Shape into four ¾-inch /2 cm thick patties.

● Grill on greased grill over medium heat, turning once, until no longer pink inside or digital thermometer registers 165°F/74°C, about 15 minutes.

● Serve burgers in buns with bocconcini, tomato and basil leaves.

Makes 4 burgers.

Photo, page 96

PER BURGER: about 499 cal, 39 g pro, 20 g total fat (8 g sat. fat), 40 g carb, 3 g fibre, 170 mg chol, 904 mg sodium, 534 mg potassium. % RDI: 35% calcium, 29% iron, 12% vit A, 15% vit C, 40% folate.

Gourmet Teriyaki Chicken Sandwich

4 **boneless skinless chicken breasts**

2 tsp / 10 mL **vegetable oil**

⅓ cup / 75 mL **Teriyaki Sauce** (page 531)

4 thick slices **crusty bread**

4 leaves **leaf lettuce** or frisée

4 tsp / 20 mL toasted **sesame seeds**

CAPER MAYONNAISE:

½ cup / 125 mL light or regular **mayonnaise**

2 tbsp / 30 mL **extra-virgin olive oil**

1 tbsp / 15 mL minced drained **capers**

2 tsp / 10 mL **Dijon mustard**

2 tsp / 10 mL **lemon juice**

¼ tsp / 1 mL **white pepper**

● **Caper Mayonnaise:** Mix together mayonnaise, oil, capers, mustard, lemon juice and pepper.

● Brush chicken all over with oil. Grill, covered, on greased grill over medium-high heat, turning once, for 8 minutes. Brush both sides with some of the Teriyaki Sauce; grill, covered, turning and brushing with remaining sauce, until no longer pink inside, about 2 minutes. Let stand for 3 minutes before slicing.

● Spread Caper Mayonnaise on bread; top with lettuce then chicken. Sprinkle with sesame seeds.

Makes 4 sandwiches.

PER SANDWICH: about 447 cal, 35 g pro, 23 g total fat (4 g sat. fat), 23 g carb, 1 g fibre, 88 mg chol, 1,299 mg sodium. % RDI: 4% calcium, 16% iron, 3% vit A, 5% vit C, 20% folate.

"Wild" Turkey Burgers

You can make these well-spiced burgers with either turkey or pork.
Serve on a bun with lettuce and tomatoes.

1 **egg**

¼ cup / 60 mL **dry bread crumbs**

2 tbsp / 30 mL **bourbon** or Tennessee whisky

2 tbsp / 30 mL **tomato ketchup**

1 tbsp / 15 mL **fancy molasses**

1 small **onion**, minced

2 cloves **garlic**, minced

1 tbsp / 15 mL **chili powder**

1 tsp / 5 mL **crumbled dried sage**

½ tsp / 2 mL **salt**

1 lb / 500 g **ground turkey**

4 slices **smoked cheese**

Sliced pickled jalapeño peppers

● Whisk together egg, bread crumbs, bourbon, ketchup, molasses, onion, garlic, chili powder, sage and salt; mix in turkey. Shape into four ¾-inch/2 cm thick patties.

● Grill over medium heat, turning halfway through and topping with cheese, until no longer pink inside or digital thermometer registers 165°F/74°C, about 15 minutes. Serve with jalapeños.

Makes 4 burgers.

PER BURGER (WITHOUT BUN): about 321 cal, 27 g pro, 16 g total fat (6 g sat. fat), 14 g carb, 1 g fibre, 156 mg chol, 735 mg sodium. % RDI: 17% calcium, 19% iron, 13% vit A, 7% vit C, 10% folate.

Grilled Eggplant & Pepper Panini

1 **eggplant**, cut into ¼-inch/5 mm thick slices

2 **sweet red peppers**, quartered

2 tbsp / 30 mL **extra-virgin olive oil**

2 cloves **garlic**, minced

¼ tsp / 1 mL each **salt** and **black pepper**

4 **panini buns**

2 tsp / 10 mL **hot** or Dijon **mustard**

12 whole **fresh basil leaves**

4 oz / 125 g thinly sliced **provolone cheese**

● Toss together eggplant, peppers, oil, garlic, salt and pepper until coated. Grill, covered, on greased grill over medium-high heat, turning once, until tender, about 10 minutes.

● Cut buns in half horizontally; spread with mustard. Sandwich eggplant, peppers, basil, then cheese in buns.

● Grill, covered, on greased grill over medium heat, pressing often to flatten and turning once, until buns are crusty and cheese is melted, about 5 minutes.

Makes 4 sandwiches.

PER SANDWICH: about 393 cal, 15 g pro, 18 g total fat (6 g sat. fat), 45 g carb, 5 g fibre, 20 mg chol, 770 mg sodium. % RDI: 27% calcium, 21% iron, 30% vit A, 167% vit C, 40% folate.

Bulgur & Mushroom Burgers

Serve these burgers on whole wheat kaiser rolls with lettuce and tomato slices.

¾ cup / 175 mL **bulgur**

1 **egg**, beaten

1 cup / 250 mL **fresh whole wheat bread crumbs**

¼ cup / 60 mL minced **fresh parsley**

8 oz / 250 g **mushrooms**

2 tbsp / 30 mL **extra-virgin olive oil**

1 small **onion**, finely chopped

2 cloves **garlic**, minced

¼ cup / 60 mL **dry white wine** or vegetable stock

½ tsp / 2 mL **salt**

¼ tsp / 1 mL **black pepper**

¼ tsp / 1 mL **dried thyme**

● In heatproof bowl, pour 1 cup/250 mL boiling water over bulgur; let stand until doubled in bulk, about 20 minutes. Mix in egg, bread crumbs and parsley.

● Meanwhile, roughly break mushrooms into pieces; in food processor, pulse until very finely chopped. In skillet, heat oil over medium heat; fry onion and garlic until softened, about 3 minutes. Stir in mushrooms, wine, salt, pepper and thyme; cook over medium-high heat, stirring occasionally, until liquid is evaporated and mushrooms begin to brown, about 8 minutes.

● Mix into bulgur mixture. Shape into four ¾-inch/2 cm thick patties.

● Grill on greased grill over medium heat, turning once, until heated through and crispy, about 15 minutes.

Makes 4 burgers.

PER BURGER (WITHOUT BUN): about 220 cal, 7 g pro, 9 g total fat (1 g sat. fat), 30 g carb, 5 g fibre, 47 mg chol, 370 mg sodium. % RDI: 4% calcium, 19% iron, 4% vit A, 12% vit C, 20% folate.

Portobello Burger Melts

Grilled portobello mushrooms make as nice a sandwich as any grilled meat.

2 tbsp / 30 mL **olive oil**

2 tbsp / 30 mL **balsamic vinegar**

1 tbsp / 15 mL **Dijon mustard**

2 cloves **garlic**, minced

½ tsp / 2 mL **Worcestershire sauce** (optional)

Pinch each **salt** and **black pepper**

4 large **portobello mushrooms**, stemmed

4 **kaiser rolls** or buns

¼ cup / 60 mL light or regular **mayonnaise**

4 slices **tomato**

1 cup / 250 mL shredded **aged Cheddar** or Monterey Jack **cheese**

● Whisk together oil, vinegar, mustard, garlic, Worcestershire sauce (if using), salt and pepper; brush all over mushrooms. Let stand for 10 minutes. Grill, covered, on greased grill over medium-high heat, turning once, until browned and tender, about 10 minutes.

● Meanwhile, cut rolls in half horizontally; spread with mayonnaise. Sandwich tomato slice, mushroom then cheese in rolls. Grill, turning once, until rolls are crusty and cheese is melted, about 2 minutes.

Makes 4 sandwiches.

PER SANDWICH: about 438 cal, 15 g pro, 24 g total fat (8 g sat. fat), 42 g carb, 5 g fibre, 30 mg chol, 668 mg sodium. % RDI: 25% calcium, 25% iron, 10% vit A, 15% vit C, 35% folate.

Bison Burger (page 98) with Brandied Mushrooms
(page 101), Fresh Salmon Burger (opposite)
with Tart-Sweet Cucumber Slices (page 101)

Fresh Salmon Burgers

Enjoy these moist and tasty fish burgers with Tart-Sweet Cucumber Slices (page 101).

1 lb / 500 g **boneless skinless salmon**, cut into chunks

1 small **onion**, grated

¼ cup / 60 mL light or regular **mayonnaise**

2 tbsp / 30 mL **dry bread crumbs**

1 tbsp / 15 mL minced **fresh parsley**

½ tsp / 2 mL **salt**

¼ tsp / 1 mL **lemon juice**

¼ tsp / 1 mL **black pepper**

Dash **hot pepper sauce**

4 **buns**

● In food processor, pulse together salmon, onion, mayonnaise, bread crumbs, parsley, salt, lemon juice, pepper and hot pepper sauce until finely chopped. Shape into four ¾-inch/2 cm thick patties.

● Grill on greased grill over medium-high heat, turning once, until digital thermometer registers 158°F/70°C, about 10 minutes. Serve in buns.

Makes 4 burgers.

PER BURGER: about 423 cal, 25 g pro, 19 g total fat (3 g sat. fat), 36 g carb, 2 g fibre, 61 mg chol, 804 mg sodium. % RDI: 10% calcium, 19% iron, 3% vit A, 8% vit C, 43% folate.

Pickerel Sandwich with Grilled Onion

4 **skinless pickerel fillets**, each 6 oz/175 g

1½ tsp / 7 mL **salt**

½ tsp / 2 mL **white pepper**

2 tbsp / 30 mL **olive oil**

4 slices (½ inch/1 cm thick) **sweet onion**

4 **buns** or 8 thick slices bread

2 cups / 500 mL (approx) **arugula leaves**

CAPER-HERB MAYONNAISE:

⅓ cup / 75 mL **mayonnaise**

¼ cup / 60 mL finely chopped **fresh chives**

2 tbsp / 30 mL drained **capers**, finely chopped

2 tbsp / 30 mL minced **fresh parsley**

4 tsp / 20 mL chopped **fresh tarragon** or ½ tsp/2 mL dried

4 tsp / 20 mL **extra-virgin olive oil**

1 tbsp / 15 mL **grainy mustard**

2 tsp / 10 mL **lemon juice**

● **Caper-Herb Mayonnaise:** Whisk together mayonnaise, chives, capers, parsley, tarragon, oil, mustard and lemon juice.

● Sprinkle fish with 1 tsp/5 mL of the salt and pepper; brush with 4 tsp/20 mL of the oil. Sprinkle onion with remaining salt; brush with remaining oil.

● Grill fish and onion on greased grill over medium-high heat, turning once, until fish flakes easily and onion is tender, about 6 minutes. Serve fish in buns with onion, arugula and Caper-Herb Mayonnaise.

Makes 4 sandwiches.

PER SANDWICH: about 538 cal, 40 g pro, 25 g total fat (3 g sat. fat), 38 g carb, 3 g fibre, 153 mg chol, 1,581 mg sodium, 970 mg potassium. % RDI: 31% calcium, 37% iron, 14% vit A, 20% vit C, 58% folate.

Grilled Salmon Sandwich with Bok Choy Slaw

4 **skinless salmon fillets**, each 6 oz/175 g

½ tsp / 2 mL **salt**

¼ tsp / 1 mL **white pepper**

4 tsp / 20 mL **sesame oil**

4 **sesame buns**

BOK CHOY SLAW:

2 cups / 500 mL julienned **bok choy** or napa cabbage

1 tsp / 5 mL **salt**

½ cup / 125 mL **grated carrot**

¼ cup / 60 mL minced **fresh coriander**

4 tsp / 20 mL **rice vinegar**

GREEN ONION MAYONNAISE:

½ cup / 125 mL very finely sliced **green onions**

⅓ cup / 75 mL **mayonnaise**

4 tsp / 20 mL **sesame oil**

4 tsp / 20 mL **rice vinegar**

1 tsp / 5 mL **granulated sugar**

Generous pinch **white pepper**

● **Bok Choy Slaw:** Toss bok choy with salt; let stand for 15 minutes. Using hands, squeeze out moisture; toss together bok choy, carrot, coriander and vinegar.

● **Green Onion Mayonnaise:** Mix together onions, mayonnaise, sesame oil, vinegar, sugar and pepper.

● Sprinkle fish all over with salt and pepper; brush with oil. Grill on greased grill over medium-high heat, turning once, until just slightly pink in centre and fish flakes easily, 6 to 8 minutes. Serve in buns with Green Onion Mayonnaise and Bok Choy Slaw.

Makes 4 sandwiches.

PER SANDWICH: about 681 cal, 36 g pro, 43 g total fat (7 g sat. fat), 36 g carb, 3 g fibre, 91 mg chol, 1,128 mg sodium, 777 mg potassium. % RDI: 14% calcium, 21% iron, 38% vit A, 40% vit C, 63% folate.

Spiced Tilapia Sandwich with Onion Salad

1 tsp / 5 mL **paprika**

1 tsp / 5 mL **ground coriander**

1 tsp / 5 mL **ground cumin**

1 tsp / 5 mL each **salt** and **black pepper**

½ tsp / 2 mL **cayenne pepper**

4 **tilapia** or catfish **fillets**, each 6 oz/175 g

4 tsp / 20 mL **olive oil**

8 thick slices **bread**

ONION SALAD:

1 cup / 250 mL thinly sliced **white** or sweet **onion**

1 tsp / 5 mL + pinch **salt**

¼ cup / 60 mL chopped **fresh parsley**

4 tsp / 20 mL **lemon juice**

2 tsp / 10 mL **extra-virgin olive oil**

½ tsp / 2 mL **paprika**

TAHINI YOGURT SAUCE:

¼ cup / 60 mL **plain yogurt**

3 tbsp / 45 mL **tahini**

2 tbsp / 30 mL **lemon juice**

¼ tsp / 1 mL **ground cumin**

½ tsp / 2 mL **hot pepper sauce**

● **Onion Salad:** Toss onion with 1 tsp/5 mL salt; let stand for 20 minutes. Using hands, squeeze out moisture; rinse under cold water and drain, pressing to remove excess moisture. Toss together onions, parsley, lemon juice, oil, paprika and pinch salt.

● **Tahini Yogurt Sauce:** Mix together yogurt, tahini, lemon juice, cumin and hot pepper sauce.

● Mix together paprika, coriander, cumin, salt, pepper and cayenne; sprinkle all over fish. Brush with oil. Grill on greased grill over medium-high heat, turning once, until fish flakes easily, about 6 minutes. Serve on bread with Tahini Yogurt Sauce and Onion Salad.

Makes 4 sandwiches.

PER SANDWICH: about 481 cal, 43 g pro, 19 g total fat (4 g sat. fat), 37 g carb, 4 g fibre, 78 mg chol, 1,125 mg sodium, 777 mg potassium. % RDI: 16% calcium, 35% iron, 9% vit A, 18% vit C, 40% folate.

Grilled Whitefish BLT

Whitefish is one of the special pleasures of central Canadian waters. Its delicate white flesh is versatile, as in this sandwich inspired by Ontario chef Paul Johnston.

2 **skin-on whitefish fillets**, each about 12 oz/375 g

2 tbsp / 30 mL **extra-virgin olive oil**

1 tbsp / 15 mL chopped **fresh tarragon**, thyme or coriander

1 tsp / 5 mL grated **lime rind**

1 tsp / 5 mL **lime juice**

¼ tsp / 1 mL each **salt** and **black pepper**

4 pieces **focaccia**, each 4 inches/10 cm square

4 **lettuce leaves**

4 slices **prosciutto**

1 **yellow** or red **tomato**, sliced

DILL PICKLE AIOLI:

2 cloves **garlic**, minced

Pinch **salt**

½ cup / 125 mL light or regular **mayonnaise**

2 tbsp / 30 mL finely chopped **dill pickle**

2 tsp / 10 mL **lemon juice**

Pinch each **turmeric** and **cayenne pepper**

● **Dill Pickle Aioli:** Mash garlic with salt to make paste; transfer to bowl. Whisk in mayonnaise, pickle, lemon juice, turmeric and cayenne.

● Cut each fillet in half diagonally. Whisk together oil, tarragon, lime rind and juice, salt and pepper; rub all over fish. Let stand for 30 minutes.

● Grill, skin side down, on greased grill over medium-high heat, turning once, until fish flakes easily, about 8 minutes.

● Cut each piece of the focaccia in half horizontally; serve fish on focaccia with Dill Pickle Aioli, lettuce, prosciutto and tomato.

Makes 4 sandwiches.

PER SANDWICH: about 731 cal, 42 g pro, 31 g total fat (4 g sat. fat), 69 g carb, 4 g fibre, 100 mg chol, 1,626 mg sodium. % RDI: 13% calcium, 32% iron, 12% vit A, 17% vit C, 85% folate.

Hoisin-Glazed Halibut Sandwich with Spinach Salad

¼ cup / 60 mL **hoisin sauce**

2 tsp / 10 mL finely grated **fresh ginger**

2 tsp / 10 mL **sesame oil**

½ tsp / 2 mL **hot pepper sauce**

4 **skinless halibut fillets**, each 6 oz/175 g

4 **buns**

SPINACH SALAD:

1 bunch **spinach**

1 tsp / 5 mL toasted **sesame seeds**

1 tsp / 5 mL **sesame oil**

1 tsp / 5 mL **rice vinegar**

¼ tsp / 1 mL **salt**

¼ tsp / 1 mL **granulated sugar**

WASABI MAYONNAISE:

⅓ cup / 75 mL **mayonnaise**

1 tbsp / 15 mL **prepared wasabi**

2 tsp / 10 mL **rice vinegar**

● **Spinach Salad:** In pot of boiling salted water, blanch spinach; drain, chill under cold water and drain well, lightly squeezing out excess moisture. Chop; mix with sesame seeds and oil, vinegar, salt and sugar until sugar is dissolved.

● **Wasabi Mayonnaise:** Whisk together mayonnaise, wasabi and vinegar.

● Mix together hoisin sauce, ginger, sesame oil and hot pepper sauce. Place fish on greased grill over medium-high heat; brush with hoisin mixture. Grill for 3 to 4 minutes; turn and brush again. Grill until fish flakes easily, 3 to 4 minutes. Serve in buns with Wasabi Mayonnaise and Spinach Salad.

Makes 4 sandwiches.

PER SANDWICH: about 585 cal, 44 g pro, 26 g total fat (4 g sat. fat), 43 g carb, 4 g fibre, 62 mg chol, 1,006 mg sodium, 1,361 mg potassium. % RDI: 23% calcium, 43% iron, 89% vit A, 40% vit C, 112% folate.

Sausages & Patties

Italian Sausage Coil

It takes a bit of skill to fill the casing evenly for this sausage coil, but it is wonderfully easy to grill and makes a stunning presentation.

3 lb / 1.5 kg **boneless pork shoulder**, cut into 1½-inch/4 cm chunks

2 tbsp / 30 mL chopped **fresh parsley**

2 tbsp / 30 mL chopped drained **oil-packed sun-dried tomatoes**

2 tsp / 10 mL **salt**

1½ tsp / 7 mL **black pepper**

1 tsp / 5 mL minced **garlic**

Sausage casings

● Using coarse disc on sausage grinder, grind pork. Mix in parsley, sun-dried tomatoes, salt, pepper and garlic. Chill well, in refrigerator for 3 to 4 hours or in freezer for 1½ to 2 hours.

● Prepare casings, and grinding and stuffing equipment according to preferred method (see Sausage Tips, page 138).

● Grind meat mixture through medium disc, sprinkling with up to ½ cup/125 mL ice water, if needed, to keep mixture moist. Fill casings, without tying into links; spiral together to form coil.

● Insert two 12-inch/30 cm skewers, perpendicular to each other, through side of coil to secure. Prick sausage in several places.

● Grill over medium-high heat, turning occasionally, until browned and no longer pink inside, 20 to 30 minutes.

Makes one 3-lb/1.5 kg sausage coil, about 8 to 10 servings.

Photo, page 134

VARIATION

Italian Sausage Patties
Omit casings; shape ground meat mixture into 12 patties. Grill on greased grill over medium-high heat, turning once, until no longer pink inside, about 15 minutes.

PER EACH OF 10 SERVINGS: about 251 cal, 24 g pro, 16 g total fat (6 g sat. fat), 1 g carb, trace fibre, 84 mg chol, 538 mg sodium, 343 mg potassium. % RDI: 1% calcium, 11% iron, 1% vit A, 3% vit C, 3% folate.

Sausage Tips

Preparing Casings

Soak fresh or frozen salted casings in plenty of water to cover for 15 minutes. Rinse under cold water, running water through inside. Keep casings well moistened for stuffing, leaving in water if not using immediately.

Preparing Meat Mixture

The colder the mixture, the easier it is to grind. Cold keeps the fat from softening and making the mixture sticky. Chilled water is often added to the mixture to give it extra moisture – add up to ½ cup/ 125 mL ice water per 3 lb/1.5 kg meat as necessary during last grinding or stuffing.

Stuffing Methods

Grinder with Sausage Stuffing Tube Attachment

With this attachment, you can grind meat directly into casings during the last grinding. For narrow casings or firmer mixtures, this can be difficult. For easier stuffing, grind meat first, then remove the grinding disc; run mixture again, through open tube, into casings.

- Attach stuffing tube to grinder. Thread 1 length of casing onto tube, leaving about 3 inches/7.5 cm hanging off.

- Grind meat mixture directly into casings, being careful not to leave air pockets or overstuff. Prick any small air pockets with needle and press out air.

- Twist or tie to form links.

Stuffing by Hand with Piping Bag

For this method, it's convenient to have one person squeezing and refilling the bag and another handling the casing.

- Place widest round tip in piping bag. Thread casing onto tip, leaving about 3 inches/7.5 cm hanging off.

- Stuff bag with meat mixture. Squeeze mixture into casing, being careful not to leave air pockets or overstuff. Prick any small air pockets with needle and press out air.

- Twist or tie to form links.

Stuffing by Hand with Funnel

This method takes some practice, but in no time, you'll be an expert. It's the easiest method for one person to fill sausages without a machine.

- Use funnel with ½- to ¾-inch/1 to 2 cm diameter opening. Thread casing onto opening, leaving about 3 inches/7.5 cm hanging off.

- Place handful of meat mixture in funnel. With thumb, press meat mixture into casing, being careful not to leave air pockets or overstuff. Prick any small air pockets with needle and press out air.

- Twist or tie to form links.

Hot Italian Sausages

Here's a basic and simple sausage that is good for novices. You can play around with the flavourings to taste, of course, adding a little dried oregano or marjoram, for instance. Other common seasonings include ground coriander and paprika.

3 lb / 1.5 kg **boneless pork shoulder**, cut into 1½-inch/4 cm chunks

1 tbsp / 15 mL dried **red chilies**

2 tsp / 10 mL **fennel seeds**

2 tsp / 10 mL **salt**

1 tsp / 5 mL **black pepper**

Sausage casings

● Using coarse disc on sausage grinder, grind pork. Mix in chilies, fennel, salt and pepper. Chill well, in refrigerator for 3 to 4 hours or in freezer for 1½ to 2 hours.

● Prepare casings, and grinding and stuffing equipment according to preferred method (see Sausage Tips, opposite).

● Grind meat mixture through medium disc, sprinkling with up to ½ cup/125 mL ice water, if needed, to keep mixture moist. Fill casings; twist into 6-inch/15 cm links. Prick each in 3 or 4 places.

● Grill over medium-high heat, turning once, until browned and juices run clear, 20 to 25 minutes.

Makes 8 to 10 sausages.

VARIATION
Hot Italian Sausage Patties
Omit casings; shape ground meat mixture into 12 patties. Grill on greased grill over medium-high heat, turning once, until no longer pink inside, about 15 minutes.

PER EACH OF 10 SAUSAGES: about 250 cal, 24 g pro, 16 g total fat (6 g sat. fat), 1 g carb, trace fibre, 84 mg chol, 521 mg sodium, 321 mg potassium. % RDI: 1% calcium, 11% iron, 1% vit A, 2% vit C, 2% folate.

Beef & Pork Bratwurst

These fairly lean, mainly beef bratwurst-type sausages are just touched with garlic and sweet spices, making them exceptionally tasty.

3 lb / 1.5 kg **boneless beef blade roast**, cut into 1-inch/2.5 cm cubes

2 lb / 1 kg **skinless pork belly**, cut into 1-inch/2.5 cm cubes

3 tbsp / 45 mL **salt**

4 tsp / 20 mL **granulated sugar**

4 cloves **garlic**, pressed or minced

4 tsp / 20 mL **paprika**

1¼ tsp / 6 mL finely ground **caraway seeds**

1 tsp / 5 mL **nutmeg**

¾ tsp / 4 mL **black pepper**

½ tsp / 2 mL **white pepper**

Generous ¼ tsp / 1.5 mL **ground cloves**

Generous ¼ tsp / 1.5 mL **saltpeter** (optional)

⅓ cup / 75 mL chilled **beef** or pork **stock** (or ice water)

Sausage casings

● Toss beef with pork belly. Mix together salt, sugar, garlic, paprika, caraway, nutmeg, black and white peppers, cloves, and saltpeter (if using); sprinkle over meat, tossing to coat. Transfer to freezer bag; refrigerate for 2 days, turning once or twice a day.

● Mix in stock. Chill in freezer for 2 to 3 hours.

● Place large bowl over another bowl of ice. Using coarse disc on sausage grinder, grind meat mixture into chilled bowl. Change to fine disc; grind through again, keeping bowl and meat mixture as chilled as possible.

● Prepare casings, and grinding and stuffing equipment according to preferred method (see Sausage Tips, page 138).

● Grind meat mixture a second time through fine disc. Fill casings; twist into 5-inch/12 cm links. Prick each in 3 or 4 places.

● Grill over medium-high heat, turning occasionally, until browned and cooked through, 20 to 30 minutes.

Makes about twenty 5-inch/12 cm sausages.

TIP

Saltpeter (potassium nitrate) is a natural preservative and gives the sausage a pinkish hue, but it isn't necessary for the flavour.

PER SAUSAGE: about 344 cal, 18 g pro, 30 g total fat (11 g sat. fat), 2 g carb, trace fibre, 69 mg chol, 1,098 mg sodium, 204 mg potassium. % RDI: 1% calcium, 12% iron, 2% vit A, 2% vit C, 1% folate.

Turkey Sausages

These tasty turkey sausages have a really old-style North American flavour.

8 oz / 250 g **salt pork** (cured not dry salted), diced

⅓ cup / 75 mL **gin**

1½ lb / 750 g cubed (½ inch/1 cm) **boneless skinless turkey thigh**

1 lb / 500 mL **boneless skinless turkey breast**, cut into ½-inch/1 cm cubes

1½ tsp / 7 mL **ground savory**

1¼ tsp / 6 mL **celery salt**

1 tsp / 5 mL **ground sage**

¾ tsp / 4 mL **ground thyme**

½ tsp / 2 mL **white pepper**

Generous ¼ tsp / 1.5 mL **ground cloves**

¼ tsp / 1 mL each **salt** and **black pepper**

Generous pinch **cayenne pepper**

2 cloves **garlic**, pressed or pounded into paste

Sausage casings

- In large bowl, mix salt pork with gin; let stand for 30 minutes. Mix in turkey thigh and breast meat. Mix together savory, celery salt, sage, thyme, white pepper, cloves, salt, black pepper, cayenne and garlic; sprinkle over meat, tossing to coat. Transfer to freezer bag; let stand for at least 1 hour or, preferably, refrigerate overnight.

- Mix in ¼ cup/60 mL ice water. Chill in freezer for 2 to 3 hours.

- Place large bowl over another bowl of ice. Using fine disc on sausage grinder, grind turkey mixture into chilled bowl.

- Prepare casings, and grinding and stuffing equipment according to preferred method (see Sausage Tips, page 138).

- Grind meat mixture a second time through fine disc. Fill casings; twist into 5-inch/12 cm links. Prick each in 3 or 4 places.

- Grill over medium-high heat, turning occasionally, until browned and no longer pink inside, 20 to 30 minutes.

Makes about fourteen 5-inch/12 cm sausages.

TIP

Turkey thighs aren't sold boneless and skinless, so you'll need at least 2½ lb/1.25 kg whole turkey thighs to make the 1½ lb/750 g cubed.

PER SAUSAGE: about 226 cal, 18 g pro, 16 g total fat (6 g sat. fat), 1 g carb, trace fibre, 75 mg chol, 422 mg sodium, 203 mg potassium. % RDI: 2% calcium, 11% iron, 3% folate.

Indonesian Lamb Sausage in Banana Leaves

After grilling, open these gorgeously fragrant packets with scissors at the table and serve with Indonesian Tomato-Chili Sauce (page 146) spooned over top.

1 can (398 mL) **coconut milk**

¾ cup / 175 mL chopped **shallots**

½ cup / 125 mL **raw cashews**

6 cloves **garlic**, smashed

6 **Thai (bird-eye) chilies** or 2 red finger hot peppers, chopped

2-inch / 5 cm piece **galangal** or 1-inch/2.5 cm piece fresh ginger, chopped

2½ tbsp / 40 mL **ground dried hot peppers**

2 tsp / 10 mL **ground coriander**

2 tsp / 10 mL **ground fennel seeds**

1½ tsp / 7 mL **black pepper**

¾ tsp / 4 mL **ground cumin**

¼ tsp / 1 mL each **ground cloves**, **cinnamon**, **nutmeg** and **turmeric**

2 lb / 1 kg **ground lamb**

1 **egg**, beaten

2½ tsp / 12 mL **salt**

Banana leaves

Indonesian Tomato-Chili Sauce (page 146)

• In blender, purée together coconut milk, shallots, cashews, garlic, chilies and galangal until smooth. In dry skillet over low heat, lightly toast hot peppers, coriander, fennel, black pepper, cumin, cloves, cinnamon, nutmeg and turmeric, stirring, until very fragrant, 5 to 7 minutes. Mix together lamb, egg, salt, coconut milk mixture and spice mixture. Set aside.

• With moist towel, wipe banana leaves. Cut out central rib from each and trim to make fifteen 10-inch/25 cm squares (you only need 12, but make extras in case of tearing). Over hot grill or heating element on stove, heat banana leaves, without charring or browning, until shiny and any natural white leaf mould disappears.

• For each sausage, shape ½ cup/125 mL lamb mixture into 4- x 2-inch/10 x 5 cm rectangular patty. Place 1 leaf square, shiny side down, on work surface with point down like diamond; place patty on bottom third of leaf. Fold in bottom then sides; roll to enclose completely. Tear off strip of leftover leaf; tie around package.

• Grill packages over medium-high heat, turning once, until leaves are well browned and digital thermometer inserted into meat registers 160°F/71°C, about 15 minutes. Serve with Indonesian Tomato-Chili Sauce.

Makes about 12 sausages.

TIP

Look for frozen banana leaves at Chinese, South and Southeast Asian, and Latin American stores. Always grill or steam them before wrapping food to make them stronger and more flexible.

PER SAUSAGE (WITH 2 TBSP/30 ML SAUCE): about 304 cal, 16 g pro, 22 g total fat (11 g sat. fat), 12 g carb, 2 g fibre, 66 mg chol, 864 mg sodium, 421 mg potassium. % RDI: 4% calcium, 26% iron, 11% vit A, 8% vit C, 11% folate.

Indonesian Tomato-Chili Sauce

2 tbsp / 30 mL **ground dried hot peppers**

1½ tbsp / 22 mL **peanut** or vegetable **oil**

¼ cup / 60 mL minced **onion**

4 cloves **garlic**, minced

6 whole **cloves**

2 tsp / 10 mL **shrimp paste** (or 1½ tbsp/22 mL fish sauce)

1 tsp / 5 mL finely grated **fresh ginger**

2 tbsp / 30 mL **palm sugar** or light brown sugar

½ tsp / 2 mL **salt**

1½ cups / 375 mL strained or crushed **tomatoes**

1 tbsp / 15 mL concentrated **tamarind paste**

● Mix hot peppers with ¼ cup/60 mL water to make paste; let stand for 10 minutes. In small saucepan, heat oil over medium heat; fry onion until light golden. Add garlic, cloves, shrimp paste, ginger and hot pepper paste; fry, stirring, for 2 minutes. Stir in sugar and salt; fry, stirring, until sugar is dissolved. Stir in tomatoes and tamarind paste; bring to boil. Reduce heat and simmer, stirring often, for 15 minutes. Let cool to room temperature before serving. Serve with Indonesian Lamb Sausage in Banana Leaves (page 145).

Makes about 1½ cups/ 375 mL.

Merguez Sausages

These popular North African sausages are flavoured with harissa, a spice paste available in tubes at gourmet and specialty stores, and even some supermarkets. Lamb casings are narrow and a bit tougher to fill, so you might not want to grind the meat and fill the casings at the same time.

3 lb / 1.5 kg **boneless lamb shoulder,** cut into 2-inch/5 cm chunks

4 cloves **garlic**, chopped

1 tbsp / 15 mL **harissa**

2 tsp / 10 mL **salt**

1 tsp / 5 mL **black pepper**

1 tsp / 5 mL **ground fennel seeds**

½ tsp / 2 mL **ground allspice**

½ tsp / 2 mL **cayenne pepper**

Sausage casings, preferably lamb

● Toss together lamb, garlic, harissa, salt, pepper, fennel, allspice and cayenne. Transfer to freezer bag; refrigerate overnight or for up to 1 day, turning once or twice.

● Using coarse disc on sausage grinder, grind lamb mixture. Chill well, in refrigerator for 3 to 4 hours or in freezer for 1½ to 2 hours.

● Prepare casings, and grinding and stuffing equipment according to preferred method (see Sausage Tips, page 138).

● Grind meat mixture through medium disc, sprinkling with up to ½ cup/125 mL ice water, if needed, to keep mixture moist. Fill casings; twist or tie into 6-inch/ 15 cm links. Prick each in 3 or 4 places.

● Grill over medium heat until browned and crisp, 15 to 20 minutes.

Makes about 24 sausages.

VARIATION

Merguez Patties

Omit casings; shape ground meat mixture into 12 patties. Grill on greased grill over medium heat, turning once, until no longer pink inside, about 15 minutes.

PER SAUSAGE: about 120 cal, 10 g pro, 9 g total fat (4 g sat. fat), 1 g carb, trace fibre, 39 mg chol, 226 mg sodium, 121 mg potassium. % RDI: 1% calcium, 6% iron, 1% vit A, 4% folate.

Chorizo Patties with Pebre

Many South American feasts, especially in Argentina and Chile,
involve a mixed grill, including chorizo. Here, it is made into a simple patty.
Serve with Chilean Pickled Onions (below).

⅓ cup / 75 mL **dry red wine**

2 cloves **garlic**, minced

1 tbsp / 15 mL **paprika**

1 tsp / 5 mL **ground coriander**

¾ tsp / 4 mL **salt**

½ tsp / 2 mL each **nutmeg** and **white pepper**

⅛ tsp / 0.5 mL each **cayenne pepper** and **ground cloves**

⅓ cup / 75 mL finely diced **salt pork** (cured not dry salted)

1⅓ lb / 670 g **lean ground pork**

⅔ lb / 350 g **lean ground beef**

Pebre Sauce (page 182)

● Whisk together wine, garlic, paprika, coriander, salt, nutmeg, pepper, cayenne and cloves; mix in salt pork. Let stand for 30 to 60 minutes. Mix in pork and beef; refrigerate for at least 1 or up to 3 days.

● Shape into 8 patties. Grill on greased grill over medium heat, turning once, until no longer pink inside, about 15 minutes. Serve with Pebre Sauce.

Makes 8 patties.

Chilean Pickled Onions

1 each **Spanish** and **red onion**

1 or 2 **hot peppers**

½ cup / 125 mL **lime juice**

2 tbsp / 30 mL **granulated sugar**

2 tbsp / 30 mL **white wine vinegar** or cider vinegar

½ tsp / 2 mL **salt**

● Slice onions into thin rings; place in heatproof bowl. Pour in enough boiling water to cover; let stand for 15 minutes. Drain; chill under cool water. Drain again; return to bowl. Slice peppers into thin rings; mix with onions.

● Whisk together lime juice, sugar, vinegar and salt; pour over onions. Refrigerate for at least 6 hours or up to 1 week.

Makes 4 cups/1 L.

PER PATTY (WITHOUT SAUCE OR ONIONS): about 232 cal, 24 g pro, 14 g total fat (5 g sat. fat), 1 g carb, 0 g fibre, 63 mg chol, 348 mg sodium. % RDI: 1% calcium, 12% iron, 6% vit A, 2% vit C, 5% folate.

Steaks, Chops & Ribs

Peppercorn-Crusted Steak

For extra flavour, top the steak off with a dab of blue cheese, such as Roquefort, Gorgonzola, Borgonzola, Blu Bénédictin or Danish creamy blue cheese (make sure to bring the cheese to room temperature before using.

2 tbsp / 30 mL **black peppercorns**

2 cloves **garlic**, minced

2 tbsp / 30 mL **Dijon mustard**

2 tbsp / 30 mL **olive oil**

4 **beef grilling steaks**, about 8 oz/ 250 g each

¼ tsp / 1 mL **salt**

● Crush peppercorns until size of sesame seeds; mix together peppercorns, garlic, mustard and oil. Trim any fat around edges of steaks to ⅛-inch/3 mm thickness; spread all over with pepper mixture. Sprinkle with salt.

● For rare, grill on greased grill over high heat, or for medium-rare to well-done, grill over medium-high heat, turning once, until desired doneness (see Tip, below).

Makes 4 servings.

Every grill is different, so there are ranges of times and temperatures that will deliver a perfectly done steak. Here are general guidelines for a 1-inch/2.5 cm thick unmarinated steak: Grill over high heat for rare (125 to 130°F/52 to 55°C), 5 to 6 minutes. Grill over medium-high heat for medium-rare (135 to 140°F/57 to 60°C), 8 to 10 minutes; medium (145 to 150°F/63 to 66°C), 10 to 12 minutes; or well-done (160°F/71°C), about 14 minutes. Grill with the lid down in cool or windy weather and let the grilled steak rest for a few minutes before digging in.

PER SERVING: about 341 cal, 43 g pro, 17 g total fat (5 g sat. fat), 3 g carb, trace fibre, 103 mg chol, 326 mg sodium. % RDI: 5% calcium, 39% iron, 6% folate.

Grilled Steak with Roquefort
Cheese Butter (variation)

Grilled Steak au Poivre

Steak au poivre is traditionally prepared in a skillet. However, grilled steak with peppercorn sauce is just as appealing.

2 tbsp / 30 mL **mixed peppercorns** or black peppercorns

4 **beef grilling medallions**, about 6 oz/175 g each

2 tsp / 10 mL **vegetable oil**

½ tsp / 2 mL **salt**

PEPPERCORN SAUCE:

¼ cup / 60 mL **butter**

2 tbsp / 30 mL minced **shallot**

¼ cup / 60 mL **brandy**

¼ cup / 60 mL **red wine**

½ cup / 125 mL **beef stock**

¼ cup / 60 mL **whipping cream**

● Crush peppercorns until size of sesame seeds. Brush steaks all over with oil; coat with peppercorns. For rare, grill on greased grill over high heat, or for medium-rare to well-done, grill over medium-high heat, turning once, until desired doneness (see Tip, page 153). Sprinkle with salt.

● **Peppercorn Sauce:** In skillet, melt butter over medium heat; fry shallot until softened, about 1 minute. Add brandy and wine; increase heat to medium-high and cook until reduced by half. Add stock; cook until reduced by half. Add cream; simmer until thickened. Add any accumulated juices from steak. Serve over steaks.

Makes 4 servings.

VARIATION
Grilled Steak with Roquefort Cheese Butter

Omit Peppercorn Sauce. Mash together ½ cup/125 mL Roquefort or other blue cheese; ¼ cup/60 mL butter, softened; 2 tbsp/30 mL minced shallots; and 2 tbsp/ 30 mL minced fresh parsley. Refrigerate until firm. Grill steaks as directed; top each with dab of butter.

PER SERVING: about 420 cal, 35 g pro, 26 g total fat (14 g sat. fat), 4 g carb, 1 g fibre, 129 mg chol, 520 mg sodium. % RDI: 4% calcium, 31% iron, 15% vit A, 2% vit C, 5% folate.

Peppercorn Thyme T-Bones

4 **beef T-bone** or other **grilling steaks**, about 8 oz/250 g each

1 tbsp / 15 mL **mixed peppercorns**

1 tbsp / 15 mL **mustard seeds**

6 cloves **garlic**, pressed or minced

1 tbsp / 15 mL chopped **fresh thyme**

1 tbsp / 15 mL **olive** or vegetable **oil**

¼ tsp / 1 mL **salt**

● Trim off all but ⅛ inch/3 mm fat around edges of steaks; slash remaining fat at 1-inch/2.5 cm intervals to prevent curling.

● Coarsely grind peppercorns with mustard seeds; mix in garlic, thyme, oil and salt. Rub all over steaks.

● For rare, grill on greased grill over high heat, or for medium-rare to well-done, grill over medium-high heat, turning once, until desired doneness (see Tip, page 153).

Makes 4 servings.

Chefs generally use touch to tell when steaks are done. Here's how: Press centre of steak with your finger. Rare steak feels quite soft to the touch. Medium-rare steak has some resistance but yields to the touch. Medium steak starts to feel firm but still has some give in centre. Well-done steak feels very firm.

PER SERVING: about 294 cal, 34 g pro, 15 g total fat (4 g sat. fat), 4 g carb, 1 g fibre, 62 mg chol, 231 mg sodium. % RDI: 4% calcium, 34% iron, 3% vit C, 5% folate.

Mexican-Style Rib-Eye Medallions with Peppers

2 tbsp / 30 mL **extra-virgin olive oil**

2 cloves **garlic**, pressed or minced

1 tsp / 5 mL **black pepper**

1 tsp / 5 mL **dried oregano**, crumbled

¾ tsp / 4 mL **salt**

½ tsp / 2 mL **ground cumin**

½ tsp / 2 mL **ground coriander**

4 **beef rib-eye grilling medallions**, about 6 oz/175 g each

3 **poblano peppers**, or 1 green bell pepper and 3 jalapeño peppers

2 **sweet red peppers**

● Mix together 4 tsp/20 mL of the oil, garlic, pepper, oregano, salt, cumin and coriander; rub all over beef. Let stand for 15 minutes.

● Meanwhile, grill poblano and red peppers, covered, over high heat, turning often, until charred. Place in bowl and cover tightly; let cool. Peel, core and seed; cut into thick strips. Toss with remaining oil.

● For rare, grill beef on greased grill over high heat, or for medium-rare to well-done, grill over medium-high heat, turning once, until desired doneness (see Tip, page 153). Serve topped with peppers.

Makes 4 servings.

PER SERVING: about 342 cal, 25 g pro, 23 g total fat (8 g sat. fat), 9 g carb, 2 g fibre, 60 mg chol, 481 mg sodium. % RDI: 3% calcium, 29% iron, 23% vit A, 235% vit C, 11% folate.

Grilled Tenderloin Steak with Mushrooms & Peppers

2 **sweet peppers**, halved

1 lb / 500 g **oyster mushrooms**, trimmed

2 tbsp / 30 mL **extra-virgin olive oil**

4 tsp / 20 mL **sherry vinegar** or wine vinegar

1 clove **garlic**, pressed or minced

1 tsp / 5 mL **fresh thyme leaves**

1¼ tsp / 6 mL **salt**

¾ tsp / 4 mL **black pepper**

4 **beef tenderloin grilling steaks**, about 4 oz/125 g each

● Grill peppers over medium-high heat for 3 minutes. Turn; grease grill and add mushrooms. Grill, turning occasionally, until tender and lightly charred, about 5 minutes. Cut peppers into strips. In large bowl, whisk together oil, vinegar, garlic, thyme and ¼ tsp/1 mL each of the salt and pepper; add hot vegetables and toss to coat.

● Sprinkle steaks with remaining salt and pepper. For rare, grill on greased grill over high heat, or for medium-rare to well-done, grill over medium-high heat, turning once, until desired doneness (see Tip, page 153). Serve topped with grilled vegetables.

Makes 4 servings.

PER SERVING: about 273 cal, 24 g pro, 15 g total fat (4 g sat. fat), 10 g carb, 3 g fibre, 53 mg chol, 790 mg sodium. % RDI: 2% calcium, 34% iron, 22% vit A, 163% vit C, 19% folate.

Shish Kabob–Style Steaks

We've combined Middle Eastern and Canadian grill favourites by using traditional shish kabob seasonings to marinate steaks. Serve with grilled tomatoes.

4 **beef grilling steaks**, 8 oz/250 g each

2 **onions**, cut into ½-inch/1 cm thick slices

¼ cup / 60 mL **lemon juice**

¼ cup / 60 mL **extra-virgin olive oil**

4 cloves **garlic**, pressed or minced

1 tsp / 5 mL **ground allspice**

½ tsp / 2 mL **black pepper**

¼ tsp / 1 mL **cinnamon**

¼ tsp / 1 mL **cayenne pepper**

¾ tsp / 4 mL **salt**

● In large dish, cover steaks with onions. Whisk together lemon juice, oil, garlic, allspice, pepper, cinnamon and cayenne; pour over onions and steaks, turning to coat. Marinate, refrigerated, for at least 4 hours or up to 1 day.

● Remove steaks and onions from marinade; bring to room temperature. Sprinkle both sides of steaks with salt. For rare, grill steaks on greased grill over high heat, or for medium-rare to well-done, grill over medium-high heat, turning once, until desired doneness (see Tip, page 153). Meanwhile, grill onions, turning once, until tender and lightly charred.

Makes 4 servings.

VARIATION

Shish Kabob–Style Lamb Steaks or Chops
Substitute 2 lb/1 kg lamb leg steaks or loin chops for beef.

PER SERVING: about 345 cal, 43 g pro, 16 g total fat (5 g sat. fat), 6 g carb, 1 g fibre, 103 mg chol, 514 mg sodium. % RDI: 4% calcium, 34% iron, 7% vit C, 10% folate.

Rib Steak with Beer Marinade

⅓ cup / 75 mL **beer**

1 tbsp / 15 mL **extra-virgin olive oil**

2 tsp / 10 mL **coarse salt**

2 tsp / 10 mL **cracked pepper**

4 cloves **garlic**, minced

2 **beef rib grilling steaks with bone**, each 1 rib thick, 3 lb/1.5 kg total

4 tsp / 20 mL **grainy mustard**

● In large dish, whisk together beer, oil, salt, pepper and garlic; add steaks, turning to coat and massaging into meat. Marinate, refrigerated, for at least 4 hours or up to 1 day.

● Reserving marinade, remove steak; brush both sides with mustard. Place on greased grill over medium-high heat; drizzle with marinade. Grill, turning once, until desired doneness, 10 to 12 minutes for rare. Transfer to cutting board; let stand for 5 minutes before carving off bone and slicing.

Makes 6 to 8 servings.

PER EACH OF 8 SERVINGS: about 204 cal, 22 g pro, 11 g total fat (4 g sat. fat), 1 g carb, trace fibre, 51 mg chol, 475 mg sodium. % RDI: 2% calcium, 15% iron, 3% folate.

Thick-Cut Sirloin Steak

Ask the butcher to cut the steak 2 inches/5 cm thick for this party-size dish.

3 lb / 1.5 kg **beef top sirloin grilling steak**, 1½ to 2 inches/4 to 5 cm thick

2 tbsp / 30 mL chopped **fresh rosemary** or thyme (or 1 tsp/5 mL dried)

2 tbsp / 30 mL **olive** or vegetable **oil**

2 tbsp / 30 mL **wine vinegar**

4 cloves **garlic**, smashed

2 tsp / 10 mL **Worcestershire sauce**

¾ tsp / 4 mL each **salt** and **black pepper**

● Trim fat around edge of steak to ⅛-inch/3 mm thickness; slash remaining fat at 1-inch/2.5 cm intervals to prevent curling. In large dish, whisk together rosemary, oil, vinegar, garlic, Worcestershire sauce, salt and pepper; add steak, turning to coat. Marinate for 20 minutes or, refrigerated, up to 1 day.

● Reserving marinade, place steak on greased grill over medium-high heat; brush generously with remaining marinade. Grill, covered, turning once, until desired doneness, 18 to 20 minutes for rare or 20 to 24 minutes for medium-rare. Transfer to cutting board; let stand for 5 minutes before slicing thinly across the grain.

Makes 8 to 12 servings.

PER EACH OF 12 SERVINGS: about 207 cal, 22 g pro, 12 g total fat (4 g sat. fat), 1 g carb, 0 g fibre, 69 mg chol, 202 mg sodium. % RDI: 1% calcium, 18% iron, 3% folate.

Old-Style Red Wine Marinated "London Broil"

Long marinating in wine is a time-tested method of flavouring and tenderizing less-expensive cuts of beef. The sauce is divine, but the steak is wonderful just plain grilled.

3 lb / 1.5 kg **beef top sirloin grilling steak**, 1½ to 2 inches/4 to 5 cm thick

1 **onion**, thinly sliced

3 cloves **garlic**, smashed

Few sprigs **fresh parsley**

Few sprigs **fresh thyme** or ¾ tsp/ 4 mL dried

8 **fresh sage leaves** or ¾ tsp/4 mL crumbled dried sage

2 **bay leaves**

½ tsp / 2 mL **black peppercorns**, crushed

8 **juniper berries**, crushed, or 2 tbsp/ 30 mL gin

5 **whole cloves**

¼ tsp / 1 mL (approx) **salt**

1½ cups / 375 mL (approx) **dry red wine**

1 tsp / 5 mL **granulated sugar**

2 tbsp / 30 mL **butter**

Sea salt

Freshly grated **black pepper**

● In resealable freezer bag, combine beef, onion, garlic, parsley, thyme, sage, bay leaves, peppercorns, juniper berries, cloves and ¼ tsp/1 mL salt; pour in enough wine to cover completely. Marinate, refrigerated, for at least 2 or up to 6 days.

● Reserving marinade, remove beef. Strain marinade into saucepan, discarding solids; stir in sugar and pinch salt. Bring to boil over high heat; boil, skimming off foam, until syrupy and reduced to about 2 tbsp/30 mL. Remove from heat; whisk in butter until fully incorporated. Keep warm.

● Grill beef, covered, on greased grill over medium-high heat, turning once, until rare to medium (do not overcook), 20 to 30 minutes. Transfer to cutting board; let stand for 5 minutes before slicing across the grain. Season with sea salt and pepper to taste. Drizzle with sauce.

Makes 8 to 10 servings.

TIPS

● Patience is a virtue: this steak is good after 2 days of marinating, but it's best after 5 or even 6 days.

● Marinating the beef in a freezer bag instead of a dish frees up lots of room in the refrigerator.

PER EACH OF 10 SERVINGS: about 190 cal, 27 g pro, 8 g total fat (4 g sat. fat), 1 g carb, 0 g fibre, 69 mg chol, 129 mg sodium, 366 mg potassium. % RDI: 1% calcium, 20% iron, 2% vit A, 3% folate.

Korean Steak Barbecue

Koreans usually eat grilled steak cut up and wrapped in lettuce or perilla (Korean shiso) leaves with raw garlic, hot sauce, green onions and rice. It's an appetizing and nutritious way to enjoy a good cut of beef.

1½ lb / 750 g **beef rib-eye**, strip loin or sirloin **grilling steak(s)**

¼ cup / 60 mL **Korean Barbecue Sauce** (page 531)

2 tsp / 10 mL toasted **sesame seeds**

2 heads **leaf lettuce**, separated into leaves

4 large cloves **garlic**, sliced

4 **green onions**, cut into 1½-inch/ 4 cm lengths

4 **finger hot peppers**, cut into 4 or 5 pieces each

Hot cooked **short-grain rice**

HOT SAUCE FOR STEAK:

⅓ cup / 75 mL **Korean hot pepper paste** (kochujang)

2 tbsp / 30 mL **sesame oil**

2 tbsp / 30 mL **rice vinegar**

2 tsp / 10 mL toasted **sesame seeds**

2 tsp / 10 mL **granulated sugar**

2 tsp / 10 mL **soy sauce**

● **Hot Sauce for Steak:** Mix together hot pepper paste, sesame oil, vinegar, sesame seeds, sugar and soy sauce to make smooth paste.

● Score both sides of steak, making crisscross pattern about ¼ inch/5 mm deep. Place steak in dish; add Korean Barbecue Sauce and sesame seeds, turning to coat. Marinate for 15 minutes or, refrigerated, up to 2 hours.

● Grill on greased grill over medium-high heat until desired doneness, 10 to 12 minutes for medium-rare.

● Slice; serve with lettuce, garlic, green onions, hot peppers, rice and Hot Sauce for Steak.

Makes 4 to 6 servings.

TIPS

● To eat this the traditional Korean way, put a spoonful of rice on a leaf, top it with a slice of steak, some garlic dipped in hot sauce to taste, green onion and hot pepper, then wrap it all up in the leaf.

● Look for Korean hot pepper paste, or *kochujang*, at Korean and larger Chinese grocery stores. Unfortunately, there is no comparable substitute.

PER EACH OF 6 SERVINGS, INCLUDING ½ CUP/125 ML RICE AND 2 TBSP/30 ML HOT SAUCE: about 479 cal, 28 g pro, 20 g total fat (7 g sat. fat), 45 g carb, 3 g fibre, 54 mg chol, 857 mg sodium. % RDI: 9% calcium, 42% iron, 28% vit A, 55% vit C, 35% folate.

Rib Steak with Cherry Tomato Salsa

Buy a thick-cut one-rib roast for this spectacular grill.

1-rib **prime rib steak with bone**, about 2 lb/1 kg

1 tbsp / 15 mL **olive** or vegetable **oil**

2 tsp / 10 mL **ancho chili powder**

2 tsp / 10 mL **ground coriander**

1 tsp / 5 mL **ground cumin**

1 tsp / 5 mL **salt**

3 cloves **garlic**, pressed or minced

CHERRY TOMATO SALSA:

2 cups / 500 mL **cherry tomatoes**

Half **white** or sweet **onion**

2 to 4 **jalapeño peppers**

⅓ cup / 75 mL finely chopped **fresh coriander**

4 tsp / 20 mL **lime juice**

1 tsp / 5 mL **salt**

● At ½-inch/1 cm intervals, diagonally score both sides of steak with series of scant ¼-inch/5 mm deep cuts. Mix together oil, ancho chili powder, coriander, cumin, salt and garlic; rub all over steak, pushing into cuts. Marinate for 30 minutes or, refrigerated, up to 1 day.

● **Cherry Tomato Salsa:** Grill tomatoes, onion and peppers in greased grill basket or wok over high heat until lightly charred; let cool. Skin and seed peppers; finely chop tomatoes, onion and peppers. Toss vegetables together with coriander, lime juice and salt.

● Grill steak on greased grill over medium-high heat, turning once, until desired doneness, about 12 minutes for rare, or 14 to 16 minutes for medium-rare. Transfer to cutting board; let stand for 5 minutes before carving off bone and slicing thinly across the grain. Serve with Cherry Tomato Salsa.

Makes 4 to 6 servings.

PER EACH OF 6 SERVINGS: about 207 cal, 22 g pro, 11 g total fat (4 g sat. fat), 6 g carb, 2 g fibre, 48 mg chol, 830 mg sodium. % RDI: 3% calcium, 18% iron, 7% vit A, 23% vit C, 10% folate.

Salt & Pepper T-Bone Steaks

Smoked sea salt delivers woody aroma and unbeatable flavour for an almost effortless dish. Use your best and most fragrant olive oil.

2 **beef T-bone grilling steaks**, 1½ inches/4 cm thick, about 1 lb/ 500 g each

2 tsp / 10 mL **smoked** or plain **sea salt**

2 tsp / 10 mL coarsely ground **black pepper**

2 tbsp / 30 mL **extra-virgin olive oil**

1 **lemon**, cut into wedges

• Sprinkle both sides of steaks with salt and pepper, pressing into steak to adhere to surface. For rare, grill on greased grill over high heat, or for medium-rare to well-done, grill over medium-high heat, turning once, until desired doneness, 16 to 20 minutes for medium-rare.

• Transfer to cutting board; let stand for 5 minutes. To carve, cut strip loin and tenderloin sections off either side of bone; slice each thinly across the grain. Arrange on platter; drizzle with oil. Serve with lemon.

Makes 8 servings.

PER SERVING: about 355 cal, 38 g pro, 22 g total fat (8 g sat. fat), 1 g carb, trace fibre, 86 mg chol, 471 mg sodium. % RDI: 3% calcium, 27% iron, 5% vit C, 4% folate.

Cumin Flank Steak with Avocado Salad

Flank steak is usually considered a marinating steak, but if you cook it to no more than medium-rare and slice it thinly across the grain, it doesn't need marinating.

1 tbsp / 15 mL **olive** or vegetable **oil**

1 tsp / 5 mL **ground cumin**

¼ tsp / 1 mL each **salt** and **black pepper**

1 lb / 500 g **beef flank steak**

AVOCADO SALAD:

2 tbsp / 30 mL **wine vinegar**

1 tbsp / 15 mL **extra-virgin olive oil**

½ tsp / 2 mL **hot pepper sauce**

¼ tsp / 1 mL **salt**

1 **sweet red pepper**, thinly sliced

½ cup / 125 mL thinly sliced **red onion**

2 **avocados**, peeled, pitted and sliced

½ cup / 125 mL chopped **fresh coriander**

● **Avocado Salad:** In large bowl, whisk together vinegar, oil, hot pepper sauce and salt. Add red pepper and onion; toss to coat. Set aside.

● Mix together oil, cumin, salt and pepper; brush over both sides of steak. Let stand for 15 to 30 minutes.

● Grill on greased grill over medium-high heat, turning once, until desired doneness, 8 to 10 minutes for medium-rare. Transfer to cutting board; let stand for 5 minutes before slicing thinly across the grain.

● Meanwhile, add avocado to red pepper mixture. Gently toss with coriander; serve with steak.

Makes 4 servings.

PER SERVING: about 429 cal, 29 g pro, 31 g total fat (7 g sat. fat), 11 g carb, 6 g fibre, 46 mg chol, 358 mg sodium. % RDI: 3% calcium, 24% iron, 24% vit A, 110% vit C, 35% folate.

Hoisin-Glazed Round Steak

½ cup / 125 mL **hoisin sauce**

¼ cup / 60 mL **rice vinegar**

4 cloves **garlic**, minced

1 tbsp / 15 mL minced **fresh ginger**

½ tsp / 2 mL **Chinese five-spice powder**, or ¼ tsp/1 mL each black pepper, cinnamon and ground cloves

½ tsp / 2 mL **salt**

2 lb / 1 kg **beef inside round** or other **marinating steak**, at least 1 inch/ 2.5 cm thick

In large dish, whisk together hoisin sauce, vinegar, garlic, ginger, five-spice powder and salt. With fork, prick steak several times on each side; add to marinade, turning to coat. Marinate, refrigerated, for at least 12 hours or up to 1 day, turning once.

Reserving marinade, place steak on greased grill over medium-high heat; brush generously with marinade. Grill, covered, turning once, until desired doneness, about 10 minutes per inch/2.5 cm for medium-rare. Transfer to cutting board; let stand for 5 minutes before slicing thinly diagonally across the grain.

Makes 6 servings.

173

PER SERVING: about 195 cal, 31 g pro, 4 g total fat (1 g sat. fat), 7 g carb, trace fibre, 65 mg chol, 374 mg sodium. % RDI: 1% calcium, 21% iron, 7% folate.

Grilled Steak Diable

It may seem like a lot of pepper on this devilishly tasty steak, but inevitably some will fall through the grill. Serve the sliced steak with fresh radishes and a cellar of sea salt on the side.

3 lb / 1.5 kg **beef sirloin steak**, 1½ inches/4 cm thick

6 sprigs **fresh thyme**

4 cloves **garlic**, crushed

3 **bay leaves**, broken into pieces

¾ cup / 175 mL **dry red wine**

¼ cup / 60 mL **extra-virgin olive oil**

¼ cup / 60 mL **black peppercorns**

¼ cup / 60 mL **Dijon mustard**

Sea salt

● In large dish, combine steak, thyme, garlic and bay leaves. Whisk wine with oil; pour over steak, turning to coat. Marinate, refrigerated, overnight or up to 1 day, turning a few times. Bring to room temperature.

● Coarsely crush peppercorns. Remove steak from marinade; pat dry. Brush mustard all over steak; sprinkle as evenly as possible all over with cracked pepper, pressing to adhere.

● Grill, covered, on greased grill over medium-high heat, turning once, until desired doneness, about 10 minutes for rare or 13 minutes for medium-rare. Transfer to cutting board; tent with foil and let stand for 5 minutes before slicing thinly across the grain. Season with sea salt to taste.

Makes 8 to 10 servings.

PER EACH OF 10 SERVINGS: about 243 cal, 31 g pro, 11 g total fat (3 g sat. fat), 3 g carb, 0 g fibre, 73 mg chol, 140 mg sodium. % RDI: 4% calcium, 30% iron, 2% vit C, 5% folate.

Gibson Flatiron Steak

The juniper, herbs and other flavourings in the gin and vermouth, along with the pickled onions, of a classic Gibson cocktail brilliantly spike a marinating steak.

⅔ cup / 150 mL **gin**

⅓ cup / 75 mL **dry white vermouth**

4 cloves **garlic**, crushed

2 **onions**, thinly sliced

1 wide strip **lemon rind**

½ tsp / 2 mL **black pepper**

Sea salt

3 lb / 1.5 kg **beef top blade flatiron** or top sirloin **grilling steak**

1 tbsp / 15 mL **vegetable oil**

Pickled cocktail onions

● In resealable freezer bag, mix together gin, vermouth, garlic, onions, lemon rind, pepper and pinch salt; add steak. Marinate, refrigerated, overnight or up to 2 days, turning occasionally.

● Brush steak with oil. Grill over medium-high heat, turning once, until desired doneness, about 10 minutes for rare or 13 minutes for medium-rare. Transfer to cutting board; let stand for 5 minutes before slicing thinly across the grain. Season with salt to taste; garnish with cocktail onions.

Makes 6 to 8 servings.

PER EACH OF 8 SERVINGS: about 222 cal, 26 g pro, 12 g total fat (4 g sat. fat), 1 g carb, 0 g fibre, 70 mg chol, 53 mg sodium. % RDI: 3% calcium, 19% iron, 2% vit C, 3% folate.

Trimming a Flatiron Steak

Making the Cut

Flatiron steak (see Gibson Flatiron Steak, opposite), also known as top blade steak, is a cut of meat you generally see in restaurants rather than home kitchens. Recently, this flavourful cut is more widely available. It's actually two steaks with a layer of connective tissue running through the centre. Sometimes you can buy it already trimmed and halved down the middle, but grocery stores usually sell it whole, so you'll have to trim it yourself. It's actually quite simple.

Step 1
Using sharp, preferably flexible, boning knife, trim off exterior connective tissue.

Step 2
Cut steak in half through centre, moving knife along interior connective tissue, butterflying it (as seen here) or cutting into two steaks, if desired.

Step 3
Trim off connective tissue.

Mustard Garlic Flank Steak

3 cloves **garlic**, pressed or minced

2 tbsp / 30 mL **Dijon mustard**

1 tbsp / 15 mL **balsamic vinegar**

1 tbsp / 15 mL **vegetable oil**

1½ lb / 750 g **beef flank steak**

4 sprigs **fresh rosemary**

¼ tsp / 1 mL each **salt** and **black pepper**

● In large dish, whisk together garlic, mustard, vinegar and oil; add steak, turning to coat. Place 2 sprigs of the rosemary on top of and 2 underneath steak. Marinate, refrigerated, for at least 4 hours or up to 1 day. Discard rosemary.

● Grill on greased grill over medium-high heat, turning once, until desired doneness, 8 to 10 minutes for medium-rare. Transfer to cutting board; sprinkle with salt and pepper. Let stand for 5 minutes before slicing thinly across the grain.

Makes 6 to 8 servings.

Flank steaks are best grilled rare to medium-rare; never grill them more than medium or they will be tough and dry. Slice the cooked steak very thinly on the diagonal across the grain.

PER EACH OF 8 SERVINGS: about 140 cal, 18 g pro, 7 g total fat (2 g sat. fat), 1 g carb, trace fibre, 36 mg chol, 147 mg sodium. % RDI: 1% calcium, 11% iron, 1% folate.

Flank Steak à la Grecque

1 tsp / 5 mL grated **lemon rind**

1 tbsp / 15 mL **lemon juice**

1 tbsp / 15 mL **olive oil**

2 cloves **garlic**, pressed or minced

½ tsp / 2 mL **dried oregano**

¼ tsp / 1 mL each **salt** and **black pepper**

1 lb / 500 g **beef flank steak**

● In large dish, whisk together lemon rind and juice, oil, garlic, oregano, salt and pepper; add steak, turning to coat. Let stand for 10 minutes.

● Grill on greased grill over medium-high heat, turning once, until desired doneness, 8 to 10 minutes for medium-rare. Transfer to cutting board; let stand for 2 to 3 minutes before slicing thinly across the grain.

Makes 4 servings.

PER SERVING: about 215 cal, 25 g pro, 12 g total fat (4 g sat. fat), 1 g carb, trace fibre, 44 mg chol, 197 mg sodium. % RDI: 1% calcium, 12% iron, 3% vit C, 3% folate.

Soy-Marinated Flank Steak

Serve this steak with refreshing Quick Pickled Cucumbers (below).

¼ cup / 60 mL **sodium-reduced soy sauce**

1 tbsp / 15 mL **mirin** or granulated sugar

5 tsp / 25 mL **sesame oil**

2 tsp / 10 mL minced **fresh ginger**

3 cloves **garlic**, thinly sliced

8 **green onions**, trimmed

2 lb / 1 kg **beef flank steak**

● In large dish, whisk together soy sauce, mirin, 1 tbsp/ 15 mL of the sesame oil, ginger and garlic. Add green onions; add steak, turning to coat. Marinate for 20 minutes or, refrigerated, up to 8 hours.

● Remove steak from marinade; in small saucepan, bring marinade to boil over medium-high heat. Reduce heat and simmer for 3 minutes.

● Grill steak on greased grill over medium-high heat, turning once and basting with marinade, until desired doneness, 8 to 10 minutes for medium-rare. Transfer to cutting board; let stand for 2 to 3 minutes before slicing thinly across the grain.

● Meanwhile, brush onions with remaining 2 tsp/10 mL sesame oil; grill until tender, about 4 minutes. Serve with steak.

Makes 6 to 8 servings.

Quick Pickled Cucumbers

● Toss 1 **English cucumber**, very thinly sliced, with ½ tsp/2 mL **salt**; let stand for 15 minutes. Squeeze out excess moisture. Toss together cucumber, 2 tbsp/ 30 mL **rice vinegar**; 2 tsp/10 mL each **granulated sugar** and **sesame oil**; 3 cloves **garlic**, minced; and ½ tsp/ 2 mL **hot pepper flakes**.

Makes 4 servings.

PER EACH OF 8 SERVINGS (WITHOUT CUCUMBERS): about 215 cal, 25 g pro, 9 g total fat (3 g sat. fat), 6 g carb, 1 g fibre, 48 mg chol, 406 mg sodium, 360 mg potassium. % RDI: 3% calcium, 18% iron, 2% vit A, 7% vit C, 7% folate.

Grilled Flank Steak & Pebre

This piquant Chilean fresh herb salsa, similar to Argentine chimichurri, serves as both marinade and condiment. Serve with Chilean Pickled Onions (page 149) for authentic flavour. Flank steak is more tender if it's not cooked past medium-rare. If you like your beef more well-done, choose a top sirloin grilling steak instead.

2 lb / 1 kg **beef flank steak**

Pebre Sauce (below)

● Place steak in large dish; spoon half of the Pebre Sauce (without tomatoes) over steak, turning to coat. Cover; refrigerate steak and remaining Pebre Sauce separately for at least 4 hours or overnight.

● Reserving marinade, grill steak on greased grill over medium-high heat, turning and basting with reserved marinade once, until desired doneness, 8 to 10 minutes for medium-rare. Transfer to cutting board; let stand for 2 to 3 minutes before slicing thinly across the grain.

● Meanwhile, stir tomatoes into remaining Pebre Sauce; serve with steak.

Makes 6 to 8 servings.

Pebre Sauce

2 **green onions**, chopped

1 cup / 250 mL each packed **fresh coriander** and **parsley leaves**

2 **jalapeño peppers**, seeded and chopped

¼ cup / 60 mL **corn oil** or olive oil

¼ cup / 60 mL **sherry vinegar** or red wine vinegar

2 cloves **garlic**, minced

¼ tsp / 1 mL **salt**

2 **tomatoes**, finely diced

● In food processor, pulse together onions, coriander, parsley, jalapeños and ½ cup/125 mL water until finely chopped. Transfer to bowl; stir in oil, vinegar, garlic and salt. Stir in tomatoes just before serving.

PER EACH OF 8 SERVINGS: about 262 cal, 26 g pro, 16 g total fat (4 g sat. fat), 3 g carb, 1 g fibre, 44 mg chol, 135 mg sodium. % RDI: 2% calcium, 17% iron, 9% vit A, 37% vit C, 11% folate.

Devilled Beef Ribs

In traditional culinary terminology, devilled *refers to mustard-spiked foods.*

1 tbsp / 15 mL **vegetable oil**

1 **onion**, chopped

3 cloves **garlic**, minced

2 tsp / 10 mL **dried thyme**

½ tsp / 2 mL each **salt** and **black pepper**

½ cup / 125 mL **Dijon mustard**

½ cup / 125 mL **grainy mustard**

⅓ cup / 75 mL **white wine** or chicken stock

¼ cup / 60 mL **liquid honey**

2 tbsp / 30 mL prepared **horseradish**

1 rack **beef back ribs**, 3 to 4 lb/1.5 to 2 kg

2 tbsp / 30 mL minced **fresh parsley**

● In saucepan, heat oil over medium heat; fry onion, garlic, thyme, salt and pepper, stirring occasionally, until softened, about 5 minutes. Let cool.

● Whisk in Dijon and grainy mustards, wine, honey and horseradish; remove ½ cup/125 mL and reserve for basting.

● Cut ribs into 1-rib portions; arrange in large shallow dish. Spread both sides with remaining sauce. Marinate, refrigerated, for 4 hours or up to 1 day.

● Grill ribs, covered and curved side down, on greased grill over medium heat for 5 minutes. Turn; brush with some of the reserved mustard mixture. Grill, brushing with mustard mixture and turning often, until glazed and crusty, about 25 minutes. Sprinkle with parsley.

Makes 3 to 4 servings.

PER EACH OF 4 SERVINGS: about 448 cal, 28 g pro, 26 g total fat (8 g sat. fat), 26 g carb, 1 g fibre, 66 mg chol, 1,158 mg sodium. % RDI: 10% calcium, 28% iron, 2% vit A, 6% vit C, 34% folate.

Korean Beef Short Ribs

Koreans prize short ribs (kalbi) *more than any other cut of beef; they love their rich flavour and slight chewiness. See page 186 for a guide to choosing and cutting Korean short ribs.*

½ cup / 125 mL **Korean Barbecue Sauce** (page 531)

4 **green onions**, minced

2 tsp / 10 mL toasted **sesame seeds**

2 lb / 1 kg **beef short ribs**, prepared (page 186)

● Mix together Korean Barbecue Sauce, green onions and sesame seeds; add prepared short ribs, tossing to coat. Marinate for 30 minutes or, refrigerated, up to 3 hours.

● Grill on greased grill over high heat, reducing heat to medium-high if outside is blackening, just until crusty outside and a hint of pink remains in centre, about 6 minutes.

Makes 4 to 6 servings.

PER EACH OF 6 SERVINGS: about 349 cal, 18 g pro, 26 g total fat (11 g sat. fat), 9 g carb, trace fibre, 56 mg chol, 828 mg sodium. % RDI: 2% calcium, 13% iron, 1% vit A, 2% vit C, 5% folate.

How to Cut Traditional Kalbi

Korean Short Ribs

Two cuts of beef short ribs are grilled in Korean cuisine, but it can be confusing trying to find the type you want. In Canada, you can buy both cuts at Korean grocery stores, but some are also easy to find under different names in other ethnic or large chain grocery stores.

Traditional kalbi: A single thick piece of short rib is cut into one long, thin piece. You can buy the thick chunks of short ribs needed for traditional kalbi at most supermarkets, all Korean food shops and at specialty and Jewish butcher shops, where they are called flanken-style.

L.A.-style kalbi: This refers to thinly cut, multi-boned strips of short ribs first popularized in the large Korean-American community in Los Angeles. Outside of Korean stores, the L.A.-style cut is often called Miami-style short ribs or simply braising short ribs.

Step 1

Place short rib, bone side down, on cutting surface.

Step 2

With knife parallel to cutting surface, cut across rib about ¼ inch/5 mm from bone, cutting to edge of bone but without cutting off rest of meat.

Step 3

Continue cutting about ¼-inch/5 mm thick through meat, folding out and cutting remaining meat, until a long evenly thick strip extends from bone. Lightly score meat in crisscross pattern.

Hot-Smoked Spiced Beef Back Ribs

This spice rub is inspired by Jewish Romanian-style pastrami seasoning. Slow smoke cooking releases most of the fat from the meat, leaving succulent and well-spiced ribs.

6 **dried hot peppers**, seeded and broken into small pieces, or 2 tsp/10 mL Indian or Mexican ground dried chilies

4 tsp / 20 mL **coriander seeds** or 1 tbsp/15 mL ground coriander

2 tsp / 10 mL **whole allspice** or 1½ tsp/ 7 mL ground allspice

1½ tsp / 7 mL **dill seeds**

1½ tsp / 7 mL **black peppercorns**

2 tsp / 10 mL **paprika**

1¼ tsp / 6 mL **garlic powder**

1¼ tsp / 6 mL **granulated sugar**

1 tsp / 5 mL **salt**

2 racks **beef back ribs**, 3 to 4 lb/1.5 to 2 kg each

● Grind together hot peppers, coriander seeds, allspice, dill seeds and peppercorns; mix in paprika, garlic, sugar and salt. Rub all over ribs. Marinate for 3 to 4 hours or, refrigerated, up to 2 days.

● Soak 3 cups/750 mL wood chips in water for 1 hour; drain. Place in pan over gas flame or on coals in barbecue (or according to manufacturer's instructions). Grill ribs, covered, over indirect medium heat (see Tip, page 214) until fork-tender and pulling away from bones, about 1½ hours.

Makes 6 servings.

Photo, page 150

TIP

For best flavour, grind your own whole spices for this recipe.

PER SERVING: about 302 cal, 26 g pro, 20 g total fat (8 g sat. fat), 4 g carb, 1 g fibre, 66 mg chol, 447 mg sodium, 361 mg potassium. % RDI: 3% calcium, 19% iron, 6% vit A, 3% vit C, 3% folate.

Steak House Beef Ribs with Stout Barbecue Sauce

Slow-roasting ribs in the oven before finishing them on the grill makes them fall-from-the-bone tender.

2 racks **beef back ribs**, 3 to 4 lb/1.5 to 2 kg each

3 cloves **garlic**, minced

2 tbsp / 30 mL **paprika**

2 tbsp / 30 mL **chili powder**

1½ tsp / 7 mL **salt**

1 tsp / 5 mL **cayenne pepper**

1 tsp / 5 mL **ground cumin**

1 tsp / 5 mL **dry mustard**

½ tsp / 2 mL **black pepper**

Pinch **cinnamon**

STOUT BARBECUE SAUCE:

2 tbsp / 30 mL **vegetable oil**

1 **onion**, diced

2 cloves **garlic**, sliced

1⅓ cups / 325 mL **bottled strained tomatoes**

1 cup / 250 mL **stout**

¼ cup / 60 mL **fancy molasses**

2 tbsp / 30 mL **cider vinegar**

1 tbsp / 15 mL packed **brown sugar**

¼ tsp / 1 mL **salt**

● Cut ribs into 1- or 2-rib portions. Mix together garlic, paprika, chili powder, salt, cayenne, cumin, mustard, pepper and cinnamon; rub all over ribs. Let stand for 30 minutes.

● Place, meaty side up, in shallow roasting pan. Cover and roast in 325°F/160°C oven until meat is tender, about 75 minutes. (Refrigerate for up to 1 day.)

● **Stout Barbecue Sauce:** In saucepan, heat oil over medium heat; fry onion and garlic, stirring occasionally, until softened, about 6 minutes. Stir in strained tomatoes, stout, molasses, vinegar, sugar and salt; bring to boil. Reduce heat and simmer, stirring occasionally, until reduced to about 2 cups/500 mL, 35 to 40 minutes. Strain into bowl.

● Toss ribs with half of the sauce. Grill, covered, on greased grill over medium heat, turning once and basting with remaining sauce, until glazed and browned, 12 to 15 minutes.

Makes 8 servings.

189

PER SERVING: about 327 cal, 21 g pro, 18 g total fat (7 g sat. fat), 19 g carb, 2 g fibre, 51 mg chol, 588 mg sodium, 689 mg potassium. % RDI: 5% calcium, 27% iron, 17% vit A, 13% vit C, 6% folate.

Steak Tacos

1 lb / 500 g **thin beef grilling steak**, cut into 2-inch/5 cm strips

¼ cup / 60 mL **lime juice**

1 **onion**, sliced

2 **sweet peppers**, sliced

1 tsp / 5 mL minced **garlic**

½ tsp / 2 mL **black pepper**

6 small **flour tortillas**

SERRANO SALSA:

4 **tomatoes**

2 **serrano peppers** or 1 jalapeño pepper, seeded

1 clove **garlic**

½ tsp / 2 mL **salt**

¼ cup / 60 mL chopped **fresh coriander**

● Toss together beef, lime juice, onion, sweet peppers, garlic and pepper. Marinate for 30 minutes or, refrigerated, up to 4 hours.

● **Serrano Salsa:** Core tomatoes and blanch for 1 minute; drain and peel. In blender, purée together tomatoes, serranos, garlic and salt; stir in coriander.

● Grill steak, onion and peppers on greased grill over high heat, turning once, until onion and peppers are soft and grill-marked and steak is rare to medium-rare, 3 to 4 minutes. Slice peppers. Serve steak, onion and peppers in tortillas with Serrano Salsa.

Makes 6 tacos.

PER TACO: about 229 cal, 19 g pro, 6 g total fat (2 g sat. fat), 26 g carb, 3 g fibre, 35 mg chol, 381 mg sodium, 504 mg potassium. % RDI: 3% calcium, 21% iron, 7% vit A, 90% vit C, 28% folate.

Arugula & Beefsteak Salad with Tomato Vinaigrette

8 oz / 250 g **beef grilling steak**

¼ tsp / 1 mL **black pepper**

8 cups / 2 L **arugula leaves**

2 **mini-cucumbers** (or half English cucumber)

⅓ cup / 75 mL thinly sliced **sweet onion**

⅓ cup / 75 mL **shaved** or shredded **Parmesan cheese**

TOMATO VINAIGRETTE:

Half small clove **garlic**, pressed

2 tsp / 10 mL **balsamic vinegar**

2 tsp / 10 mL **red wine vinegar**

¼ tsp / 1 mL **salt**

¼ tsp / 1 mL **anchovy paste**

¼ cup / 60 mL **extra-virgin olive oil**

⅓ cup / 75 mL finely chopped seeded drained **canned tomatoes**

● Sprinkle steak with pepper. For rare, grill, covered, over high heat, or for medium-rare to well-done, grill over medium-high heat, turning once, until desired doneness (see Tip, page 153). Transfer to cutting board; let stand for 5 minutes before slicing.

● **Tomato Vinaigrette:** Whisk together garlic, balsamic and wine vinegars, salt and anchovy paste. Whisk in oil; whisk in tomatoes.

● Place arugula in salad bowl (or 4 individual plates or bowls). Using mandoline, vegetable peeler or knife, slice cucumbers lengthwise as thinly as possible to form ribbons. Top arugula with cucumbers and onion. Slice steak thinly across the grain; arrange over greens. Spoon vinaigrette over salad; top with Parmesan.

Makes 4 servings.

PER SERVING: about 294 cal, 18 g pro, 22 g total fat (6 sat. fat), 8 g carb, 2 g fibre, 41 mg chol, 396 mg sodium. % RDI: 28% calcium, 24% iron, 30% vit A, 37% vit C, 55% folate.

Mekong Beef Noodle Salad

1 piece (8 inches/20 cm) **English cucumber**

1 large **carrot**

6 oz / 175 g **wide rice-stick noodles**

Quarter **red onion**, thinly sliced

3 tbsp / 45 mL each chopped **fresh coriander** and **fresh mint**

3 tbsp / 45 mL **Thai** or other **basil leaves**

¼ cup / 60 mL chopped **unsalted roasted peanuts**

STEAK:

2 tbsp / 30 mL **soy sauce**

1 tbsp / 15 mL **sesame oil**

1 tbsp / 15 mL **vegetable oil**

2 cloves **garlic**, pressed or minced

2 tbsp / 30 mL grated **fresh ginger**

1 tbsp / 15 mL **granulated sugar**

1 lb / 500 g **beef flank steak**

DRESSING:

½ cup / 125 mL **hot water**

¼ cup / 60 mL **granulated sugar**

2 tbsp / 30 mL **lime juice**

2 tbsp / 30 mL **fish sauce**

2 **Thai (bird-eye) chilies**, sliced, or serrano peppers, seeded and thinly sliced

● **Steak:** In large dish, mix together soy sauce, sesame and vegetable oils, garlic, ginger and sugar; add steak, turning to coat. Marinate, refrigerated, for at least 4 or up to 12 hours, turning occasionally.

● **Dressing:** Stir water with sugar until dissolved; stir in lime juice, fish sauce and chilies.

● Using vegetable peeler, slice cucumber lengthwise, discarding soft core and seeds, into thin strips. Slice carrot lengthwise into thin strips.

● In large pot of boiling salted water, cook rice noodles according to package instructions until tender. Drain and chill under cold water; drain and transfer to large bowl. Toss with Dressing.

● Grill steak on greased grill over medium-high heat, turning once, until desired doneness, 8 to 10 minutes for medium-rare. Transfer to cutting board; let stand for 5 to 10 minutes before slicing thinly across the grain.

● Add cucumber, carrot, onion, coriander, mint and basil to noodle mixture; toss until coated. Divide among bowls or plates; top with steak and sprinkle with peanuts.

Makes 4 to 6 servings.

PER EACH OF 6 SERVINGS: about 363 cal, 21 g pro, 13 g total fat (3 g sat. fat), 41 g carb, 3 g fibre, 31 mg chol, 873 mg sodium. % RDI: 4% calcium, 15% iron, 26% vit A, 20% vit C, 14% folate.

Grilled Flank Steak Salad

You can vary the greens for the salad as you wish or add, for example, cherry tomatoes, cucumber or shaved fennel. The steak is best if marinated overnight, but even one hour adds delicious flavour.

2 cloves **garlic**, pressed or pounded into paste

2 tbsp / 30 mL **extra-virgin olive oil**

1½ tbsp / 22 mL finely minced **fresh coriander stems**

1½ tsp / 7 mL **fish sauce**

½ tsp / 2 mL **smoked** or sweet **paprika**

¼ tsp / 1 mL **cayenne pepper**

1 lb / 500 g **beef flank steak**

Sea salt

SALAD:

4 cups / 1 L **arugula leaves**

Half head **Boston lettuce**

Half head **frisée lettuce**

⅓ cup / 75 mL thinly sliced **sweet onion**

3 tbsp / 45 mL **extra-virgin olive oil**

1 tbsp / 15 mL **sherry vinegar** or other vinegar

Pinch each **salt** and **black pepper**

● Mix together garlic, oil, coriander stems, fish sauce, paprika and cayenne; spread over both sides of steak. Wrap in plastic. Marinate for 1 hour or, refrigerated, up to 3 days.

● Grill on greased grill over medium-high heat, turning once, until desired doneness, 8 to 10 minutes for medium-rare. Transfer to cutting board; let stand for 5 to 10 minutes before slicing thinly diagonally across the grain.

● **Salad:** Meanwhile, toss together arugula, Boston and frisée lettuces, onion, oil, vinegar, salt and pepper. Arrange on 4 plates; top with steak. Season with sea salt to taste.

Makes 4 servings.

PER SERVING: about 338 cal, 26 g pro, 24 g total fat (5 g sat. fat), 5 g carb, 2 g fibre, 48 mg chol, 239 mg sodium, 590 mg potassium. % RDI: 11% calcium, 24% iron, 22% vit A, 22% vit C, 51% folate.

Deli-Style Spiced
Bison Steaks

Bison (buffalo) is lean, exceptionally tasty meat, like very rich beef, and is suited to this Montreal-style spicing. Of course, you can substitute beef steaks for the bison.

4 **bison rib-eye** or strip loin **steaks**, about 1 lb/500 g each

4 tsp / 20 mL **extra-virgin olive oil**

DELI-STYLE STEAK SPICE MIX:

1 tbsp / 15 mL **coriander seeds**, lightly toasted

1 tbsp / 15 mL **black peppercorns**

1 tsp / 5 mL **dill seeds**

4 tsp / 20 mL **coarse sea salt** or kosher salt

2 tsp / 10 mL **paprika**

2 tsp / 10 mL **hot pepper flakes**

1½ tsp / 7 mL **granulated garlic** (or 1 tsp/5 mL garlic powder)

- **Deli-Style Steak Spice Mix:** Coarsely grind together coriander seeds, peppercorns and dill seeds; mix in salt, paprika, hot pepper flakes and garlic.

- Rub each steak with 1 tsp/5 mL of the oil; sprinkle each with 2 tsp/10 mL to 1 tbsp/15 mL of the Deli-Style Steak Spice Mix, according to taste. For rare, grill steaks on greased grill over high heat, or for medium-rare to well-done, grill over medium-high heat, turning once, until desired doneness (see Tip, page 153). Transfer to cutting board; let stand for 3 minutes before slicing thinly across the grain.

Makes 8 servings.

197

PER SERVING: about 272 cal, 50 g pro, 6 g total fat (2 g sat. fat), 2 g carb, 1 g fibre, 142 mg chol, 512 mg sodium. % RDI: 2% calcium, 44% iron, 4% vit A.

Grilled Veal Chops with Fines-Herbes Butter

Delectable veal chops deserve simple grilling and lightly seasoned yet tasty sauces. If you wish, gild the lily by sautéing mushrooms and serving them atop the butter.

4 **veal chops**

½ tsp / 2 mL **black pepper**

¼ tsp / 1 mL **salt**

2 tsp / 10 mL **olive** or vegetable **oil**

FINES-HERBES BUTTER:

½ cup / 125 mL minced **shallots**

3 **anchovy fillets**, minced, or ¼ tsp/ 1 mL salt

2 cloves **garlic**, pressed or minced

½ cup / 125 mL **dry white wine** or white vermouth

⅓ cup / 75 mL **butter**, softened

2 tbsp / 30 mL finely chopped **fresh chervil** (optional)

4 tsp / 20 mL finely chopped **fresh chives**

4 tsp / 20 mL minced **fresh parsley**

2 tsp / 10 mL minced **fresh tarragon**

½ tsp / 2 mL **salt**

● **Fines-Herbes Butter:** In small saucepan over medium-high heat, boil shallots, anchovies, garlic and wine until about 2 tsp/10 mL liquid remains; transfer to bowl and let cool. Mash in butter, chervil (if using), chives, parsley, tarragon and salt until smooth. Set aside and keep cool.

● Sprinkle veal with pepper and salt; brush with oil. Grill, covered, over medium-high heat until medium-rare, 10 to 12 minutes. Transfer to warmed platter; let stand for 3 minutes. Spoon one-quarter of the Fines-Herbes Butter over each chop.

Makes 4 servings.

PER SERVING: about 505 cal, 49 g pro, 30 g total fat (15 g sat. fat), 4 g carb, 1 g fibre, 233 mg chol, 826 mg sodium. % RDI: 6% calcium, 16% iron, 17% vit A, 5% vit C, 17% folate.

Parmesan-Crusted Veal Chops

4 **veal chops**

½ cup / 125 mL **red wine**

2 **bay leaves**

1 clove **garlic**, smashed

¼ cup / 60 mL **fresh parsley leaves**

1 tsp / 5 mL **salt**

½ tsp / 2 mL **black pepper**

2 tbsp / 30 mL **dry bread crumbs**

2 tbsp / 30 mL grated **Parmesan cheese**

2 tbsp / 30 mL minced **fresh parsley**

2 tbsp / 30 mL **olive oil**

● In resealable freezer bag, combine veal, wine, bay leaves, garlic, parsley, and half each of the salt and pepper. Marinate, refrigerated, for 1 to 2 hours.

● Mix together bread crumbs, Parmesan cheese and parsley; rub in oil until evenly moistened.

● Pat veal dry; sprinkle with remaining salt and pepper. Press 1 tbsp/15 mL of the crumb mixture onto each side of each chop.

● Grill on greased grill over medium-high heat, turning once, until medium-rare, 8 to 10 minutes.

Makes 4 servings.

Chops need to be watched and turned while grilling, so it's easier to keep track of their progress in an uncovered grill. However, in cool or windy weather it's best to close the lid for even cooking.

PER SERVING: about 399 cal, 35 g pro, 26 g total fat (10 g sat. fat), 3 g carb, trace fibre, 105 mg chol, 566 mg sodium, 551 mg potassium. % RDI: 9% calcium, 20% iron, 2% vit A, 3% vit C, 11% folate.

Lemon Thyme Pork Chops

4 **bone-in pork chops**, about ½ inch/
1 cm thick

2 cloves **garlic**, minced

1 tbsp / 15 mL chopped **fresh thyme**
(or ½ tsp/2 mL dried)

1 tsp / 5 mL grated **lemon rind**

1 tbsp / 15 mL **lemon juice**

¼ tsp / 1 mL each **salt** and **black pepper**

● Trim all but ⅛ inch/3 mm fat from chops; slash remaining fat at 1-inch/2.5 cm intervals to prevent curling. Mix together garlic, thyme, lemon rind and juice, salt and pepper; rub all over chops. Let stand for 10 minutes.

● Grill on greased grill over medium-high heat, turning once, until juices run clear when pork is pierced and just a hint of pink remains inside, about 10 minutes.

Makes 4 servings.

PER SERVING: about 173 cal, 25 g pro, 7 g total fat (2 g sat. fat), 1 g carb, trace fibre, 68 mg chol, 194 mg sodium. % RDI: 3% calcium, 6% iron, 7% vit C, 3% folate.

Barbecued Peach Pork Chops

Juicy grilled peaches become an instant chutney for grilled pork.

4 **bone-in pork loin chops**, about ½ inch/1 cm thick

¼ cup / 60 mL chopped **fresh basil** or mint

¼ cup / 60 mL **red pepper jelly**, melted

2 tbsp / 30 mL **cider vinegar**

1 tbsp / 15 mL **grainy mustard**

3 cloves **garlic**, minced

¼ tsp / 1 mL **salt**

Pinch **black pepper**

2 firm ripe **peaches** (unpeeled), sliced

● Trim all but ⅛ inch/3 mm fat from chops; slash remaining fat at 1-inch/2.5 cm intervals to prevent curling. In large dish, mix together basil, red pepper jelly, vinegar, mustard, garlic, salt and pepper. Transfer 2 tbsp/30 mL to bowl; toss with peaches until coated. Add chops to remainder, turning to coat. Let stand for 20 minutes.

● Grill chops and peaches on greased grill over medium-high heat, turning once, until peaches are browned, about 6 minutes. Remove peaches; keep warm. Grill chops until juices run clear when pork is pierced and just a hint of pink remains inside, about 4 minutes.

Makes 4 servings.

PER SERVING: about 219 cal, 22 g pro, 6 g total fat (2 g sat. fat), 20 g carb, 1 g fibre, 57 mg chol, 244 mg sodium. % RDI: 4% calcium, 6% iron, 2% vit A, 5% vit C, 3% folate.

Tangy Glazed Pork Chops

Add an eastern Mediterranean touch to chops with mint and pomegranate molasses.

4 **bone-in pork loin chops**, about ½ inch/1 cm thick

¼ cup / 60 mL chopped **fresh mint** or basil

1 tsp / 5 mL grated **lemon rind**

2 tbsp / 30 mL **lemon juice**

2 tbsp / 30 mL **pomegranate molasses** or syrup

½ tsp / 2 mL each **salt** and **black pepper**

½ tsp / 2 mL **granulated sugar**

¼ tsp / 1 mL **hot pepper flakes**

● Trim all but ⅛ inch/3 mm fat from chops; slash remaining fat at 1-inch/2.5 cm intervals to prevent curling. Mix together mint, lemon rind and juice, pomegranate molasses, salt, pepper, sugar and hot pepper flakes; add pork chops, turning to coat. Marinate for 30 minutes or, refrigerated, up to 4 hours.

● Reserving marinade, place chops on greased grill over medium-high heat; brush with remaining marinade. Grill, turning once, until juices run clear when pork is pierced and just a hint of pink remains inside, about 10 minutes.

Makes 4 servings.

TIP

If you can't find pomegranate molasses or syrup in your supermarket, gourmet shop or Middle Eastern grocery store, increase lemon juice to ¼ cup/60 mL and add 1 tbsp/15 mL fancy molasses and ¼ tsp/ 1 mL bitters.

PER SERVING: about 198 cal, 25 g pro, 7 g total fat (3 g sat. fat), 7 g carb, trace fibre, 68 mg chol, 340 mg sodium. % RDI: 3% calcium, 6% iron, 2% vit A, 7% vit C, 4% folate.

Pork Chops with Chimichurri Rojo

This assertive Argentine marinade and sauce, a cousin of the popular green chimichurri, is a natural with grilled pork.

4 **boneless pork loin centre chops**,
about ½ inch/1 cm thick

⅓ cup / 75 mL **Chimichurri Rojo**
(page 531)

● Trim all but ⅛ inch/3 mm fat from chops; slash remaining fat at 1-inch/2.5 cm intervals to prevent curling. Place in large dish; pour Chimichurri Rojo over top, turning to coat. Marinate, refrigerated, for at least 4 hours or up to 1 day.

● Reserving any remaining marinade, place chops on greased grill over medium-high heat; brush with marinade. Grill, turning once, until juices run clear when pork is pierced and just a hint of pink remains inside, about 10 minutes.

Makes 4 servings.

PER SERVING: about 186 cal, 22 g pro, 10 g total fat (3 g sat. fat), 2 g carb, trace fibre, 60 mg chol, 148 mg sodium. % RDI: 2% calcium, 9% iron, 5% vit A, 5% vit C, 2% folate.

Pork Chops with Green Pepper Salsa

This recipe makes a generous amount of the flavourful green pepper salsa; mop up the extra with a side of boiled potatoes, bread or tortilla chips.

4 **pork chops**, about 1 inch/2.5 cm thick

2 tsp / 10 mL **ancho** or other **chili powder**

½ tsp / 2 mL **salt**

½ tsp / 2 mL **ground cumin**

½ tsp / 2 mL **ground coriander**

½ tsp / 2 mL **ground allspice**

½ tsp / 2 mL **garlic powder**

1 tbsp / 15 mL (approx) **olive** or vegetable **oil**

GREEN PEPPER SALSA:

1 **white onion**, thickly sliced

2 **sweet green peppers**

4 **jalapeño peppers**

½ cup / 125 mL finely chopped **fresh coriander**

2 tbsp / 30 mL **extra-virgin olive oil**

1 tbsp / 15 mL **lime** or lemon **juice**

½ tsp / 2 mL **salt**

● **Green Pepper Salsa:** Grill onion over medium-high heat until tender and lightly charred; let cool. Chop; place in bowl. Grill green and jalapeño peppers over high heat, turning often, until skins are charred all over. Place in separate bowl; cover and let cool. Peel, seed and chop peppers; add to onion. Mix in coriander, oil, lime juice and salt.

● Trim all but ⅛ inch/3 mm fat from chops; slash remaining fat at 1-inch/2.5 cm intervals to prevent curling. Mix together chili powder, salt, cumin, coriander, allspice and garlic; rub all over chops. Marinate for 15 minutes or, refrigerated, up to 1 day.

● Brush chops with oil. Grill over medium-high heat, turning once, until juices run clear when pork is pierced and just a hint of pink remains inside. Transfer to warmed platter; top each chop with spoonful of Green Pepper Salsa. Serve remainder alongside.

Makes 4 servings.

PER SERVING: about 233 cal, 24 g pro, 12 g total fat (3 g sat. fat), 7 g carb, 2 g fibre, 66 mg chol, 483 mg sodium, 450 mg potassium. % RDI: 4% calcium, 11% iron, 6% vit A, 42% vit C, 8% folate.

Grilled Lemon Pork Chops

Serve these chops with a medley of grilled vegetables, such as mini sweet peppers, sliced fennel bulbs, corn on the cob, whole small onions, wedges of squash and pole beans.

4 **pork chops**, about 1 inch/2.5 cm thick

2 tsp / 10 mL **caraway**, cumin or fennel **seeds**

4 cloves **garlic**, minced

1 tsp / 5 mL grated **lemon rind**

2 tbsp / 30 mL **lemon juice**

2 tbsp / 30 mL **extra-virgin olive oil**

1 tbsp / 15 mL chopped **fresh rosemary** (or 1 tsp/5 mL dried)

½ tsp / 2 mL **black pepper**

¼ tsp / 1 mL **salt**

2 **lemons**, halved

● Trim off all but ⅛ inch/3 mm fat from edges of chops; slash remaining fat at 1-inch/2.5 cm intervals to prevent curling.

● Lightly crush caraway seeds. Mix together caraway seeds, garlic, lemon rind and juice, half of the oil, the rosemary, pepper and salt; add chops, turning to coat. Marinate, refrigerated, for at least 4 hours or up to 1 day, turning occasionally.

● Brush lemons with remaining oil. Grill chops and lemons on greased grill over medium-high heat, turning once, until lemons are slightly charred, and juices run clear when pork is pierced and just a hint of pink remains inside, about 10 minutes. Serve chops with lemons to squeeze over top.

Makes 4 servings.

PER SERVING: about 243 cal, 24 g pro, 14 g total fat (4 g sat. fat), 5 g carb, trace fibre, 66 mg chol, 200 mg sodium. % RDI: 4% calcium, 9% iron, 27% vit C, 3% folate.

Slow & Easy Java Ribs

These tender back ribs have a satisfying crunchy texture and a whisper of coffee taste that mingles seductively with the spices.

3 racks **pork back ribs**, 5 to 6 lb/ 2 to 2.2 kg total

¼ cup / 60 mL **freshly ground coffee beans**

3 tbsp / 45 mL packed **brown sugar**

2 tbsp / 30 mL **chili powder**

2 tbsp / 30 mL **paprika**

1 tbsp / 15 mL **salt**

2 tsp / 10 mL **ground cumin**

½ tsp / 2 mL **cinnamon**

½ tsp / 2 mL **ground ginger**

2 tbsp / 30 mL **vegetable oil**

● Remove membrane from underside of ribs if attached. Mix together coffee, sugar, chili powder, paprika, salt, cumin, cinnamon and ginger; rub all over ribs. Marinate, refrigerated, for at least 4 hours or up to 1 day.

● Grill, covered, on greased grill over medium-low heat, turning every 20 minutes and brushing with oil, until tender and meat pulls away from ends of bones, 1½ to 2 hours. Cut into 1- to 3-rib portions.

Makes 6 to 8 servings.

PER EACH OF 8 SERVINGS: about 494 cal, 29 g pro, 39 g total fat (13 g sat. fat), 7 g carb, 1 g fibre, 137 mg chol, 1,005 mg sodium. % RDI: 7% calcium, 20% iron, 17% vit A, 5% vit C, 1% folate.

Barbecue Beer Ribs

Any brown ale will do for this marinade, but stout has a wonderful toasty flavour that lends itself well to the grill.

3 racks **pork back ribs**, about 5 to 6 lb/ 2 to 2.2 kg total

1½ cups / 375 mL **stout** or dark ale

1 **onion**, grated

1 clove **garlic**, minced

1 tsp / 5 mL **Worcestershire sauce**

¼ tsp / 1 mL **salt**

¼ tsp / 1 mL **ground cloves**

¼ tsp / 1 mL **hot pepper sauce**

⅔ cup / 150 mL chopped pitted **dates**

⅓ cup / 75 mL **tomato paste**

2 tbsp / 30 mL packed **brown sugar**

2 tbsp / 30 mL **white wine vinegar**

1 tbsp / 15 mL **Dijon mustard**

1 tbsp / 15 mL **fancy molasses**

● Remove membrane from underside of ribs if attached; place ribs in large dish. Mix together stout, onion, garlic, Worcestershire sauce, salt, cloves and hot pepper sauce; pour over ribs. Marinate, refrigerated, for at least 4 hours or up to 1 day.

● Reserving marinade, remove ribs and pat dry. Grill, covered, on greased grill over medium-low heat, turning 4 times, until tender, 1½ to 2 hours.

● Meanwhile, in saucepan, combine reserved marinade, dates, tomato paste, brown sugar, vinegar, mustard and molasses; bring to boil. Boil, stirring occasionally, until reduced to 2 cups/500 mL, about 10 minutes.

● Brush both sides of ribs with sauce. Increase heat to medium-high; close lid and cook, turning once, until glazed, about 15 minutes. Cut into 1- to 3-rib portions.

Makes 6 to 8 servings.

PER EACH OF 8 SERVINGS: about 521 cal, 29 g pro, 35 g total fat (13 g sat. fat), 21 g carb, 2 g fibre, 137 mg chol, 235 mg sodium. % RDI: 7% calcium, 17% iron, 3% vit A, 10% vit C, 4% folate.

Whiskey Sour Ribs

The sweet caramel taste of bourbon and tart lemon make these soused ribs irresistible.

2 racks large **pork back ribs**, 5 to 6 lb/2.2 to 2.7 kg

4 cloves **garlic**, pressed or minced

2 tbsp / 30 mL **bourbon** or Canadian whiskey

1 tbsp / 15 mL grated **fresh ginger**

1 tbsp / 15 mL **lemon juice**

1 tsp / 5 mL **black pepper**

¾ tsp / 4 mL **salt**

½ tsp / 2 mL **cayenne pepper**

WHISKEY SOUR BARBECUE SAUCE:

½ cup / 125 mL packed **brown sugar**

¼ cup / 60 mL **bourbon** or Canadian whiskey

¼ cup / 60 mL **lemon juice**

¼ cup / 60 mL **crushed tomatoes**

2 tbsp / 30 mL **fancy molasses**

2 cloves **garlic**, pressed or minced

● Cut rib racks in half; remove membrane from underside if attached. Mix together garlic, bourbon, ginger, lemon juice, pepper, salt and cayenne; rub all over ribs. Place in resealable freezer bag; marinate, refrigerated, overnight or for up to 2 days.

● Place ribs in roasting pan; cover with foil. Roast in 375°F/190°C oven until tender, about 1½ hours.

● **Whiskey Sour Barbecue Sauce:** Meanwhile, in saucepan over medium heat, mix together sugar, bourbon, lemon juice, tomatoes and molasses; boil until reduced by half, about 12 minutes. Reduce heat and stir in garlic; simmer for 1 minute.

● Grill ribs, covered, over medium-high heat, turning once, until lightly browned on both sides, about 8 minutes. Brush meaty sides of racks with some of the sauce; grill, covered, for 5 minutes. Turn; continue basting and grilling until both sides are glazed, about 5 minutes. Cut into 1- to 3-rib portions.

Makes 6 to 8 servings.

PER EACH OF 8 SERVINGS: about 467 cal, 29 g pro, 29 g total fat (11 g sat. fat), 19 g carb, 0 g fibre, 70 mg chol, 286 mg sodium. % RDI: 4% calcium, 13% iron, 1% vit A, 5% vit C, 5% folate.

Slow-Grilled Ribs

These slow-grilled succulent ribs are spiced with a touch of Asian flavours.

5 to 6 lb / 2.2 to 2.7 kg **pork back ribs**

¼ cup / 60 mL packed **brown sugar**

2 tbsp / 30 mL **paprika**

2 tbsp / 30 mL **ground coriander**

1 tbsp / 15 mL **ground cumin**

1 tbsp / 15 mL **salt**

1 tbsp / 15 mL **ground fennel or aniseed**

1 tsp / 5 mL **cayenne pepper**

1 tsp / 5 mL **cinnamon**

1 tsp / 5 mL **nutmeg**

1 tsp / 5 mL **black pepper**

¾ tsp / 4 mL **ground cloves**

LIME BARBECUE SAUCE:

2 tbsp / 30 mL **vegetable oil**

1 **onion**, minced

5 cloves **garlic**, minced

⅓ cup / 75 mL minced **fresh coriander**

1 tbsp / 15 mL grated **fresh ginger**

1 to 2 tbsp /15 to 30 mL minced **hot peppers**

1 cup / 250 mL **ground tomatoes**

¼ cup / 60 mL **fancy molasses**

2 tbsp / 30 mL **soy sauce**

1½ tsp / 7 mL grated **lime** or lemon **rind**

¼ cup / 60 mL **lime** or lemon **juice**

To grill over indirect heat on gas grill, set foil drip pan under 1 rack of 2-burner barbecue or under centre of 3-burner barbecue. Heat remaining burner(s) to temperature indicated (see Grilling Temperatures, page 10). For charcoal grill, place drip pan in centre and arrange hot charcoal on either side. Set meat on greased grill over drip pan. Grill as directed.

• Remove membrane from underside of ribs if attached; place ribs in large dish. Mix together sugar, paprika, coriander, cumin, salt, fennel, cayenne, cinnamon, nutmeg, pepper and cloves; rub all over ribs. Marinate, refrigerated, for at least 1 or up to 3 days.

• **Lime Barbecue Sauce:** Meanwhile, in saucepan, heat oil over medium heat; fry onion and garlic, stirring occasionally, until lightly browned, about 7 minutes. Add coriander, ginger and hot peppers; cook, stirring, for 2 minutes. Stir in tomatoes, molasses and soy sauce; bring to boil. Reduce heat and simmer, stirring occasionally, until thickened and reduced by about one-third, about 20 minutes. Stir in lime rind and juice; set aside.

• Grill ribs, covered, over indirect medium heat (see Tip, opposite) until tender and meat pulls away from ends of bones, about 1½ hours. Brush bone side of ribs with half of the Sauce; cook for 10 minutes. Turn and brush with remaining sauce; cook until glazed, about 15 minutes. Cut into 2- or 3-rib portions.

Makes 6 to 8 servings.

PER EACH OF 8 SERVINGS: about 508 cal, 30 g pro, 34 g total fat (11 g sat. fat), 22 g carb, 2 g fibre, 70 mg chol, 1,226 mg sodium. % RDI: 8% calcium, 26% iron, 15% vit A, 22% vit C, 8% folate.

Chinese-Style Grilled Ribs

Although Chinese cuisine rarely includes grilled meats, there is no reason that Chinese seasonings can't greatly enhance your grilling repertoire. Here's a good example.

¾ cup / 175 mL **hoisin sauce**

2 tbsp / 30 mL ground or finely minced **fresh lemongrass**, or 1 tsp/5 mL finely grated lime or lemon rind

1 tbsp / 15 mL **light soy sauce**

1 tbsp / 15 mL **dark soy sauce**

1 tbsp / 15 mL finely grated **fresh ginger**

2 cloves **garlic**, minced

1 tsp / 5 mL **Sichuan pepper** or ½ tsp/ 2 mL white pepper

3 to 4 lb / 1.5 to 2 kg **small pork ribs**

2 tsp / 10 mL **sesame oil**

1½ tsp / 7 mL **toasted sesame seeds**

½ to 1½ tsp / 2 to 7 mL **hot pepper flakes**

● In small saucepan, mix together hoisin sauce, lemongrass, light and dark soy sauces, ginger, garlic and Sichuan pepper; bring to boil. Reduce heat to low and simmer for 5 minutes. Let cool.

● Remove membrane from underside of ribs if attached; place ribs in large dish. Pour half of the hoisin mixture over top; refrigerate remaining marinade. Marinate ribs at cool room temperature for 3 hours or, preferably, refrigerated, up to 2 days.

● Grill, covered, on greased grill over medium heat, turning constantly to avoid burning, until meat is tender, 20 to 25 minutes. Cut into 1-rib portions; toss with reserved marinade until coated. Grill, turning a few times, until glazed, 2 to 3 minutes. Transfer to serving platter; sprinkle with sesame oil and seeds, and hot pepper flakes.

Makes 4 to 6 servings.

PER EACH OF 6 SERVINGS: about 403 cal, 27 g pro, 27 g total fat (10 g sat. fat), 11 g carb, 1 g fibre, 103 mg chol, 634 mg sodium, 359 mg potassium. % RDI: 4% calcium, 11% iron, 1% vit A, 2% vit C, 5% folate.

Indonesian-Style Ribs

Although most Indonesians are Muslims and don't eat pork (which is, however, consumed by the large Chinese and smaller Balinese populations), Indonesian flavours complement pork quite well, especially for ribs.

3 to 4 lb / 1.5 to 2 kg **small pork ribs**

3 cloves **garlic**, minced

2 tbsp / 30 mL ground or finely minced **fresh lemongrass**

2 tbsp / 30 mL **fish sauce**

1½ tbsp / 22 mL minced **fresh coriander**

2 tsp / 10 mL finely grated **fresh ginger**

2 **kaffir lime leaves**, centre vein removed and minced, or ½ tsp/2 mL finely grated lime rind

¼ cup / 60 mL coarsely ground **roasted peanuts**

SWEET & SPICY SAUCE:

¼ cup / 60 mL **peanut** or vegetable **oil**

⅓ cup / 75 mL sliced **shallots**

5 cloves **garlic**, sliced

4 tsp / 20 mL minced **Thai (bird-eye) chilies** or other hot peppers

½ cup / 125 mL **sweet soy sauce** (kecap manis; see Tip, right)

⅓ cup / 75 mL **lime juice**

● Remove membrane from underside of ribs if attached. Mix together garlic, lemongrass, fish sauce, coriander, ginger and lime leaves; rub all over ribs. Marinate for 2 hours or, refrigerated, up to 1 day.

● **Sweet & Spicy Sauce:** In small saucepan, heat oil over medium-high heat; fry shallots until golden. With slotted spoon, transfer shallots to paper towel and let drain. Add garlic to pan; fry until golden. Transfer to paper towel and let drain. In mortar with pestle, pound chilies until paste; add shallots and garlic and pound until almost smooth (or mince together as finely as possible). Transfer to large bowl; mix in sweet soy sauce and lime juice.

● Grill ribs, covered, on greased grill over medium heat, turning constantly to avoid burning, until meat is tender, 20 to 25 minutes. Cut into 1-rib portions; toss with Sweet and Spicy Sauce until coated. Grill, turning a few times, until glazed, 2 to 3 minutes. Transfer to serving platter; sprinkle with peanuts.

Makes 4 to 6 servings.

Photo, page 218

TIP

If you can't find kecap manis for this recipe, boil together ½ cup/125 mL granulated sugar, ⅓ cup/75 mL soy sauce and 2 tbsp/30 mL fancy molasses until sugar is dissolved.

PER EACH OF 6 SERVINGS: about 555 cal, 29 g pro, 36 g total fat (12 g sat. fat), 29 g carb, 1 g fibre, 103 mg chol, 1,410 mg sodium, 577 mg potassium. % RDI: 7% calcium, 16% iron, 2% vit A, 13% vit C, 9% folate.

Indonesian-Style Ribs
(page 217)

Smoked Garlic Ribs with Fresh Tomato Barbecue Sauce

Smoke-grilling the ribs gives them a deep, sweet flavour that makes a nice backdrop for a fresh tomato barbecue sauce with Spanish flavourings.

3 to 4 lb / 1.5 to 2 kg **small pork ribs**

6 cloves **garlic**

1 tsp / 5 mL **salt**

1 tbsp / 15 mL minced **fresh rosemary**

2 tsp / 10 mL **sherry vinegar** or red wine vinegar

¾ tsp / 4 mL **ground cumin**

FRESH TOMATO BARBECUE SAUCE:

3 ripe **tomatoes**

2 tbsp / 30 mL **olive oil**

1 New Mexico **hot red pepper**, seeded and coarsely ground, or 2 tsp/10 mL New Mexico or ancho chili powder

Half **onion**, minced

1 small clove **garlic**, minced

½ tsp / 2 mL **salt**

1 sprig **fresh rosemary**

½ tsp / 2 mL **sherry vinegar**

¼ tsp / 1 mL **granulated sugar**

¼ tsp / 1 mL **smoked paprika**

● Remove membrane from underside of ribs if attached. In mortar with pestle, pound garlic and salt together until paste (or mince garlic; using side and back of knife, rub with salt on cutting board until paste). Mix together garlic paste, rosemary, vinegar and cumin; rub all over ribs. Marinate for 1 hour or, preferably, refrigerated, up to 1 day.

● Soak 3 cups/750 mL wood chips in water for 1 hour; drain. Place in pan over gas flame or on coals in barbecue (or according to manufacturer's instructions). Grill ribs, covered, over indirect medium heat (see Tip, page 214) until fork-tender and meat pulls away from ends of bones, about 1½ hours.

● **Fresh Tomato Barbecue Sauce:** Meanwhile, halve tomatoes crosswise; on coarse side of box grater, grate flesh, discarding skin. In saucepan, heat oil over medium-low heat; fry hot pepper, onion, garlic and salt until onion is softened. Add tomatoes and juices, rosemary, vinegar, sugar and paprika. Increase heat to medium; simmer, uncovered, until thickened, about 15 minutes. Discard rosemary.

● Cut ribs into 1-rib portions. Toss with Fresh Tomato Barbecue Sauce until coated.

Makes 4 to 6 servings.

PER EACH OF 6 SERVINGS: about 397 cal, 27 g pro, 30 g total fat (10 g sat. fat), 5 g carb, 1 g fibre, 103 mg chol, 706 mg sodium, 493 mg potassium. % RDI: 5% calcium, 12% iron, 8% vit A, 15% vit C, 5% folate.

Gremolata Rack of Lamb

*To french chops is to scrape clean the end of each rib bone to within
1 inch/2.5 cm of the eye of the raw meat.*

2 **racks of lamb**, frenched, about
1¼ lb/625 g each

¼ tsp / 1 mL each **salt** and **black pepper**

GREMOLATA:

½ cup / 125 mL minced **fresh parsley**

2 tbsp / 30 mL **extra-virgin olive oil**

4 tsp / 20 mL grated **lemon rind**

½ tsp / 2 mL **ground coriander**

2 cloves **garlic**, minced

¼ tsp / 1 mL each **salt** and **black pepper**

● **Gremolata:** Mix together parsley, oil, lemon rind, coriander, garlic, salt and pepper.

● Trim excess fat from lamb, leaving thin layer over meat; sprinkle with salt and pepper. Press Gremolata onto rounded side. Grill, covered and bare side down, on greased grill over medium heat until medium-rare, 20 to 25 minutes.

● Transfer to cutting board and tent with foil; let stand for 5 minutes before carving between bones.

Makes 4 servings.

PER SERVING: about 253 cal, 24 g pro, 16 g total fat (5 g sat. fat), 2 g carb, 1 g fibre, 89 mg chol, 337 mg sodium. % RDI:
3% calcium, 17% iron, 4% vit A, 20% vit C, 5% folate.

Lamb Chops with Chunky Greek Salad

3 tbsp / 45 mL **extra-virgin olive oil**

2 cloves **garlic**, minced

½ tsp / 2 mL grated **lemon rind**

1 tbsp / 15 mL **lemon juice**

1 tsp / 5 mL **dried oregano**

½ tsp / 2 mL each **salt** and **black pepper**

8 **lamb loin chops**, about 1½ lb/750 g, trimmed

2 **tomatoes**, cut into wedges

1 **sweet yellow** or red **pepper**, cut into ½-inch/1 cm pieces

Half **English cucumber**, cut into ½-inch/1 cm pieces

2 cups / 500 mL torn **leaf lettuce**

½ cup / 125 mL thinly sliced **red onion**

2 tbsp / 30 mL minced **fresh parsley**

2 tsp / 10 mL **red wine vinegar**

● In large dish, whisk together oil, garlic, lemon rind and juice, oregano, salt and pepper; transfer half to large salad bowl. Add lamb chops to remainder, turning to coat. Let stand for 20 minutes.

● Grill, covered, on greased grill over medium-high heat, turning once, until desired doneness, about 8 minutes for medium-rare.

● Add tomatoes, pepper, cucumber, lettuce, onion, parsley and vinegar to reserved oil mixture; toss until coated. Serve with chops.

Makes 4 servings.

PER SERVING: about 227 cal, 19 g pro, 13 g total fat (3 g sat. fat), 9 g carb, 2 g fibre, 68 mg chol, 259 mg sodium. % RDI: 4% calcium, 17% iron, 8% vit A, 127% vit C, 20% folate.

Teriyaki Orange Lamb Chops

⅓ cup / 75 mL **Teriyaki Sauce** (page 531)

2 tbsp / 30 mL thawed **orange juice concentrate**

1 tbsp / 15 mL minced **fresh ginger**

2 tsp / 10 mL grated **orange rind**

2 cloves **garlic**, minced

¼ tsp / 1 mL **salt**

Pinch **black pepper**

12 **lamb loin** or rib **chops**, 2 lb/1 kg total

2 **green onions**, sliced

● Mix together Teriyaki Sauce, orange juice concentrate, ginger, orange rind, garlic, salt and pepper; add lamb, turning to coat. Marinate, refrigerated, for at least 4 hours or up to 1 day.

● Reserving marinade, place chops on greased grill over medium-high heat; brush with marinade. Grill, turning once, until desired doneness, about 8 minutes for medium-rare. Serve sprinkled with green onions.

Makes 4 servings.

PER SERVING: about 183 cal, 24 g pro, 7 g total fat (3 g sat. fat), 5 g carb, trace fibre, 91 mg chol, 486 mg sodium. % RDI: 3% calcium, 16% iron, 12% vit C, 5% folate.

Mojito Rack of Lamb

Mint and rum define this famous Cuban drink; here we infuse lamb with rum, garlic and spices, then top it with a fragrant mint chutney.

2 **racks of lamb**, about 1 lb/500 g each

2 cloves **garlic**, pressed or minced

4 tsp / 20 mL **amber** or dark **rum**

¼ tsp / 1 mL each **salt** and **black pepper**

¼ tsp / 1 mL **cayenne pepper**

¼ tsp / 1 mL **ground cumin**

¼ tsp / 1 mL **turmeric**

MINT CHUTNEY:

½ cup / 125 mL packed **fresh mint leaves**

1 **green onion**, chopped

1 **hot green pepper**, seeded and chopped

1 tbsp / 15 mL **lime juice**

2 tsp / 10 mL **granulated sugar**

2 tsp / 10 mL **amber rum**

¼ tsp / 1 mL **salt**

● Trim excess fat from lamb, leaving thin layer over meat. Mix together garlic, rum, salt, pepper, cayenne, cumin and turmeric; rub all over lamb. Marinate for 1 hour or, refrigerated, up to 1 day.

● **Mint Chutney:** In food processor, pulse together mint, onion, hot pepper, lime juice, sugar, rum and salt until finely minced.

● Grill racks, covered, on greased grill over medium-high heat, turning once, until medium-rare, about 20 minutes. Transfer to cutting board; tent with foil and let stand for 5 minutes before cutting into 1-chop portions. Spoon dollop of Mint Chutney over each chop.

Makes 4 servings.

PER SERVING: about 210 cal, 22 g pro, 10 g total fat (4 g sat. fat), 4 g carb, 0 g fibre, 72 mg chol, 358 mg sodium. % RDI: 2% calcium, 20% iron, 4% vit A, 6% vit C, 12% folate.

Moroccan-Style Lamb Chops with Tomato Olive Salsa

1 tbsp / 15 mL **extra-virgin olive oil**

1 clove **garlic**, minced

1 tsp / 5 mL **ground coriander**

1 tsp / 5 mL **ground cumin**

1 tsp / 5 mL **black pepper**

½ tsp / 2 mL **cinnamon**

½ tsp / 2 mL **salt**

¼ tsp / 1 mL **cayenne pepper**

Pinch **ground cloves**

8 **lamb loin chops**, about 2 lb/1 kg total, trimmed

TOMATO OLIVE SALSA:

1½ cups / 375 mL **grape** or cherry **tomatoes**, halved

⅓ cup / 75 mL chopped **green olives**

2 tbsp / 30 mL minced **fresh mint** and/or **parsley**

1 tbsp / 15 mL **extra-virgin olive oil**

1 clove **garlic**, minced

2 tsp / 10 mL **lemon juice**

Pinch each **salt** and **black pepper**

● **Tomato Olive Salsa:** Toss together tomatoes, olives, mint, oil, garlic, lemon juice, salt and pepper until coated.

● Mix together oil, garlic, coriander, cumin, pepper, cinnamon, salt, cayenne and cloves; add lamb, turning to coat. Let stand for 20 minutes.

● Grill on greased grill over medium-high heat, turning once, until desired doneness, about 8 minutes for medium-rare. Serve with Tomato Olive Salsa.

Makes 4 servings.

PER SERVING: about 254 cal, 24 g pro, 15 g total fat (4 g sat. fat), 5 g carb, 2 g fibre, 91 mg chol, 507 mg sodium. % RDI: 4% calcium, 21% iron, 6% vit A, 15% vit C, 5% folate.

Peppered Lamb with Mint Butter

Cuts such as ¾-inch/2 cm thick boneless lamb leg steaks or loin chops can be used instead of medallions.

8 **lamb medallions**, 1¼ lb/625 g total, or 8 lamb loin chops, about 2 lb/1 kg total, trimmed

2 tsp / 10 mL **vegetable oil**

1 tbsp / 15 mL coarsely cracked **black pepper**

MINT BUTTER:

¼ cup / 60 mL **butter**, softened

1 tbsp / 15 mL chopped **fresh mint** (or ¾ tsp/4 mL dried)

2 tsp / 10 mL **white wine vinegar**

1 **shallot**, minced

½ tsp / 2 mL **black pepper**

● **Mint Butter:** Mash together butter, mint, vinegar, shallot and pepper. On plastic wrap, shape into 3-inch/8 cm long log; seal ends. Refrigerate until firm, about 30 minutes.

● Rub lamb with oil; sprinkle with pepper. Grill on greased grill over medium-high heat, turning once, until desired doneness, about 8 minutes for medium-rare. Transfer to platter. Cut Mint Butter into 8 slices; place 1 on each medallion.

Makes 4 servings.

PER SERVING: about 330 cal, 30 g pro, 22 g total fat (11 g sat. fat), 2 g carb, trace fibre, 152 mg chol, 174 mg sodium. % RDI: 3% calcium, 22% iron, 11% vit A, 2% vit C, 1% folate.

Herbed Lamb Medallions or Chops

1 tbsp / 15 mL chopped **fresh thyme** (or ¾ tsp/4 mL dried)

1 tbsp / 15 mL chopped **fresh oregano** (or 1 tsp/5 mL dried)

1 tbsp / 15 mL chopped **fresh rosemary**

1 tbsp / 15 mL **extra-virgin olive oil**

1 tsp / 5 mL **fennel seeds**, crushed

1 clove **garlic**, minced

½ tsp / 2 mL **black pepper**

¼ tsp / 1 mL **salt**

8 **lamb medallions**, 1¼ lb/625 g total, or 8 lamb loin chops, about 2 lb/1 kg total, trimmed

● Mix together thyme, oregano, rosemary, oil, fennel seeds, garlic, pepper and salt; rub all over lamb.

● Grill, covered, on greased grill over medium-high heat, turning once, until desired doneness, about 8 minutes for medium-rare.

Makes 4 servings.

PER SERVING: about 196 cal, 24 g pro, 10 g total fat (3 g sat. fat), 1 g carb, trace fibre, 92 mg chol, 189 mg sodium. % RDI: 3% calcium, 16% iron, 1% vit A, 2% vit C.

Grilled Venison Chops (opposite),
Creamy Potato Salad (page 483)

Grilled Venison Chops

If you're not a hunter or a lucky friend of a hunter with game to spare, venison chops are an expensive but wonderful luxury. This recipe is easily doubled or tripled for more than just two chops. Don't cook venison chops past medium or they'll be dry.

¼ cup / 60 mL **gin**

¼ cup / 60 mL grated **onion**

2 cloves **garlic**, pressed or minced

2 tsp / 10 mL minced **fresh rosemary**

¾ tsp / 4 mL **black pepper**

Pinch (approx) **salt**

2 **venison chops**, about 1 lb/500 g total

¾ tsp / 4 mL **Indian ground red chilies**, or ancho or other chili powder

¼ tsp / 1 mL **ground cumin**

1 tbsp / 15 mL **lard** or butter, melted, or olive oil

● Mix together gin, onion, garlic, rosemary, ½ tsp/2 mL of the pepper and pinch salt; add chops, turning to coat. Marinate, refrigerated, for 4 to 8 hours, turning once or twice.

● Remove chops from marinade, brushing off onions; sprinkle both sides with ground chilies, cumin and remaining pepper.

● Grill over medium-high heat, basting with lard and turning once, until desired doneness, about 10 minutes for medium-rare. Season with salt to taste.

Makes 2 servings.

PER SERVING: about 327 cal, 51 g pro, 11 g total fat (4 g sat. fat), 1 g carb, trace fibre, 139 mg chol, 106 mg sodium, 701 mg potassium. % RDI: 2% calcium, 52% iron, 3% vit A, 2% vit C, 7% folate.

Grilled Liver with Mushrooms & Onions

3 cups / 750 mL sliced **mushrooms** (8 oz/250 g)

1 **onion**, finely chopped

3 tbsp / 45 mL **balsamic vinegar**

1 tbsp / 15 mL **butter**, melted

½ tsp / 2 mL crumbled **dried sage**

½ tsp / 2 mL each **salt** and **black pepper**

1 tsp / 5 mL **Dijon mustard**

1 lb / 500 g thinly sliced **calves'** or beef **liver**

1 tbsp / 15 mL **vegetable oil**

2 tbsp / 30 mL minced **fresh parsley**

● Arrange mushrooms and onion on heavy-duty foil; drizzle with 1 tbsp/15 mL of the vinegar and butter. Sprinkle with sage and half each of the salt and pepper; seal to form packet. Grill over medium heat, turning once, until tender, about 10 minutes.

● Meanwhile, whisk remaining vinegar with mustard. Pat liver dry; brush with oil and sprinkle with remaining salt and pepper. Grill over medium-high heat, turning and brushing twice with vinegar mixture, until glazed, browned on both sides and still slightly pink inside, about 4 minutes. Sprinkle with parsley; serve with mushrooms and onions.

Makes 3 servings.

TIP

Calves' liver is mild, tender and pricey. Improve less-expensive beef liver by soaking it in milk in the refrigerator for up to 4 hours. Drain, pat dry and proceed with recipe.

PER SERVING: about 336 cal, 32 g pro, 15 g total fat (5 g sat. fat), 19 g carb, 1 g fibre, 547 mg chol, 557 mg sodium. % RDI: 3% calcium, 83% iron, 1,196% vit A, 53% vit C, 119% folate.

Liver with Garlic Wine Sauce

¾ cup / 175 mL **dry red wine**

5 tsp / 25 mL **balsamic vinegar**

4 cloves **garlic**, pressed or minced

2 **anchovy fillets**, minced, or ¼ tsp/
1 mL salt

1 lb / 500 g sliced **calves'**, beef, lamb or
pork **liver**

¼ tsp / 1 mL each **salt** and **black pepper**

3 tbsp / 45 mL **all-purpose flour**

2 tbsp / 30 mL **olive oil**

1 tbsp / 15 mL finely chopped **fresh
parsley**

In small saucepan, bring wine, vinegar, garlic and anchovies to boil; reduce heat to medium and boil until thickened and reduced to about 2 tbsp/30 mL, about 15 minutes. Set aside at room temperature for up to 8 hours.

If necessary, peel off outer membrane from liver; sprinkle all over with salt and pepper. Dredge with flour; brush lightly with oil. Grill over medium-high heat, turning once, until lightly browned and still slightly pink in centre, about 4 minutes. Transfer to warmed platter; spoon sauce (rewarming, if necessary) over top. Sprinkle with parsley.

Makes 3 servings.

Supermarket liver is often cut too thin to grill, so look for liver that's sliced at least ¼ inch/ 5 mm – or preferably ½ inch/1 cm – thick at the butcher counter.

PER SERVING: about 469 cal, 37 g pro, 23 g total fat (5 g sat. fat), 21 g carb, trace fibre, 635 mg chol, 533 mg sodium, 639 mg potassium. % RDI: 4% calcium, 68% iron, 1,407% vit A, 56% vit C, 140% folate.

Grilled Calves' Liver with Green Onions

Milk-fed calves' liver is unsurpassed in taste and delicacy. Grain-fed veal liver, baby beef liver, or lamb or pork liver are good, too.

1 lb / 500 g **calves' liver**, cut into ⅓- to ½-inch/8 mm to 1 cm thick slices

1 tsp / 5 mL **red wine vinegar**

½ tsp / 2 mL (approx) **salt**

¼ tsp / 1 mL **black pepper**

¼ tsp / 1 mL **ground sage**

¼ tsp / 1 mL **ground savory**

Pinch **cayenne pepper**

3 tbsp / 45 mL **butter**

1 small clove **garlic**, pressed or minced

¼ tsp / 1 mL **smoked paprika** (or sweet paprika)

8 **green onions**

● Sprinkle liver with vinegar, rubbing to coat evenly; let stand for 5 minutes. Pat dry. Sprinkle both sides with ½ tsp/2 mL salt, pepper, sage, savory and cayenne.

● In small saucepan or in microwave, melt together butter, garlic, paprika and pinch salt.

● Brush liver and onions with butter mixture. Grill over medium-high heat, turning once, until onions are tender, 2 to 3 minutes, and liver is lightly browned and still slightly pink in centre, 3 to 6 minutes.

Makes 3 servings.

PER SERVING: about 315 cal, 29 g pro, 18 g total fat (10 g sat. fat), 8 g carb, 1 g fibre, 527 mg chol, 558 mg sodium, 488 mg potassium. % RDI: 4% calcium, 49% iron, 2,069% vit A, 10% vit C, 172% folate.

Roasts

Rotisserie Prime Rib

This simple but sophisticated recipe is a household favourite of Winnipeg chef Michael Dacquisto.

6 lb / 2.7 kg **beef prime rib roast**

⅓ cup / 75 mL minced **garlic**

⅓ cup / 75 mL **vegetable oil**

¼ cup / 60 mL **coarse sea salt**

¼ cup / 60 mL **cracked black peppercorns**

¼ cup / 60 mL **fresh thyme leaves**

¼ cup / 60 mL **Dijon mustard**

10 **fresh rosemary sprigs**

● Trim all but ¼-inch/5 mm thick layer of fat from outside of roast. With fork or lightly in mortar with pestle, mash together garlic, oil, salt, peppercorns, thyme and mustard until paste; spread evenly over top of roast. Lay rosemary over top; with kitchen string, tie tightly at 1-inch/2.5 cm intervals. Refrigerate for 1 to 2 days.

● Secure rotisserie prong to 1 end of roast; push spit through centre and secure other end with prong. Grill, covered, on rotisserie over indirect medium-low heat (see Tip, below), 2 to 2½ hours for rare to medium (see Tip, page 241).

● Transfer to cutting board; tent with foil. Let stand for 10 minutes. Remove string and rosemary before carving.

Makes 10 to 12 servings.

To grill over indirect heat on gas grill, set foil drip pan under 1 rack of 2-burner barbecue or under centre rack of 3-burner barbecue. Heat remaining burner(s) to temperature indicated (see Grilling Temperatures, page 10). For charcoal grill, place drip pan in centre and arrange hot charcoal on either side. Set meat on greased grill or rotisserie and centre over drip pan. Grill as directed.

PER EACH OF 12 SERVINGS: about 307 cal, 32 g pro, 18 g total fat (5 g sat. fat), 3 g carb, trace fibre, 72 mg chol, 2,447 mg sodium. % RDI: 3% calcium, 24% iron, 5% vit C, 4% folate.

Garlicky Prime Rib

Think big when entertaining and grill a succulent roast of beef that will surely satisfy a crowd.

6 cloves **garlic**, minced

2 tbsp / 30 mL chopped **fresh thyme**

1 tsp / 5 mL **salt**

2 tbsp / 30 mL **coriander seeds**

1 tbsp / 15 mL **black peppercorns**

1 tbsp / 15 mL **dill seeds**

1 tbsp / 15 mL **vegetable oil**

8 lb / 3.5 kg **beef prime rib roast**

● In mortar with pestle or on cutting board with side of knife, mash together garlic, thyme and salt until smooth paste; transfer to small dish. Coarsely crush together coriander seeds, peppercorns and dill seeds; add to garlic mixture. Mix in oil; spread over roast. Let stand for 1 hour or, refrigerated, up to 1 day.

● Grill, covered and bone side down, on greased grill over indirect medium heat (see Tip, page 239), 2 to 2½ hours for rare or medium-rare (see Tip, below). Transfer to cutting board; tent with foil and let stand for 10 minutes before carving.

Makes 12 servings.

Use an instant-read thermometer or ovenproof meat thermometer to test the internal temperature of beef roasts: rare (125 to 130°F/53 to 55°C), medium-rare (131 to 140°F/56 to 60°C), medium (141 to 150°F/ 61 to 65°C), medium-well (151 to 155°F/67 to 69°C) and well-done (156 to 160°F/70 to 71°C). The lower ends of the temperatures here are obviously less well-done than the higher, but you should be able to satisfy diners if your roast falls within the ranges given.

PER SERVING: about 334 cal, 42 g pro, 17 g total fat (6 g sat. fat), 2 g carb, 1 g fibre, 97 mg chol, 295 mg sodium. % RDI: 3% calcium, 27% iron, 5% folate.

Beef Tenderloin Roast with Oyster Mushrooms

Beef tenderloin roast is so lean that it's best to cook it over direct high heat like a steak. This luxurious, rich roast bastes itself from the inside with porcini-flavoured butter.

½ oz / 15 g **dried porcini (cep) mushrooms**

1 tbsp / 15 mL **brandy** or dry sherry

½ cup / 125 mL **butter**, softened

1 clove **garlic**, pressed or minced

2 tbsp / 30 mL minced **fresh parsley**

2 tbsp / 30 mL finely chopped **fresh chives**

1 tsp / 5 mL minced **fresh thyme** or ½ tsp/2 mL minced fresh rosemary

1¼ tsp / 6 mL (approx) **salt**

¾ tsp / 4 mL **black pepper**

3 lb / 1.5 kg **beef tenderloin roast**, tied

1 lb / 500 g **oyster mushrooms**

Banana leaf or heavy-duty foil

● In spice grinder, grind porcini to fine powder; set aside 2 tsp/10 mL. Stir brandy into remainder; mash together moistened porcini powder, butter, garlic, parsley, chives, thyme, and ¼ tsp/1 mL each of the salt and pepper. Set aside ¼ cup/60 mL of the butter mixture.

● With long thin sharp knife, make slit all the way through centre of tenderloin from both ends; stuff remaining butter mixture evenly into slit. Mix together reserved porcini powder, 1 tsp/5 mL of the remaining salt and remaining pepper; sprinkle all over roast.

● Place oyster mushrooms on banana leaf (see Tip, page 145) or foil; top with reserved butter mixture and pinch salt. Wrap to make package, securing with string or strip of leaf (omit string if using foil).

● Grill beef, covered, on greased grill over high heat, turning often, until rare to medium (do not cook tenderloin past medium), about 16 minutes for medium-rare (see Tip, page 241). Transfer to cutting board; tent with foil and let stand for 10 minutes before slicing.

● Meanwhile, grill mushroom package over high heat for 10 minutes. Serve mushrooms with their juices over sliced roast.

Makes 8 servings.

PER SERVING: about 350 cal, 38 g pro, 19 g total fat (11 g sat. fat), 4 g carb, 1 g fibre, 110 mg chol, 528 mg sodium, 604 mg potassium. % RDI: 2% calcium, 36% iron, 11% vit A, 3% vit C, 11% folate.

Roast Sirloin with Orange Barbecue Sauce

This roast, sliced and topped with zesty orange barbecue sauce, is great on crusty rolls, but you could also serve it on its own with potatoes or rice.

3 lb / 1.5 kg **beef top sirloin roast**

1 tbsp / 15 mL **vegetable oil**

¼ tsp / 1 mL each **salt** and **black pepper**

8 **kaiser rolls**, halved

ORANGE BARBECUE SAUCE:

1 tbsp / 15 mL **vegetable oil**

1 small **onion**, chopped

2 cloves **garlic**, minced

1 tbsp / 15 mL **paprika**

1 tbsp / 15 mL **chili powder**

¼ tsp / 1 mL each **salt** and **black pepper**

1 can (19 oz/540 mL) **stewed tomatoes**

1 can (5½ oz/156 mL) **tomato paste**

⅓ cup / 75 mL packed **brown sugar**

⅓ cup / 75 mL **cider vinegar**

1 tbsp / 15 mL grated **orange rind**

⅓ cup / 75 mL **orange juice**

2 tbsp / 30 mL **Dijon mustard**

● Brush roast with oil; sprinkle with salt and pepper. Grill, covered, on greased grill over indirect medium heat (see Tip, page 239), 1½ to 2½ hours for rare to medium (see Tip, page 241).

● Orange Barbecue Sauce: Meanwhile, in saucepan, heat oil over medium heat; fry onion, garlic, paprika, chili powder, salt and pepper, stirring occasionally, until onion is softened, about 5 minutes. Mash in tomatoes, tomato paste, sugar, vinegar, orange rind and juice, and mustard; bring to boil. Reduce heat and simmer, stirring occasionally, until thickened and reduced by one-third, about 40 minutes.

● Transfer roast to cutting board; tent with foil and let stand for 10 minutes before carving into thin slices. Serve on rolls with Orange Barbecue Sauce.

Makes 8 servings.

243

PER SERVING: about 503 cal, 40 g pro, 14 g total fat (3 g sat. fat), 55 g carb, 6 g fibre, 77 mg chol, 806 mg sodium. % RDI: 12% calcium, 52% iron, 18% vit A, 43% vit C, 36% folate.

Texas Barbecue Brisket

Starting the brisket in the oven lets you recreate this American classic on a home grill.

1 tbsp / 15 mL **chili powder**

1 tbsp / 15 mL **smoked paprika**

1 tbsp / 15 mL **kosher** or coarse sea **salt**

2 tsp / 10 mL **granulated sugar**

1 tsp / 5 mL **ground cumin**

1 tsp / 5 mL **black pepper**

5 to 6 lb / 2.2 to 2.7 kg **beef brisket**

BRISKET SAUCE:

1 tbsp / 15 mL **vegetable oil**

Half **onion**, finely chopped

2 cloves **garlic**, minced

2 cups / 500 mL **dark ale** or sodium-reduced beef stock

¼ cup / 60 mL packed **brown sugar**

¼ cup / 60 mL **Worcestershire sauce**

¼ cup / 60 mL **cider vinegar**

2 tsp / 10 mL **dry mustard**

1 tbsp / 15 mL **salt**

2 tbsp / 30 mL **tomato paste**

● Mix together chili powder, paprika, salt, sugar, cumin and pepper; rub all over brisket. Let stand for 1 hour or, refrigerated, up to 1 day.

● **Brisket Sauce:** In small saucepan, heat oil over medium heat; fry onion and garlic until soft and translucent. Stir in ale, sugar, Worcestershire sauce, vinegar, mustard and salt (if using beef stock, reduce salt to 1½ tsp/7 mL); bring to boil. Reduce heat and simmer for 10 minutes.

● Place roast in roasting pan; loosely cover with foil. Roast in 300°F/150°C oven, basting with Brisket Sauce every 30 minutes after first hour, until falling-apart tender, about 3 hours. Transfer brisket to plate; skim fat off juices in pan. Add juices to remaining sauce. Set aside. (Refrigerate brisket and sauce separately overnight.)

● Soak 4 cups/1 L wood chips in water for 30 minutes. Prepare barbecue for indirect grilling (see Tip, page 239). For gas barbecue, follow manufacturer's instructions or seal soaked chips in foil to make packet; poke several holes in top. Place over lit burner; close lid. For charcoal barbecue, place soaked chips directly on coals. Grill, covered and basting with some of the remaining sauce every 15 minutes (without allowing too much smoke to escape), until dark brown and crisp, about 1 hour. Transfer to cutting board; tent with foil and let stand for 15 minutes before slicing thinly across the grain.

● Meanwhile, in saucepan over medium-high heat, whisk remaining sauce with tomato paste; simmer until thickened, about 10 minutes. Serve with brisket.

Makes 8 to 10 servings.

PER EACH OF 10 SERVINGS: about 355 cal, 35 g pro, 18 g total fat (6 g sat. fat), 12 g carb, 1 g fibre, 89 mg chol, 1,323 mg sodium, 506 mg potassium. % RDI: 3% calcium, 31% iron, 6% vit A, 5% vit C, 6% folate.

Rolled Veal Roast

5 lb / 2.2 kg **veal outside round roast**

1 tsp / 5 mL each **salt** and **black pepper**

4 oz / 125 g thinly sliced **pancetta** or bacon

¼ cup / 60 mL grated **Parmesan cheese**

¼ cup / 60 mL chopped **fresh parsley**

1 tbsp / 15 mL minced **garlic**

● Place veal, fat side down, on cutting board; cut horizontally in half along 1 long side, leaving 3 inches/ 7.5 cm attached. Open like book; sprinkle with ½ tsp/ 2 mL each of the salt and pepper. Lay pancetta over top; sprinkle with Parmesan cheese, parsley and garlic. Roll up roast, ensuring that fat is on outside; with kitchen string, tie tightly at 2-inch/5 cm intervals. Sprinkle with remaining salt and pepper.

● Secure rotisserie prong to 1 end of roast; push spit through centre and secure other end with prong. Grill, covered, on rotisserie over indirect medium-high heat (see Tip, page 239) until medium-rare to medium (140 to 150°F/60 to 65°C), 1 to 1½ hours.

● Transfer to cutting board; tent with foil and let stand for 15 minutes. Remove string before carving.

Makes 8 to 10 servings.

TIP

If you don't have a rotisserie, grill over indirect heat, turning roast every 15 minutes.

PER EACH OF 10 SERVINGS: about 328 cal, 52 g pro, 12 g total fat (6 g sat. fat), 1 g carb, trace fibre, 191 mg chol, 459 mg sodium, 726 mg potassium. % RDI: 4% calcium, 13% iron, 2% vit A, 3% vit C, 14% folate.

Veal Loin Rib Roast

A luxurious cut of meat, veal rib roast should be absolutely tender and lusciously rich. White, milk-fed veal yields the finest result, while grain-fed veal produces a slightly coarser, beefier roast.

1 tbsp / 15 mL chopped **fresh sage**

6 **anchovy fillets**

3 cloves **garlic**, smashed

½ tsp / 2 mL **salt**

1 tbsp / 15 mL **olive oil**

1 tsp / 5 mL **fennel seeds**, coarsely crushed

½ tsp / 2 mL coarsely ground **black pepper**

3-rib **veal loin rib roast**, about 3 lb/1.5 kg

¼ cup / 60 mL **dry white wine** or dry white vermouth

¼ cup / 60 mL **butter**, melted

● In mortar with pestle or on cutting board with side of knife, mash together sage, anchovies, garlic and salt until smooth paste; transfer to small dish. Mix in oil, fennel seeds and pepper; rub all over roast. Let stand for 1 hour or, refrigerated, up to 1 day.

● Mix wine with butter. Grill roast, covered and bone side down, over indirect medium heat (see Tip, page 239), basting often with wine mixture, until medium-rare to medium (140 to 150°F/60 to 65°C), 1¼ to 1½ hours. Transfer to cutting board; tent with foil and let stand for 10 minutes before carving.

Makes 4 or 5 servings.

PER EACH OF 5 SERVINGS: about 309 cal, 35 g pro, 18 g total fat (6 g sat. fat), 1 g carb, trace fibre, 165 mg chol, 564 mg sodium, 452 mg potassium. % RDI: 4% calcium, 12% iron, 4% vit A, 2% vit C, 9% folate.

Rotisserie Pork Rib Roast

A rotisserie-grilled pork roast dazzles the senses with its crisp, browned crust and tender, juicy, smoke-touched flesh. Make sure your butcher hasn't trimmed off too much of the fat cap on the top of the roast; a thin layer will keep the meat moist.

3 lb / 1.5 kg **pork rib roast** (French rack)

3 cloves **garlic**, cut into slivers

1¼ tsp / 6 mL **salt**

½ tsp / 2 mL **black pepper**

8 sprigs (approx) **fresh rosemary**

1 **onion**, coarsely chopped

3 **anchovy fillets**

1½ cups / 375 mL **dry white wine**

● Cut slits all over roast; insert 1 garlic sliver into each. Sprinkle with ¾ tsp/4 mL of the salt and pepper. Lay rosemary over top; with kitchen string, tie tightly at 1-inch/2.5 cm intervals (if roast is already tied, thread rosemary under string).

● Place roast in resealable freezer bag. In blender, purée together onion, anchovies and wine; pour over roast. Refrigerate for at least 8 hours or, preferably, 1 or 2 days, turning occasionally.

● Reserving marinade, remove roast; let come to room temperature. Secure rotisserie prong to 1 end of roast; push spit through centre and secure other end with prong. Grill, covered, on rotisserie over indirect medium heat (see Tip, page 239), basting with reserved marinade every 10 minutes, for 1 hour. Sprinkle roast with remaining salt; grill, without basting, until just a hint of pink remains in centre (160°F/71°C), about 1 hour.

● Transfer to cutting board; tent with foil and let stand for 10 to 15 minutes. Remove string and rosemary before carving.

Makes 8 servings.

Photo, page 236

PER SERVING: about 186 cal, 23 g pro, 9 g total fat (3 g sat. fat), 2 g carb, trace fibre, 56 mg chol, 438 mg sodium, 391 mg potassium. % RDI: 3% calcium, 7% iron, 2% vit C, 2% folate.

Herbed Pork Rib Roast

The spectacular look of this succulent roast belies how simple it is to make.
If you can only find smaller short roasts, you can tie two racks together.

¾ tsp / 4 mL **fennel seeds**

3 tbsp / 45 mL **extra-virgin olive oil**

4 cloves **garlic**, minced

2 tbsp / 30 mL minced **fresh rosemary**

1 tbsp / 15 mL minced **fresh sage**

1 tbsp / 15 mL **lemon juice**

½ tsp / 2 mL each **salt** and **black pepper**

3½ lb / 1.75 kg **pork rib roast**
(French rack)

● In small skillet over low heat, lightly toast fennel seeds, about 2 minutes. Let cool; gently crush. Mix together fennel seeds, oil, garlic, rosemary, sage, lemon juice, salt and pepper.

● With long thin sharp knife, make 2-inch/5 cm slit all the way through centre of roast from both ends; stuff 1 tbsp/15 mL of the fennel mixture evenly into slit. Spread remainder over top of roast. Refrigerate for at least 2 hours or up to 1 day.

● Prepare barbecue for indirect grilling (see Tip, page 239), adding 1 inch/2.5 cm water to drip pan. Grill roast, covered and bone side down, on greased grill over indirect medium-high heat, turning every 20 minutes, until just a hint of pink remains in centre (160°F/71°C), 1½ to 2 hours.

● Transfer to cutting board; tent with foil and let stand for 15 minutes before carving.

Makes 6 to 8 servings.

For French-cut rib roasts, you can wrap the bones in foil to keep them from charring, if desired.

PER EACH OF 8 SERVINGS: about 250 cal, 26 g pro, 15 g total fat (5 g sat. fat), 1 g carb, trace fibre, 64 mg chol, 187 mg sodium. % RDI: 3% calcium, 7% iron, 2% vit C, 1% folate.

Plum-Glazed Pork Loin

2 tbsp / 30 mL **soy sauce**

2 tbsp / 30 mL **lime juice**

2 tsp / 10 mL finely grated or minced **fresh ginger**

2 cloves **garlic**, pressed or minced

½ tsp / 2 mL **black pepper**

3 lb / 1.5 kg **boneless pork loin roast**

¼ cup / 60 mL **plum sauce** or apricot jam

● Mix together soy sauce, lime juice, ginger, garlic and pepper; rub all over roast. Refrigerate for at least 8 hours or up to 1 day, turning occasionally.

● Reserving marinade, place roast on greased grill over medium heat; brush with marinade. Grill, covered, turning and basting with any reserved marinade occasionally, for 1½ hours. Brush with plum sauce; grill, turning occasionally, until just a hint of pink remains in centre (160°F/71°C), about 10 minutes.

● Transfer to cutting board; tent with foil and let stand for 10 minutes before carving.

Makes 8 servings.

PER SERVING: about 186 cal, 25 g pro, 7 g total fat (2 g sat. fat), 4 g carb, trace fibre, 68 mg chol, 313 mg sodium. % RDI: 3% calcium, 6% iron, 2% vit C, 3% folate.

Smoked Pork Loin

You can also cook this pork loin without a rotisserie over indirect heat; stand it bone side down.

½ cup / 125 mL packed **brown sugar**

1 tbsp / 15 mL **paprika**

2 cloves **garlic**, minced

2 tsp / 10 mL **ground cumin**

2 tsp / 10 mL **salt**

1 tsp / 5 mL minced **fresh thyme**

1 tsp / 5 mL **black pepper**

4 lb / 2 kg **bone-in pork loin roast**

● Mix together sugar, paprika, garlic, cumin, salt, thyme and pepper; rub all over roast. Refrigerate for at least 6 hours or up to 1 day.

● Soak 6 cups/1.5 L hickory wood chips in water for 1 hour. Secure rotisserie prong to 1 end of roast; push spit through centre and secure other end with prong. Prepare barbecue for indirect grilling (see Tip, page 239). For gas barbecue, follow manufacturer's instructions or seal soaked chips in foil to make packet; poke several holes in top. Place over lit burner; close lid. For charcoal barbecue, place soaked chips directly on coals. Grill pork, covered, on rotisserie over indirect medium heat until crisp but just a hint of pink remains in centre (160°C/71°C), 1¼ to 1½ hours.

● Transfer to cutting board; tent with foil and let stand for 10 minutes before carving.

Makes 6 to 8 servings.

253

PER EACH OF 8 SERVINGS: about 279 cal, 31 g pro, 10 g total fat (4 g sat. fat), 15 g carb, 1 g fibre, 88 mg chol, 653 mg sodium, 487 mg potassium. % RDI: 4% calcium, 15% iron, 4% vit A, 3% vit C, 3% folate.

Mushroom-Stuffed Pork Loin

3 lb / 1.5 kg **boneless centre-cut pork loin roast**

¼ tsp / 1 mL each **salt** and **black pepper**

5 slices **bacon**

½ cup / 125 mL (approx) **chicken stock**

1 tbsp / 15 mL **cornstarch**

MUSHROOM STUFFING:

2 tbsp / 30 mL **olive** or vegetable **oil**

8 cups / 2 L diced **mixed mushrooms** (1 lb/500 g)

3 cloves **garlic**, minced

1 **onion**, finely chopped

1 cup / 250 mL diced **sweet red pepper**

¼ tsp / 1 mL each **salt** and **black pepper**

½ cup / 125 mL **dry white wine** (or ½ cup/125 mL chicken stock and 1 tsp/5 mL white wine vinegar)

2 tbsp / 30 mL minced **fresh parsley**

1 tbsp / 15 mL minced **fresh thyme**

1 cup / 250 mL **fresh bread crumbs**

- **Mushroom Stuffing:** In large skillet, heat oil over medium heat; fry mushrooms, garlic, onion, red pepper, salt and pepper until no liquid remains, about 15 minutes. Add wine; bring to boil. Reduce heat and simmer until evaporated, about 8 minutes. Stir in parsley and thyme. Let cool. Stir in bread crumbs.

- Meanwhile, place pork, fat side up, on cutting board with short end closest. Starting at right side, cut in half horizontally almost but not all the way through; open like book. Starting in centre of opened loin, cut left side in half horizontally almost but not all the way through; repeat on right side. Open flat; cover with waxed paper. With mallet, pound to even ½-inch/ 1 cm thickness.

- Leaving 1-inch/2.5 cm border on 1 short side, spread Mushroom Stuffing over meat. Starting at other short side, roll up tightly. Sprinkle with salt and pepper; lay bacon over top. With kitchen string, tie at 2-inch/5 cm intervals.

- Grill, covered, on greased grill over indirect medium heat (see Tip, page 239) until just a hint of pink remains in centre (160°F/71°C), 1¼ to 1½ hours. Transfer to cutting board; tent with foil and let stand for 10 minutes before slicing.

- Skim fat from drippings in drip pan; pour into glass measure; add enough stock to make 1 cup/250 mL. Transfer to saucepan; bring to boil. Mix cornstarch with 2 tbsp/30 mL water; whisk into pan. Cook until thickened, about 1 minute. Serve with pork.

Makes 8 to 10 servings.

PER EACH OF 10 SERVINGS: about 295 cal, 29 g pro, 13 g total fat (4 g sat. fat), 13 g carb, 2 g fibre, 75 mg chol, 359 mg sodium. % RDI: 5% calcium, 19% iron, 6% vit A, 48% vit C, 9% folate.

Suckling Pig Filipino-Style

Suckling pig, or lechon de leche, *is a national obsession in the Philippines. The meat of a milk-fed piglet is one of the meat lover's greatest treasures — silky smooth flesh, crispy skin and full yet delicate flavour. For a home grill, you'll need to get a true suckling pig, no bigger than 16 lb/7 kg.*

12 to 16 lb / 5.5 to 7 kg **suckling pig**

2 tsp + 1 tbsp / 10 mL + 15 mL **salt**

1 tsp / 5 mL **black pepper**

2 tbsp / 30 mL minced **garlic**

¼ cup / 60 mL finely minced **fresh lemongrass**, or 4 stalks lemongrass (preferably with leaves), smashed (optional)

3 tbsp / 45 mL **lard**, melted, or vegetable oil

Lechon Sauce (opposite)

● Wipe cavity of pig dry; remove liver (save for Lechon Sauce, opposite). If desired, leave kidneys and heart inside (or remove and sauté as cook's treat). Mix 2 tsp/10 mL of the salt with pepper. Rub cavity with half of the salt mixture, garlic and, if using, minced lemongrass (if using stalks, crumble and place inside cavity). Skewer or sew cavity shut.

● Mount pig on rotisserie through mouth and opening under tail, stretching legs out in front and behind; with kitchen string, tie tightly in several places. Brush all over with lard; sprinkle with remaining salt mixture.

● Mix 2 cups/500 mL water with remaining salt. Grill, covered, on rotisserie over indirect medium-low heat (see Tip, page 239) until light golden, about 40 minutes. Uncover and continue grilling, basting every 10 to 15 minutes with salt solution, until skin is crisp and deep reddish-brown, about 2½ hours. Serve with Lechon Sauce.

Makes 8 servings.

TIP

If your rotisserie is too short to mount the suckling pig with legs stretched out (which is preferable), then tuck the hind legs in toward the belly. This will arch the back a little and make the pig a bit less well-balanced, but as long as it's tied tightly with kitchen string, there should be no problem.

PER SERVING WITH ¼ CUP/60 mL LECHON SAUCE : about 481 cal, 54 g pro, 24 g total fat (8 g sat. fat), 10 g carb, 1 g fibre, 185 mg chol, 967 mg sodium, 725 mg potassium. % RDI: 6% calcium, 30% iron, 54% vit A, 7% vit C, 16% folate.

Lechon Sauce

This sauce always accompanies roast suckling pig in the Philippines.
Any leftover meat or other pork is often stewed in the leftover sauce (thinned
with stock) the next day to eat with rice. You can make the sauce up
to 1 day before roasting the pig; bring to room temperature before serving.

1 **suckling pig liver**, 7 to 8 oz/
200 to 250 g, or 2 chicken livers

¼ cup / 60 mL **palm**, cane or cider
vinegar

1 cup / 250 mL chopped **shallots**

6 cloves **garlic**, smashed

1 tsp / 5 mL chopped **fresh ginger**

2 tbsp / 30 mL **peanut** or vegetable **oil**

½ tsp / 2 mL each **salt** and **black pepper**

¼ tsp / 1 mL **cayenne pepper**

Pinch **ground cloves**

3 tbsp / 45 mL **palm sugar**, or natural
cane or brown sugar

2 tbsp / 30 mL **oyster sauce** or
soy sauce

1 tbsp / 15 mL **soy sauce**

2 cups / 500 mL **pork** or chicken **stock**

¾ cup / 175 mL **bread crumbs**

● Trim any connective tissues off liver; slice. Bring saucepan of salted water to boil; add 1 tbsp/15 mL of the vinegar. Add liver; reduce heat to low and poach until still pink in centre of thickest slices, 2 to 3 minutes. Drain. In food processor, purée liver until smooth.

● In clean food processor or using knife, pulse or mince together shallots, garlic and ginger until almost smooth paste.

● In saucepan, heat oil over medium heat; fry shallot mixture until light golden. Stir in salt, pepper, cayenne and cloves; fry for 1 minute. Stir in sugar; fry, stirring, until melted and slightly darkened. Stir in liver purée, remaining vinegar and oyster and soy sauces. Stir in stock; bring to boil. Stir in bread crumbs; reduce heat to low. Simmer, covered and stirring often, until a bit thicker than thick applesauce, about 50 minutes, adding a little more stock or lightly salted water if mixture is too thick. Let cool to room temperature before serving.

Makes 4 cups/1 L.

PER ¼ CUP/60 mL: about 73 cal, 4 g pro, 2 g total fat (1 g sat. fat), 9 g carb, 1 g fibre, 34 mg chol, 292 mg sodium, 75 mg potassium. % RDI: 2% calcium, 16% iron, 53% vit A, 5% vit C, 11% folate.

Balsamic Honey Tenderloin

Succulent pork tenderloin is perfect for the grill. It needs little time for cooking and is a great medium for marinades and spices. Simple cupboard-friendly standbys — mustard, honey and vinegar — glaze the meat to create a delicious crust.

2 **pork tenderloins**, about 12 oz/
375 g each

2 tbsp / 30 mL **liquid honey**

2 tbsp / 30 mL **grainy mustard**

2 tbsp / 30 mL **balsamic vinegar**

1 tbsp / 15 mL **olive oil**

1 clove **garlic**, minced

¼ tsp / 1 mL each **salt** and **black pepper**

● Remove any silverskin (connective tissue) from pork. Mix together honey, mustard, vinegar, oil, garlic, salt and pepper; add pork, turning to coat. Marinate for 20 minutes or, refrigerated, up to 1 day.

● Reserving marinade, place pork on greased grill over medium-high heat; brush with marinade. Grill, covered, turning occasionally, until just a hint of pink remains in centre (160°F/71°C), about 18 minutes.

● Transfer to cutting board; tent with foil and let stand for 5 minutes before slicing.

Makes 4 to 6 servings.

Try to get smaller pork tenderloins, about 12 oz/375 g, for the best flavour and delicate texture. Avoid any that are labelled "seasoned" – they have been injected with brine and are inferior.

PER EACH OF 6 SERVINGS: about 182 cal, 27 g pro, 5 g total fat (1 g sat. fat), 5 g carb, 0 g fibre, 61 mg chol, 167 mg sodium. % RDI: 1% calcium, 10% iron, 2% folate.

Pork Tenderloin with Romano Cheese

Flattening the tenderloin ensures quick cooking and, thus, juicy meat.

2 **pork tenderloins**, about 12 oz/ 375 g each

2 tbsp / 30 mL **olive oil**

2 tbsp / 30 mL **dry white wine**

2 cloves **garlic**, pressed or pounded into paste

1 tsp / 5 mL **fennel seeds**, crushed

¾ tsp / 4 mL **salt**

½ tsp / 2 mL finely grated **lemon rind**

½ tsp / 2 mL **black pepper**

½ tsp / 2 mL **hot pepper flakes**

8 **fresh sage leaves**, finely sliced into chiffonade, or 1 tsp/5 mL crumbled dried sage

½ cup / 125 mL grated **Romano cheese**

Lemon wedges

● Remove any silverskin (connective tissue) from pork. Cut horizontally almost but not all the way through; open like book. Between sheets of waxed paper or plastic wrap, pound each to even ½-inch/1 cm thickness; halve crosswise.

● Whisk together oil, wine, garlic, fennel seeds, salt, lemon rind, pepper, hot pepper flakes and sage; rub all over pork. Marinate for 30 minutes or, refrigerated, up to 8 hours.

● Grill on greased grill over high heat, turning once and sprinkling cheese evenly over top during last minute, until just a hint of pink remains in centre (160°F/71°C), 4 to 6 minutes. Serve with lemon wedges.

Makes 4 servings.

PER SERVING (WITHOUT LEMON WEDGES): about 339 cal, 48 g pro, 14 g total fat (5 g sat. fat), 2 g carb, 1 g fibre, 120 mg chol, 671 mg sodium, 660 mg potassium. % RDI: 14% calcium, 17% iron, 3% vit A, 3% vit C, 5% folate.

Gorgonzola Pork Tenderloin Steaks

As in the previous recipe, tenderloin benefits from quick, hot cooking, so pounding it into steaks makes sense. The Gorgonzola melts over the meat for an instant sauce.

2 **pork tenderloins**, about 12 oz/ 375 g each

2 tbsp / 30 mL **extra-virgin olive oil**

1 tsp / 5 mL minced **fresh rosemary** or thyme

1 clove **garlic**, pressed or pounded into paste

½ tsp / 2 mL each **salt** and **black pepper**

4 oz / 125 g **Gorgonzola cheese**, at room temperature

4 tsp / 20 mL finely chopped **fresh chives**

● Remove any silverskin (connective tissue) from pork. Halve each tenderloin crosswise; cut each lengthwise, halfway through. Open like book. Between sheets of waxed paper or plastic wrap, pound each to even ½-inch/1 cm thickness. Mix together oil, rosemary, garlic, salt and pepper; rub all over pork.

● Grill on greased grill over high heat, turning once, until just a hint of pink remains in centre (160°F/71°C), 4 to 6 minutes. Transfer to warmed platter. Cut cheese into 4 slices; lay 1 on each tenderloin piece. Sprinkle with chives.

Makes 4 servings.

TIP

For a mild taste, choose sweet (dolce) Gorgonzola.

PER SERVING: about 390 cal, 47 g pro, 21 g total fat (9 g sat. fat), 1 g carb, trace fibre, 119 mg chol, 843 mg sodium. % RDI: 17% calcium, 16% iron, 10% vit A, 2% vit C, 10% folate.

Sweet & Sour Pork Tenderloin

2 tbsp / 30 mL **cider vinegar**

1 tbsp / 15 mL **Dijon mustard**

1 tbsp / 15 mL **vegetable oil**

2 tsp / 10 mL chopped **fresh thyme** (or ½ tsp/2 mL dried)

¼ tsp / 1 mL each **salt** and **black pepper**

2 **pork tenderloins**, about 12 oz/ 375 g each

2 tbsp / 30 mL **orange marmalade**

● Remove any silverskin (connective tissue) from pork. Mix together vinegar, mustard, oil, thyme, salt and pepper; add pork, turning to coat. Marinate, refrigerated, for at least 2 hours or up to 1 day.

● Reserving marinade, place pork on greased grill over medium-high heat; brush with marinade. Grill, covered, turning once, until just a hint of pink remains in centre (160°F/71°C), about 20 minutes.

● Brush both sides of pork with marmalade, turning after 30 seconds. Transfer to cutting board; tent with foil and let stand for 5 minutes before slicing.

Makes 4 servings.

PER SERVING: about 276 cal, 41 g pro, 9 g total fat (2 g sat. fat), 8 g carb, 0 g fibre, 92 mg chol, 275 mg sodium.
% RDI: 2% calcium, 17% iron, 3% vit C, 6% folate.

Garlic & Anchovy Stuffed Pork Tenderloins

2 **pork tenderloins**, about 12 oz/
375 g each

4 **anchovy fillets**

2 cloves **garlic**

2 tsp / 10 mL **fennel seeds**

1 tsp / 5 mL coarsely ground
black pepper

½ tsp / 2 mL **hot pepper flakes**

½ tsp / 2 mL **salt**

2 tsp / 10 mL **olive oil**

● Remove any silverskin (connective tissue) from pork. Trim flat ends from tenderloins (reserve for stir-frying). Push anchovies and garlic through garlic press (or crush in mortar with pestle) until paste. Push long chopstick or metal skewer lengthwise through centre of each tenderloin; spoon one-quarter of the anchovy mixture into hole at each end; press paste into centre of tenderloin, ensuring filling is evenly distributed.

● On plate, mix together fennel seeds, pepper, hot pepper flakes and salt; roll pork in mixture until coated. Wrap in plastic wrap; marinate for 30 minutes or, refrigerated, up to 8 hours (bring to room temperature before grilling).

● Brush pork with oil. Grill, covered, on greased grill over medium-high heat, turning once, until just a hint of pink remains in centre (160°F/71°C), 18 to 20 minutes. Transfer to cutting board; tent with foil and let stand for 5 minutes before slicing.

Makes 4 servings.

PER SERVING: about 207 cal, 36 g pro, 6 g total fat (2 g sat. fat), 2 g carb, 1 g fibre, 87 mg chol, 503 mg sodium. % RDI: 3% calcium, 15% iron, 2% vit A, 3% vit C, 3% folate.

Barbecued Pork Tenderloin with
Southwestern Marinade

Barbecued Pork Tenderloin Two Ways

2 **pork tenderloins**, about 12 oz/ 375 g each

Southwestern Marinade or Peanut Curry Marinade (below)

2 tsp / 10 mL **cornstarch**

1 **green onion**, finely chopped

2 tbsp / 30 mL finely chopped **fresh coriander**

● Remove silverskin from pork; coat pork in marinade. Refrigerate for at least 2 hours or up to 1 day. Remove pork; pour marinade and ¾ cup/175 mL water into small saucepan. Bring to boil; reduce heat and simmer until reduced to 1 cup/250 mL, 7 minutes. Mix cornstarch with 1 tbsp/15 mL cold water; whisk into sauce. Simmer until thickened and glossy, about 1 minute. Keep warm.

● Grill pork, covered, on greased grill over medium heat, turning often, until just a hint of pink remains in centre (160°F/71°C), 20 minutes. Transfer to cutting board; tent with foil and let stand for 10 minutes before slicing. Sprinkle with onion and coriander; serve with sauce.

Makes 4 to 6 servings.

MARINADES

Southwestern Marinade

● Mix together ½ cup/125 mL **orange juice**; ¼ cup/ 60 mL **tomato paste**; 2 tbsp/30 mL **grainy mustard**; 3 cloves **garlic**, minced; 4 tsp/20 mL **chili powder**; 1½ tsp/7 mL **granulated sugar**; 1 tsp/5 mL each **ground cumin** and **coriander**; ½ tsp/2 mL **Worcestershire sauce**; and ¼ tsp/1 mL **salt**.

Peanut Curry Marinade

● Mix together ⅔ cup/150 mL **coconut milk**; 3 tbsp/ 45 mL **chunky natural peanut butter**; 2 tbsp/30 mL **fish sauce**; 1 tbsp/15 mL **lime juice**; 2 tsp/10 mL each **curry paste** and grated **fresh ginger**; 2 cloves **garlic**, minced; ½ tsp/2 mL packed **brown sugar**; and pinch **turmeric**.

PER EACH OF 6 SERVINGS (WITH SOUTHWESTERN MARINADE): about 186 cal, 29 g pro, 4 g total fat (1 g sat. fat), 8 g carb, 1 g fibre, 61 mg chol, 244 mg sodium. % RDI: 3% calcium, 17% iron, 9% vit A, 22% vit C, 7% folate.

Saucy Pulled Pork on a Bun

Rubbed with a spicy mixture, this slow-barbecued pork is shredded, tossed with sauce and piled high on crusty rolls.

2 tbsp / 30 mL **paprika**

2 tbsp / 30 mL packed **brown sugar**

1 tbsp / 15 mL **chili powder**

1 tbsp / 15 mL **ground cumin**

1 tbsp / 15 mL **dried thyme**

1 tsp / 5 mL each **salt** and **black pepper**

1 **boneless pork butt (shoulder) roast**, about 3 lb/1.5 kg

1 recipe **Smoky Barbecue Sauce** (page 528) or 1 bottle (455 mL) hickory barbecue sauce

¼ cup / 60 mL **cider vinegar**

¼ cup / 60 mL packed **brown sugar**

½ tsp / 2 mL **hot pepper sauce**

8 **kaiser rolls**, halved

● Mix together paprika, sugar, chili powder, cumin, thyme, salt and pepper. Untie pork if necessary; rub all over with spice mixture. Refrigerate for at least 4 hours or up to 1 day.

● Grill pork, covered and fat side up, on greased grill over indirect medium heat (see Tip, page 239), until meat is fork-tender, about 3 hours. Transfer to cutting board; tent with foil and let stand for 20 minutes. Using 2 forks or hands, pull into shreds; place in bowl.

● Meanwhile, in saucepan, combine Smoky Barbecue Sauce, vinegar, brown sugar and hot pepper sauce; bring to boil. Reduce heat and simmer, stirring occasionally, for 5 minutes.

● Pour 1½ cups/375 mL of the sauce over pork, tossing to coat. Serve on rolls with remaining sauce.

Makes 8 servings.

PER SERVING: about 652 cal, 37 g pro, 30 g total fat (10 g sat. fat), 57 g carb, 3 g fibre, 95 mg chol, 1,262 mg sodium. % RDI: 9% calcium, 40% iron, 19% vit A, 12% vit C, 31% folate.

Mexican Pork Shoulder

This pork is wonderful on its own but it makes great tacos, too. Just shred the meat instead of slicing and serve it in corn tortillas with avocado and fresh cilantro.

4 **dried ancho chilies**, stemmed and seeded

2 **dried chipotle peppers**

⅓ cup / 75 mL **cider vinegar**

3 cloves **garlic**, smashed

½ cup / 125 mL chopped **onion**

1 tbsp / 15 mL **dried oregano**

3 to 4 lb / 1.5 to 2 kg **pork butt (shoulder) roast**

2 tsp / 10 mL **salt**

¼ cup / 60 mL **butter**, softened

● In dry small skillet over medium-low heat, toast anchos and chipotles, turning once, until dark and pliable, 1 to 2 minutes. In small saucepan, combine anchos, chipotles and just enough water to cover; bring to boil. Reduce heat and simmer over medium heat until soft, about 15 minutes. Reserving ½ cup/125 mL of the cooking liquid, drain.

● In blender, purée together anchos, chipotles, vinegar, garlic, onion and oregano, adding some of the reserved cooking liquid to make smooth paste. Sprinkle pork all over with salt; rub all over with butter. Rub chili paste over roast, pressing into every crevice. Refrigerate for at least 4 hours or up to 1 day.

● Soak 6 cups/1.5 L mesquite or other wood chips in water for 1 hour. Prepare barbecue for indirect grilling (see Tip, page 239). For gas barbecue, follow manufacturer's instructions or seal soaked chips in foil to make packet; poke holes in top. Place over lit burner; close lid. For charcoal barbecue, place soaked chips directly on coals. Grill roast, covered, over indirect medium heat until dark brown and crisp and meat is fork-tender, 2 to 2¼ hours. Transfer to cutting board; tent with foil and let stand for 15 minutes before slicing.

Makes 8 to 10 servings.

PER EACH OF 10 SERVINGS: about 273 cal, 28 g pro, 16 g total fat (7 g sat. fat), 5 g carb, 2 g fibre, 96 mg chol, 576 mg sodium, 515 mg potassium. % RDI: 2% calcium, 17% iron, 19% vit A, 3% vit C, 7% folate.

Smoke-Grilled Lamb Shoulder

Fairly fatty lamb shoulder calls for slow grilling. Highly spiced and lightly smoked, this shoulder cooks undisturbed on the grill for about two hours to produce succulent, flavourful meat.

½ cup / 125 mL chopped **fresh coriander** (roots, stems and leaves)

2 tbsp / 30 mL chopped **fresh ginger**

4 cloves **garlic**, smashed

1 tbsp / 15 mL **lemon juice**

1¼ tsp / 6 mL **salt**

2 tbsp / 30 mL **ground dried hot peppers** or chili powder of choice

2 tsp / 10 mL **ground coriander**

1 tsp / 5 mL **turmeric**

¾ tsp / 4 mL **ground allspice**

¾ tsp / 4 mL **ground cumin**

½ tsp / 2 mL **black pepper**

1 **lamb shoulder**, foreshank attached, about 5 lb/2.2 kg

● In food processor, purée together chopped coriander, ginger, garlic, lemon juice and salt; mix in hot pepper, ground coriander, turmeric, allspice, cumin and pepper. With tip of sharp knife, make deep slashes all over lamb; rub spice mixture all over lamb and into slashes. Let stand for 1 hour or, refrigerated, up to 1 day.

● Soak 3 cups/750 mL wood chips in water for 1 hour. Prepare barbecue for indirect grilling (see Tip, page 239). For gas barbecue, follow manufacturer's instructions or seal soaked chips in foil to make packet; poke several holes in top. Place over lit burner; close lid. For charcoal barbecue, place soaked chips directly on coals. Grill lamb, covered, over medium-high heat, until fork-tender and crisp outside, about 2 hours.

● Transfer to cutting board; tent with foil and let stand for 10 minutes before carving.

Makes 8 servings.

PER SERVING: about 291 cal, 34 g pro, 15 g total fat (6 g sat. fat), 3 g carb, 1 g fibre, 118 mg chol, 472 mg sodium, 440 mg potassium. % RDI: 4% calcium, 26% iron, 6% vit A, 5% vit C, 17% folate.

How to Butterfly a Leg of Lamb

Step 1
Using boning knife, trim excess fat from lamb, leaving a thin layer of fat and membrane to hold lamb together. Starting at wide end close to bone and using short strokes with tip of knife, cut around flat pelvic bone to loosen.

Step 2
Holding pelvic bone, cut through tendons of ball-and-socket joint connecting pelvic bone to thigh bone.

Step 3
Turn lamb fat side up. Cutting right to thigh bone, cut leg open lengthwise. Following close to bone and using short strokes, cut meat and tendons away from bone to reveal another ball-and-socket joint connecting thinner shank bone.

Step 4
Repeat cutting meat away from shank bone; save bones for stock or discard. Lay meat membrane side down. From inside edge of 1 of 2 thickest lobes of meat and holding knife blade flat, cut in half horizontally almost through; repeat on other lobe. Open like book.

Grilled Butterflied Leg of Lamb Three Ways

1 **butterflied leg of lamb**, 2½ to
3 lb/1.25 to 1.5 kg (page 269)

Smoked Paprika Marinade, Ginger Soy
Marinade or Orange Rosemary
Marinade (below)

Salt and **black pepper**

● In large dish, combine lamb with marinade, turning
to coat. Refrigerate for at least 6 hours or up to 1 day,
turning occasionally. For best results, thread onto 3 long
flat metal skewers to make as even thickness as possible.

● Grill, covered, on greased grill over medium-high
heat, turning 4 times, until desired doneness, 20 to
30 minutes for medium-rare (140°F/60°C). Transfer to
cutting board; tent with foil and let stand for 10 minutes
before carving. Sprinkle with salt and pepper to taste.

Make 8 to 10 servings.

MARINADES

Smoked Paprika Marinade

● Mix together ½ cup/125 mL **dry white wine**;
¼ cup/60 mL minced **onion**; 2 tbsp/30 mL **smoked
paprika**; 1 tsp/5 mL **dried marjoram**; 2 cloves **garlic**,
minced; and ¼ tsp/1 mL each **salt** and **black pepper**.

Ginger Soy Marinade

● Mix ⅓ cup/75 mL **soy sauce**; 2 tbsp/30 mL minced
fresh ginger; 2 tbsp/30 mL **mirin** (Japanese sweet rice
wine) or white vermouth; 1 tbsp/15 mL **Dijon mustard**;
3 cloves **garlic**, minced; and 1 **green onion**, chopped.

Orange Rosemary Marinade

● Mix together 2 tbsp/30 mL grated **orange rind**;
¼ cup/60 mL each **orange juice** and **wine vinegar**;
2 tbsp/30 mL chopped **fresh rosemary**; 2 cloves **garlic**,
minced; 1 tsp/5 mL **anchovy paste**; and ¼ tsp/1 mL
each **salt** and **black pepper**.

PER EACH OF 10 SERVINGS: about 159 cal, 24 g pro, 6 g total fat (3 g sat. fat), trace carb, 0 g fibre, 87 mg chol, 48 mg sodium.
% RDI: 1% calcium, 14% iron, 1% vit A.

Armenian Butterflied Leg of Lamb

In this dish, adapted from a favourite Armenian recipe for roasted lamb leg, the perfect combination of spices flavours a grilled butterflied leg.

¼ cup / 60 mL chopped **fresh parsley**

1 tsp / 5 mL grated **lemon rind**

¼ cup / 60 mL **lemon juice**

3 tbsp / 45 mL **olive oil**

4 cloves **garlic**, minced

1 tbsp / 15 mL chopped **fresh marjoram** (or 1 tsp/5 mL dried)

2 tsp / 10 mL **caraway seeds**, crushed

¼ tsp / 1 mL each **salt** and **black pepper**

1 **butterflied leg of lamb**, 2½ to 3 lb/1.25 to 1.5 kg (page 269)

2 slices **bacon**, chopped

● Mix together parsley, lemon rind and juice, oil, garlic, marjoram, caraway seeds, salt and pepper.

● Trim fat from lamb. Using tip of sharp knife, cut slits all over; insert bacon piece into each. Add lamb to marinade, turning to coat. Refrigerate for at least 8 hours or up to 2 days, turning occasionally. For best results, thread onto 3 long flat metal skewers to produce as even thickness as possible.

● Grill, covered, on greased grill over medium-high heat, turning once, until desired doneness, 20 to 30 minutes for medium-rare (140°F/60°C).

● Transfer to cutting board; tent with foil and let stand for 10 minutes before slicing thinly across the grain. Serve with any accumulated juices.

Makes 8 to 10 servings.

PER EACH OF 10 SERVINGS: about 166 cal, 20 g pro, 9 g total fat (4 g sat. fat), 1 g carb, trace fibre, 74 mg chol, 102 mg sodium. % RDI: 1% calcium, 13% iron, 1% vit A, 3% vit C, 1% folate.

Wine-Marinated Leg of Lamb

A simple wine marinade transforms an already beautiful butterflied leg of lamb into something decadently delicious.

4 cloves **garlic**, pressed or pounded into paste

1 tbsp / 15 mL minced **fresh rosemary** or 2 tsp/10 mL dried oregano

2 tsp / 10 mL **fennel seeds**

2 **bay leaves**, crumbled

¾ tsp / 4 mL **black pepper**

¾ tsp / 4 mL **ground allspice**

½ tsp / 2 mL **salt**

1 **butterflied leg of lamb**, 2½ to 3 lb/1.25 to 1.5 kg (page 269)

1 to 1½ cups / 250 to 375 mL **dry red wine**

2 tbsp / 30 mL **extra-virgin olive oil**

Sea salt

● Mix together garlic, rosemary, fennel seeds, bay leaves, pepper, allspice and salt; rub all over lamb. In resealable freezer bag, combine lamb, wine and oil; turn until coated. Marinate at cool room temperature for 4 hours, or, refrigerated, up to 2 days. For best results, thread onto 3 long flat metal skewers to produce as even thickness as possible.

● Reserving marinade, remove lamb with spices still clinging to meat. Grill, covered, on greased grill over medium-high heat, turning once and basting with reserved marinade for first 10 minutes, until desired doneness, 20 to 25 minutes for medium-rare (140°F/60°C).

● Transfer to cutting board; tent with foil and let stand for 10 minutes before slicing thinly across the grain. Season with sea salt to taste.

Makes 8 to 10 servings.

PER EACH OF 10 SERVINGS: about 167 cal, 24 g pro, 7 g total fat (2 g sat. fat), trace carb, trace fibre, 75 mg chol, 80 mg sodium, 292 mg potassium. % RDI: 1% calcium, 13% iron, 9% folate.

Butterflied Leg of Lamb with Apricot Pepper Sauce

1 small **onion**, chopped

4 cloves **garlic**, minced

⅓ cup / 75 mL chopped **fresh parsley**

¼ cup / 60 mL **extra-virgin olive oil**

3 tbsp / 45 mL chopped **fresh herbs** (such as thyme, sage or rosemary or combination)

1 **butterflied leg of lamb**, 2½ to 3 lb/1.25 to 1.5 kg (page 269)

½ tsp / 2 mL each **salt** and **black pepper**

Apricot Pepper Sauce (below)

● Mix together onion, garlic, parsley, oil and herbs; rub all over lamb. Marinate, refrigerated, for at least 4 hours or up to 1 day.

● Remove lamb from marinade; sprinkle with salt and pepper. For best results, thread onto 3 long flat metal skewers to produce as even thickness as possible. Grill, covered, on greased grill over medium-high heat, turning once, until desired doneness, 20 to 30 minutes for medium-rare (140°F/60°C).

● Transfer to cutting board; tent with foil and let stand for 10 minutes before slicing thinly across the grain. Serve with Apricot Pepper Sauce.

Makes 8 to 10 servings.

Apricot Pepper Sauce

● Grill 1 **sweet red pepper** over high heat, turning often, until charred all over. Let cool enough to handle; peel, seed and chop. Combine ¼ cup/60 mL each chopped **dried apricots** and **boiling water**; soak for 15 minutes. In skillet, heat 3 tbsp/45 mL **extra-virgin olive oil** over medium-low heat. Add red pepper; 3 **shallots**, sliced (or ¼ cup/60 mL chopped onion); 3 cloves **garlic**, sliced; and 1 **Scotch bonnet** or jalapeño **pepper**, seeded and chopped. Fry until very soft, about 15 minutes. In food processor, pulse pepper mixture, apricots and soaking liquid, 2 tbsp/30 mL **white wine vinegar**, and pinch each **granulated sugar** and **salt** until slightly chunky.

PER EACH OF 10 SERVINGS: about 277 cal, 29 g pro, 15 g total fat (4 g sat. fat), 5 g carb, 1 g fibre, 102 mg chol, 163 mg sodium. % RDI: 2% calcium, 19% iron, 7% vit A, 38% vit C, 3% folate.

Rotisserie Greek-Style
Leg of Lamb (page 278)

Rotisserie Greek-Style Leg of Lamb

A large leg of lamb roasts to perfection on the rotisserie.

1 large **whole leg of lamb**, 6 to 7 lb/ 2.7 to 3.15 kg

4 cloves **garlic**, quartered lengthwise

2 tbsp / 30 mL **lemon juice**

1½ tsp / 7 mL **fennel seeds**

1 tsp / 5 mL **salt**

1 tsp / 5 mL **dried (preferably Greek) oregano**, crumbled

¾ tsp / 4 mL **black pepper**

½ tsp / 2 mL **ground allspice**

BASTING SAUCE:

¼ cup / 60 mL **butter**, melted

2 tbsp / 30 mL **extra-virgin olive oil**

2 tbsp / 30 mL **lemon juice**

2 tsp / 10 mL **dried (preferably Greek) oregano**, crumbled

¼ tsp / 1 mL **salt**

● With tip of knife, make 16 slits all over lamb; insert 1 piece garlic into each. Rub all over with lemon juice. Pound fennel seeds to coarse powder; mix in salt, oregano, pepper and allspice. Sprinkle all over lamb. Marinate for 1 hour or, refrigerated, up to 1 day (bring to room temperature before grilling).

● **Basting Sauce:** Whisk together butter, oil, lemon juice, oregano and salt.

● Secure rotisserie prong to haunch end of leg; push spit through leg. Secure shank end with prong; tie tightly with string (prong might not stay stuck into narrow shank end). Grill, covered, on rotisserie over indirect medium heat (see Tip, page 239), basting often with Basting Sauce after first 20 minutes, until desired doneness, 1½ to 2 hours for medium-rare to medium (150 to 160°F/65 to 71°C).

Makes 8 servings.

Photo, page 276

V A R I A T I O N

Greek-Style Leg of Lamb for a Crowd

For more than 8 people, use 2 legs or 1 half-lamb. For either, double all remaining ingredients. Tie 2 legs to rotisserie spit, keeping flatter sides facing in and each haunch facing the other leg's shank. Secure prong on 1 side; push spit through centre. Secure other prong; tie legs together in 2 or 3 places. For half-lamb, have butcher cut back leg from main saddle section halfway down length. Secure back leg section, then saddle and foreleg onto rotisserie spit with prongs; tie in several places.

PER SERVING: about 360 cal, 47 g pro, 17 g total fat (7 g sat. fat), 2 g carb, trace fibre, 153 mg chol, 456 mg sodium, 582 mg potassium. % RDI: 3% calcium, 27% iron, 3% vit A, 3% vit C, 18% folate.

Leg of Lamb with Red Currant Mint Sauce

¼ cup / 60 mL **red wine vinegar**

3 tbsp / 45 mL **extra-virgin olive oil**

3 cloves **garlic**, minced

1 tbsp / 15 mL chopped **fresh thyme** (or 1 tsp/5 mL dried)

1 **butterflied leg of lamb**, about 3 lb/ 1.5 kg (page 269)

½ tsp / 2 mL each **salt** and **black pepper**

RED CURRANT MINT SAUCE:

½ cup / 125 mL **red currant jelly**

⅓ cup / 75 mL packed chopped **fresh mint leaves**

2 tbsp / 30 mL **Port wine** (optional)

2 tbsp / 30 mL **red wine vinegar**

Pinch each **salt** and **black pepper**

● Mix together vinegar, oil, garlic and thyme; add lamb, turning to coat. Marinate, refrigerated, for at least 4 hours or up to 1 day.

● **Red Currant Mint Sauce:** In food processor, purée together jelly, mint, Port (if using), vinegar, salt and pepper.

● Remove lamb from marinade; sprinkle with salt and pepper. For best results, thread onto 3 long flat metal skewers to produce as even thickness as possible. Grill, covered, on greased grill over medium-high heat until desired doneness, 20 to 30 minutes for medium-rare (140°C/60°C).

● Transfer to cutting board; tent with foil and let stand for 10 minutes before slicing thinly across the grain. Serve with Red Currant Mint Sauce.

Makes 8 to 10 servings.

PER EACH OF 10 SERVINGS: about 191 cal, 23 g pro, 5 g total fat (2 g sat. fat), 11 g carb, trace fibre, 84 mg chol, 157 mg sodium. % RDI: 1% calcium, 16% iron, 1% vit A.

Poultry

Mediterranean Lemon & Rosemary Rotisserie Chickens

If you don't have a rotisserie, grill whole chickens over indirect heat, giving them a quarter-turn every 15 minutes or so. It's easy to halve this recipe, but roast two chickens no matter how many people are eating; they're so good for leftovers.

2 **whole chickens**, about 4 lb/2 kg each

2 tsp / 10 mL **salt**

1 tsp / 5 mL **black pepper**

2 cloves **garlic**, pressed or minced

14 sprigs **fresh rosemary**

BASTING LIQUID:

1 **lemon**

2 cloves **garlic**, smashed

2 tbsp / 30 mL **olive oil**

Pinch **salt**

● Sprinkle inside of each chicken with ½ tsp/2 mL of the salt and ¼ tsp/1 mL of the pepper; rub garlic all over inside.

● **Basting Liquid:** Reserving rinds, halve and juice lemon; stir together lemon juice, garlic, oil and salt.

● Place 1 of the squeezed-out lemon halves and 3 sprigs rosemary inside each chicken. With kitchen string, truss together legs and tail to close each cavity. Secure rotisserie prong to 1 end of 1 of the chickens; push spit through centre of both chickens and secure other end with prong. Sprinkle each chicken all over with ½ tsp/ 2 mL of the remaining salt and ¼ tsp/1 mL of the remaining pepper. Lay 2 sprigs rosemary on top and bottom of each chicken; tie string around each chicken, securing rosemary, wings and legs against body.

● Grill, covered, on rotisserie over indirect medium-high heat (see Tip, below). After first 30 minutes, brush chicken every 10 minutes with Basting Liquid and pan drippings, grilling until juices run clear when thickest part of thigh is pierced, about 1½ hours total.

Makes 6 to 8 servings.

To grill over indirect heat on gas grill, set foil drip pan under 1 rack of 2-burner barbecue or under centre rack of 3-burner barbecue. Heat remaining burner(s) to temperature indicated (see Grilling Temperatures, page 10). For charcoal grill, place drip pan in centre and arrange hot charcoal on either side. Set meat on greased grill or rotisserie and centre over drip pan. Grill as directed.

PER EACH OF 8 SERVINGS: about 517 cal, 48 g pro, 34 g total fat (9 g sat. fat), 1 g carb, trace fibre, 188 mg chol, 460 mg sodium. % RDI: 2% calcium, 18% iron, 8% vit A, 8% vit C, 5% folate.

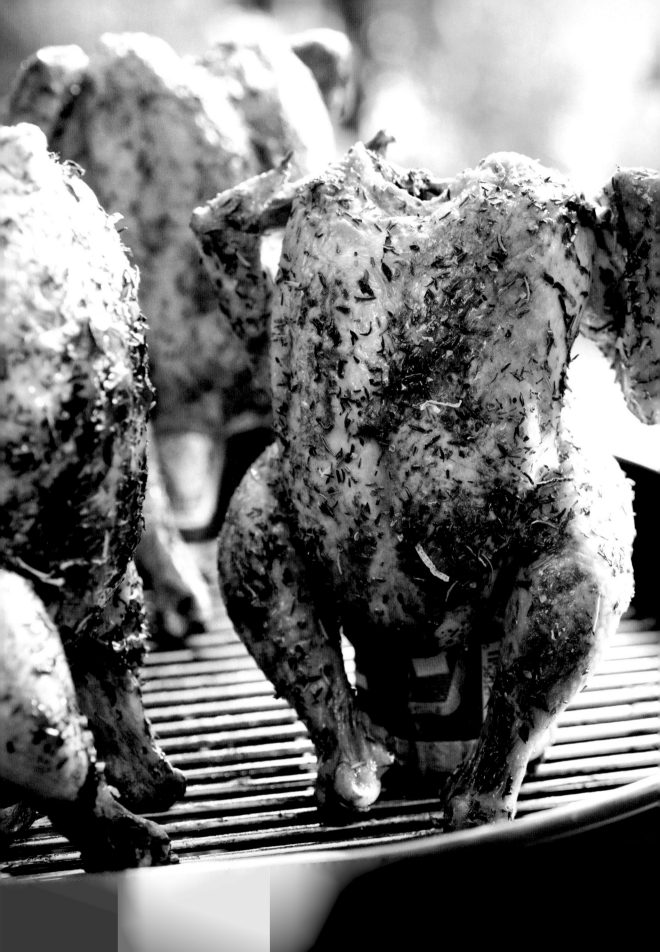

Beer-Can Chicken with Greek Spices

Popular in the United States, this method yields chicken that's tender and very juicy. The Greek spicing makes it just a bit more special for a backyard or tailgate barbecue.

1 **whole chicken**, about 3½ lb/1.75 kg

1 can (355 mL) **beer**

Lemon wedges

GREEK SPICE RUB:

1 tbsp / 15 mL **dried (preferably Greek) oregano**, crumbled

2 tsp / 10 mL **dried mint**

1 tsp / 5 mL **ground cumin**

1 tsp / 5 mL **black pepper**

¾ tsp / 4 mL **salt**

¾ tsp / 4 mL **cinnamon**

- **Greek Spice Rub:** Mix together oregano, mint, cumin, pepper, salt and cinnamon; sprinkle 2 tsp/10 mL all over inside of chicken. Rub 1 tbsp/15 mL all over outside.

- Pour off ⅓ cup/75 mL of the beer. With can opener, make 5 holes in top of can; spoon in remaining spice rub. Holding chicken upright, push cavity down onto can.

- Prepare barbecue for indirect grilling (see Tip, page 283). Stand chicken on grill over drip pan. Grill, covered, over indirect medium heat until juices run clear when thickest part of thigh is pierced, 1 to 1¼ hours. Serve with lemon wedges.

Makes 6 servings.

VARIATION

Beer-Can Chicken with Italian Herbs
Prepare as above, substituting the Greek Spice Rub with 2 tbsp/30 mL dried Italian herb seasoning, 1 tbsp/15 mL grated lemon rind and ¾ tsp/4 mL each salt and black pepper.

285

PER SERVING (WITHOUT LEMON WEDGES): about 169 cal, 25 g pro, 7 g total fat (2 g sat. fat), 1 g carb, trace fibre, 75 mg chol, 244 mg sodium. % RDI: 2% calcium, 11% iron, 2% vit A, 3% folate.

Rotisserie Piri-Piri Chickens

Piri-piri is a pan-African word for hot peppers and often particularly refers to African small red hot peppers, similar in heat and flavour to Thai (bird-eye) chilies. Even with the 18 hot peppers here, the chicken is just mildly hot. Because of the lemon, the skin will not roast as crisply as on other grilled chickens, but it is every bit as delicious.

2 **whole chickens**, about 3 lb/1.5 kg each

PIRI-PIRI MARINADE:

18 **Thai (bird-eye) chilies** or other small red hot peppers, finely chopped

4 cloves **garlic**, smashed

¼ cup / 60 mL **lemon juice**

2 tbsp / 30 mL **red wine vinegar**

½ cup / 125 mL **extra-virgin olive oil**

2½ tsp / 12 mL **paprika**

2 tsp / 10 mL **salt**

½ tsp / 2 mL **ground cumin**

● **Piri-Piri Marinade:** In blender, purée together hot peppers, garlic, lemon juice and vinegar until very smooth (seeds are no longer visible) and liquefied (if blender does not have purée function, in mortar with pestle, pound hot peppers with garlic until seeds are crushed and mixture is paste, then blend with lemon juice). Blend in oil, paprika, salt and cumin.

● Rub chicken inside and out with Piri-Piri Marinade. Marinate, refrigerated, for at least 4 hours or up to 1 day.

● Reserving marinade, remove chicken. With kitchen string, truss together legs and tail to close each cavity. Secure rotisserie prong to 1 end of 1 of the chickens; push spit through centre of both chickens and secure other end with prong. Tie string around each chicken, securing wings and legs against body.

● Grill, covered, on rotisserie over indirect medium-high heat (see Tip, page 283), uncovering for final 10 to 15 minutes of grilling. After first 20 minutes and until 10 minutes before chicken is finished, brush about every 10 minutes with reserved marinade until used up, grilling until juices run clear when thickest part of thigh is pierced, about 1½ hours total.

Makes 6 to 8 servings.

TIP

If you don't have a rotisserie, you can grill the whole chickens on the grate over indirect heat, turning every 15 minutes.

PER EACH OF 8 SERVINGS: about 438 cal, 33 g pro, 32 g total fat (7 g sat. fat), 3 g carb, 1 g fibre, 119 mg chol, 677 mg sodium, 445 mg potassium. % RDI: 2% calcium, 11% iron, 21% vit A, 52% vit C, 5% folate.

Spatchcock Dijon Chicken

Spatchcock, which means removing the backbone of a chicken and flattening it out, is an old Irish term, abbreviated from "dispatch cock," an order barked at cooks to get the chicken off the spit and out to the customer. Flattening a whole chicken means that you can grill it over direct heat in half the time.

¼ cup / 60 mL **Dijon mustard**

2 tbsp / 30 mL chopped **fresh herbs**, such as tarragon, rosemary or savory

2 tbsp / 30 mL **wine vinegar**

2 tbsp / 30 mL **vegetable oil**

½ tsp / 2 mL each **salt** and **black pepper**

1 **whole chicken**, about 3 lb/1.5 kg

- Mix together mustard, herbs, vinegar, oil, salt and pepper.

- Using kitchen shears, cut chicken down each side of backbone; remove backbone (save for stockpot). Turn chicken breast side up; press firmly on breastbone to flatten. Tuck wings behind back; brush all over with mustard mixture. Marinate, refrigerated, for at least 8 hours or up to 1 day, turning occasionally.

- Grill, covered and bone side down, on greased grill over medium heat, turning once, until juices run clear when thickest part of thigh is pierced, 35 to 45 minutes.

Makes 4 servings.

PER SERVING: 257 cal, 29 g pro, 15 g total fat (3 g sat. fat), 1 g carb, trace fibre, 102 mg chol, 332 mg sodium. % RDI: 2% calcium, 9% iron, 4% vit A, 3% folate.

Spatchcock Spiced Lemon Chicken

It's a nice touch to grill halved lemons beside the chicken. Squeeze the warm, lightly smoky lemon juice over the cooked chicken and/or an accompanying green vegetable.

2 tbsp / 30 mL **extra-virgin olive oil**

1 tbsp / 15 mL grated **lemon rind**

1 tbsp / 15 mL **lemon juice**

2 tsp / 10 mL **ground coriander**

1 tsp / 5 mL **fennel seeds**, crushed

¾ tsp / 4 mL **salt**

Pinch **turmeric**

Pinch **cayenne pepper**

2 cloves **garlic**, minced

1 **shallot**, minced

1 **whole chicken**, about 3 lb/1.5 kg

● Mix together oil, lemon rind and juice, coriander, fennel seeds, salt, turmeric, cayenne, garlic and shallot.

● Using kitchen shears, cut chicken down each side of backbone; remove backbone (save for stockpot). Turn chicken breast side up; press firmly on breastbone to flatten. Tuck wings behind back; brush all over with lemon mixture. Marinate, refrigerated, for at least 1 hour or up to 1 day.

● Grill, covered and bone side down, on greased grill over medium heat, turning once, until juices run clear when thickest part of thigh is pierced, 35 to 45 minutes.

Makes 4 servings.

PER SERVING: about 377 cal, 33 g pro, 26 g total fat (6 g sat. fat), 2 g carb, 1 g fibre, 119 mg chol, 533 mg sodium, 407 mg potassium. % RDI: 3% calcium, 10% iron, 6% vit A, 7% vit C, 4% folate.

Carnival Chicken

Celebrate the sunny Caribbean with this hot and spicy chicken, inspired by the flavours of the islands.

1 **whole chicken**, 3 lb/1.5 kg, cut into serving-size portions, or 3 lb/1.5 kg chicken pieces

3 **green onions**, minced

3 **Scotch bonnet (habanero) peppers**, seeded and minced, or 1 tbsp/15 mL Caribbean hot sauce

3 cloves **garlic**, pressed or minced

½ tsp / 2 mL finely grated **orange rind**

½ tsp / 2 mL finely grated **lime rind**

3 tbsp / 45 mL **orange juice**

2 tbsp / 30 mL **lime juice**

2 tbsp / 30 mL **vegetable oil**

2 tsp / 10 mL grated **fresh ginger**

1 tsp / 5 mL crumbled **dried oregano**

1 tsp / 5 mL **salt**

¾ tsp / 4 mL **ground allspice**

¾ tsp / 4 mL **ground cumin**

¼ tsp / 1 mL **nutmeg**

¼ tsp / 1 mL **black pepper**

• Toss together chicken, onions, hot peppers, garlic, orange and lime rind and juices, oil, ginger, oregano, salt, allspice, cumin, nutmeg and pepper until coated. Marinate, refrigerated, for at least 3 hours or, preferably, up to 1 day, turning occasionally. Bring to room temperature.

• Grill over medium heat, turning often, until juices run clear when thickest part is pierced, about 30 minutes.

Makes 4 to 6 servings.

Scotch bonnet or habanero hot peppers are essential to Caribbean cuisine, but they should be handled with caution. If you're not used to handling hot peppers, wear kitchen gloves when you seed and chop them.

PER EACH OF 6 SERVINGS: about 254 cal, 22 g pro, 17 g total fat (4 g sat. fat), 3 g carb, 1 g fibre, 79 mg chol, 451 mg sodium. % RDI: 2% calcium, 9% iron, 5% vit A, 13% vit C, 6% folate.

Burnished Hoisin Chicken

½ cup / 125 mL **hoisin sauce**

2 tbsp / 30 mL **soy sauce**

2 tbsp / 30 mL **rice vinegar**

2 cloves **garlic**, minced

1 tbsp / 15 mL minced **fresh ginger**

2 tsp / 10 mL **sesame oil**

¼ tsp / 1 mL each **salt** and **black pepper**

2 lb / 1 kg **chicken pieces**

1 tbsp / 15 mL **toasted sesame seeds**

● Mix together hoisin sauce, soy sauce, vinegar, garlic, ginger, sesame oil, salt and pepper; add chicken, turning to coat. Marinate, refrigerated, for at least 4 or up to 12 hours.

● Reserving any remaining marinade, place chicken, bone side down, on greased grill over medium heat; brush with marinade. Grill, covered, for 25 minutes. Turn; grill until juices run clear when thickest part is pierced, about 10 minutes. Sprinkle with sesame seeds.

Makes 4 servings.

PER SERVING: about 376 cal, 32 g pro, 20 g total fat (5 g sat. fat), 17 g carb, 1 g fibre, 111 mg chol, 1,272 mg sodium. % RDI: 2% calcium, 12% iron, 5% vit A, 2% vit C, 8% folate.

Thai Grilled Chicken

All over Southeast Asia, chicken is marinated with aromatics, such as garlic, ginger, coriander and lime, then grilled and served with a dipping sauce.

½ cup / 125 mL chopped **fresh coriander** (leaves, stems and roots)

4 cloves **garlic**, chopped

2 tbsp / 30 mL **fish sauce**

2 tbsp / 30 mL **lime juice**

1½ tsp / 7 mL chopped **fresh ginger**

2 tsp / 10 mL grated **lime rind**

1½ tsp / 7 mL **coriander seeds**

1 tsp / 5 mL packed **brown sugar**

½ tsp / 2 mL **black pepper**

¼ tsp / 1 mL **cayenne pepper**

4 lb / 2 kg **chicken pieces**

Fresh coriander sprigs

THAI DIPPING SAUCE:

¼ cup / 60 mL **lime juice**

2 tbsp / 30 mL **fish sauce**

1 clove **garlic**, minced

1½ tsp / 7 mL **granulated sugar**

½ to 1½ tsp / 2 to 7 mL finely chopped **Thai (bird-eye) chilies** (or 1 jalapeño or other hot pepper, finely chopped)

- In food processor, purée together chopped coriander, garlic, fish sauce, lime juice and ginger. Add lime rind, coriander seeds, sugar, pepper and cayenne; purée until smooth, scraping down side of bowl often. Place chicken in large bowl; add coriander mixture, turning to coat. Marinate, refrigerated, for at least 8 hours or up to 1 day, turning often.

- **Thai Dipping Sauce:** Mix together lime juice, fish sauce, garlic, sugar and chilies.

- Reserving any marinade, place chicken, bone side down, on greased grill over medium heat. Grill, covered and basting once with marinade, for 15 minutes. Turn; grill until juices run clear when thickest part is pierced, about 30 minutes. Garnish with coriander sprigs; serve with Thai Dipping Sauce.

Makes 6 to 8 servings.

PER EACH OF 8 SERVINGS: about 206 cal, 30 g pro, 8 g total fat (2 g sat. fat), 4 g carb, trace fibre, 89 mg chol, 785 mg sodium. % RDI: 3% calcium, 11% iron, 3% vit A, 5% vit C, 5% folate.

Top to bottom: Jerk Pork Kabobs
(page 30), Caribbean Coleslaw
(page 480), Chicken with Puerto
Rican Adobo Seasoning (opposite)

Chicken with Puerto Rican Adobo Seasoning

Puerto Rican adobo seasoning is a favourite among the island's cooks and always includes garlic, onion, oregano and other spices. Here's our tasty version.

⅓ cup / 75 mL **tomato paste**

3 tbsp / 45 mL **orange juice**

2 tbsp / 30 mL **lime juice**

2 tbsp / 30 mL **olive oil**

3 cloves **garlic**, pressed

1 tsp / 5 mL **salt**

1 tsp / 5 mL **paprika**

½ tsp / 2 mL **onion powder**

½ tsp / 2 mL **dried oregano**, crumbled

¼ tsp / 1 mL **cayenne pepper**

¼ tsp / 1 mL **black pepper**

¼ tsp / 1 mL **ground cumin**

1 **whole chicken**, 3 lb/1.5 kg, cut into serving-size portions, or 3 lb/1.5 kg chicken pieces

● Mix together tomato paste, orange and lime juices, oil, garlic, salt, paprika, onion powder, oregano, cayenne, pepper and cumin; set aside half. Toss remainder with chicken until coated.

● Grill chicken, covered, on greased grill over medium heat, turning occasionally, for 20 minutes. Grill, brushing with reserved spice mixture, until juices run clear when thickest part is pierced, 10 to 15 minutes.

Makes 4 to 6 servings.

PER EACH OF 6 SERVINGS: about 207 cal, 20 g pro, 12 g total fat (3 g sat. fat), 5 g carb, 1 g fibre, 68 mg chol, 452 mg sodium. % RDI: 2% calcium, 10% iron, 9% vit A, 17% vit C, 5% folate.

Coriander Chicken

¾ cup / 175 mL **Balkan-style plain yogurt**

4 cloves **garlic**, minced

3 tbsp / 45 mL **lemon juice**

1 tbsp / 15 mL **paprika**

1 tbsp / 15 mL **ground coriander**

1 tbsp / 15 mL **olive** or vegetable **oil**

1 tsp / 5 mL **ground cumin**

½ tsp / 2 mL each **salt** and **cayenne pepper**

8 **chicken thighs**, about 2 lb/1 kg, or 4 legs, skinned

¼ cup / 60 mL **fresh coriander leaves**

● Mix together yogurt, garlic, lemon juice, paprika, ground coriander, oil, cumin, salt and cayenne; add chicken, tossing to coat. Marinate, refrigerated, for at least 8 hours or up to 1 day.

● Reserving marinade, place chicken, bone side down, on greased grill over medium heat; brush generously with marinade. Grill, covered, turning once, until juices run clear when chicken is pierced, 20 to 30 minutes for thighs, 45 minutes for legs. Serve sprinkled with fresh coriander.

Makes 4 servings.

PER SERVING: about 247 cal, 29 g pro, 12 g total fat (3 g sat. fat), 4 g carb, trace fibre, 126 mg chol, 347 mg sodium. % RDI: 7% calcium, 16% iron, 11% vit A, 13% vit C, 6% folate.

Oregano Chicken with Tomato Salsa

Smashing garlic with the side of a knife instead of mincing it lets it flavour the marinade without little bits of it burning on the grill.

3 tbsp / 45 mL **wine vinegar**

2 tbsp / 30 mL chopped **fresh oregano** (or ½ tsp/2 mL dried)

2 tbsp / 30 mL **extra-virgin olive oil**

4 cloves **garlic**, smashed

½ tsp / 2 mL each **salt** and **black pepper**

4 **bone-in chicken breasts**

TOMATO SALSA:

2 cups / 500 mL **cherry tomatoes**, quartered

⅓ cup / 75 mL diced **red onion**

2 tbsp / 30 mL chopped **fresh mint**

8 **olives**, halved and pitted

1 tbsp / 15 mL **wine vinegar**

1 tbsp / 15 mL **extra-virgin olive oil**

¼ tsp / 1 mL each **salt** and **black pepper**

● Mix together vinegar, oregano, oil, garlic, salt and pepper; add chicken, turning to coat. Marinate for 20 minutes or, refrigerated, up to 1 day.

● Reserving marinade, place chicken, bone side down, on greased grill over medium heat; brush with half of the reserved marinade. Grill, covered, for 25 minutes. Turn; brush with remaining marinade. Grill, covered, until no longer pink inside, about 20 minutes.

● **Tomato Salsa:** Meanwhile, toss together tomatoes, onion, mint, olives, vinegar, oil, salt and pepper; serve over chicken.

Makes 4 servings.

PER SERVING: about 301 cal, 30 g pro, 17 g total fat (3 g sat. fat), 7 g carb, 1 g fibre, 93 mg chol, 579 mg sodium. % RDI: 3% calcium, 11% iron, 7% vit A, 23% vit C, 8% folate.

Spicy Orange-Paprika Grilled Chicken

1 tbsp / 15 mL grated **orange rind**

1 tbsp / 15 mL **orange juice**

1 tbsp / 15 mL **extra-virgin olive oil**

1 tbsp / 15 mL **liquid honey**

2 tsp / 10 mL **paprika**

1 tsp / 5 mL **ground coriander**

1 tsp / 5 mL **ground ginger**

¾ tsp / 4 mL **salt**

½ tsp / 2 mL **cayenne pepper**

2 small cloves **garlic**, minced

1 **whole chicken**, about 3 lb/1.5 kg, cut in half

● Mix together orange rind and juice, oil, honey, paprika, coriander, ginger, salt, cayenne and garlic; brush over chicken. Marinate for 20 minutes or, refrigerated, up to 1 day.

● Grill chicken, covered and bone side down, on greased grill over indirect medium heat (see Tip, page 283), turning once, until juices run clear when thickest part of thigh is pierced, about 45 minutes. If skin is not crisped, move over direct heat for a few minutes.

Makes 4 servings.

PER SERVING (WITHOUT SKIN): about 277 cal, 29 g pro, 15 g total fat (4 g sat. fat), 7 g carb, 1 g fibre, 102 mg chol, 520 mg sodium, 388 mg potassium. % RDI: 2% calcium, 11% iron, 10% vit A, 8% vit C, 5% folate.

Crisp & Juicy Barbecued Chicken

Grilling chicken pieces over indirect heat, then moving them over direct heat to crisp and colour makes for perfectly cooked chicken with crispy skin — a perfect combination.

4 **green onions**, chopped

4 cloves **garlic**

2 **jalapeño peppers**, seeded and chopped

½ cup / 125 mL packed **fresh basil leaves**

¼ cup / 60 mL **extra-virgin olive oil**

2 tbsp / 30 mL **wine vinegar**

1 tsp / 5 mL **salt**

1 tsp / 5 mL **smoked** or sweet **paprika**

½ tsp / 2 mL **hot pepper flakes**

3½ lb / 1.75 kg **chicken pieces**

In food processor, purée together onions, garlic, jalapeños, basil, oil, vinegar, salt, paprika and hot pepper flakes until loose paste forms; toss with chicken until coated. Marinate, refrigerated, for at least 6 hours or up to 1 day, turning occasionally.

Grill, covered and bone side down, on greased grill over indirect medium heat (see Tip, page 283) until bottom is grill marked, about 25 minutes. Turn; grill until juices run clear when thickest part is pierced, about 20 minutes. If skin is not crisped, move over direct heat for a few minutes.

Makes 6 servings.

PER SERVING: about 363 cal, 32 g pro, 24 g total fat (6 g sat. fat), 2 g carb, 1 g fibre, 120 mg chol, 389 mg sodium, 443 mg potassium. % RDI: 2% calcium, 9% iron, 10% vit A, 5% vit C, 6% folate.

Citrus Sesame Chicken

1 each **orange**, **lemon** and **lime**

2 tbsp / 30 mL **soy sauce**

2 tbsp / 30 mL **sesame oil**

½ tsp / 2 mL **hot pepper sauce**

3 lb / 1.5 kg **bone-in chicken breasts** or legs, skinned

1 tbsp / 15 mL **sesame seeds**

1 tbsp / 15 mL **liquid honey**

● Finely grate rinds of orange, lemon and lime into large bowl; squeeze out juices and add to bowl. Mix in soy sauce, half of the sesame oil and hot pepper sauce; add chicken, turning to coat. Marinate for at least 30 minutes or, refrigerated, up to 1 day.

● Reserving marinade, place chicken, bone side down, on greased grill over medium heat; brush generously with some of the marinade. Grill, covered, for 25 minutes. Turn; brush with remaining marinade. Grill for 10 minutes.

● Meanwhile, combine sesame seeds, remaining sesame oil and honey; brush over both sides of chicken. Grill, turning once, until no longer pink inside for breasts or juices run clear when legs are pierced, about 10 minutes.

Makes 6 servings.

PER SERVING: about 249 cal, 39 g pro, 7 g total fat (1 g sat. fat), 6 g carb, trace fibre, 99 mg chol, 302 mg sodium. % RDI: 1% calcium, 6% iron, 1% vit A, 17% vit C, 4% folate.

Buttermilk & Spice Grilled Drumsticks

2 lb / 1 kg **chicken drumsticks**

2 tsp / 10 mL **paprika**

1 tsp / 5 mL **dried thyme**, crumbled

¾ tsp / 4 mL **salt**

½ tsp / 2 mL **black pepper**

½ tsp / 2 mL finely grated **lemon rind**

¼ tsp / 1 mL **cayenne pepper**

BUTTERMILK MARINADE:

1 cup / 250 mL **buttermilk**

2 tbsp / 30 mL **lemon juice**

2 cloves **garlic**, pressed or minced

● **Buttermilk Marinade:** Mix together buttermilk, lemon juice and garlic; add drumsticks, rolling to coat. Marinate, refrigerated, for at least 3 or up to 12 hours, turning occasionally. Drain well.

● In large bowl, whisk together paprika, thyme, salt, pepper, lemon rind and cayenne; add chicken, tossing to coat. Let stand for 10 minutes. Grill on greased grill over medium heat, turning often, until juices run clear when thickest part is pierced, 20 to 25 minutes.

Makes 4 to 6 servings.

PER EACH OF 6 SERVINGS: about 178 cal, 17 g pro, 11 g total fat (3 g sat. fat), 3 g carb, trace fibre, 69 mg chol, 377 mg sodium. % RDI: 5% calcium, 11% iron, 7% vit A, 5% vit C, 4% folate.

Old-Fashioned Barbecued Drumsticks

Drumsticks are very inexpensive and a favourite with kids and nostalgic adults, too, especially when they're covered in delicious homemade barbecue sauce.

1½ cups / 375 mL **Hot & Spicy Chipotle Barbecue Sauce** (page 529) or other homemade barbecue sauce (pages 525, 528 and 530)

2 lb / 1 kg **chicken drumsticks** or pieces

● Set aside ½ cup/125 mL of the Hot & Spicy Chipotle Barbecue Sauce for serving; pour remainder into large bowl.

● Grill chicken, covered, on greased grill over medium heat, turning once, until juices run clear when thickest part is pierced, about 30 minutes. Add to bowl of barbecue sauce; toss to coat. Grill until slightly crusty but still saucy, about 5 minutes. Serve with reserved barbecue sauce.

Makes 6 servings.

PER SERVING: about 217 cal, 17 g pro, 11 g total fat (3 g sat. fat), 14 g carb, 1 g fibre, 66 mg chol, 184 mg sodium, 457 mg potassium. % RDI: 4% calcium, 15% iron, 8% vit A, 10% vit C, 4% folate.

Chipotle Grilled Chicken

1 can (5½ oz/156 mL) **tomato paste**

¾ cup / 175 mL **dry white wine**
(or chicken stock and 2 tbsp/30 mL
wine vinegar)

2 **canned chipotle peppers**

1 tbsp / 15 mL **adobo sauce** from
canned chipotles

2 cloves **garlic**, minced

¾ tsp / 4 mL **salt**

½ tsp / 2 mL **black pepper**

6 **bone-in chicken breasts** or legs,
skinned

● In blender or food processor, purée together tomato paste, wine, chipotles, adobo sauce, garlic, salt and pepper until smooth; transfer to large bowl. Add chicken, turning to coat. Marinate, refrigerated, for at least 4 hours or up to 1 day.

● Reserving marinade, place chicken, bone side down, on greased grill over medium heat; brush with marinade. Grill, covered, turning occasionally, until breasts are no longer pink inside or juices run clear when legs are pierced, about 45 minutes.

Makes 6 servings.

PER SERVING: about 209 cal, 37 g pro, 3 g total fat (1 g sat. fat), 7 g carb, 1 g fibre, 92 mg chol, 431 mg sodium. % RDI:
2% calcium, 12% iron, 11% vit A, 22% vit C, 4% folate.

Grilled Chicken Cutlets with Peaches

Cutlets, or scaloppine, cook so quickly. If you can't find them ready-cut, choose boneless skinless chicken breasts and slice horizontally into two thin cutlets.

1 tsp / 5 mL grated **lime rind**

¼ cup / 60 mL **lime juice**

2 tbsp / 30 mL **olive** or vegetable **oil**

2 tbsp / 30 mL **liquid honey**

½ tsp / 2 mL each **salt** and **black pepper**

1 tbsp / 15 mL chopped **fresh coriander**

1 tsp / 5 mL minced **jalapeño pepper**

1 clove **garlic**, minced

½ tsp / 2 mL **ground cumin**

½ tsp / 2 mL **ground coriander**

1 lb / 500 g **chicken cutlets**

4 **peaches**, pitted and quartered

4 cups / 1 L torn **mixed salad greens**

● Mix together lime rind and juice, oil, honey and pinch each of the salt and pepper; set half aside for basting. Stir fresh coriander and jalapeño into remainder to make dressing.

● Mix together garlic, cumin, ground coriander and remaining salt and pepper; rub all over chicken.

● Place chicken and peaches on greased grill over medium-high heat; brush with basting mixture. Grill, covered, turning once, until chicken is no longer pink inside and peaches are tender, 6 to 8 minutes. Serve over greens; drizzle with dressing.

Makes 4 servings.

PER SERVING: about 271 cal, 28 g pro, 9 g total fat (1 g sat. fat), 22 g carb, 3 g fibre, 67 mg chol, 360 mg sodium. % RDI: 5% calcium, 9% iron, 17% vit A, 32% vit C, 24% folate.

Flash-Grilled Chicken Breasts with Oyster Mushrooms

Splitting and flattening the breasts lets them quickly absorb the simple Spanish-style marinade, so they grill fast and stay moist. The mushrooms make an elegant topping.

4 **boneless skinless chicken breasts**

2 tbsp / 30 mL **extra-virgin olive oil**

2 cloves **garlic**, pressed or minced

1 tsp / 5 mL minced **fresh thyme leaves** or scant ½ tsp/2 mL dried thyme

½ tsp / 2 mL **salt**

Generous ¼ tsp / 1.5 mL **smoked paprika**

OYSTER MUSHROOM PACKET:

12 oz / 375 g **oyster mushrooms**

⅓ cup / 75 mL chopped **fresh parsley**

1 tbsp / 15 mL **extra-virgin olive oil**

1 tsp / 5 mL **sherry vinegar**

1 small **shallot**, very thinly sliced

¼ tsp / 1 mL **salt**

● Cut each chicken breast in half horizontally, almost but not all the way through; open like book. Between sheets of plastic wrap or waxed paper, pound each to even ¼-inch/5 mm thickness. Mix together oil, garlic, thyme, salt and paprika; add chicken, turning to coat. Marinate for 20 minutes or, refrigerated, up to 12 hours.

● **Oyster Mushroom Packet:** Trim off and discard tough stem ends from mushrooms; tear large mushrooms into smaller pieces. Place on heavy-duty foil; sprinkle with parsley, oil, vinegar, shallot and salt. Toss until coated; seal to form packet. Prick 2 or 3 steam vents in top. Grill over high heat until tender, about 8 minutes. Keep warm.

● Grill chicken over high heat, turning once, until no longer pink inside, 3 to 4 minutes. Serve topped with mushroom mixture.

Makes 4 servings.

PER SERVING: about 272 cal, 33 g pro, 12 g total fat (2 g sat. fat), 7 g carb, 2 g fibre, 79 mg chol, 516 mg sodium. % RDI: 2% calcium, 15% iron, 6% vit A, 10% vit C, 12% folate.

Mango Chicken

Combining fresh mango and mango chutney in the sauce brings the mango flavour front and centre.

1 tbsp / 15 mL **vegetable oil**

1 small **onion**, chopped

1 clove **garlic**, minced

1 tbsp / 15 mL **chili powder**

Half **mango**, peeled and chopped

¼ cup / 60 mL **mango chutney**

1 tsp / 5 mL grated **lime rind**

3 tbsp / 45 mL **lime juice**

2 tbsp / 30 mL **granulated sugar**

½ tsp / 2 mL **salt**

¼ tsp / 1 mL **black pepper**

4 **bone-in chicken breasts**, skinned

Lime wedges

● In saucepan, heat oil over medium heat; fry onion, garlic and chili powder, stirring occasionally, until onion is softened, about 5 minutes.

● Stir in mango, chutney, lime rind and juice, sugar, salt and pepper; bring to boil. Reduce heat and simmer, stirring occasionally, until mango is very tender, about 8 minutes. Let cool.

● In blender or food processor, purée mango mixture until smooth. Transfer to large bowl; add chicken, turning to coat. Marinate, refrigerated, for at least 4 hours or up to 1 day, turning occasionally.

● Reserving any remaining marinade, place chicken on greased grill over medium heat; brush with marinade. Grill, covered, turning once, until no longer pink inside, 30 to 45 minutes. Serve with lime wedges.

Makes 4 servings.

PER SERVING: about 281 cal, 33 g pro, 6 g total fat (1 g sat. fat), 24 g carb, 1 g fibre, 84 mg chol, 721 mg sodium. % RDI: 2% calcium, 7% iron, 16% vit A, 18% vit C, 4% folate.

Quick Korean Chicken

This is an instant Korean-style barbecued chicken, great for last-minute cooking.

8 **boneless skinless chicken thighs**, about 1½ lb/750 g total

¼ cup / 60 mL **sodium-reduced soy sauce**

2 tbsp / 30 mL **sesame oil**

4 tsp / 20 mL **granulated sugar**

2 tsp / 10 mL minced **fresh ginger**

2 tsp / 10 mL **sesame seeds**

½ tsp / 2 mL **black pepper**

4 cloves **garlic**, thinly sliced

4 **green onions**, trimmed

● Trim any fat from thighs. Between 2 sheets of plastic wrap or waxed paper, pound to even scant ½-inch/ 1 cm thickness. Mix together soy sauce, oil, sugar, ginger, sesame seeds, pepper and garlic; add chicken and onions, turning to coat. Let stand for 15 minutes, turning occasionally.

● Brush garlic off chicken and onions. Grill chicken, covered, on greased grill over medium-high heat, turning once, for 6 minutes. Add onions; grill, covered, until juices run clear when chicken is pierced and onions are slightly charred, about 2 minutes. Cut onions into bite-size pieces.

Makes 4 servings.

PER SERVING: about 250 cal, 33 g pro, 12 g total fat (3 g sat. fat), 2 g carb, trace fibre, 123 mg chol, 167 mg sodium. % RDI: 3% calcium, 14% iron, 3% vit A, 3% vit C, 8% folate.

Chinese Chicken Breast Salad

Savoury Chinese sesame dressing makes this salad irresistible. Use homemade teriyaki sauce (page 531) or bottled — it's up to you.

2 tbsp / 30 mL **teriyaki sauce**

1 tbsp / 15 mL **sesame oil**

½ tsp / 2 mL **hot pepper flakes**

¼ tsp / 1 mL **white pepper**

4 **boneless skinless chicken breasts**

SESAME DRESSING:

¼ cup / 60 mL **Asian sesame paste** or tahini

1 tbsp / 15 mL **sesame oil**

1 tbsp / 15 mL **soy sauce**

2 tsp / 10 mL **rice vinegar** or cider vinegar

2 tsp / 10 mL **hot mustard**

2 cloves **garlic**, pressed or minced

1 tsp / 5 mL **granulated sugar**

¼ tsp / 1 mL **salt**

Pinch **white pepper**

SALAD:

4 stalks **celery**

4 cups / 1 L shredded **napa cabbage** or Chinese lettuce

1 bunch **radishes**, sliced

Half **English cucumber**, sliced

2 **green onions**, thinly sliced

- Mix together teriyaki sauce, oil, hot pepper flakes and pepper; add chicken, turning to coat. Marinate for at least 30 minutes or, refrigerated, up to 1 day.

- **Sesame Dressing:** With fork, whisk together sesame paste, sesame oil, soy sauce, rice vinegar, hot mustard, garlic, sugar, salt and pepper; whisk in enough cold water (¼ to ⅓ cup/60 to 75 mL) to make smooth and pourable.

- Grill chicken over medium-high heat, turning once, until no longer pink inside, about 12 minutes. Transfer to cutting board; let stand for 5 minutes before slicing.

- **Salad:** Meanwhile, in pot of boiling salted water, blanch celery until tender-crisp, 20 to 30 seconds; drain. Chill under cold water; drain. Cut into bite-size pieces. Arrange cabbage on 4 plates; top with celery, radishes and cucumber. Top each with chicken; spoon Sesame Dressing over top. Sprinkle with onions.

Makes 4 servings.

311

PER SERVING: about 343 cal, 36 g pro, 17 g total fat (3 g sat. fat), 15 g carb, 5 g fibre, 79 mg chol, 822 mg sodium. % RDI: 17% calcium, 21% iron, 9% vit A, 55% vit C, 58% folate.

Spanish Chicken Breast Salad

Good-quality olive oil and sherry vinegar are all you need to dress this Spanish-inspired grilled chicken salad.

1 tbsp / 15 mL **brandy**

1 tbsp / 15 mL **extra-virgin olive oil**

1½ tsp / 7 mL chopped **fresh thyme** or ½ tsp/2 mL dried

1 tsp / 5 mL **smoked paprika**

½ tsp / 2 mL **salt**

4 **boneless skinless chicken breasts**

SHERRY VINAIGRETTE:

½ cup / 125 mL **extra-virgin olive oil**

3 tbsp / 45 mL **sherry vinegar**

¼ tsp / 1 mL **salt**

Pinch **black pepper**

SALAD:

1 head **Boston lettuce**, separated into leaves

2 **roasted red peppers**, peeled and cut into strips

16 thick spears **white** or green **asparagus**, cooked

● Mix together brandy, oil, thyme, paprika and salt; add chicken, turning to coat. Marinate for 30 minutes or, refrigerated, up to 1 day.

● **Sherry Vinaigrette:** Whisk together oil, vinegar, salt and pepper.

● Grill chicken over medium-high heat, turning once, until no longer pink inside, about 12 minutes. Transfer to cutting board; let stand for 5 minutes before slicing.

● **Salad:** Meanwhile, arrange lettuce leaves on 4 plates; top with peppers and asparagus. Top with chicken; spoon Sherry Vinaigrette over top.

Makes 4 servings.

313

PER SERVING: about 446 cal, 33 g pro, 32 g total fat (5 g sat. fat), 10 g carb, 2 g fibre, 79 mg chol, 501 mg sodium. % RDI: 4% calcium, 14% iron, 26% vit A, 118% vit C, 59% folate.

Russian Chicken Breast Salad

Russian dressing is an old-fashioned, classic mix of numerous flavourings that's definitely worth revisiting.

2 tbsp / 30 mL **tomato-based chili sauce** or ketchup

1½ tbsp / 22 mL chopped **fresh dill** or 1 tsp/5 mL dried dillweed

1 tbsp / 15 mL **vegetable oil**

½ tsp / 2 mL each **salt** and **black pepper**

4 **boneless skinless chicken breasts**

SALAD:

1 head **iceberg lettuce**, coarsely shredded

Quarter small **red cabbage**, finely shredded

4 **beets**, cooked and quartered

12 small **new potatoes**, cooked and quartered

1 bunch **baby carrots**, cooked if desired, or 4 small carrots, sliced

2 small **cucumbers**, sliced

Russian Dressing (right)

● Mix together chili sauce, dill, oil, salt and pepper; add chicken, turning to coat. Marinate for at least 30 minutes or, refrigerated, up to 1 day.

● Grill over medium-high heat, turning once, until no longer pink inside, about 12 minutes. Transfer to cutting board; let stand for 5 minutes before slicing.

● **Salad:** Meanwhile, arrange lettuce and cabbage on 4 plates; top with beets, potatoes, carrots and cucumbers. Top with chicken; spoon Russian Dressing over top.

Makes 4 servings.

Russian Dressing

● Stir together ¾ cup/175 mL **mayonnaise**; 1 **hard-cooked egg**, finely chopped; 1 ripe **tomato**, peeled, seeded and finely chopped; half **dill pickle**, finely chopped; 2 tbsp/30 mL each chopped **fresh parsley** and **chives**; 2 tbsp/30 mL **tomato-based chili sauce** or ketchup; 1 tbsp/15 mL chopped **fresh dill** (or ¾ tsp/ 4 mL dried dillweed); 1 tbsp/15 mL **cider vinegar**; 2 tsp/10 mL chopped drained **capers**; ¾ tsp/4 mL **paprika**; ¼ tsp/1 mL **black pepper**; and pinch **salt**.

Makes about 1½ cups/375 mL.

PER SERVING: about 716 cal, 41 g pro, 38 g total fat (6 g sat. fat), 57 g carb, 11 g fibre, 141 mg chol, 909 mg sodium. % RDI: 13% calcium, 36% iron, 115% vit A, 102% vit C, 137% folate.

Indonesian Chicken Breast Salad

Indonesian salads often include a mix of raw and cooked vegetables and fruit. Raid your refrigerator and use your imagination for the salad ingredients.

1 tsp / 5 mL grated **lime rind**

1 tbsp / 15 mL **lime juice**

1 tbsp / 15 mL **peanut** or vegetable **oil**

2 tsp / 10 mL grated **fresh ginger**

½ tsp / 2 mL **salt**

¼ tsp / 1 mL **turmeric**

¼ tsp / 1 mL **cayenne pepper**

4 **boneless skinless chicken breasts**

SALAD:

1 small head **iceberg lettuce**, shredded

8 oz / 250 g **green beans**, cooked

1 **sweet pepper**, sliced

1 **star fruit** or half small pineapple, sliced

Half **English cucumber**, sliced

Half **jicama**, sliced

2 cups / 500 mL cubed **medium tofu**, blanched and drained

Indonesian Peanut Dressing (right)

● Mix together lime rind and juice, oil, ginger, salt, turmeric and cayenne; add chicken, turning to coat. Marinate for 30 minutes or, refrigerated, up to 1 day.

● Grill over medium-high heat, turning once, until no longer pink inside, about 12 minutes. Transfer to cutting board; let stand for 5 minutes before slicing.

● **Salad:** Meanwhile, arrange lettuce, beans, pepper, star fruit, cucumber, jicama and tofu on 4 plates. Top with chicken; spoon Indonesian Peanut Dressing over top.

Makes 4 servings.

Indonesian Peanut Dressing

● In small skillet, heat 2 tbsp/30 mL **peanut** or vegetable **oil** over medium-high heat; fry 2 **shallots**, thinly sliced, and 3 cloves **garlic**, thinly sliced, until golden. Drain through sieve into heatproof bowl; mince shallots and garlic and add to bowl with oil. Stir in ⅓ cup/75 mL **natural peanut butter**; 3 tbsp/45 mL **soy sauce**; 1 to 2 tbsp/15 to 30 mL minced **hot pepper**; 1 tbsp/15 mL **fancy molasses**; 1 tbsp/15 mL **lime juice**; ¼ tsp/1 mL **five-spice powder**. Stir in enough cold water (3 to 4 tbsp/45 to 60 mL) to make smooth and pourable.

Makes about 1 cup/250 mL.

PER SERVING: about 558 cal, 49 g pro, 28 g total fat (5 g sat. fat), 34 g carb, 11 g fibre, 79 mg chol, 980 mg sodium. % RDI: 23% calcium, 38% iron, 13% vit A, 100% vit C, 73% folate.

Middle Eastern Chicken Breast Salad

This summery grilled Middle Eastern—inspired salad gets delicious nuttiness from the tahini and pistachios.

¼ cup / 60 mL chopped **fresh dill**

2 tbsp / 30 mL **extra-virgin olive oil**

1 **shallot** (or half small onion), minced

1 tbsp / 15 mL grated **lemon rind**

¼ tsp / 1 mL each **salt** and **black pepper**

4 **boneless skinless chicken breasts**

TAHINI DRESSING:

¼ cup / 60 mL **Balkan-style plain yogurt**

¼ cup / 60 mL **tahini**

3 tbsp / 45 mL **lemon juice**

2 tbsp / 30 mL **warm water**

½ tsp / 2 mL **ground cumin**

¼ tsp / 1 mL each **salt** and **black pepper**

SALAD:

2 heads **Belgian endive**, chopped

1 **bunch watercress** (tough stems removed), coarsely chopped

Half head **radicchio**, chopped

1 each stalk **celery** and **green onion**, thinly sliced

1 cup / 250 mL halved **grape** or cherry **tomatoes**

¼ cup / 60 mL hulled **pistachios** or slivered almonds

2 tbsp / 30 mL chopped **fresh mint** or parsley

● Mix together dill, oil, shallot, lemon rind, salt and pepper; add chicken, turning to coat. Marinate, refrigerated, for at least 4 or up to 12 hours, turning chicken occasionally.

● **Tahini Dressing:** Whisk together yogurt, tahini, lemon juice, water, cumin, salt and pepper until smooth.

● Grill chicken over medium-high heat, turning once, until no longer pink inside, about 12 minutes. Transfer to cutting board; let stand for 5 minutes before slicing.

● **Salad:** Meanwhile, toss together endive, watercress, radicchio, celery, onion, tomatoes, half of the pistachios and the mint; toss with all but 2 tbsp/30 mL of the Tahini Dressing.

● Divide salad among 4 plates; top with chicken. Spoon remaining dressing over top; sprinkle with remaining pistachios.

Makes 4 servings.

PER SERVING: about 338 cal, 36 g pro, 18 g total fat (3 g sat. fat), 11 g carb, 5 g fibre, 81 mg chol, 405 mg sodium. % RDI: 15% calcium, 21% iron, 20% vit A, 45% vit C, 29% folate.

Five-Spice Chicken Wings

2 tbsp / 30 mL **soy sauce**

2 tbsp / 30 mL **hoisin sauce**

2 tbsp / 30 mL **rice vinegar**

1 tbsp / 15 mL **five-spice powder**

1 tbsp / 15 mL **sesame** or vegetable **oil**

½ tsp / 2 mL each **salt** and **black pepper**

2 cloves **garlic**, minced

2½ lb / 1.25 kg **chicken wing drumettes** and **winglets** (midsections)

3 tbsp / 45 mL **liquid honey**

● Mix together soy sauce, hoisin sauce, vinegar, five-spice powder, oil, salt, pepper and garlic; add wings, tossing to coat. Marinate, refrigerated, for at least 2 hours or up to 1 day.

● Grill wings, covered, on greased grill or in greased grill basket over medium heat, turning occasionally, until crisp and no longer pink at joints, 20 to 25 minutes. Brush all over with honey; grill, covered, turning once, for 3 minutes.

Makes about 30 pieces.

PER PIECE: about 56 cal, 4 g pro, 3 g total fat (1 g sat. fat), 2 g carb, 0 g fibre, 13 mg chol, 119 mg sodium. % RDI: 2% iron, 1% vit A.

Indian Hot Wings with Mint Dipping Sauce

¼ cup / 60 mL minced **fresh coriander**

2 tbsp / 30 mL **Madras** or other Indian **curry paste**

2 tbsp / 30 mL **lemon juice**

1 tbsp / 15 mL **vegetable oil**

1½ tsp / 7 mL **ground ginger**

¾ tsp / 4 mL **turmeric**

¾ tsp / 4 mL **ground coriander**

¼ tsp / 1 mL **salt**

2 lb / 1 kg **chicken wing drumettes** and **winglets** (midsections)

MINT DIPPING SAUCE:

⅓ cup / 75 mL **Balkan-style plain yogurt**

¼ cup / 60 mL minced **fresh mint** (or 1 tbsp/15 mL dried)

2 tsp / 10 mL **lemon juice**

1 tbsp / 15 mL minced seeded **jalapeño pepper**

¼ tsp / 1 mL **ground cumin**

¼ tsp / 1 mL **black pepper**

Pinch **granulated sugar**

Pinch **salt**

● Mix together fresh coriander, curry paste, lemon juice, oil, ginger, turmeric, ground coriander and salt; add wings, tossing to coat. Marinate, refrigerated, for at least 2 hours or up to 1 day.

● **Mint Dipping Sauce:** In bowl, mix together yogurt, mint, lemon juice, jalapeño, cumin, pepper, sugar and salt.

● Grill wings, covered, on greased grill or in greased grill basket over medium heat, turning occasionally, until crisp and no longer pink at joints, 15 to 25 minutes. Serve with Mint Dipping Sauce.

Makes about 25 pieces.

Photo, page 323

PER PIECE (WITHOUT SAUCE): about 45 cal, 3 g pro, 3 g total fat (1 g sat. fat), 1 g carb, 0 g fibre, 10 mg chol, 31 mg sodium. **% RDI:** 1% calcium, 2% iron, 1% vit A, 2% vit C.

Left to right: Chili Chicken Wings (page 324), Indian Hot Wings with Mint Dipping Sauce (page 321)

Chili Chicken Wings

Skewered lengthwise, these spicy wings stay flat and are easy to handle on the grill.

3 lb / 1.5 kg **chicken wings**

¼ cup / 60 mL **Chili Spice Mix**
(page 526)

ANCHO CHILI TOMATO SAUCE:

1 tbsp / 15 mL **vegetable oil**

¼ cup / 60 mL minced **onion**

2 cloves **garlic**, minced

¾ cup / 175 mL **ketchup** or tomato-
based chili sauce

2 tbsp / 30 mL **fancy molasses**

1 tbsp / 15 mL **cider vinegar**

1 tsp / 5 mL **dry mustard**

1 tsp / 5 mL **hot pepper sauce**

2 tsp / 10 mL **ancho chili powder**

● Straighten each chicken wing; push skewer through length from base to tip. Rub all over with Chili Spice Mix. Marinate for 30 minutes or, refrigerated, up to 1 day, turning occasionally.

● **Ancho Chili Tomato Sauce:** Meanwhile, in saucepan, heat oil over medium heat; fry onion and garlic, stirring occasionally, until softened, about 3 minutes. Stir in ketchup, molasses, vinegar, mustard, hot pepper sauce and ancho chili powder; reduce heat and simmer, stirring occasionally, until bubbly, about 5 minutes. Let cool.

● Grill wings, covered, on greased grill over medium heat, turning once, for 10 minutes. Baste with sauce; grill, basting and turning occasionally, until crisp and no longer pink at joints, 15 to 25 minutes.

Makes about 30 pieces.

Photo, page 322

PER PIECE: about 93 cal, 7 g pro, 5 g total fat (1 g sat. fat), 4 g carb, trace fibre, 21 mg chol, 137 mg sodium. % RDI: 1% calcium, 5% iron, 6% vit A, 3% vit C, 1% folate.

Three-Pepper Chicken Wings

*Black, white and cayenne peppers combine to make an intensely flavoured
wing marinade that's equally appealing on chicken pieces.*

5 cloves **garlic**, pressed or minced

1 tbsp / 15 mL grated **fresh ginger**

1 tsp / 5 mL **black pepper**

1 tsp / 5 mL **white pepper**

1 tsp / 5 mL **cayenne pepper**

¾ tsp / 4 mL **salt**

¼ cup / 60 mL **sesame oil**

2 tbsp / 30 mL **Chinese black vinegar** or
balsamic vinegar

2 lb / 1 kg **chicken wing drumettes** and
winglets (midsections)

● In large heatproof bowl, mix together garlic; ginger;
black, white and cayenne peppers; and salt. In small
skillet or saucepan, heat sesame oil over medium-high
heat until haze forms over surface but oil is not
smoking; pour over garlic mixture. Add vinegar to
skillet; bring to boil (this will happen almost
immediately) and pour into bowl. Add wings, tossing
to coat. Marinate for 30 minutes or, refrigerated, up
to 1 day.

● Reserving any remaining marinade, place wings on
grill over medium heat; brush with marinade. Grill,
covered, turning occasionally, until crisp and no longer
pink at joints, 15 to 25 minutes.

Makes about 25 pieces.

325

PER PIECE: about 57 cal, 4 g pro, 4 g total fat (1 g sat. fat), 1 g carb, trace fibre, 11 mg chol, 80 mg sodium, 33 mg potassium.
% RDI: 1% iron, 1% vit A.

"Paris Wings" with Crudités

"Toto, we're not in Buffalo anymore. We've been upgraded to Paris!" Serve these classy Parisian wings along with French-style vegetable crudités, such as haricots verts, Belgian endive, baby carrots and French breakfast radishes to dip in the cheese sauce.

3 lb / 1.5 kg **chicken wing drumettes** and **winglets** (midsections)

¼ cup / 60 mL **dry white vermouth**

3 tbsp / 45 mL **Dijon mustard**

2 cloves **garlic**, pressed or minced

1 tbsp / 15 mL minced **fresh thyme** or 1 tsp/5 mL dried

2 tsp / 10 mL minced **fresh tarragon** or ¾ tsp/4 mL crumbled dried

¾ tsp / 4 mL **salt**

¼ tsp / 1 mL **black pepper**

1 tbsp / 15 mL **olive** or vegetable **oil**

Hot pepper sauce

Vegetable crudités

ROQUEFORT DIPPING SAUCE:

3 oz / 90 g **Roquefort cheese**

3 to 4 tbsp / 45 to 60 mL **buttermilk** or milk

2 tsp / 10 mL **sherry vinegar** or cider vinegar

Pinch **salt**

Pinch white or black **pepper**

2 tbsp / 30 mL finely chopped **fresh chives**

Milk (optional)

● Toss together wings, vermouth, mustard, garlic, thyme, tarragon, salt and pepper until wings are coated. Marinate, refrigerated, for at least 2 hours or up to 1 day. Bring to room temperature; toss with oil until coated.

● **Roquefort Dipping Sauce:** With fork, mash together Roquefort cheese, buttermilk, vinegar, salt and pepper until almost smooth. Stir in chives (add a little milk to thin, if desired).

● Grill wings on greased grill over medium heat until crisp and no longer pink at joints, 15 to 25 minutes. Serve with Roquefort Dipping Sauce, hot pepper sauce and crudités.

Makes about 35 pieces.

327

PER PIECE WITH 1 TSP/5 ML ROQUEFORT DIPPING SAUCE (WITHOUT HOT PEPPER SAUCE OR CRUDITÉS): about 95 cal, 7 g pro, 7 g total fat (2 g sat. fat), 1 g carb, trace fibre, 24 mg chol, 172 mg sodium. % RDI: 2% calcium, 3% iron, 2% vit A.

Mexican Wings & Green Salsa

Tomatillos, sometimes called Spanish or Mexican green tomatoes, have a delicate, lightly acidic flavour that's nice with the rich, smoky chipotles. The green salsa is also good with tortilla chips.

2 **canned chipotle peppers**

2 tbsp / 30 mL **adobo sauce** from canned chipotles

2 tbsp / 30 mL **lime juice**

1 tbsp / 15 mL **vegetable oil**

1 tsp / 5 mL **dried oregano**

¼ tsp / 1 mL **cinnamon**

¼ tsp / 1 mL **salt**

2 cloves **garlic**, chopped

2 lb / 1 kg **chicken wing drumettes** and **winglets** (midsections)

Green Salsa (right)

● Mash together chipotle peppers, adobo sauce, lime juice, oil, oregano, cinnamon, salt and garlic until smooth; add wings, tossing to coat. Marinate, refrigerated, for at least 2 hours or up to 1 day.

● Grill wings, covered, on greased grill or in greased grill basket over medium heat, turning occasionally, until crisp and no longer pink at joints, 20 to 25 minutes. Serve with Green Salsa.

Makes about 25 pieces.

Green Salsa

● In bowl, mix together ⅓ cup/75 mL grilled fresh or chopped drained canned **tomatillos** or green tomatoes; 1 or 2 **jalapeño** or serrano **pepper(s)**, seeded and minced; 2 tbsp/30 mL minced **green onions** (white part only); 4 tsp/20 mL chopped **fresh coriander** or parsley; 2 tsp/10 mL **lime juice**; and pinch each **granulated sugar** and **salt**.

Makes about ¾ cup/175 mL.

PER PIECE: about 40 cal, 3 g pro, 3 g total fat (1 g sat. fat), 1 g carb, trace fibre, 9 mg chol, 46 mg sodium. % RDI: 1% iron, 2% vit A.

Tuscan Cornish Hens

Cornish hens are tender, with juicy, delicate yet tasty flesh. They're perfect candidates for the grill — simple enough for family meals and special enough for entertaining.

⅓ cup / 75 mL **lemon juice**

¼ cup / 60 mL **extra-virgin olive oil**

4 cloves **garlic**, minced

1 tbsp / 15 mL chopped **fresh rosemary**

2 tsp / 10 mL **fennel seeds**, crushed

½ tsp / 2 mL each **salt** and **black pepper**

4 small **Cornish hens**, about 1 lb/500 g each

● Mix together lemon juice, oil, garlic, rosemary, fennel, salt and pepper.

● Using kitchen shears, cut hens down each side of backbone; remove backbone (save for stockpot). Turn hens breast side up; press firmly on breastbone to flatten. Tuck wings behind back; add to oil mixture, turning to coat. Marinate, refrigerated, for at least 4 hours or up to 1 day, turning occasionally.

● Grill hens, covered and bone side down, on greased grill over medium heat, turning occasionally, until juices run clear when thickest part of thigh is pierced and skin is crisp, 25 to 30 minutes.

Makes 4 servings.

PER SERVING: about 586 cal, 45 g pro, 43 g total fat (11 g sat. fat), 2 g carb, trace fibre, 262 mg chol, 274 mg sodium. % RDI: 3% calcium, 15% iron, 7% vit A, 5% vit C, 2% folate.

Lemon Pepper Cornish Hens

2 large **Cornish hens**, about 1½ lb/
750 g each

1½ tsp / 7 mL grated **lemon rind**

¼ cup / 60 mL **lemon juice**

3 cloves **garlic**, pressed

1 tbsp / 15 mL **black pepper**

2 tsp / 10 mL packed **brown sugar**

2 tsp / 10 mL grated **fresh ginger**

1½ tsp / 7 mL **dried oregano**, crumbled

1 tsp / 5 mL **salt**

½ tsp / 2 mL **ground cumin**

¼ tsp / 1 mL **ground cloves**

Extra-virgin olive oil

● Using kitchen shears, cut hens down each side of backbone; remove backbone (save for stockpot). Snip through breastbone to separate each hen into halves. Mix together lemon rind and juice, garlic, pepper, sugar, ginger, oregano, salt, cumin and cloves; add hens, turning to coat. Marinate, refrigerated, for at least 2 hours or up to 1 day. Bring to room temperature.

● Brush hens lightly with oil; grill, covered and bone side down, over medium heat, turning occasionally and basting with a little more oil, until juices run clear when thickest part of thigh is pierced and skin is crisp, 25 to 30 minutes.

Makes 4 servings.

PER SERVING: about 454 cal, 32 g pro, 33 g total fat (8 g sat. fat), 6 g carb, 1 g fibre, 186 mg chol, 668 mg sodium. % RDI: 4% calcium, 16% iron, 5% vit A, 17% vit C, 3% folate.

Grilled Brined Whole Turkey

Cooking the turkey in a pan makes it easy to move around and cook on the barbecue. Soaking the turkey in brine before cooking adds flavour and guarantees a moist and juicy bird.

1 **whole turkey**, about 10 lb/4.5 kg

¼ tsp / 1 mL **black pepper**

4 sprigs **fresh thyme**

3 sprigs **fresh parsley**

2 cloves **garlic**

1 **onion**, halved

BRINE:

1 cup / 250 mL **pickling salt**

¼ cup / 60 mL packed **brown sugar**

12 cups / 3 L **cold water**

1 tbsp / 15 mL **black peppercorns**

3 **bay leaves**

GLAZE:

¼ cup / 60 mL **maple syrup**

¼ cup / 60 mL **beer**

3 tbsp / 45 mL **grainy mustard**

2 tbsp / 30 mL **vegetable oil**

1 tbsp / 15 mL chopped **fresh thyme** (or 1 tsp/5 mL dried)

● **Brine:** In very large bowl, stockpot or resealable plastic bag, dissolve salt and sugar in water; add peppercorns and bay leaves.

● Remove neck and giblets from turkey (save for stockpot); add turkey to brine. Cover or seal; set on tray. Refrigerate for at least 12 hours or up to 1 day.

● **Glaze:** Mix together maple syrup, beer, mustard, oil and thyme.

● Remove turkey from brine; rinse under cold water and pat dry. Sprinkle pepper in cavity; stuff with thyme, parsley, garlic and onion. Skewer neck skin to back to close. Place on greased rack in large disposable foil roasting pan; pour in 2 cups/500 mL water.

● Grill turkey, covered, in pan on grill over indirect medium heat (see Tip, page 283), brushing with glaze every 45 minutes and maintaining level of water in pan, until digital thermometer inserted in thickest part of thigh registers 175°F/80°C, 2¼ to 2½ hours. Let stand for 15 minutes before carving.

Makes 8 to 10 servings.

TIP

When you brine a turkey, the pan drippings are too salty for gravy, so don't use them. If you want gravy, make a simple one from the neck, gizzard and heart.

333

PER EACH OF 10 SERVINGS: about 536 cal, 65 g pro, 26 g total fat (7 g sat. fat), 7 g carb, trace fibre, 190 mg chol, 1,137 mg sodium. % RDI: 7% calcium, 32% iron, 3% vit C, 8% folate.

Grilled Turkey Breast with Sautéed Banana Peppers

6 long **fresh rosemary** or thyme **sprigs**

4 **bay leaves**

2 to 2½ lb / 1 to 1.25 kg **single skin-on boneless turkey breast**

½ tsp / 2 mL **salt**

¼ tsp / 1 mL **black pepper**

2 tbsp / 30 mL **olive oil**

SAUTÉED BANANA PEPPERS:

4 **hot banana peppers**

4 **sweet banana peppers**, or 3 Cubanelle or 2 green bell peppers

3 tbsp / 45 mL **olive oil**

3 **anchovy fillets** (optional), chopped

½ cup / 125 mL minced **white onion**

2 cloves **garlic**, minced

½ tsp / 2 mL **white wine vinegar**

¼ tsp / 1 mL **ground cumin**

¼ tsp / 1 mL **smoked paprika**

Generous ¼ tsp / 1.5 mL **salt**

3 tbsp / 45 mL finely chopped **fresh parsley**

● **Sautéed Banana Peppers:** Grill hot and sweet peppers, covered, over high heat, turning often, until charred all over. Transfer to bowl; cover and let cool. Peel, seed and julienne peppers. In skillet, heat oil over medium-high heat; fry anchovies (if using) until beginning to break down, about 1 minute. Reduce heat to medium; add onion and garlic and sauté until softened, reducing heat if beginning to colour. Stir in peppers, vinegar, cumin, paprika and salt (increase to ½ tsp/2 mL if not using anchovies); cook over medium-low heat for 5 minutes. Stir in parsley; cook for 30 seconds. Remove from heat.

● Lay rosemary sprigs and bay leaves over turkey breast; with kitchen string, tie tightly, slightly flattening breast. Sprinkle all over with salt and pepper.

● Grill, covered and skin side up, over medium-high heat, basting with oil and turning occasionally, until digital thermometer registers 160°F/71°C, turkey is no longer pink inside and skin is crisp, about 45 minutes. Transfer to cutting board; let stand for 5 minutes.

● Meanwhile, reheat Sautéed Banana Peppers (if desired). Remove string and herbs from turkey before slicing. Spoon peppers over slices.

Makes 8 servings.

PER SERVING: about 257 cal, 26 g pro, 15 g total fat (3 g sat. fat), 4 g carb, 2 g fibre, 64 mg chol, 349 mg sodium. % RDI: 3% calcium, 12% iron, 3% vit A, 58% vit C, 8% folate.

Lemon Sage Barbecued Turkey Breast

3 lb / 1.5 kg **single skin-on boneless turkey breast**

4 oz / 125 g thinly sliced **prosciutto** or ham

10 **fresh sage leaves**

LEMON SAGE BASTING SAUCE:

1 tbsp / 15 mL grated **lemon rind**

3 tbsp / 45 mL **lemon juice**

2 tbsp / 30 mL **extra-virgin olive oil**

1 tbsp / 15 mL chopped **fresh sage**

¼ tsp / 1 mL **black pepper**

● **Lemon Sage Basting Sauce:** Mix together lemon rind and juice, oil, sage and pepper.

● Place turkey, skin side down, on work surface with tapered end closest to you; cut horizontally between fillet and breast almost but not all the way through. Open like book. Brush with 2 tbsp/30 mL of the Lemon Sage Basting Sauce. Arrange prosciutto down 1 half of turkey breast; top with sage leaves. Fold uncovered side over; with kitchen string, tie tightly at 2-inch/5 cm intervals.

● Place turkey, skin side down, on greased grill over indirect medium heat (see Tip, page 283); baste with 2 tbsp/30 mL of the remaining basting sauce. Grill, covered, for 1½ hours. Turn; brush with half of the remaining basting sauce; grill, basting occasionally, until digital thermometer registers 160°F/71°C, turkey is no longer pink inside and skin is crisp, about 1 hour.

Makes 8 servings.

PER SERVING: about 229 cal, 36 g pro, 8 g total fat (2 g sat. fat), 1 g carb, trace fibre, 84 mg chol, 252 mg sodium. % RDI: 2% calcium, 12% iron, 5% vit C, 4% folate.

Mushroom-Stuffed Turkey Breast Rolls

Turkey scaloppine rolled around a moist stuffing is a fast, lean main.
Try this dish also with veal or pork scaloppine.

2 tbsp / 30 mL **olive oil**

⅓ cup / 75 mL minced **shallots**

2 tbsp / 30 mL chopped **fresh sage**

8 oz / 250 g **mushrooms**, finely chopped

¾ tsp / 4 mL **salt**

¼ tsp / 1 mL (approx) **black pepper**

¼ cup / 60 mL **dry sherry**, dry white vermouth or white wine

⅓ cup / 75 mL **fresh bread crumbs**

2 tsp / 10 mL **lemon juice**

4 pieces **turkey breast scaloppine**, about 1 lb/500 g total

¼ tsp / 1 mL **paprika**

● In nonstick skillet, heat half of the oil over medium-high heat; fry shallots until softened, about 2 minutes. Stir in sage; fry for 1 minute. Add mushrooms, ½ tsp/ 2 mL of the salt and pinch of the pepper; sauté until mushrooms are softened, 2 to 3 minutes. Stir in sherry; cook until liquid no longer pools on bottom of pan, about 2 minutes. Remove from heat; mix in bread crumbs and lemon juice.

● Spread each turkey slice with one-quarter of the mushroom mixture; starting at 1 short end, roll up around filling. Thread all 4 rolls crosswise onto 2 skewers, about 1 inch/2.5 cm in from each end, leaving a little space between rolls. Brush with remaining oil; sprinkle with paprika and remaining salt and ¼ tsp/1 mL of the remaining pepper.

● Grill over medium-high heat until turkey is no longer pink inside, 10 to 12 minutes.

Makes 4 servings.

Carefully check your turkey scaloppine. Make sure they are cut across the grain – not with it – or they will be chewy.

PER SERVING: about 227 cal, 28 g pro, 8 g total fat (1 g sat. fat), 8 g carb, 1 g fibre, 74 mg chol, 500 mg sodium. % RDI: 3% calcium, 18% iron, 2% vit A, 3% vit C, 9% folate.

Last-Minute Turkey Scaloppine

Instant low-calorie cooking that's tasty and fresh — what more could you want?

2 **tomatoes**, diced

⅓ cup / 75 mL shredded **fresh basil** (or ½ tsp/2 mL dried)

1 clove **garlic**, minced

2 tbsp / 30 mL **extra-virgin olive oil**

1 tbsp / 15 mL **wine vinegar**

½ tsp / 2 mL **salt**

¼ tsp / 1 mL **black pepper**

1 lb / 500 g **turkey breast scaloppine**

● Toss together tomatoes, basil, garlic, half of the oil, the vinegar and half each of the salt and pepper.

● Brush remaining oil all over turkey; sprinkle with remaining salt and pepper. Grill, covered, on greased grill over medium-high heat, turning once, until no longer pink inside, about 6 minutes. Serve topped with tomato-basil mixture.

Makes 4 servings.

PER SERVING: about 214 cal, 27 g pro, 10 g total fat (2 g sat. fat), 4 g carb, 1 g fibre, 61 mg chol, 349 mg sodium. % RDI: 3% calcium, 12% iron, 5% vit A, 22% vit C, 8% folate.

Chipotle-Glazed Turkey Thighs

No need to make a complicated barbecue sauce to coat these moist turkey thighs — the chipotle mixture is a simple, ready-in-an-instant sauce.

4 **turkey thighs**

1½ tsp / 7 mL **ground cumin**

½ tsp / 2 mL each **salt** and **black pepper**

1 tbsp / 15 mL **vegetable oil**

2 **canned chipotle peppers**

2 tbsp/30 mL **adobo sauce** from canned chipotle peppers

3 cloves **garlic**, minced

2 tbsp / 30 mL **lime juice**

1 tbsp / 15 mL **liquid honey**

● Sprinkle turkey with cumin, salt and pepper; brush with oil. Grill, covered, on greased grill over medium heat, turning once, until juices run clear when thickest part is pierced, about 45 minutes.

● Meanwhile, seed and mince chipotles. Mix together chipotles, adobo sauce, garlic, lime juice and honey; brush over turkey during last 2 minutes of cooking.

Makes 4 servings.

VARIATION

Chipotle-Glazed Turkey Brochettes
Instead of thighs, cut 1½ lb/750 g turkey breast into 1½-inch/4 cm cubes. Thread onto skewers; grill until no longer pink inside, 10 to 12 minutes.

PER SERVING: about 446 cal, 48 g pro, 24 g total fat (6 g sat. fat), 9 g carb, 1 g fibre, 151 mg chol, 835 mg sodium. % RDI: 7% calcium, 34% iron, 10% vit A, 5% vit C, 7% folate.

Cider & Maple Grilled Duck

This innovative recipe moves duck from the roasting pan to the barbecue.

2 tbsp / 30 mL **coarse salt**

5 **bay leaves**, broken into pieces

5 cloves **garlic**, minced

4 tsp / 20 mL minced **fresh thyme** (or 1½ tsp/7 mL dried)

2 tsp / 10 mL coarsely ground **black pepper**

1 **whole duck**, about 4 lb/2 kg

⅓ cup / 75 mL **maple syrup**

3 cups / 750 mL **dry hard cider** or sweet (nonalcoholic) cider

1 tbsp / 15 mL **cider vinegar**

2 **red-skinned apples**, cored

• Mix together salt, bay leaves, garlic, thyme and pepper.

• Cut off tailbone, excess neck skin and fat in duck cavity. With kitchen shears, cut out backbone and wing tips. Cut legs off breast; separate wings from breast. Cut breast in half. Place pieces in large dish; rub all over with salt mixture. Refrigerate for 1 to 2 days, turning once.

• Rinse well; pat dry. Using skewer, prick skin all over, being careful not to prick into meat under fat. Brush with 2 tbsp/30 mL of the maple syrup.

• In wok or large pot, bring cider to boil. Place duck pieces, close together and skin side up, in steamer or on rack above cider. Cover and steam over medium heat for 1 hour, adding water to wok to maintain level if necessary.

• Remove duck from steamer; skim fat off cider. Bring to boil; boil until reduced to ½ cup/125 mL, about 12 minutes. Add vinegar and remaining maple syrup. (Let cool. Refrigerate duck and cider separately for up to 1 day.)

• Grill duck, covered and bone side down, on greased grill over medium heat, turning and basting with maple mixture every 5 minutes, until skin is crisp and golden, about 25 minutes.

• Meanwhile, cut apples crosswise into ½-inch/1 cm thick slices. Grill, basting with maple mixture and turning once, until slightly softened and grill-marked, about 6 minutes. Serve with duck along with any remaining maple mixture.

Makes 4 servings.

PER SERVING: about 737 cal, 29 g pro, 46 g total fat (15 g sat. fat), 55 g carb, 2 g fibre, 128 mg chol, 1,241 mg sodium. % RDI: 6% calcium, 41% iron, 10% vit A, 10% vit C, 5% folate.

Grilled Orange Duck

Because of its high fat content, a raw duck causes huge flare-ups on the grill, making it inconvenient to cook that way, so we steam it first to flavour and precook it.

1 **whole young duck**, 4 to 5 lb/2 to 2.2 kg

1 tsp / 5 mL **salt**

½ tsp / 2 mL **black pepper**

¼ tsp / 1 mL **cinnamon**

¼ tsp / 1 mL **ground cloves**

¼ tsp / 1 mL **nutmeg**

4 **bay leaves**

12 thin slices **fresh ginger**

1 **orange**, thinly sliced

1 strip **orange rind**

½ cup / 125 mL **orange juice**

2 tbsp / 30 mL **liquid honey**

1 tbsp / 15 mL **soy sauce**

2 cloves **garlic**, pressed or minced

● If not grilling whole, using kitchen shears, cut duck down each side of backbone; remove backbone (save for stockpot). Snip through breastbone to separate duck into halves. With tip of knife, prick skin, without piercing meat, all over at 1-inch/2.5 cm intervals. Sprinkle all over with salt, pepper, cinnamon, cloves and nutmeg; place duck, skin side up, on heatproof plate. Lay bay leaves and ginger over top; cover with orange slices.

● Place plate in hot steamer or on rack above boiling water; steam, covered, over medium-high heat, adding more boiling water if necessary, until meat feels tender when pierced and leg joints are slightly loose, about 1¼ hours. Remove bay leaves, ginger and orange slices. Discarding fat and juices, transfer duck to rack and let dry, about 30 minutes. (Refrigerate for up to 1 day.)

● Meanwhile, in small saucepan over high heat, stir together orange rind and juice, honey, soy sauce and garlic; bring to boil. Reduce heat to medium; boil until reduced by about half and thin syrupy consistency. Strain through fine sieve, discarding solids.

● Grill duck over medium heat, turning occasionally and basting with orange mixture for last 5 minutes, until skin is crisp and meat is heated through, 15 to 20 minutes.

Makes 4 servings.

PER SERVING: about 716 cal, 38 g pro, 56 g total fat (19 g sat. fat), 13 g carb, trace fibre, 165 mg chol, 917 mg sodium. % RDI: 3% calcium, 41% iron, 13% vit A, 20% vit C, 8% folate.

Rosemary Skewered Quails

Quails are a special treat on the grill. Whole quails are the only way to go for best flavour and juiciness.

6 **whole quails**

¼ cup / 60 mL **red wine**

2 tbsp / 30 mL **liquid honey**

2 tbsp / 30 mL **balsamic vinegar**

2 tbsp / 30 mL **olive oil**

2 tbsp / 30 mL chopped **fresh rosemary**

1 tsp / 5 mL **salt**

½ tsp / 2 mL **black pepper**

3 cloves **garlic**, halved

● Rinse quails; pat dry. Mix together red wine, honey, vinegar, oil, rosemary, salt and pepper; add quails, turning to coat. Marinate, refrigerated, for at least 4 hours or up to 1 day.

● Place 1 piece garlic in cavity of each quail. Line up quails on work surface, alternating breast and leg ends. Insert long metal skewer into first quail, through breast just above wing and out other side; repeat with next quail through legs, pushing close together. Continue skewering remaining quails in same manner. Repeat on other side with second skewer.

● Grill, breast side down, over medium heat, turning once, until dark golden outside and no longer pink inside at joint where thigh meets body, 20 to 25 minutes.

Makes 6 servings.

If you can't find quails in your local supermarket, buy them from specialty butchers or Chinese grocery stores. Be careful not to overcook them or they will dry out.

PER SERVING: about 276 cal, 25 g pro, 17 g total fat (4 g sat. fat), 5 g carb, trace fibre, 86 mg chol, 272 mg sodium, 237 mg potassium. % RDI: 2% calcium, 33% iron, 7% vit A, 5% vit C, 3% folate.

Lemon Thyme Quails

2 tbsp / 30 mL chopped **fresh thyme**

2 tbsp / 30 mL **olive oil**

2 tbsp / 30 mL **lemon juice**

2 tbsp / 30 mL **brandy**

2 **bay leaves**, broken into pieces

4 tsp / 20 mL **fish sauce** or soy sauce

1 tsp / 5 mL **ground cumin**

¼ tsp / 1 mL **black pepper**

¼ tsp / 1 mL **ground cloves**

Pinch **cayenne pepper**

6 **whole quails**

Lemon wedges

● Mix together thyme, oil, lemon juice, brandy, bay leaves, fish sauce, cumin, pepper, cloves and cayenne.

● Using kitchen shears, cut quails down each side of backbone; remove backbone (save for stockpot). Turn quails breast side up; press on breastbone to flatten. Add to thyme mixture, turning to coat. Marinate, refrigerated, for at least 4 hours or up to 1 day, turning occasionally.

● Brush off bay leaves. Grill quails, covered and skin side down, on greased grill over medium heat, turning once, until no longer pink inside at joint where thigh meets body, 18 to 20 minutes. Serve with lemon wedges.

Makes 6 servings.

PER SERVING: about 357 cal, 34 g pro, 23 g total fat (6 g sat. fat), 1 g carb, trace fibre, 129 mg chol, 285 mg sodium. % RDI: 3% calcium, 51% iron, 10% vit A, 15% vit C, 5% folate.

Korean Grilled Quails

Once you've made the Korean Barbecue Sauce (which keeps for the whole barbecue season), these quails are some of the easiest, tastiest things you can make on your grill.

¼ cup / 60 mL **Korean Barbecue Sauce** (page 531)

2 **green onions**, minced

2 tsp / 10 mL **Korean ground hot pepper**

2 tsp / 10 mL **toasted sesame seeds**

2 tsp / 10 mL **sesame oil**

6 **whole quails**

● Mix together Korean Barbecue Sauce, onions, hot pepper, sesame seeds and sesame oil.

● Using kitchen shears, cut quails down each side of backbone; remove backbone (save for stockpot). Turn quails breast side up; press on breastbone to flatten. Add to sauce mixture, turning to coat. Marinate for 30 minutes or, refrigerated, up to 3 hours.

● Grill, covered and skin side down, on greased grill over medium-high heat, turning once, until skin is crisp and meat is no longer pink inside at joint where thigh meets body, 12 to 15 minutes.

Makes 6 servings.

PER SERVING: about 268 cal, 26 g pro, 16 g total fat (4 g sat. fat), 4 g carb, trace fibre, 86 mg chol, 385 mg sodium. % RDI: 2% calcium, 34% iron, 9% vit A, 5% vit C, 5% folate.

Barbecued Rabbit

Rabbit in a poultry chapter? Definitely! Rabbit is often grouped with chicken because of its delicate white meat, which tastes only slightly earthier than chicken.

½ cup / 125 mL **plain yogurt**

2 tbsp / 30 mL **olive oil**

1 tbsp / 15 mL grated **fresh ginger**

1 tsp / 5 mL pressed or minced **garlic**

1 tsp / 5 mL **salt**

¼ tsp / 1 mL **black pepper**

¼ tsp / 1 mL **cayenne pepper**

1 **whole rabbit**, cut into 8 pieces

1 tbsp / 15 mL chopped **fresh coriander**

1 tbsp / 15 mL chopped **fresh mint**

● Mix together yogurt, oil, ginger, garlic, salt, pepper and cayenne. In resealable freezer bag, combine rabbit with yogurt mixture, turning to coat. Marinate, refrigerated, for at least 4 hours or up to overnight.

● Grill rabbit, covered, on greased grill over medium heat, turning once, until no longer pink inside, about 20 minutes.

● Serve sprinkled with coriander and mint.

Makes 4 servings.

PER SERVING: about 436 cal, 54 g pro, 22 g total fat (6 g sat. fat), 3 g carb, trace fibre, 148 mg chol, 679 mg sodium, 781 mg potassium. % RDI: 8% calcium, 31% iron, 2% vit A, 2% vit C, 11% folate.

Fish & Seafood

Whole Lake Trout with Fennel Salad

Other large trout or any fish suitable for grilling whole can be made this way. Or use skin-on fillets instead; just sprinkle tops with fennel fronds and grill skin side down.

1 whole **lake trout**, 2 lb/1 kg, cleaned

½ tsp / 2 mL **salt**

¼ tsp / 1 mL **black pepper**

FENNEL SALAD:

1 small **fennel bulb**

3 tbsp / 45 mL chopped **fresh parsley**

2 tbsp / 30 mL **extra-virgin olive oil**

1 tbsp / 15 mL **wine vinegar**

1 clove **garlic**, minced

½ tsp / 2 mL **salt**

¼ tsp / 1 mL **black pepper**

TARRAGON MAYONNAISE:

½ cup / 125 mL **mayonnaise**

2 tbsp / 30 mL chopped **fresh tarragon**

2 tbsp / 30 mL **extra-virgin olive oil** (optional)

1 tsp / 5 mL **Dijon mustard**

½ tsp / 2 mL **wine vinegar**

● **Fennel Salad:** Reserving tops and fronds, slice fennel paper-thin. Whisk together parsley, oil, vinegar, garlic, salt and pepper; toss with fennel until coated. Let stand for 30 minutes or, refrigerated, up to 1 day.

● **Tarragon Mayonnaise:** Mix together mayonnaise, tarragon, oil (if using), mustard and vinegar.

● Sprinkle fish inside and out with salt and pepper; stuff cavity with reserved fennel tops and fronds. Grill, covered, in greased fish basket or on greased grill over medium-high heat, turning once, until fish flakes easily, 25 to 30 minutes. Serve with Fennel Salad and Tarragon Mayonnaise.

Makes 4 to 6 servings.

Adding a little fragrant extra-virgin olive oil to store-bought mayonnaise will boost and enrich the flavour and make it taste more like homemade.

PER EACH OF 6 SERVINGS: about 295 cal, 27 g pro, 18 g total fat (4 g sat. fat), 4 g carb, 1 g fibre, 79 mg chol, 601 mg sodium. % RDI: 10% calcium, 6% iron, 11% vit A, 17% vit C, 17% folate.

Whole Trout with Lemon Parsley Butter

Grilling a whole fish is easy — just remember to grease the grill so the skin doesn't stick to it.

2 **whole trout**, about 1 lb/500 g each, cleaned

1½ tsp / 7 mL **sea salt** or salt

½ tsp / 2 mL **black pepper**

1 **lemon**, sliced

Half bunch **parsley**

1 bunch **thyme** (optional)

LEMON PARSLEY BUTTER:

¼ cup / 60 mL **unsalted butter**, softened

1 tbsp / 15 mL chopped **fresh parsley**

2 tsp / 10 mL grated **lemon rind**

1 tsp / 5 mL **lemon juice**

Pinch each **salt** and **black pepper**

Lemon Parsley Butter: Mash together butter, parsley, lemon rind and juice, salt and pepper. Scrape into shallow serving dish, smoothing top; refrigerate until firm, about 1 hour (or scrape onto plastic wrap, shape into 1-inch/2.5 cm diameter log and wrap tightly; cut chilled butter into ½-inch/1 cm rounds).

Sprinkle trout cavities with half each of the salt and pepper. Stuff cavities with lemon slices, parsley, and thyme (if using); skewer closed. Sprinkle outside of fish with remaining salt and pepper.

Grill, covered, on greased grill over medium-high heat, turning once, until fish flakes easily, about 10 minutes per inch/2.5 cm of thickness. Transfer to platter. Serve with Lemon Parsley Butter.

Makes 6 servings.

To serve whole fish, run knife along backbone to cut through skin; pull back skin, then ease knife between flesh and bone on top side. Ease off top fillet; scrape bottom fillet off long rib bones. Turn fish and repeat.

PER SERVING: about 210 cal, 20 g pro, 14 g total fat (7 g sat. fat), 3 g carb, 1 g fibre, 75 mg chol, 425 mg sodium.
% RDI: 8% calcium, 6% iron, 18% vit A, 40% vit C, 13% folate.

Trout with Tomato Tomatillo Salsa

Buy tomatillos fresh during late summer or canned year-round. Or substitute two small green tomatoes.

1 tbsp / 15 mL **olive** or vegetable **oil**

½ tsp / 2 mL **ground coriander**

½ tsp / 2 mL **ground cumin**

¼ tsp / 1 mL each **salt** and **black pepper**

4 **trout fillets**, 8 oz/250 g each

TOMATO TOMATILLO SALSA:

2 **tomatoes**, peeled, seeded and diced

2 **tomatillos** (see Tip, below), diced

Half small **red onion**, diced

1 or 2 **jalapeño pepper(s)**, seeded and minced

1 clove **garlic**, minced

⅓ cup / 75 mL chopped **fresh coriander**

2 tbsp / 30 mL **orange juice**

2 tbsp / 30 mL **extra-virgin olive oil**

Pinch each **salt** and **black pepper**

● **Tomato Tomatillo Salsa:** Toss together tomatoes, tomatillos, onion, jalapeño(s), garlic, coriander, orange juice, oil, salt and pepper.

● Stir together oil, coriander, cumin, salt and pepper; brush over fish. Grill, covered and skin side down, on greased grill over medium-high heat, turning once, until fish flakes easily, about 8 minutes. Serve with Tomato Tomatillo Salsa.

Makes 4 servings.

TIP

Fresh tomatillos should be quickly blanched in boiling water or lightly grilled before using; this intensifies the flavour and removes any mouth-puckering resins that are a natural part of the fruit. Canned tomatillos can be used as is.

PER SERVING: about 418 cal, 44 g pro, 23 g total fat (5 g sat. fat), 6 g carb, 1 g fibre, 120 mg chol, 224 mg sodium. % RDI: 15% calcium, 9% iron, 20% vit A, 33% vit C, 27% folate.

Dill Grilled Trout Fillets

2 **green onions**, minced

2 tbsp / 30 mL chopped **fresh dill**
(or 2 tsp/10 mL dried dillweed)

¼ tsp / 1 mL grated **lemon rind**

4 **trout** or salmon **fillets**, about
6 oz/175 g each

1 tbsp / 15 mL **butter**, melted

½ tsp / 2 mL **salt**

¼ tsp / 1 mL **black pepper**

Lemon wedges

● Mix together green onions, dill and lemon rind. Brush flesh side of fish with butter; sprinkle with onion mixture, salt and pepper.

● Grill, covered and skin side down, on greased grill over medium-high heat, turning once, until fish flakes easily, about 4 minutes for trout, 12 minutes for salmon. Serve with lemon wedges.

Makes 4 servings.

PER SERVING: about 228 cal, 29 g pro, 11 g total fat (4 g sat. fat), 1 g carb, trace fibre, 89 mg chol, 367 mg sodium. % RDI: 10% calcium, 4% iron, 13% vit A, 13% vit C, 15% folate.

Trout with Herb Stuffing

Boning whole trout is actually quite easy, and you don't need to worry about the flesh of the fish getting a bit nicked — you won't be able to tell after it's stuffed. Arctic char or other types of trout are also wonderful prepared this way, and you could grill pickerel or whitefish with this stuffing, too.

1 large whole **trout**, about 1½ lb/750 g

½ tsp / 2 mL (approx) **salt**

¼ tsp / 1 mL (approx) **white pepper**

1½ cups / 375 mL **fresh bread crumbs**

2 tbsp / 30 mL **butter**

¼ cup / 60 mL finely chopped **shallots**

¼ cup / 60 mL finely diced **celery**

1 clove **garlic**, minced

3 tbsp / 45 mL finely chopped **fresh chives**

2 tbsp / 30 mL finely chopped **fresh parsley**

1 tbsp / 15 mL finely chopped **celery leaves**

1 tbsp / 15 mL finely chopped **fresh tarragon**

¼ tsp / 1 mL finely grated **lemon rind**

1½ tsp / 7 mL **lemon juice**

Pinch **nutmeg**

1 **egg yolk**

2 tsp / 10 mL **butter**, melted

Pinch **black pepper**

- From inside of fish, cut through spine to break at head and tail. Starting at head, slide sharp, fine knife under ribs down each side of fish, then, holding head end of spine, pull out spine along with attached rib bones. Cut out remaining row of bones that run straight down centre from head to tail; trim edges of belly, removing any bones. Feel for and remove any missed bones. Open and flatten fish, skin side down, on work surface; sprinkle with ¼ tsp/1 mL of the salt and half of the white pepper.

- Place bread crumbs in large bowl. In skillet, melt butter over medium heat; fry shallots, celery, garlic and pinch of the remaining salt until softened, about 4 minutes. Scrape over bread crumbs; toss in chives, parsley, celery leaves, tarragon, lemon rind and juice, nutmeg and remaining white pepper until thoroughly mixed. Stir in egg yolk; spoon evenly over fish. Close around mixture; with toothpicks, fasten edges together at 1½-inch/4 cm intervals. Lace kitchen string back and forth around toothpicks to secure. Brush butter all over skin; sprinkle with generous pinch of the remaining salt and black pepper.

- Grill, covered, on greased grill over medium-high heat, turning once, until digital thermometer inserted in centre of stuffing registers 155°F/68°C, about 20 minutes.

Makes 4 servings.

PER SERVING: about 316 cal, 28 g pro, 17 g total fat (8 g sat. fat), 11 g carb, 1 g fibre, 143 mg chol, 483 mg sodium. % RDI: 12% calcium, 10% iron, 22% vit A, 13% vit C, 25% folate.

Whole Arctic Char with Green Onion Butter Sauce

Arctic char from northern Canadian waters is really special; its delicate pink flesh tastes somewhat like speckled or brook trout with a whiff of wild salmon, so it only requires a light touch of flavouring. And it's beautiful, too.

1 whole **Arctic char**, 2½ to 3 lb/1.25 to 1.5 kg

2 tsp / 10 mL **coarse sea salt**

2 tsp / 10 mL coarsely ground **black pepper**

GREEN ONION BUTTER SAUCE:

1½ cups / 375 mL thinly sliced **green onions**

3 cloves **garlic**, minced

⅓ cup / 75 mL **butter**

3 tbsp / 45 mL **lemon juice**

½ tsp / 2 mL **smoked paprika** or 1 tsp/5 mL sweet paprika

½ tsp / 2 mL **salt**

¼ tsp / 1 mL **white pepper**

● Sprinkle fish inside and out with salt and pepper. Grill, covered, on greased grill over medium heat (keep some water on hand to sprinkle over burner or coals at beginning when fish oils cause flare-ups), turning once, until fish flakes easily, 20 to 25 minutes.

● **Green Onion Butter Sauce:** Meanwhile, place onions on heavy-duty foil; top with garlic, butter, lemon juice, paprika, salt and pepper. Seal to form packet; place on grill for last 5 minutes while grilling fish.

● To serve fish, lift crispy skin from belly and roll up to back; spoon some of the Green Onion Butter Sauce over fish. Serve remainder on side.

Makes 4 to 6 servings.

PER EACH OF 6 SERVINGS: about 220 cal, 23 g pro, 13 g total fat (7 g sat. fat), 4 g carb, 1 g fibre, 93 mg chol, 854 mg sodium, 448 mg potassium. % RDI: 4% calcium, 9% iron, 15% vit A, 10% vit C, 6% folate.

Fishing for Facts

Buying

- Buy fish from a supermarket or fish market with rapid turnover; ask what is freshest and adjust your menu.

- Fresh fish should have a pleasant (not fishy) smell. Whole fish should be firm, with bright red gills, clear eyes and scales that adhere tightly. Have the fishmonger scale it, clean it and remove the gills.

- Fish fillets and steaks should be moist and elastic throughout, with no dry or discoloured edges.

- The best fish for grilling whole are those with firm or flaky (not soft) flesh and skin that will crisp nicely, such as pickerel, whitefish, salmon, trout, Arctic char, bass or snapper. For fillets and steaks, use any type except soft-fleshed fish, such as cod, flounder, sole or fluke, which can be cooked successfully in packets.

Storing

- It is best to use fish the same day it's purchased. Wrap lightly in plastic wrap and place in the coldest part of the refrigerator, preferably on ice or an ice pack. If storing for a day or more, wrap fish in paper towels then plastic; change after 24 hours.

Prepping

- Before cooking whole fish, remove any remaining scales by scraping from tail to head with knife. From cavity, pull out any innards and walls of air bladder. Run knife point down spine inside cavity; rinse out any blood with cold water. Cut out gills if still attached. Pat dry.

Grilling

- To grill fish, use tongs and 2 wide spatulas, which are great at getting under and supporting fish when turning. A fish basket (page 11) makes grilling whole fish a snap.

- Always clean the grill thoroughly with a wire brush and preheat well.

Cedar-Planked Salmon

Grilling salmon on water-soaked cedar planks infuses it with a delightfully woody and smoky taste.

1½ lb / 750 g **salmon fillet**, cut into 2 to 6 pieces

2 tbsp / 30 mL **olive oil**

½ tsp / 2 mL grated **lemon rind**

2 tbsp / 30 mL **lemon juice**

1 tbsp / 15 mL chopped **fresh chives** or green onions

2 tsp / 10 mL **Dijon mustard**

Pinch each **salt** and **black pepper**

DILL SAUCE:

½ cup / 125 mL **light sour cream**

2 tbsp / 30 mL finely chopped **cucumber**

1 tbsp / 15 mL chopped **fresh dill** (or 1 tsp/5 mL dried dillweed)

2 tsp / 10 mL minced **fresh chives** or green onions

Pinch each **salt** and **black pepper**

● Soak two 12- x 7-inch/30 x 18 cm untreated cedar planks in water for at least 30 minutes or up to 1 day; place fish on planks.

● Whisk together oil, lemon rind and juice, chives, mustard, salt and pepper; brush half over salmon. Grill, covered, over medium-high heat, brushing once with remaining lemon mixture, until fish flakes easily, 20 to 25 minutes.

● **Dill Sauce:** Meanwhile, stir together sour cream, cucumber, dill, chives, salt and pepper; serve with fish.

Makes 6 servings.

PER SERVING: about 248 cal, 21 g pro, 17 g total fat (3 g sat. fat), 3 g carb, trace fibre, 59 mg chol, 94 mg sodium. % RDI: 5% calcium, 3% iron, 3% vit A, 10% vit C, 14% folate.

Salmon & Scallop Grill

Scallops from the East Coast and wild salmon from the West Coast are graced with a lively Chinese-style relish.

16 large **sea scallops**

1½ lb / 750 g **wild salmon fillet**

GINGER GREEN ONION RELISH:

12 **green onions**, minced

2 sprigs **fresh coriander**, minced

¼ cup / 60 mL grated **fresh ginger**

1 tbsp / 15 mL minced seeded **red hot pepper**

2 tsp / 10 mL **salt**

Scant ½ tsp / 2 mL **white pepper**

½ cup / 125 mL **peanut oil**

2 tbsp / 30 mL **sesame oil**

● **Ginger Green Onion Relish:** In heatproof bowl, stir onions with coriander; top with ginger, hot pepper, salt and pepper. Heat peanut oil until light haze appears on surface but oil is not smoking; remove from heat and add sesame oil. Immediately pour over green onion mixture; mix well. Let cool. Reserving oil, strain off most of it, leaving enough to keep relish quite moist.

● Brush scallops and flesh side of salmon lightly with reserved oil. Grill fish, covered and skin side down, on greased grill over medium-high heat until skin is crisp. Turn; grill until centre of thickest part just begins to turn opaque, 10 to 15 minutes total. Meanwhile, grill scallops, turning once, just until centres begin to turn opaque, about 5 minutes. Place salmon on platter; surround with scallops. Top each scallop with dollop of Ginger Green Onion Relish; spoon line of relish over salmon.

Makes 8 servings.

PER SERVING: about 276 cal, 28 g pro, 16 g total fat (2 g sat. fat), 6 g carb, 1 g fibre, 66 mg chol, 1,008 mg sodium. % RDI: 6% calcium, 10% iron, 6% vit A, 16% vit C, 18% folate.

Salmon with Lemon & Onion Relish

Loaded with chunks of juicy lemon, the relish is powerfully tangy, so you only need a small amount.

2 large **lemons**

½ cup / 125 mL finely diced **red onion**

2 tbsp / 30 mL minced **fresh dill**

2 tbsp / 30 mL **extra-virgin olive oil**

1 tbsp / 15 mL minced **fresh parsley**

1 tbsp / 15 mL drained **capers**, chopped

1 large clove **garlic**, minced

½ tsp / 2 mL **salt**

¼ tsp / 1 mL **cayenne pepper**

4 **salmon steaks** or fillets, or 2 whole trout, about 1¼ lb/625 g each

● Peel and remove pith from lemons; seed and dice flesh. Transfer lemons and any juices to bowl; stir in onion, dill, oil, parsley, capers, garlic, half of the salt, and the cayenne.

● Sprinkle fish inside and out with remaining salt. Grill, covered, on greased grill over medium-high heat, turning once, until fish flakes easily, about 15 minutes. Serve with lemon relish.

Makes 4 servings.

PER SERVING: about 350 cal, 39 g pro, 18 g total fat (4 g sat. fat), 6 g carb, 1 g fibre, 108 mg chol, 420 mg sodium. % RDI: 14% calcium, 7% iron, 15% vit A, 52% vit C, 22% folate.

Garlic Rosemary Salmon

Try this simple herb-and-spice rub also on lake trout, pickerel or whitefish.

2 cloves **garlic**, minced

1 tbsp / 15 mL minced **fresh rosemary**

2 tsp / 10 mL **fennel seeds**, coarsely crushed

2 tsp / 10 mL **extra-virgin olive oil**

½ tsp / 2 mL **salt**

¼ tsp / 1 mL **black pepper**

1½ lb / 750 g **salmon fillet(s)**

Lemon wedges

● Mix together garlic, rosemary, fennel seeds, oil, salt and pepper; rub over flesh side of fish. Let stand for 20 minutes or, refrigerated, up to 8 hours.

● Grill, covered and skin side down, on greased grill over medium-high heat for 10 minutes. Turn; grill until fish flakes easily, about 2 minutes. Serve with lemon wedges.

Makes 4 servings.

PER SERVING: about 265 cal, 26 g pro, 17 g total fat (3 g sat. fat), 1 g carb, trace fibre, 74 mg chol, 359 mg sodium. % RDI: 2% calcium, 4% iron, 2% vit A, 8% vit C, 18% folate.

Whole Salmon with Basil Sauce

Grilling a whole salmon keeps the flesh juicy and tender, and is wonderful for a really large crowd. Large and fatty Atlantic salmon is especially suited for grilling whole.

1 **whole salmon**, 8 to 10 lb/3.5 to 4.5 kg

2 tsp / 10 mL each **salt** and **black pepper**

BASIL SAUCE:

2 cups / 500 mL cubed crustless **white bread**

2 cups / 500 mL packed **fresh basil leaves**

1 clove **garlic**, smashed

1 tsp / 5 mL **salt**

¼ tsp / 1 mL **black pepper**

1 cup / 250 mL **extra-virgin olive oil**

2 tbsp / 30 mL **lemon juice**

● **Basil Sauce:** In food processor, pulse together bread, basil, garlic, salt and pepper until minced. With motor running, slowly pour in oil; pulse in lemon juice.

● Sprinkle fish inside and out with salt and pepper. Grill, covered, on greased grill over indirect medium-low heat (see Tip, below), turning once after bottom skin is crisp, until flesh in thickest part flakes easily from backbone, about 25 minutes per side. Serve with Basil Sauce.

Makes 12 to 18 servings.

VARIATION

Grilled Salmon Fillet with Basil Sauce

Halve Basil Sauce recipe; prepare as directed. Replace whole fish with 3 lb/1.5 kg skin-on salmon fillet; sprinkle both sides with 1 tsp/5 mL each salt and pepper. Grill, covered and skin side down, on greased grill over medium heat until fish flakes easily, 15 to 25 minutes depending on salmon variety and thickness. Serve with Basil Sauce.

Makes 7 to 9 servings.

To grill over indirect heat on gas grill, set foil drip pan under 1 rack of 2-burner barbecue or under centre rack of 3-burner barbecue. Heat remaining burner(s) to temperature indicated (see Grilling Temperatures, page 10). For charcoal grill, place drip pan in centre and arrange hot charcoal on either side. Set meat on greased grill or rotisserie and centre over drip pan. Grill as directed.

PER EACH OF 18 SERVINGS: about 304 cal, 21 g pro, 23 g total fat (4 g sat. fat), 2 g carb, trace fibre, 57 mg chol, 457 mg sodium, 380 mg potassium. % RDI: 2% calcium, 5% iron, 4% vit A, 8% vit C, 17% folate.

Maple-Glazed Salmon Steaks

4 **salmon steaks**, about 6 oz/175 g each

1 tbsp / 15 mL **vegetable oil**

½ tsp / 2 mL **salt**

½ tsp / 2 mL **black pepper**

3 tbsp / 45 mL **maple syrup**

1 tbsp / 15 mL **grainy mustard**

1 tbsp / 15 mL **cider vinegar**

● Shape each steak into circle by wrapping belly ends around body cavity; secure with string. Brush with oil; sprinkle both sides with salt and pepper. Mix together maple syrup, mustard and vinegar.

● Place salmon on greased grill over medium heat; brush with half of the maple mixture. Grill, covered, for 5 minutes. Turn; brush with remaining maple mixture. Grill for 4 minutes. Turn; grill until fish flakes easily, about 1 minute. Transfer to platter; let stand for 2 minutes before removing string.

Makes 4 servings.

PER SERVING: about 307 cal, 26 g pro, 18 g total fat (3 g sat. fat), 9 g carb, trace fibre, 74 mg chol, 400 mg sodium, 485 mg potassium. % RDI: 3% calcium, 5% iron, 2% vit A, 7% vit C, 18% folate.

Masala Salmon

You only wish your local Pakistani grill (tikka) restaurant offered fish this good.

¼ cup / 60 mL **peanut** or vegetable **oil**

1½ cups / 375 mL sliced **onions**

¼ cup / 60 mL **plain yogurt**

¼ cup / 60 mL minced **fresh coriander**

1 tbsp / 15 mL **lemon juice**

2 **green hot peppers**, minced

2 cloves **garlic**, minced

2 tsp / 10 mL grated **fresh ginger**

2 tsp / 10 mL **curry powder** or paste

1 tsp / 5 mL **salt**

4 **skinless salmon fillets** or steaks, about 6 oz/175 g each

Fresh coriander sprigs

● In skillet, heat oil over medium-high heat; sauté onions, reducing heat if blackening, until browned and slightly crispy, about 10 minutes. Reserving oil, drain through sieve over heatproof bowl; let cool. In food processor, purée together onions, yogurt, minced coriander, lemon juice, hot peppers, garlic, ginger, curry powder, salt and 1 tbsp/15 mL of the reserved oil. Scrape into large bowl; add salmon, turning to coat. Let stand for 15 minutes.

● Grill, covered, on greased grill over medium-high heat, turning once and topping with any leftover spice mixture, until fish flakes easily, 10 to 12 minutes. Garnish with coriander sprigs.

Makes 4 servings.

373

PER SERVING: about 398 cal, 28 g pro, 29 g total fat (6 g sat. fat), 7 g carb, 1 g fibre, 75 mg chol, 658 mg sodium.
% RDI: 5% calcium, 6% iron, 3% vit A, 17% vit C, 24% folate.

Salmon with Coriander Oil

This recipe, with its Portuguese sauce, is so simple it's almost not a recipe — but the result is utterly elegant. Use the finest extra-virgin olive oil you have.

4 **salmon fillets** or steaks, about 6 oz/175 g each

¼ cup / 60 mL **extra-virgin olive oil**

¾ tsp / 4 mL **salt**

¼ tsp / 1 mL **black pepper**

½ cup / 125 mL finely chopped **fresh coriander**

2 tsp / 10 mL **lemon juice**

● Lightly brush salmon all over with 2 tsp/10 mL of the oil; sprinkle with ½ tsp/2 mL of the salt and the pepper. Place coriander on cutting board and sprinkle with remaining salt; mince vigorously until almost paste. In small bowl, stir together coriander paste, lemon juice and remaining oil.

● Grill fish, covered and skin side down, over medium-high heat until skin is crisp and fish flakes easily, about 10 minutes. Transfer to platter; spoon coriander oil over and around salmon.

Makes 4 servings.

PER SERVING: about 394 cal, 29 g pro, 30 g total fat (5 g sat. fat), trace carb, trace fibre, 84 mg chol, 513 mg sodium. % RDI: 2% calcium, 4% iron, 3% vit A, 10% vit C, 21% folate.

Mustard Grilled Salmon or Halibut with Prosciutto

Use whole large slices of prosciutto to cover the fish well.

¼ cup / 60 mL **Dijon mustard**

2 tbsp / 30 mL chopped **fresh chives** or minced green onions

¼ tsp / 1 mL **black pepper**

4 **skinless salmon** or halibut **fillets**, about 6 oz/175 g each

4 thin slices **prosciutto**

● Mix together mustard, chives and pepper; spread over both sides of salmon. Place fish on prosciutto; wrap around fish.

● Grill on greased grill over medium heat, turning once, until fish flakes easily, about 10 minutes.

Makes 4 servings.

PER SERVING: about 311 cal, 33 g pro, 19 g total fat (4 g sat. fat), 1 g carb, 0 g fibre, 91 mg chol, 463 mg sodium. % RDI: 4% calcium, 6% iron, 3% vit A, 8% vit C, 21% folate.

Pickerel or Whitefish with Cherry Tomato Relish

1 **whole pickerel** or whitefish, about 2 lb/1 kg

½ tsp / 2 mL each **salt** and **black pepper**

CHERRY TOMATO RELISH:

2 cups / 500 mL quartered **cherry tomatoes**

½ cup / 125 mL chopped **fresh coriander**

1 **jalapeño pepper**, seeded and minced

2 tbsp / 30 mL finely chopped **onion**

2 tbsp / 30 mL **extra-virgin olive oil**

½ tsp / 2 mL grated **lime rind**

2 tbsp / 30 mL **lime juice**

1½ tsp / 7 mL grated or minced **fresh ginger**

½ tsp / 2 mL **salt**

2 tsp / 10 mL **ground coriander**

½ tsp / 2 mL **black pepper**

● **Cherry Tomato Relish:** Toss together cherry tomatoes, fresh coriander, jalapeño, onion, oil, lime rind and juice, ginger and salt. In small skillet over medium-low heat, lightly toast ground coriander and pepper until fragrant, about 2 minutes; stir into relish.

● Cut 2 diagonal slashes into each side of fish; sprinkle inside and out with salt and pepper. Grill, covered, in greased fish basket or on greased grill over medium-high heat, turning once, until fish flakes easily, about 20 to 25 minutes. Serve with Cherry Tomato Relish.

Makes 4 servings.

377

PER SERVING: about 203 cal, 26 g pro, 9 g total fat (1 g sat. fat), 5 g carb, 1 g fibre, 111 mg chol, 574 mg sodium. % RDI: 14% calcium, 17% iron, 10% vit A, 35% vit C, 13% folate.

Whitefish with Grilled Ratatouille Salad

Here, ratatouille, a stew of late-summer vegetables, turns into a perfect grilled salad. Skewering the vegetables by type ensures that they all cook through in the same time.

378

1 small **eggplant**, peeled and cut into 1-inch/2.5 cm chunks

1 **zucchini**, cut into 1-inch/2.5 cm chunks

Half each **sweet red** and **green pepper**, cut into 1-inch/2.5 cm chunks

1 small **red onion**, cut into 1-inch/ 2.5 cm chunks

1½ cups / 375 mL **cherry tomatoes**

⅓ cup / 75 mL **extra-virgin olive oil**

¼ cup / 60 mL chopped **fresh oregano**

3 tbsp / 45 mL **wine vinegar**

2 tsp / 10 mL **Dijon mustard**

2 cloves **garlic**, minced

1 tsp / 5 mL each **salt** and **black pepper**

1½ lb / 750 g **skin-on whitefish** or pickerel **fillets**, or saltwater fish, such as snapper or striped bass

● In large bowl, combine eggplant, zucchini, red and green peppers, onion and cherry tomatoes. Drizzle with 2 tbsp/30 mL of the oil; toss until coated. Thread onto long skewers, grouping same vegetables together.

● Grill, covered, on greased grill over medium-high heat, turning occasionally, until browned and tender, about 12 minutes. Remove from skewers and return to bowl. Whisk together remaining oil, oregano, vinegar, mustard, garlic and half each of the salt and pepper; toss ¼ cup/60 mL with vegetables until coated.

● Sprinkle fish with remaining salt and pepper; brush both sides with remaining oil mixture. Grill, covered and skin side down, on greased grill over medium-high heat until fish flakes easily, 8 to 10 minutes. Serve with salad.

Makes 4 to 6 servings.

PER EACH OF 6 SERVINGS: about 296 cal, 21 g pro, 18 g total fat (3 g sat. fat), 12 g carb, 3 g fibre, 62 mg chol, 486 mg sodium. % RDI: 5% calcium, 10% iron, 12% vit A, 53% vit C, 17% folate.

Tilapia Tacos

2 **tilapia fillets**, about 8 oz/250 g each

1 tsp / 5 mL **smoked paprika**

¾ tsp / 4 mL **salt**

½ tsp / 2 mL **ground cumin**

¼ tsp / 1 mL **black pepper**

1 tbsp / 15 mL **vegetable oil**

8 **corn tortillas**, warmed

1 **avocado**, peeled, pitted and sliced

4 **lime wedges**

RED ONION & JALAPEÑO PICKLE:

1 **red onion**, thinly sliced

2 **jalapeño peppers**, thinly sliced

2 tbsp / 30 mL **lime juice**

2 tbsp / 30 mL **cider vinegar**

½ tsp / 2 mL **salt**

½ tsp / 2 mL **granulated sugar**

● **Red Onion & Jalapeño Pickle:** Mix together onion, jalapeños, lime juice, vinegar, salt and sugar; let stand for 20 minutes or, refrigerated, up to 8 hours.

● Cut each fillet in half crosswise. Mix together paprika, salt, cumin and pepper; sprinkle over both sides of fish. Brush with oil. Grill, covered and flat side down, over medium-high heat, turning once, until fish flakes easily, 6 to 8 minutes.

● For each serving, divide each portion of fish in half; place in warm tortillas. Top with Red Onion & Jalapeño Pickle and avocado slices; garnish with lime wedge.

Makes 4 servings.

PER SERVING: about 342 cal, 27 g pro, 14 g total fat (2 g sat. fat), 30 g carb, 7 g fibre, 50 mg chol, 794 mg sodium, 798 mg potassium. % RDI: 7% calcium, 14% iron, 4% vit A, 28% vit C, 32% folate.

Fish Tikka

This is an extremely popular way to eat fish throughout India and Pakistan and wherever South Asians have settled. Fish tikka is often cooked in a tandoor oven, but at home it's a breeze on the grill. Use fish that's at least ¾ inch/2 cm thick; you can cut it into large chunks as it is here, or marinate and cook whole fish steaks.

1½ lb / 750 g thick firm **fish fillets**

¾ cup / 175 mL **1% to full-fat yogurt**

4 cloves **garlic**, pressed, grated or pounded into paste

2 tbsp / 30 mL **lime** or lemon **juice**

5 tsp / 25 mL **Indian red chili powder** or ground dried hot peppers, or 2 tsp/10 mL cayenne pepper

2 tsp / 10 mL **paprika**

1½ tsp / 7 mL finely grated **fresh ginger**

1½ tsp / 7 mL **ground coriander**

1 tsp / 5 mL **ground cumin**

1 tsp / 5 mL **salt**

¾ tsp / 4 mL **turmeric**

½ tsp / 2 mL **ground mace** or nutmeg

½ tsp / 2 mL **ground ajwain seeds**, or dried thyme, crumbled

¼ tsp / 1 mL each **black pepper** and **ground cinnamon**

Pinch **ground cloves**

1 large **Cubanelle** or other sweet **pepper**, cut into 2-inch/5 cm chunks

1 **white**, red or sweet **onion**, cut into ½-inch/1 cm wide wedges

2 tbsp / 30 mL **peanut** or vegetable **oil** or butter, melted

Lime halves or wedges

● Cut fish into about 2-inch/5 cm chunks; place in large nonreactive bowl. In separate bowl, stir together yogurt, garlic, lime juice, chili powder, paprika, ginger, coriander, cumin, salt, turmeric, mace, ajwain, pepper, cinnamon and cloves. Scrape over fish; mix well. Refrigerate for 2 to 4 hours.

● Add pepper and onion; toss until lightly coated. Let stand for 15 minutes. Alternately thread fish, pepper and onion onto long skewers. Drizzle with oil.

● Grill, covered, on greased grill over indirect high heat (see Tip, page 370), turning once or twice, until fish flakes easily, about 15 minutes. Serve with lime.

Makes 6 servings.

TIP

Look for ajwain seeds at Indian grocery stores or in the spice aisle of supermarkets. Ajwain seeds contain thymol, the same substance that gives thyme much of its distinctive flavour, so dried thyme is an acceptable substitute.

PER SERVING: about 205 cal, 25 g pro, 8 g total fat (1 g sat. fat), 8 g carb, 2 g fibre, 37 mg chol, 277 mg sodium, 685 mg potassium. % RDI: 9% calcium, 11% iron, 10% vit A, 12% vit C, 11% folate.

Thai-Style Grilled Bass

Freshwater small-mouth, large-mouth or rock bass are all good prepared this way, as is ocean striped bass, croaker or any other full-flavoured white-fleshed saltwater fish.

2 tbsp / 30 mL **lime juice**

1 tbsp / 15 mL minced **fresh lemongrass**

1 tbsp / 15 mL **fish sauce**

1 tbsp / 15 mL **peanut** or vegetable **oil**

4 tsp / 20 mL **Thai red curry paste**

1 tsp / 5 mL finely grated **fresh ginger**

1 clove **garlic**, pressed, pounded or grated into paste

1 tsp / 5 mL **palm sugar** or light brown sugar

1 **kaffir lime leaf**, centre rib removed and finely julienned, or ¼ tsp/1 mL finely grated lime rind

¼ tsp / 1 mL **white pepper**

1 **whole bass**, 1½ to 2 lb/750 g to 1 kg

Lime wedges

Fresh coriander sprigs

● Mix together lime juice, lemongrass, fish sauce, oil, curry paste, ginger, garlic, palm sugar, lime leaf and pepper.

● Cut 3 X-shaped slits diagonally deep into each side of fish; pat dry with paper towels inside and out. Rub spice mixture all over inside and outside of fish, rubbing into slits. Refrigerate for 2 to 3 hours.

● Grill, covered, on greased grill over medium heat, turning once, until fish flakes easily, 14 to 16 minutes. Serve garnished with lime wedges and coriander sprigs.

Makes 4 servings.

Photo, page 350

PER SERVING: about 174 cal, 19 g pro, 9 g total fat (2 g sat. fat), 4 g carb, trace fibre, 66 mg chol, 418 mg sodium, 400 mg potassium. % RDI: 8% calcium, 13% iron, 4% vit A, 7% vit C, 6% folate.

Smoky Grilled Capelin

Capelin are a Maritimes specialty. These small roe-filled fish are scooped up in large quantities on their annual ocean spawning run. Adored by locals and East Asians, they are basically ignored by the rest of Canada. Look for inexpensive frozen capelin in Chinese and Japanese grocery stores. Enjoy simply grilled or smoked as in this recipe.

2 tbsp / 30 mL **sea**, pickling or kosher **salt**

1 tbsp / 15 mL grated **fresh ginger**

2 tsp / 10 mL **granulated sugar**

1 lb / 500 g **whole capelin**

1 tbsp / 15 mL **vegetable oil**

HOT MUSTARD DIPPING SAUCE:

1 tbsp / 15 mL **hot mustard powder**

½ tsp / 2 mL **rice vinegar** or cider vinegar

¼ tsp / 1 mL **granulated sugar**

1 tbsp / 30 mL **soy sauce**

● Mix together 2 cups/500 mL water, salt, ginger and sugar; add fish and cure for 1½ hours. Drain; pat dry. Place capelin on tray in single layer; refrigerate, uncovered, for at least 2 or up to 8 hours.

● **Hot Mustard Dipping Sauce:** Mix mustard powder with 1 tbsp/15 mL cold water to make paste; let stand for 10 minutes. Stir in vinegar and sugar until sugar is dissolved. Transfer to small dipping sauce plate; stir in soy sauce.

● Soak 1 cup/250 mL wood chips in water for 1 hour. For gas barbecue, follow manufacturer's instructions or seal soaked chips in foil to make packet; poke several holes in top. Place over lit burner; close lid. For charcoal barbecue, place soaked chips directly on coals.

● Brush fish with oil. Grill, covered, over medium-high heat, turning once, until golden, 8 to 10 minutes. Serve with Hot Mustard Dipping Sauce.

Makes 4 to 6 servings.

TIP

Eat capelin bones and all – everything but the head.

PER EACH OF 6 SERVINGS: about 97 cal, 13 g pro, 4 g total fat (1 g sat. fat), 1 g carb, 0 g fibre, 50 mg chol, 855 mg sodium, 221 mg potassium. % RDI: 4% calcium, 6% iron, 1% vit A, 1% folate.

Spiced Catfish Fillets with Thai Mango Relish

Catfish takes to highly spiced preparations exceedingly well. To keep the fillets from breaking up, be sure your fish is fully grilled on one side before flipping it.

4 cloves **garlic**, pressed or minced

1 tbsp / 15 mL **lime juice**

1 tbsp / 15 mL **peanut** or vegetable **oil**

2 tsp / 10 mL finely grated **fresh ginger**

1½ tsp / 7 mL **black pepper**

½ tsp / 2 mL each **ground cumin**, **turmeric** and **salt**

¼ tsp / 1 mL **cayenne pepper**

¼ tsp / 1 mL **granulated sugar**

4 **catfish fillets**, 8 to 10 oz/250 to 300 g each

THAI MANGO RELISH:

1 hard half-ripe **mango**

¼ cup / 60 mL minced **red onion**

2 to 4 **Thai (bird-eye) chilies**, finely chopped

1 tbsp / 15 mL chopped **fresh coriander**

1 tbsp / 15 mL **palm sugar** or light brown sugar

1 tbsp / 15 mL **palm vinegar** or rice vinegar

1 tbsp / 15 mL **fish sauce**

1½ tsp / 7 mL each finely chopped **fresh Thai basil** and **mint**

● Mix together garlic, lime juice, oil, ginger, pepper, cumin, turmeric, salt, cayenne and sugar; rub all over fish. Let stand for 20 minutes or, refrigerated, up to 2 hours.

● **Thai Mango Relish:** Peel and pit mango; cut flesh into fine julienne or shred on coarse grater to make about 2 cups/500 mL. Toss together mango, onion, chilies, coriander, sugar, vinegar, fish sauce, basil and mint.

● Grill fish, covered, on greased grill over medium heat until bottoms are golden, about 7 minutes. Turn; grill until fish flakes easily, 3 to 5 minutes. Serve topped with some of the Thai Mango Relish; serve remainder on side.

Makes 4 servings.

PER SERVING: about 382 cal, 36 g pro, 19 g total fat (4 g sat. fat), 17 g carb, 2 g fibre, 120 mg chol, 792 mg sodium, 791 mg potassium. % RDI: 4% calcium, 18% iron, 25% vit A, 35% vit C, 14% folate.

Fish Grilled in Banana Leaves

Try this tasty preparation with catfish, tilapia, perch, snapper, pollock, kingfish or Spanish mackerel. Grilling fish in banana leaves keeps in all the juices and adds a distinctive smoky taste, complemented here with an aromatic spice paste.

5 to 10 **dried hot peppers**

1 stalk **fresh lemongrass** (or 1 tsp/5 mL grated lemon rind)

½ cup / 125 mL unsalted **roasted cashews**

1 **roasted sweet red pepper**, peeled and seeded

Half **onion**, coarsely chopped

4 cloves **garlic**

2 tbsp / 30 mL **lime** or lemon **juice**

1 tbsp / 15 mL **vegetable oil**

2 tsp / 10 mL chopped **fresh ginger**

2 tsp / 10 mL **fish sauce**

1 pkg (14 oz/397 g) **banana leaves**

4 **fish fillets**, 6 to 8 oz/175 to 250 g each

Lime wedges

● In skillet over medium heat, toast hot peppers until slightly darkened and fragrant, about 1 minute; grind to powder. Remove tough outer layer of lemongrass. Trim off and discard green and dried tops; mince stalk. In food processor, purée together hot pepper powder, lemongrass, cashews, red pepper, onion, garlic, lime juice, oil, ginger and fish sauce until fine paste.

● With moist towel, wipe banana leaves. Cut out central rib from each; cut into 4 pieces, about 14 x 10 inches/ 35 x 25 cm each. Over hot grill or heating element on stove, heat banana leaves, without charring or browning, until shiny and any natural white leaf mould disappears.

● Place 1 leaf square, shiny side down, on work surface, with point down like diamond; spoon one-eighth of the spice paste onto bottom half of leaf; cover with fish fillet. Spread another eighth of the spice paste over fish. Fold in bottom then sides; roll to enclose completely (if leaf cracks, cover with small piece of leftover leaf). Tear off strip of leftover leaf; tie around package.

● Grill packages over medium-high heat, turning once, until leaves are well browned, 14 to 16 minutes. To serve, cut open with scissors, corner to corner. Serve with lime.

Makes 4 servings.

TIP

Look for frozen banana leaves at Chinese, South and Southeast Asian, and Latin American stores. Always grill or steam them before wrapping food to make them stronger and more flexible.

PER SERVING: about 311 cal, 33 g pro, 16 g total fat (2 g sat. fat), 10 g carb, 2 g fibre, 78 mg chol, 381 mg sodium. % RDI: 3% calcium, 9% iron, 30% vit A, 58% vit C, 13% folate.

Lemongrass Barbecued Halibut Fillets

1 cup / 250 mL **coconut milk**

2 tbsp / 30 mL chopped **fresh lemongrass**

1 tbsp / 15 mL chopped **fresh coriander**

1 **shallot**, chopped

1 tbsp / 15 mL packed **brown sugar**

1 tbsp / 15 mL **lime juice**

1 tbsp / 15 mL **fish sauce**

¼ tsp / 1 mL **salt**

4 **halibut fillets**, about 5 oz/150 g each

8 heads **baby bok choy**

1 tbsp / 15 mL **vegetable oil**

● In blender, purée together coconut milk, lemongrass, coriander, shallot, brown sugar, lime juice, fish sauce and salt; rub half over fish. Refrigerate for at least 30 minutes or up to 2 hours.

● Cut each head of bok choy in half lengthwise; toss with oil.

● Grill halibut and bok choy on greased grill over medium heat, basting bok choy often with remaining coconut mixture and turning both once, until fish flakes easily and bok choy is wilted, about 8 minutes. Transfer to platter; spoon any remaining coconut mixture over fish and bok choy.

Make 4 servings.

PER SERVING: about 322 cal, 33 g pro, 18 g total fat (10 g sat. fat), 9 g carb, 2 g fibre, 45 mg chol, 972 mg sodium, 1,389 mg potassium. % RDI: 21% calcium, 34% iron, 74% vit A, 70% vit C, 41% folate.

Grilled Halibut with Oyster Mushrooms

You can use other white-fleshed fish or other mushrooms, such as wild chanterelles or black trumpets, or sliced cultivated mushrooms like king oyster, button or cremini.

8 oz / 250 g **oyster mushrooms**

2 cloves **garlic**, minced

2 tbsp / 30 mL chopped **fresh parsley**

2 tbsp / 30 mL chopped **fresh basil**

2 tbsp / 30 mL chopped **fresh chives**

2 tbsp / 30 mL **butter**

¼ cup / 60 mL **fish**, chicken or vegetable **stock**

1 tbsp / 15 mL **soy sauce**

2 tsp / 10 mL **lemon juice**

4 **halibut steaks**, about 6 oz/175 g each

2 tsp / 10 mL **vegetable oil**

¼ tsp / 1 mL each **salt** and **black pepper**

● Pull mushrooms apart into wide shreds; place on heavy-duty foil. Scatter garlic, parsley, basil and chives over top; dot with butter. Sprinkle with stock, soy sauce and lemon juice; seal to form packet.

● Brush fish with oil; sprinkle with salt and pepper. Grill mushroom packet and fish, covered, on greased grill over medium-high heat, turning fish once, until fish flakes easily, 8 to 10 minutes. To serve, spoon mushroom mixture over fish.

Makes 4 servings.

PER SERVING: about 276 cal, 37 g pro, 12 g total fat (4 g sat. fat), 3 g carb, 1 g fibre, 70 mg chol, 603 mg sodium. % RDI: 9% calcium, 17% iron, 15% vit A, 8% vit C, 14% folate.

Salt-Grilled Mackerel-Family Fish

Sprinkling fresh fish with salt, grilling it over hot coals and serving with citrus wedges or a simple dipping sauce (right) is one of the greatest pleasures of the grill. It's a common practice from Lisbon to Seoul, from Toronto to Santiago, from Manila to Melbourne. And, as far as we are concerned, few fish deserve this simple treatment more than the richly tasty mackerel and sardine families. Every type, from whole Atlantic mackerel to whole sardines from the Mediterranean region to whole pike mackerel from the eastern Pacific to whole horse mackerel from the Atlantic or Pacific, is wonderful. Equally good are kingfish steaks or Spanish mackerel cut into sections and slashed with diagonal cuts. If you love fish, try these; they're incredibly tasty, good for you, an ecologically sound choice and (except, perhaps, for kingfish) quite inexpensive.

Filipino Hot Pepper Dipping Sauce

● Mix together 2 tbsp/30 mL **palm**, cane or rice **vinegar**; 1 tbsp/15 mL chopped pickled or fresh **hot peppers**; 2 tsp/ 10 mL **fish sauce**; 2 tsp/10 mL **lime** or lemon **juice**; 1 tsp/5 mL minced **garlic**; and 1 tsp/5 mL coarsely ground **black pepper**.

Citrus Soy Dipping Sauce

● Mix together 4 tsp/20 mL **soy sauce**; 1 tbsp/15 mL **lemon juice**; and 1½ tsp/7 mL prepared **wasabi** or hot mustard. If desired, add pinch finely grated **lemon rind**.

Chinese Ginger Dipping Sauce

● Mix together 2 tbsp/30 mL red, aged or clear **rice vinegar**; 1 tbsp/15 mL finely julienned **fresh ginger**; and pinch **salt**.

Salt-Grilled Fish

1 lb / 500 g **whole fish**, cleaned, or steaks

1½ tsp / 7 mL **coarse sea salt**

Lemon or lime **wedges**, or dipping sauce (opposite)

● Sprinkle fish inside and out with salt (if using steaks, brush lightly with olive or vegetable oil, then sprinkle with salt). Grill, covered, on greased grill over medium-high heat, turning once, until fish flakes easily, 8 to 10 minutes per inch / 2.5 cm of thickness. Serve with lemon wedges or dipping sauce.

Makes 2 or 3 servings.

VARIATION

Mediterranean-Style Grilled Fish with Salt

This is especially good for whole grilled sardines or horse mackerel but is also tasty with red mullet or snapper, Mediterranean sea bass or porgy.

● Prepare as directed above, sprinkling fish with ½ tsp / 2 mL black pepper before grilling. To serve, drizzle with 2 to 3 tbsp / 30 to 45 mL extra-virgin olive oil; top with ⅓ cup / 75 mL sliced sweet onion, 2 tsp / 10 mL drained capers and sprinkle chopped fresh parsley. Garnish with whole black or green olives. Serve with lemon wedges.

PER EACH OF 3 SERVINGS: about 311 cal, 28 g pro, 21 g total fat (5 g sat. fat), 0 g carb, 0 g fibre, 89 mg chol, 872 mg sodium, 477 mg potassium. % RDI: 2% calcium, 14% iron, 6% vit A, 1% folate.

Portuguese Grilled Sardines with Potatoes & Peppers

Grilled sardines are beloved throughout the Mediterranean region but are especially emblematic of Portuguese cuisine.

1⅔ lb / 800 g fresh or thawed frozen **sardines**, cleaned

¾ tsp / 4 mL **salt**

½ tsp / 2 mL **black pepper**

1½ lb / 750 g **potatoes**, peeled

2 **sweet green peppers**

Half **sweet onion**, cut into rings

⅓ cup / 75 mL **olives**

2 tbsp / 30 mL chopped **fresh parsley**

¼ cup / 60 mL **extra-virgin olive oil**

1 tbsp / 15 mL **red wine vinegar**

Lemon wedges

● Sprinkle fish inside and out with pinch each of the salt and pepper. Let stand for 30 minutes.

● In saucepan of boiling salted water, cook potatoes until tender, about 20 minutes. Drain; keep warm.

● Meanwhile, grill green peppers, covered, over high heat, turning often, until charred all over. Let cool enough to handle. Peel, seed and cut into ¾-inch/2 cm wide strips. Place in large bowl.

● Grill fish, covered, in greased fish basket or on greased grill over high heat, turning once, until skin is golden and crisp, 6 to 12 minutes, depending on size. Arrange in centre of serving platter.

● Cut warm potatoes into chunks (or leave whole, if desired); add to peppers along with onion, olives and parsley. Whisk together oil, vinegar and remaining salt and pepper; toss with potato mixture until coated. Arrange around fish; garnish with lemon wedges.

Makes 4 servings.

Fresh sardines are hard to come by in Canada, but excellent individually quick frozen (IQF) ones, usually from Portugal and sold in inexpensive 800-gram packages, are easy to find. Look for them in grocery stores in or near Portuguese, Greek or Italian neighbourhoods.

PER SERVING: about 428 cal, 21 g pro, 24 g total fat (5 g sat. fat), 35 g carb, 4 g fibre, 103 mg chol, 1,058 mg sodium, 923 mg potassium. % RDI: 10% calcium, 17% iron, 4% vit A, 93% vit C, 16% folate.

Grilled Marinated Sardines

Boned and marinated, sardines can make an elegant starter or main course.

1⅔ lb / 800 g fresh or thawed frozen **sardines**

3 cloves **garlic**, pressed or minced

2 tbsp / 30 mL minced **fresh parsley**

2 tbsp / 30 mL **extra-virgin olive oil**

1 tbsp / 15 mL **lemon juice**

½ tsp / 2 mL **salt**

¼ tsp / 1 mL **black pepper**

Pinch **cayenne pepper**

● Under cold running water, scale sardines by running fingers up body from tail to head. With scissors, trim off top fin. Slit belly from tail to head; remove gills and innards. Slide finger down both sides of backbone to loosen; pull out backbone. With scissors, cut off tail and head; trim sides, removing any missed bones.

● Lay pieces flat, skin side down, on plate; sprinkle with garlic, parsley, oil, lemon juice, salt, pepper and cayenne. Refrigerate for at least 30 minutes or up to 4 hours.

● Grill, covered and skin side down, over high heat until skin is browned on bottom and fish just begins to flake, 5 to 7 minutes.

Makes 8 to 12 pieces.

PER EACH OF 12 PIECES: about 73 cal, 7 g pro, 5 g total fat (1 g sat. fat), trace carb, trace fibre, 37 mg chol, 134 mg sodium. % RDI: 3% calcium, 4% iron, 1% vit A, 2% vit C, 1% folate.

Tuna & Grilled Jalapeño Salsa

This salsa is also good with mahi-mahi (dolphin-fish), marlin and swordfish. Tuna should be rare or medium-rare, but other fish should be cooked until it flakes easily. Jalapeños vary widely in heat, so taste your peppers and adjust the amount. For milder salsa, mix in ½ cup/125 mL finely chopped grilled fresh or canned tomatillos.

6 **tuna steaks**, about 6 oz/175 g each

¾ tsp / 4 mL **salt**

Generous ¼ tsp / 1.5 mL **black pepper**

4 tsp / 20 mL **extra-virgin olive oil**

GRILLED JALAPEÑO SALSA:

1 **white onion**, halved

4 cloves **garlic** (unpeeled)

6 **jalapeño peppers**

⅓ cup / 75 mL finely chopped **fresh coriander**

3 tbsp / 45 mL **lime juice**

2 tbsp / 30 mL **extra-virgin olive oil**

½ tsp / 2 mL **salt**

½ tsp / 2 mL **ground cumin**

● **Grilled Jalapeño Salsa:** Grill onion, garlic and peppers, turning often, over medium-high heat until peppers are charred and onion and garlic are tender. Place peppers in bowl; cover and let cool. Let onion and garlic cool. Peel off and discard blackened outside layer of onion; finely chop onion and place in clean bowl. Peel and seed peppers; chop and add to onion. Peel garlic; with fork or side of knife, mash into paste and add to onion mixture. Mix in coriander, lime juice, oil, salt and cumin.

● Sprinkle fish all over with salt and pepper; brush with oil. Grill over high heat, turning once, until centre is still rare to medium-rare, 5 to 7 minutes, respectively, for 1-inch/2.5 cm thick steak. Serve with dollop of Grilled Jalapeño Salsa on top; serve remainder on side.

Makes 6 servings.

PER SERVING: about 338 cal, 40 g pro, 16 g total fat (3 g sat. fat), 6 g carb, 1 g fibre, 65 mg chol, 551 mg sodium. % RDI: 3% calcium, 16% iron, 102% vit A, 15% vit C, 9% folate.

Tuna Steaks with Mediterranean Tomato Relish

Grilled tuna should be eaten rare to medium like a good steak, so make sure your tuna steaks are the freshest possible. If you cook tuna all the way through, it can be quite dry.

4 **tuna steaks**, 6 oz/175 g each

1½ tbsp / 22 mL **extra-virgin olive oil**

¾ tsp / 4 mL each **salt** and **black pepper**

MEDITERRANEAN TOMATO RELISH:

¾ cup / 175 mL chopped **ripe tomatoes**

3 tbsp / 45 mL finely chopped **red onion**

2 tbsp / 30 mL chopped **olives**

2 tbsp / 30 mL finely sliced **caper berries** or 1½ tbsp/22 mL chopped drained capers

2 tbsp / 30 mL finely chopped **fresh parsley**

1 clove **garlic**, minced

2 tbsp / 30 mL **extra-virgin olive oil**

1½ tbsp / 22 mL **lemon juice**

1 tsp / 5 mL **red wine vinegar**

½ tsp / 2 mL **dried oregano**, crumbled

¼ tsp / 1 mL **hot pepper flakes**

¼ tsp / 1 mL **salt**

Pinch **black pepper**

● **Mediterranean Tomato Relish:** Mix together tomatoes, onion, olives, caper berries, parsley, garlic, oil, lemon juice, vinegar, oregano, hot pepper flakes, salt and pepper; let stand for 15 minutes.

● Brush both sides of fish with oil; sprinkle with salt and pepper. Grill over high heat, turning once, until centre is still rare to medium-rare, about 5 to 7 minutes, respectively, for 1-inch/2.5 cm thick steak. Serve topped with some of the Mediterranean Tomato Relish; serve remainder on side.

Makes 4 servings.

PER SERVING: about 367 cal, 40 g pro, 21 g total fat (4 g sat. fat), 4 g carb, 1 g fibre, 65 mg chol, 774 mg sodium, 549 mg potassium. % RDI: 3% calcium, 18% iron, 105% vit A, 15% vit C, 7% folate.

Cod in Grape Leaf Packets

Grape leaves add distinctive flavour and hold delicate fish together on the grill. You can make these packets, which are also perfect as hors d'oeuvres, with many other fish, such as haddock, pollock, sole, flounder, halibut, turbot or sablefish (black cod).

12 brined **grape leaves**

1 lb / 500 g **cod fillets**

⅓ cup / 75 mL chopped **fresh parsley**

⅓ cup / 75 mL chopped **fresh mint**

⅓ cup / 75 mL chopped **green onions**

⅓ cup / 75 mL **extra-virgin olive oil**

3 tbsp / 45 mL **lemon juice**

½ tsp / 2 mL **salt**

¼ tsp / 1 mL **black pepper**

8 thin **lemon wedges**

● Rinse grape leaves; soak in large bowl of cold water for 1 hour. Rinse; pat dry.

● Cut fish into twelve 2½- x 1- x 1-inch/6 x 2.5 x 2.5 cm pieces. Mix together parsley, mint, onions, all but 2 tbsp/30 mL of the oil, the lemon juice, salt and pepper. For each packet, place grape leaf, vein side up and stem closest, on work surface. Spoon 1 tsp/5 mL of the herb mixture onto bottom of leaf; cover with 1 piece of the fish then another 1 tsp/5 mL of the herb mixture. Fold leaf sides over and roll into secure package.

● Alternately with 2 lemon wedges, thread 3 packets crosswise onto 2 parallel skewers to hold firmly. Repeat with remaining packets and lemon wedges. Brush with remaining oil. Grill, covered, on greased grill over medium-high heat, turning once, for 15 minutes.

Makes 4 servings.

PER SERVING: about 265 cal, 22 g pro, 19 g total fat (3 g sat. fat), 4 g carb, 2 g fibre, 49 mg chol, 1,018 mg sodium. % RDI: 14% calcium, 58% iron, 14% vit A, 20% vit C, 10% folate.

Caribbean Snapper with Pepper Sauce

Striped bass, red mullet, porgy or rockfish are all good prepared this way.

1 **whole red** or white **snapper**, about 1¾ lb/875 g, cleaned

1½ tsp / 7 mL **salt**

½ cup / 125 mL **lime juice**

1 tbsp / 15 mL minced **Scotch bonnet (habanero)** or other hot pepper

1 **green onion**, finely chopped

2 cloves **garlic**, minced

3 tbsp / 45 mL **malt** or cider **vinegar**

4 tsp / 20 mL **grainy mustard**

● Cut 2 or 3 diagonal slashes into each side of fish. Rub 1 tsp/5 mL of the salt into slashes and over inside and outside of fish. Place in shallow glass dish; pour lime juice over top, turning fish to coat. Refrigerate for 30 minutes, turning once.

● Meanwhile, in small heatproof bowl, mix together Scotch bonnet pepper, green onion, garlic and remaining salt. In small saucepan, bring vinegar and 2 tbsp/30 mL water to boil; pour over hot pepper mixture. Stir in mustard.

● Drain fish; pat dry. Grill, covered, in greased fish basket or on greased grill over medium-high heat, turning once, until fish flakes easily, 20 to 25 minutes. Serve with pepper sauce.

Makes 4 servings.

401

Marinating the fish briefly in lime juice and salt is a Caribbean technique that rids it of any "fishy" taste and helps firm the flesh.

PER SERVING: about 210 cal, 41 g pro, 3 g total fat (1 g sat. fat), 2 g carb, trace fibre, 73 mg chol, 848 mg sodium. % RDI: 7% calcium, 4% iron, 7% vit A, 10% vit C, 4% folate.

Snapper with Green Salsa

Tomatillos add a slightly acidic flavour to the fresh salsa that livens up this smoky grilled red snapper. For a grilled salsa, grill whole fresh tomatillos until lightly charred on the outside before chopping; if desired, the jalapeño peppers can also be grilled until charred then peeled.

1 **whole red snapper**, about 2 lb/1 kg, cleaned

1 tsp / 5 mL **salt**

½ cup / 125 mL **lime juice**

GREEN SALSA:

1 cup / 250 mL chopped blanched or grilled fresh or drained canned **tomatillos** (see Tip, page 356)

2 **jalapeño peppers**, seeded and minced

½ cup / 125 mL minced **green onions** (white parts only)

¼ cup / 60 mL minced **fresh coriander**

2 tbsp / 30 mL **lime juice**

¼ tsp / 1 mL **granulated sugar**

¼ tsp / 1 mL **salt**

● Cut 2 or 3 diagonal slashes into each side of fish. Rub salt into slashes and over inside and outside of fish. Place in shallow glass dish; pour lime juice over top, turning fish to coat. Refrigerate, turning once, for 30 minutes.

● **Green Salsa:** Meanwhile mix together tomatillos, jalapeños, green onions, coriander, lime juice, sugar and salt.

● Drain fish; pat dry. Grill, covered, in greased fish basket or on greased grill over medium-high heat, turning once, until fish flakes easily, 20 to 25 minutes. Serve with Green Salsa.

Makes 4 servings.

PER SERVING: about 215 cal, 41 g pro, 3 g total fat (1 g sat. fat), 4 g carb, 1 g fibre, 72 mg chol, 475 mg sodium. % RDI: 7% calcium, 6% iron, 12% vit A, 37% vit C, 10% folate.

Spiced Grilled Red Snapper

Instead of red snapper, try white snapper, red mullet, striped bass, rockfish, porgy or even freshwater fish, such as whitefish or pickerel, for this West Indian—style recipe.

2 lb / 1 kg **whole red snapper**, cleaned

1 or 2 **Scotch bonnet (habanero) peppers**, seeded and minced

2 tbsp / 30 mL grated **onion**

2 tbsp / 30 mL **lime juice**

2 tbsp / 30 mL **orange juice**

2 tsp / 10 mL grated **fresh ginger**

1 tsp / 5 mL chopped **fresh thyme**

1 tsp / 5 mL **dried oregano**, crumbled

1 tsp / 5 mL **fennel seeds**

1 tsp / 5 mL **paprika**

1 tsp / 5 mL **salt**

½ tsp / 2 mL **turmeric**

¼ tsp / 1 mL **ground allspice**

¼ tsp / 1 mL **black pepper**

2 tbsp / 30 mL **vegetable oil**

● Cut 3 diagonal slashes into each side of fish(es). Mix together peppers, onion, lime and orange juices, ginger, thyme, oregano, fennel, paprika, salt, turmeric, allspice and pepper; rub into slashes and over inside and outside of fish. Refrigerate for 30 to 60 minutes.

● Brush fish with oil. Grill, covered, in greased fish basket or on greased grill over medium-high heat, turning once, until fish flakes easily, 12 to 25 minutes, depending on size of fish(es).

Makes 6 servings.

405

PER SERVING: about 183 cal, 28 g pro, 7 g total fat (1 g sat. fat), 2 g carb, 0 g fibre, 49 mg chol, 443 mg sodium. % RDI: 5% calcium, 4% iron, 6% vit A, 8% vit C, 5% folate.

Misoyaki

Misoyaki means "miso-grilled" and is a favourite Japanese method of grilling fish. The marinade gives the fish flavour and a lovely glazed exterior. This recipe is easiest with thick firm-fleshed fillets or steaks, such as halibut, wild salmon or swordfish.

⅔ cup / 150 mL **white** or red **miso**

¼ cup / 60 mL **sake**, dry sherry or Chinese rice wine

2 tender small inner stalks **celery** with leaves, finely chopped

1 tsp / 5 mL grated or julienned **fresh ginger**

4 **green onions**

4 **fish fillets** or steaks, about 6 oz/ 175 g each

Lemon wedges

● In blender, purée together miso, sake, celery, ginger and 1 tbsp/15 mL water, adding up to 1 tbsp/15 mL more water if necessary to keep ingredients moving.

● Place onions in glass or ceramic dish. Spread miso mixture evenly over fish fillets; place over onions. Refrigerate for at least 6 or up to 12 hours.

● Scrape marinade off fish and discard. Grill fish on greased grill over medium-high heat, turning once, until golden, 12 to 14 minutes. Serve with lemon wedges.

Makes 4 servings.

TIPS

● For authentic Japanese-style grilling, thread 2 pieces fish crosswise onto 2 long metal skewers; repeat with remaining 2 pieces. Place 2 bricks on grill, 10 to 12 inches/25 to 30 cm apart; place skewers on bricks so fish is suspended over grill. Grill over high heat, turning once, until golden, 12 to 14 minutes.

● Misoyaki is also excellent with softer, fattier fish, especially sablefish (black cod). Grill all softer fish on skewers.

PER SERVING: about 198 cal, 36 g pro, 4 g total fat (1 g sat. fat), 2 g carb, 0 g fibre, 54 mg chol, 260 mg sodium. % RDI: 8% calcium, 11% iron, 7% vit A, 5% vit C, 10% folate.

Turkish Grilled Lemon Fish

Called Izgara Balik, *this basic and quick dish shows off the Mediterranean flavours of lemon, garlic and olive oil.*

¼ cup / 60 mL minced **fresh parsley**

3 tbsp / 45 mL **olive oil**

2 cloves **garlic**, minced

1 tsp / 5 mL grated **lemon rind**

2 tbsp / 30 mL **lemon juice**

¼ tsp / 1 mL each **salt** and **black pepper**

1 lb / 500 g **fish steaks** or thick fillets

4 **lemon wedges**

● Mix together parsley, oil, garlic, lemon rind and juice, salt and pepper; add fish, turning to coat.

● Grill, covered, on greased grill over medium-high heat, turning once, until fish flakes easily, 8 to 10 minutes per inch/2.5 cm of thickness. Serve with lemon wedges.

Makes 4 servings.

PER SERVING: about 219 cal, 24 g pro, 13 g total fat (2 g sat. fat), 2 g carb, trace fibre, 36 mg chol, 206 mg sodium. % RDI: 6% calcium, 9% iron, 7% vit A, 8% vit C, 8% folate.

Chili Barbecued Shrimp

Think of these juicy shrimp as shrimp cocktail on the grill.

2 lb / 1 kg **extra jumbo raw shrimp** (about 32)

½ cup / 125 mL **tomato-based chili sauce**

1 tbsp / 15 mL packed **brown sugar**

2 tsp / 10 mL **cider vinegar**

1 tsp / 5 mL **hot pepper sauce**

¾ tsp / 4 mL **paprika**

1 clove **garlic**, minced

Lemon wedges

● Peel and devein shrimp, leaving tails intact. Thread lengthwise onto skewers, 1 shrimp per skewer.

● Mix together chili sauce, brown sugar, vinegar, hot pepper sauce, paprika and garlic; brush half over shrimp.

● Grill shrimp over medium-high heat, turning once, for 5 minutes. Brush with remaining sauce; grill, turning once, until opaque and glazed, 2 to 3 minutes. Serve with lemon wedges.

Makes 8 servings.

PER SERVING (WITHOUT LEMON WEDGES): about 116 cal, 18 g pro, 2 g total fat (trace sat. fat), 6 g carb, 1 g fibre, 129 mg chol, 358 mg sodium. % RDI: 5% calcium, 16% iron, 6% vit A, 7% vit C, 4% folate.

"Shrimp on the Barbi" with Chinese Dipping Sauce

The quintessential Australian grill dish, fresh shell-on shrimp are served plain, or with a squeeze of citrus, plain or flavoured butter, or a dipping sauce like this one.

1 lb / 500 g **large shell-on (head-on if possible) shrimp**, deveined (see Tip, below)

¼ tsp / 1 mL each **salt** and **black pepper**

CHINESE HOT PEPPER & SOY DIPPING SAUCE:

4 tsp / 20 mL **peanut** or vegetable **oil**

2 **red** or green **finger chilies**, thinly sliced on the diagonal

2 **green onions**, julienned

Pinch **salt**

2 tbsp / 30 mL **soy sauce**

2 tsp / 10 mL **sesame oil**

1 tsp / 5 mL **rice vinegar**

1 tbsp / 15 mL chopped **fresh coriander**

• **Chinese Hot Pepper & Soy Dipping Sauce:** In small skillet, heat peanut oil over medium-high heat; fry chilies, green onions and salt until wilted and fragrant, about 30 seconds. Scrape into heatproof bowl. Add soy sauce to skillet; bring to simmer. Stir into bowl along with sesame oil and vinegar; top with coriander.

• Sprinkle shrimp with salt and pepper. Grill over high heat until pink and opaque in centre, 3 to 5 minutes. Serve with Chinese Hot Pepper & Soy Dipping Sauce.

Makes 4 servings.

It's easy to devein shell-on shrimp. Bend shrimp into circle; into gap between shell pieces, one or two sections back from head, insert toothpick under vein. Pull out vein between shell pieces.

PER SERVING: about 135 cal, 18 g pro, 6 g total fat (1 g sat. fat), 2 g carb, trace fibre, 129 mg chol, 428 mg sodium, 190 mg potassium. % RDI: 4% calcium, 16% iron, 6% vit A, 10% vit C, 5% folate.

Kerala Grilled Shrimp

Kerala, the tropical southwestern province of India known for its lavishly spiced coconut-based cuisine, is the origin of these extremely tasty grilled shrimp.

1½ tsp / 7 mL **coriander seeds**

¾ tsp / 4 mL **black peppercorns**

4 whole **cloves**

1 tsp / 5 mL **aniseeds** or fennel seeds

¼ tsp / 1 mL **fenugreek seeds** (optional)

1 tsp / 5 mL **turmeric**

½ to 1 tsp / 2 to 5 mL **cayenne pepper**

¼ tsp / 1 mL **cinnamon**

Half **onion**, chopped

¼ cup / 60 mL finely grated **fresh coconut** (or unsweetened desiccated coconut)

3 cloves **garlic**, chopped

2 tsp / 10 mL chopped **fresh ginger**

½ tsp / 2 mL **salt**

1 lb / 500 g **large shrimp**, peeled and deveined

2 tbsp / 30 mL **butter**, melted

Lime wedges

● In small skillet over medium heat, toast coriander seeds for 1 minute. Add peppercorns and cloves; toast for 30 seconds. Add aniseeds, and fenugreek seeds (if using); toast for 30 seconds. Grind spices to fine powder; mix in turmeric, cayenne and cinnamon.

● In food processor, purée together onion, coconut, garlic, ginger and salt, adding up to 2 tbsp/30 mL water if necessary to form paste; transfer to bowl. Mix in spice mixture; toss with shrimp until coated. Marinate for 30 minutes or, refrigerated, up to 6 hours.

● Thread onto skewers; brush with butter. Grill on greased grill over medium heat, turning once, until pink and opaque, about 12 minutes. Serve with lime wedges.

Makes 6 servings.

PER SERVING: about 138 cal, 16 g pro, 7 g total fat (4 g sat. fat), 4 g carb, 1 g fibre, 125 mg chol, 345 mg sodium. % RDI: 3% calcium, 14% iron, 8% vit A, 5% vit C, 3% folate.

Grilled Shrimp with Corn & Black Bean Salad

1 lb / 500 g **jumbo shrimp**, peeled and deveined

1 tbsp / 15 mL **peanut** or vegetable **oil**

1 tbsp / 15 mL **lime juice**

1 tsp / 5 mL **soy sauce**

1 tsp / 5 mL **sesame oil**

½ tsp / 2 mL **black pepper**

2 cloves **garlic**, minced

CORN & BLACK BEAN SALAD:

3 **cobs of corn**, husked

1 can (19 oz/540 mL) **black beans**, drained and rinsed

1 **sweet red pepper**, diced

½ cup / 125 mL chopped **red onion**

½ cup / 125 mL **fresh coriander leaves**, coarsely chopped

3 tbsp / 45 mL **peanut** or vegetable **oil**

3 tbsp / 45 mL **lime juice**

½ tsp / 2 mL **salt**

½ tsp / 2 mL **ground cumin**

¼ tsp / 1 mL **black pepper**

1 head **Boston lettuce**, separated into leaves

● Toss together shrimp, oil, lime juice, soy sauce, sesame oil, pepper and garlic. Refrigerate for 1 hour.

● **Corn & Black Bean Salad:** Meanwhile, grill corn on greased grill over medium-high heat, turning occasionally, until kernels are tender, about 15 minutes. Slice kernels off cobs; toss together corn, black beans, red pepper, onion and coriander. Whisk together oil, lime juice, salt, cumin and pepper; toss with corn mixture until coated.

● Grill shrimp on greased grill over medium-high heat, turning once, until pink and opaque, about 6 minutes. Divide lettuce leaves among plates; top with salad then shrimp.

Makes 4 servings.

PER SERVING: about 438 cal, 29 g pro, 18 g total fat (2 g sat. fat), 45 g carb, 9 g fibre, 129 mg chol, 736 mg sodium. % RDI: 7% calcium, 33% iron, 21% vit A, 100% vit C, 95% folate.

Rosemary Grilled Scallops

4 thick sprigs **fresh rosemary**

12 **sea scallops**, about 1 lb/500 g

¼ cup / 60 mL **extra-virgin olive oil**

2 tbsp / 30 mL **lemon juice**

1 clove **garlic**

¼ tsp / 1 mL **salt**

¼ tsp / 1 mL **black pepper**

6 oz / 175 g small **potatoes**

2 small **Italian eggplants**, about 8 oz/250 g total

3 **banana peppers**

¼ cup / 60 mL **fresh parsley leaves**, chopped

● Remove leaves from rosemary, leaving about 1 inch/2.5 cm intact at tops of stems; chop enough of the removed leaves to make 1 tbsp/15 mL. Thread 3 scallops, through sides, onto each rosemary stem. Mix together chopped rosemary, oil, lemon juice, garlic, salt and pepper; brush 2 tbsp/30 mL over scallops. Refrigerate for 30 minutes.

● Meanwhile, slice larger or halve smaller potatoes. Cut eggplant into ¾-inch/2 cm thick slices. Toss together potatoes, eggplant, whole peppers and 2 tbsp/30 mL of the remaining oil mixture. Grill over medium heat, turning occasionally, until tender, 8 to 10 minutes for peppers and eggplant, about 15 minutes for potatoes.

● Seed and cut peppers into ½-inch/1 cm thick slices; toss together peppers, potatoes, eggplant, remaining oil mixture and parsley.

● Grill scallops on greased grill over high heat, turning once, until just turning opaque in centre, 3 to 4 minutes. Serve on grilled vegetables.

Makes 4 servings.

PER SERVING: about 276 cal, 21 g pro, 15 g total fat (2 g sat. fat), 15 g carb, 4 g fibre, 43 mg chol, 373 mg sodium, 765 mg potassium. % RDI: 11% calcium, 25% iron, 7% vit A, 57% vit C, 18% folate.

Grilled Stuffed Squid

Inspired by Spanish and Portuguese flavours, these grilled squid make an elegant first course or part of a seafood grill. If you prefer a bit of heat, use the hot banana pepper.

1 **green bell pepper** or large Cubanelle pepper

1 **hot banana pepper** (optional)

6 large **whole squid**, 1½ to 1¾ lb/ 750 to 875 g total

¼ cup / 60 mL **olive oil**

3 cups / 750 mL finely sliced **sweet** or white **onion**

1 **bay leaf**

¾ tsp / 4 mL (approx) **salt**

⅓ cup / 75 mL chopped **green olives**

1 clove **garlic**, minced

⅓ cup / 75 mL **dry white wine**

¼ cup / 60 mL chopped **fresh parsley**

¼ tsp / 1 mL **black pepper**

Lemon wedges

● Grill green pepper, and banana pepper (if using), over high heat until charred all over. Place in bowl; cover and let cool. Peel and seed peppers; cut into thin strips.

● To clean each squid, pull tentacle section off body. Remove plastic-like quill from body; rinse inside and out. Cut off innards, beak and eyes from base of tentacle portion; cut tentacle portions into 3 or 4 pieces each. (Pull off purplish skin from body if desired; it adds extra flavour if left on.) Set aside in refrigerator.

● In skillet, heat 2 tbsp/30 mL of the oil over medium heat; fry onion, bay leaf and pinch salt, stirring often, until onions are golden, 20 to 25 minutes. Add olives, garlic, squid tentacles, peppers and ½ tsp/2 mL of the remaining salt; fry until garlic is softened, about 2 minutes. Stir in wine; increase heat to high and cook until liquid is evaporated. Stir in half of the parsley. Let cool.

● Stuff each squid body half-full of onion mixture; secure open end with short skewer or toothpick. Mix together 1 tbsp/15 mL of the remaining oil, pepper and remaining ¼ tsp/1 mL salt; add squid, turning to coat.

● Grill on greased grill over high heat, turning once, until firm but tender, 3 to 5 minutes. Transfer to platter; sprinkle with remaining parsley and oil. Serve with lemon wedges.

Makes 6 servings.

PER SERVING: about 203 cal, 15 g pro, 12 g total fat (2 g sat. fat), 9 g carb, 1 g fibre, 206 mg chol, 447 mg sodium, 349 mg potassium. % RDI: 5% calcium, 9% iron, 4% vit A, 38% vit C, 10% folate.

Greek Grilled Squid

Who doesn't go to a good Greek restaurant and order grilled squid (calamari)? Why not enjoy it more often at home? It's easy — and inexpensive to boot.

4 large **whole squid**, 1 to 1¼ lb/500 to 625 g total

5 tbsp / 75 mL **extra-virgin olive oil**

2 cloves **garlic**, minced

1 tsp / 5 mL **dried (preferably Greek) oregano**

½ tsp / 2 mL **hot pepper flakes**

½ tsp / 2 mL + pinch **salt**

¼ tsp / 1 mL + pinch **black pepper**

2 **hot banana peppers**

1 or 2 **ripe tomatoes**, sliced

Half **field cucumber** or quarter English cucumber, sliced

12 **black olives**

2 tbsp / 30 mL **lemon juice**

2 tbsp / 30 mL chopped **fresh parsley**

● To clean each squid, pull tentacle section off body. Remove plastic-like quill from body; rinse inside and out. Cut off innards, beak and eyes from base of tentacle portion. (Pull off purplish skin from body if desired; it adds extra flavour if left on.)

● At scant ½-inch/1 cm intervals, slice squid bodies crosswise three-quarters of the way through. Toss together squid bodies and tentacles, 3 tbsp/45 mL of the oil, garlic, oregano, hot pepper flakes, ½ tsp/2 mL of the salt and ¼ tsp/1 mL of the pepper until coated. Let stand for 30 to 60 minutes.

● Meanwhile, grill peppers over high heat, turning often, until charred all over. Place in bowl; cover and let cool. Peel peppers; arrange on platter along with tomatoes and cucumbers.

● Grill squid over high heat, turning often, until opaque and lightly browned, about 5 minutes. Transfer to platter; scatter olives over top. Sprinkle with remaining salt and pepper. Drizzle with remaining oil and lemon juice; sprinkle with parsley.

Makes 4 servings.

VARIATION

Buffet-Style Grilled Squid Salad

Prepare as directed, but dice grilled peppers, tomatoes and cucumber; slice grilled squid into rings. In bowl, toss with other ingredients then transfer to serving plate.

Makes 8 servings.

PER SERVING: about 270 cal, 15 g pro, 20 g total fat (3 g sat. fat), 9 g carb, 2 g fibre, 206 mg chol, 450 mg sodium, 443 mg potassium. % RDI: 6% calcium, 13% iron, 8% vit A, 50% vit C, 9% folate.

Vietnamese Squid Salad

Heady seafood salads full of fresh herbs and piqued with chilies, tart citrus and fish sauce are a hallmark of Vietnamese and other Southeast Asian cuisines. Cut all the salad ingredients into very fine julienne for the best result.

1 lb / 500 g cleaned **squid** (tubes and tentacles)

1 clove **garlic**, minced

1 **Thai (bird-eye) chili**, minced

1 tbsp / 15 mL **fish sauce**

2 tsp / 10 mL minced **fresh lemongrass**

1 tsp / 5 mL finely grated **fresh ginger**

¼ tsp / 1 mL **black pepper**

Dressing for Squid Salad (right)

¼ cup / 60 mL chopped **fresh coriander**

¼ cup / 60 mL chopped **fresh mint** and/or Thai basil

1 tbsp / 15 mL ground **roasted peanuts**

1 tbsp / 15 mL **crispy fried shallots**

1 tsp / 5 mL **crispy fried sliced garlic**

SALAD:

¼ cup / 60 mL finely julienned hard semi-ripe **mango**

¼ cup / 60 mL finely sliced **sweet onion**

¼ cup / 60 mL finely julienned **cucumber**

2 tbsp / 30 mL each finely julienned **sweet red**, **yellow** and **green peppers**

2 tbsp / 30 mL finely julienned **carrot**

2 or 3 **red hot finger peppers** or Thai (bird-eye) chilies, finely sliced

● Mix together squid tubes and tentacles, garlic, chili, fish sauce, lemongrass, ginger and pepper. Let stand for 10 to 20 minutes.

● **Salad:** Meanwhile, in large bowl, toss together mango, onion, cucumber, sweet peppers, carrot and hot peppers.

● Grill squid on greased grill over high heat, turning often, until opaque and lightly browned, about 5 minutes. Cut tubes into rings; cut tentacles into 2 or 3 pieces each. Add Salad; toss with Squid Salad Dressing. Toss in coriander and mint; transfer to platter. Sprinkle with peanuts, shallots and garlic.

Makes 6 servings.

Dressing for Squid Salad

● Mix together 3 tbsp/45 mL **lime juice**, 1 tbsp/15 mL **fish sauce**, 2 tsp/10 mL **palm** or rice **vinegar**, and 1½ tsp/7 mL **palm** or granulated **sugar** until sugar is dissolved.

TIP

You can buy crispy fried shallots and garlic in Asian markets or make them yourself: fry thinly sliced shallots or garlic in hot oil until golden; drain on paper towels.

PER SERVING: about 88 cal, 10 g pro, 2 g total fat (trace sat. fat), 8 g carb, 1 g fibre, 137 mg chol, 502 mg sodium, 271 mg potassium. % RDI: 4% calcium, 9% iron, 11% vit A, 42% vit C, 8% folate.

Grilled Octopus

From Portugal to Greece and, indeed, wherever it is found in Asia, octopus is considered a delicacy. Its meat is tender and sweet when cooked, with a taste somewhere between those of lobster and squid.

1 **onion**, quartered

1¾ tsp / 9 mL **salt**

1 tsp / 5 mL **black peppercorns**

2 **bay leaves**

3 lb / 1.5 kg fresh or thawed frozen **octopus**

3 tbsp / 45 mL **extra-virgin olive oil**

½ tsp / 2 mL **dried oregano**

Pinch **black pepper**

1 tbsp / 15 mL finely chopped **fresh parsley**

Sliced **tomato** and/or **cucumber** (optional)

Olives

Lemon wedges

● In large saucepan, bring 6 cups/1.5 L water, onion, 1½ tsp/7 mL of the salt, peppercorns and bay leaves to boil; add octopus and return to boil. Reduce heat; simmer, covered, over low heat until tender, 1½ to 2 hours for fresh, 1 to 1¼ hours for thawed. Drain; let cool. (Refrigerate for up to 1 day.)

● Separate head from tentacles; cut off and discard beak in centre where tentacles join. Cut into large pieces. Toss together octopus, 1 tbsp/15 mL of the oil, oregano, pepper and remaining salt.

● Grill on greased grill over high heat, turning once, until hot and edges are crispy, 4 to 6 minutes. Transfer to platter; drizzle with remaining oil and sprinkle with parsley. Serve with tomatoes and/or cucumber (if using), olives and lemon wedges.

Makes 6 servings.

Imported fresh octopus is occasionally available from fishmongers (particularly Portuguese, Italian or Greek), but frozen is also good and considerably lower in price. It's widely available in large grocery chains and ethnic Mediterranean and Asian markets.

PER SERVING: about 246 cal, 34 g pro, 9 g total fat (1 g sat. fat), 5 g carb, trace fibre, 109 mg chol, 618 mg sodium, 720 mg potassium. % RDI: 11% calcium, 79% iron, 10% vit A, 17% vit C, 13% folate.

Baby Octopus with Cherry Tomatoes

Baby octopus can be grilled directly without boiling first. Look for thawed or frozen baby octopus at Mediterranean or Chinese fishmongers or grocery stores.

1 lb / 500 g **baby octopus** (4 to 8, depending on size)

3 tbsp / 45 mL **extra-virgin olive oil**

2 cups / 500 mL **cherry tomatoes**, halved

3 tbsp / 45 mL torn **fresh basil leaves**

2 tbsp / 30 mL pitted **black olives**, sliced

1 tbsp / 15 mL drained **capers**, chopped

1 clove **garlic**, minced

1 tsp / 5 mL **hot pepper flakes**

½ tsp / 2 mL **salt**

¼ tsp / 1 mL **black pepper**

● If octopus are large, cut in half; toss octopus with 1 tbsp/15 mL of the oil.

● Toss together cherry tomatoes, 2 tbsp/30 mL of the basil, olives, capers, garlic, hot pepper flakes, salt, pepper and remaining oil. Place tomato mixture on heavy-duty foil; seal to form packet.

● Grill tomato packet over medium-high heat for 10 minutes. Meanwhile, grill octopus, turning often, until tentacles curl and become crispy, about 6 minutes. Serve octopus over tomatoes; top with remaining basil.

Makes 4 servings.

PER SERVING: about 205 cal, 18 g pro, 12 g total fat (2 g sat. fat), 7 g carb, 1 g fibre, 54 mg chol, 653 mg sodium, 558 mg potassium. % RDI: 7% calcium, 43% iron, 14% vit A, 23% vit C, 10% folate.

424

From top: Buttered Clams on the
Grill (page 427), Grilled Oysters
with Black Bean Sauce (page 426)

CANA

Grilled Oysters with Black Bean Sauce

A favourite Cantonese dish is oysters steamed with a dollop of garlicky black bean sauce on top, but we think these spicy grilled oysters might even be better!

1 tbsp / 15 mL **sesame oil**

2 tbsp / 30 mL minced **shallots**

1 clove **garlic**, minced

2 tbsp / 30 mL **chili black bean sauce** or black bean and garlic sauce

1 tsp / 5 mL **Chinese rice wine** or dry sherry

½ tsp / 2 mL **granulated sugar**

½ tsp / 2 mL **Chinese black vinegar** or balsamic vinegar

2 tbsp / 30 mL chopped **fresh coriander**

1 **green onion**, thinly sliced

12 **fresh oysters**

● In small saucepan, heat oil over medium-low heat; fry shallots and garlic until softened and fragrant, 2 to 3 minutes. Stir in black bean sauce, wine, sugar and vinegar; simmer for 2 minutes. Let cool. Stir in coriander and green onion.

● Shuck oysters, discarding top shell and keeping as much liquid in bottom shell as possible; spoon about ½ tsp/2 mL bean sauce onto each. Grill over high heat until juices are bubbling.

Makes 12 oysters.

Photo, page 425

PER OYSTER: about 27 cal, 1 g pro, 1 g total fat (trace sat. fat), 3 g carb, trace fibre, 3 mg chol, 56 mg sodium, 38 mg potassium. % RDI: 1% calcium, 7% iron, 2% vit C, 1% folate.

Buttered Clams on the Grill

Serve these simply delicious clams with some sliced baguette to soak up any clam juice and seasoned butter.

¼ cup / 60 mL **butter**

2 tbsp / 30 mL **lemon juice**

1 clove **garlic**, pressed or minced

2 tbsp / 30 mL chopped **fresh parsley**

1 lb / 500 g **littleneck** or small cherrystone **clams** (about 12)

● Mix together butter, lemon juice and garlic; microwave on high until butter is melted (or melt in small skillet). Stir in parsley.

● Grill clams, covered, over high heat until they open, about 8 minutes. Carefully, without spilling clam liquor in bottom shells, transfer to platter. Spoon some of the butter mixture into each.

Makes 4 servings.

Photo, page 424

PER SERVING: about 97 cal, 2 g pro, 9 g total fat (6 g sat. fat), 1 g carb, trace fibre, 30 mg chol, 77 mg sodium, 73 mg potassium. % RDI: 1% calcium, 18% iron, 11% vit A, 8% vit C, 2% folate.

Vegetables & Cheese

Grilled Corn on the Cob with Ancho Chili Glaze

Steamed or boiled **cobs of corn**

Peanut or vegetable **oil**

ANCHO CHILI SAUCE:

2 tbsp / 30 mL **ancho chili powder**

1½ tbsp / 22 mL **peanut** or vegetable **oil**

3 cloves **garlic**, pressed or minced

½ tsp / 2 mL **ground cumin**

2 tbsp / 30 mL packed **dark brown sugar**

2 tbsp / 30 mL **dark soy sauce**

2 tbsp / 30 mL **ketchup**

1½ tbsp / 22 mL **cider vinegar**

● **Ancho Chili Sauce:** Mix chili powder with 3 tbsp/ 45 mL water to make paste; let stand for 10 minutes. In small saucepan over medium heat, cook chili paste, oil, garlic and cumin until fragrant, 2 to 3 minutes. Stir in sugar, soy sauce, ketchup, vinegar and ⅓ cup/ 75 mL water; bring to boil. Reduce heat and simmer until very thick, about 10 minutes. Let cool.

● Lightly brush corn with oil; grill over medium-high heat until hot and grill-marked, 3 to 4 minutes. Brush with Ancho Chili Sauce; grill, turning, for 1 minute.

Makes about ½ cup/125 mL sauce, enough for 12 cobs of corn.

PER 2 TSP/10 mL SAUCE, ENOUGH FOR 1 COB OF CORN: about 29 cal, 0 g pro, 1 g total fat (0 g sat. fat), 4 g carb, 0 g fibre, 0 mg chol, 219 mg sodium. % RDI: 1% calcium, 3% iron, 5% vit A, 2% vit C, 1% folate.

Left to right: Spiced Olive
Oil & Butter, Basil Butter

Corn Butters & Sauces

Instead of plain butter and salt, dress up grilled cobs of corn with one of these butter, mayonnaise or olive oil toppings, then salt to taste.

- **Basil Butter:** ¼ cup/60 mL softened **butter**; 2 tbsp/30 mL grated **Parmesan cheese**; 1 clove **garlic**, minced; and 1 tbsp/15 mL minced **fresh basil**

- **Spiced Olive Oil & Butter:** 2 tbsp/30 mL **extra-virgin olive oil**; 2 tbsp/30 mL softened **butter**; 1 tbsp/15 mL minced **fresh coriander**; 1 tsp/5 mL **curry paste**; and ½ tsp/2 mL **lemon juice**

- **Provençal Butter:** ¼ cup/60 mL softened **butter**; 1 tbsp/15 mL **Dijon mustard**; and ¾ tsp/4 mL **herbes de Provence**

- **Lemon Butter:** ¼ cup/60 mL softened **butter**; ½ tsp/2 mL grated **lemon rind**; 1 tbsp/15 mL **lemon juice**; and ½ tsp/2 mL **black pepper**

- **Smoky Orange Mayonnaise:** ¼ cup/60 mL **mayonnaise**; 2 tsp/10 mL **barbecue sauce**; and 1 tsp/5 mL each chopped **canned chipotle pepper** and grated **orange rind**

- **Lemon Pepper Mayonnaise:** ¼ cup/60 mL **mayonnaise**; 1 tsp/5 mL each grated **lemon rind** and **lemon juice**; ½ tsp/2 mL **black pepper**; and ¼ tsp/1 mL **white pepper**

- **Mediterranean Olive Oil:** 3 tbsp/45 mL **extra-virgin olive oil**; 4 tsp/20 mL minced drained **oil-packed sun-dried tomatoes**; ½ tsp/2 mL **dried thyme**; and pinch **black pepper**

Each makes enough for about 6 cobs of corn.

TIP

Grill husked cobs over medium heat for 15 to 20 minutes; or soak unhusked cobs in water for 20 minutes, then grill for 15 to 20 minutes.

Chat Masala for Grilled Corn

Anyone who has walked through a South Asian shopping district in summertime has experienced the wonderful fragrance (and flavour) of Indian-style grilled corn on the cob, seasoned with the distinctive spice mix chat *(or* chaat*)* masala. *Make a jar and keep it all summer for parties or anytime you grill sweet local corn.*

434

1½ tbsp / 22 mL **coarse salt**

3 tbsp / 45 mL **coriander seeds**

5 tsp / 25 mL **cumin seeds**

2 tsp / 10 mL **fennel seeds**

1 tsp / 5 mL **black peppercorns**

8 whole **cloves**

4 tsp / 20 mL **amchur** (green mango powder)

1 tbsp / 15 mL **black salt** (or table salt)

1 tbsp / 15 mL **paprika**

1½ tsp / 7 mL **cayenne pepper**

½ tsp / 2 mL **ground ginger**

¼ tsp / 1 mL **nutmeg**

¼ tsp / 1 mL **asafetida** (or 1 tsp/5 mL garlic powder)

● In skillet over medium heat, toast coarse salt until sand-coloured; transfer to bowl to cool. One at a time, in skillet over medium-low heat, toast coriander, cumin, fennel, peppercorns and cloves until fragrant and slightly darkened, 1 to 3 minutes; add to bowl and let cool. Grind until fine powder; stir in amchur, black salt, paprika, cayenne, ginger, nutmeg and asafetida.

● To use, rub cut side of lime half all over corn to moisten; sprinkle with Chat Masala to taste.

Makes enough for about 50 cobs of corn.

TIP

It's worth the jaunt to the Indian grocer to pick up a few specialized spices, namely the distinctive, slightly sulfurous black salt; dried green mango powder, or *amchur* (also spelled *amchor* or *amchoor*), for tartness; and asafetida (*hing*) for this ground resin's distinctive garlic-like flavour. You also can buy prepared chat masala at Indian grocers, but it won't be as fresh and fragrant as your own; it's used for sprinkling over corn, fruit, nuts and many other snack foods.

One Potato, Two Potato

Lemon Grilled Potatoes

4 large **red potatoes**, scrubbed and cut into 8 wedges each

2 tbsp / 30 mL **olive oil**

2 tsp / 10 mL grated **lemon rind**

½ tsp / 2 mL **salt**

¼ tsp / 1 mL **black pepper**

• Toss together potatoes, oil, lemon rind, salt and pepper until coated.

• Reserving any oil mixture, grill potatoes, covered, on greased grill over medium-high heat, turning halfway through and brushing with oil mixture, until golden and tender, about 25 minutes.

Makes 4 servings.

PER SERVING: about 190 cal, 3 g pro, 7 g total fat (1 g sat. fat), 30 g carb, 3 g fibre, 0 mg chol, 296 mg sodium. % RDI: 1% calcium, 12% iron, 28% vit C, 6% folate.

Olive Oil Potatoes

24 small **new potatoes**

2 tbsp / 30 mL **olive oil**

¼ tsp / 1 mL **smoked** or sweet **paprika**

¼ tsp / 1 mL **salt**

• In saucepan of boiling salted water, cover and cook potatoes until almost tender, about 15 minutes. Drain; let cool. Thread onto skewers.

• Place on greased grill over medium-high heat; brush with some of the oil. Grill, covered and brushing often with remaining oil, until hot and skins are crisp, 10 to 15 minutes. Sprinkle with paprika and salt before serving.

Makes 6 to 8 servings.

PER EACH OF 8 SERVINGS: about 111 cal, 2 g pro, 3 g total fat (trace sat. fat), 19 g carb, 2 g fibre, 0 mg chol, 298 mg sodium. % RDI: 1% calcium, 6% iron, 20% vit C, 4% folate.

Salt & Pepper Potato Packets

3 lb / 1.5 kg small **potatoes**, peeled (optional) and halved

2 to 3 tbsp / 30 to 45 mL **olive oil** or butter, diced

½ tsp / 2 mL **salt**

¼ tsp / 1 mL **black pepper**

● Place potatoes on heavy-duty foil; sprinkle with oil (use 3 tbsp/45 mL for peeled potatoes), salt and pepper; seal to form packet. Grill over medium-high heat for 10 minutes; turn and cut 1 or 2 vents in top. Grill until tender, about 8 minutes.

Makes 8 servings.

PER SERVING: about 158 cal, 3 g pro, 4 g total fat (trace sat. fat), 29 g carb, 3 g fibre, 0 mg chol, 157 mg sodium. % RDI: 2% calcium, 11% iron, 22% vit C, 18% folate.

Rosemary Onion Potato Fans

4 **baking (russet) potatoes**

1 **onion**, thinly sliced

2 tbsp / 30 mL **olive oil**

1 tbsp / 15 mL **fresh rosemary leaves**

½ tsp / 2 mL each **salt** and **black pepper**

● Scrub potatoes; slice each almost all the way through at ¼-inch/5 mm intervals. Insert onion slice into each slit.

● Place each potato on heavy-duty foil. Drizzle with oil; sprinkle with rosemary, salt and pepper. Seal to form packets. Grill, covered, over medium heat, turning occasionally, until tender, about 1 hour.

Makes 4 servings.

PER SERVING: about 233 cal, 5 g pro, 7 g total fat (1 g sat. fat), 40 g carb, 4 g fibre, 0 mg chol, 305 mg sodium. % RDI: 3% calcium, 15% iron, 1% vit A, 28% vit C, 24% folate.

Grilled Green Onions

Cooking onions sweetens them and eliminates their harshness.

2 bunches **green onions**

1 tbsp / 15 mL **peanut** or vegetable **oil**

1 tbsp / 15 mL **soy sauce**

½ tsp / 2 mL **sesame oil**

¼ tsp / 1 mL **hot pepper sauce**

● Trim root ends off onions; cut off any wilted ends of tops. In bowl, toss onions with peanut oil. Grill, covered, on greased grill over medium-high heat, turning once, until lightly browned and tender, about 4 minutes.

● Toss together grilled onions, soy sauce, sesame oil and hot pepper sauce until coated.

Makes 4 servings.

VARIATIONS

Grilled Asparagus

Use 1 lb/500 g thin asparagus spears instead of onions; grill for about 6 minutes.

Grilled Carrots

Use 6 carrots, quartered lengthwise, or 16 thin carrots instead of onions; grill for about 10 minutes.

PER SERVING: about 54 cal, 1 g pro, 4 g total fat (trace sat. fat), 4 g carb, 1 g fibre, 0 mg chol, 268 mg sodium. % RDI: 4% calcium, 6% iron, 2% vit A, 10% vit C, 10% folate.

Grilled Eggplant & Garlic

2 **eggplants**, about 2½ lb/1.25 kg

2 whole heads **garlic**

⅓ cup / 75 mL minced **fresh coriander**, parsley or mint

½ tsp / 2 mL **salt**

¼ tsp / 1 mL **black pepper**

3 tbsp / 45 mL **lemon juice**

¼ cup / 60 mL **extra-virgin olive oil**

● Prick eggplants with fork a few times. Grill eggplant and garlic, covered, over medium-high heat, turning often, until eggplant is soft when thickest part is pierced and garlic cloves are tender, about 40 minutes. Let cool.

● Peel eggplant; halve lengthwise. In colander, let drain for 15 minutes. Cut into bite-size pieces; place on serving plate. Cut off tops of garlic and squeeze out cloves; scatter over eggplant. Sprinkle with coriander, salt and pepper; drizzle with lemon juice then oil.

Makes 4 to 6 servings.

439

PER EACH OF 6 SERVINGS: about 141 cal, 2 g pro, 9 g total fat (1 g sat. fat), 14 g carb, 4 g fibre, 0 mg chol, 200 mg sodium.
% RDI: 3% calcium, 6% iron, 1% vit A, 12% vit C, 10% folate.

Grilling Vegetables

● Brush **vegetable** with **olive** or vegetable **oil**; sprinkle with **salt** and **black pepper**. Grill on greased grill, on skewers or in grill basket or wok.

● Grill, covered if desired, over medium heat for time specified in chart or until lightly browned and tender-crisp to tender.

Vegetable	Prep/Size	Cooking Time
Asparagus	Snap off tough woody ends	10 minutes, turning often
Belgian endive	Halve lengthwise	15 to 20 minutes, turning once
Carrots	Lengthwise ¼-inch/5 mm strips	15 minutes, turning once
Corn on the cob	Husk; or leave in husk and soak in water (do not oil)	15 to 20 minutes, turning often
Eggplant	¼-inch/5 mm thick slices	10 minutes, turning once
Fennel bulb	Lengthwise ¼-inch/5 mm slices	15 minutes, turning once
Green onions	Trim	5 minutes, turning often
Mushrooms	Whole (1½ inches/4 cm or larger)	10 minutes, turning once
New potatoes	Whole small or ¼-inch/5 mm slices	15 to 20 minutes, turning once
Onions	Crosswise ½-inch/1 cm slices	15 minutes, turning once
Portobello mushrooms	Remove stems	10 minutes, turning once
Radicchio	Halve or quarter if large	10 minutes, turning once
Squash	Crosswise ¼-inch/5 mm slices	15 minutes, turning once
Sweet peppers	Quarter	10 minutes, turning once
Sweet potatoes	¼-inch/5 mm slices	15 minutes, turning once
Tomatoes	Halves or ½-inch/1 cm slices	5 minutes, turning once
Cherry tomatoes	Skewer	5 minutes, turning often
Zucchini	1½-inch/4 cm chunks or lengthwise ¼-inch/5 mm strips	10 minutes, turning once

Balsamic Grilled Vegetables

Grilled and lightly dressed summer vegetables are equally delicious served warm or at room temperature.

1 small **red onion**, cut into ½-inch/1 cm thick slices

4 **sweet peppers**, cut into 1-inch/2.5 cm wide strips

2 **zucchini**, cut lengthwise into ¼-inch/ 5 mm thick strips

BALSAMIC DRESSING:

⅓ cup / 75 mL **extra-virgin olive oil**

3 tbsp / 45 mL **white balsamic** or balsamic **vinegar**

1 tsp / 5 mL minced **fresh oregano** or ½ tsp/2 mL dried, crumbled

½ tsp / 2 mL each **salt** and **black pepper**

● **Balsamic Dressing:** Whisk together oil, vinegar, oregano, salt and pepper.

● Skewer onion slices through edges to keep rings intact. Toss half of the Balsamic Dressing with peppers and zucchini; brush some of the remainder over onions. Let stand for 10 minutes.

● Grill, covered, on greased grill over medium-high heat, turning once, until tender and grill-marked, 10 to 15 minutes. Transfer to platter, peeling skins off peppers, if desired; drizzle with remaining Balsamic Dressing.

Makes 6 servings.

441

PER SERVING: about 154 cal, 1 g pro, 12 g total fat (2 g sat. fat), 11 g carb, 2 g fibre, 0 mg chol, 197 mg sodium. % RDI: 2% calcium, 6% iron, 21% vit A, 210% vit C, 12% folate.

Grilled Radicchio

2 heads **radicchio**

3 tbsp / 45 mL **extra-virgin olive oil**

½ tsp / 2 mL **coarse sea salt**

¼ tsp / 1 mL **black pepper**

1 tbsp / 15 mL **balsamic vinegar**

● Leaving core intact, cut radicchio in half (cut large heads into quarters); thread onto skewers. Brush with half of the oil; sprinkle with half each of the salt and pepper.

● Grill, covered, on greased grill over medium-high heat, turning often, until wilted and lightly browned and centre is softened, about 10 minutes. Transfer to platter; drizzle with vinegar and remaining oil; sprinkle with remaining salt and pepper.

Makes 4 servings.

VARIATION

Grilled Radicchio Salad

Cut, skewer and grill radicchio as directed. Brush with 4 tsp/20 mL olive oil; grill as directed. Cut out core; thinly slice. In serving bowl, whisk together 2 tbsp/ 30 mL extra-virgin olive oil; 1 tbsp/15 mL sherry vinegar or wine vinegar; 1 clove garlic, minced; ½ tsp/2 mL Dijon mustard; and pinch granulated sugar. Add radicchio, tossing to coat. Sprinkle with 2 tbsp/30 mL shaved Parmesan cheese.

PER SERVING: about 113 cal, 1 g pro, 10 g total fat (1 g sat. fat), 5 g carb, 1 g fibre, 0 mg chol, 307 mg sodium. % RDI: 2% calcium, 5% iron, 10% vit C, 16% folate.

Oyster Mushrooms & Peppers

Grilling oyster mushrooms crisps their edges and intensifies their woodsy flavour. If you like, try this with portobellos or shiitake caps or halved large button mushrooms. Shepherd peppers are a richly flavoured seasonal alternative to red bell peppers.

1 lb / 500 g **oyster mushrooms**

3 **sweet red peppers**, quartered

⅓ cup / 75 mL **extra-virgin olive oil**

⅓ cup / 75 mL chopped **fresh basil**

2 tbsp / 30 mL **balsamic vinegar**

1 clove **garlic**, minced

½ tsp / 2 mL **salt**

¼ tsp / 1 mL **black pepper**

● Toss together mushrooms, peppers and ¼ cup/60 mL of the oil. Grill, covered, on greased grill over medium-high heat, turning once, until tender and browned, about 8 minutes for mushrooms, 12 minutes for peppers. Transfer to platter.

● Mix together remaining oil, basil, vinegar, garlic, salt and pepper; drizzle over vegetables.

Makes 6 servings.

PER SERVING: about 143 cal, 2 g pro, 12 g total fat (2 g sat. fat), 8 g carb, 2 g fibre, 0 mg chol, 194 mg sodium. % RDI: 1% calcium, 9% iron, 22% vit A, 167% vit C, 9% folate.

Grilled Asparagus with Fines Herbes Sauce

2 lb / 1 kg **asparagus**, trimmed

1 tbsp / 15 mL **olive** or vegetable **oil**

¼ tsp / 1 mL **salt**

FINES HERBES SAUCE:

1 **egg yolk**

2 tbsp / 30 mL **lemon juice**

1 tbsp / 15 mL **white wine vinegar**

1 small clove **garlic**, minced

1 tsp / 5 mL **Dijon mustard**

Pinch each **salt** and **black pepper**

½ cup / 125 mL **extra-virgin olive oil**

1 tbsp / 15 mL each chopped **fresh chives**, **tarragon**, and **chervil** or parsley

● **Fines Herbes Sauce:** In heatproof bowl set over saucepan of gently simmering water, whisk together egg yolk, lemon juice and vinegar until slightly thickened, about 2 minutes. Remove from heat; whisk in garlic, mustard, salt and pepper. Whisking constantly, drizzle in olive oil, a few drops at a time, until thick and opaque. Whisk in chives, tarragon and chervil. (Place wrap directly on surface; refrigerate for up to 1 day.)

● Toss together asparagus, oil and salt. Grill, covered, on greased grill over medium-high heat, turning occasionally, until tender-crisp, about 6 minutes. Transfer to platter; spoon Fines Herbes Sauce over grilled asparagus.

Makes 8 servings.

PER SERVING: about 104 cal, 3 g pro, 9 g total fat (1 g sat. fat), 4 g carb, 1 g fibre, 25 mg chol, 90 mg sodium. % RDI: 2% calcium, 6% iron, 6% vit A, 18% vit C, 55% folate.

Barbecued Stuffed Tomato (opposite),
grilled chicken breast with Argentine
Chimichurri Verde (page 531)

Barbecued Stuffed Tomatoes

Juicy grilled tomatoes are a robust side dish for grilled meat, poultry or fish, but they make a scrumptious component of a vegetarian meal, too.

4 **tomatoes**

1 cup / 250 mL **small croutons**

½ cup / 125 mL grated **Parmesan cheese**

¼ cup / 60 mL chopped **fresh parsley** or basil

2 cloves **garlic**, minced

1 tbsp / 15 mL **olive oil**

¼ tsp / 1 mL each **salt** and **black pepper**

● Cut off top of each tomato; scoop out and chop pulp, discarding seeds. Mix together pulp, croutons, Parmesan cheese, parsley, garlic, oil, salt and pepper; stuff into tomatoes.

● Place tomatoes in metal or foil cake pan; grill, covered, over medium-high heat until tender and stuffing is golden, about 20 minutes.

Makes 4 servings.

TIP

To make small croutons, cut bread into ½-inch/ 1 cm cubes; toss with just enough olive oil to coat. Sprinkle with salt and black pepper; spread on rimmed baking sheet. Bake in 400°F/200°C oven, turning once, until golden, 8 to 10 minutes.

PER SERVING: about 167 cal, 8 g pro, 9 g total fat (3 g sat. fat), 14 g carb, 3 g fibre, 10 mg chol, 514 mg sodium. % RDI: 18% calcium, 11% iron, 21% vit A, 42% vit C, 9% folate.

Pattypan Skewers

Look for pattypan squashes that are no more than 2 inches/5 cm wide to ensure tenderness.

3 tbsp / 45 mL **extra-virgin olive oil**

1 tbsp / 15 mL **balsamic vinegar**

1 clove **garlic**, minced

¼ tsp / 1 mL each **salt** and **black pepper**

18 mini **pattypan squash**, about 1 lb/ 500 g

4 tsp / 20 mL finely chopped drained **oil-packed sun-dried tomatoes**

1 tbsp / 15 mL minced **fresh parsley**

● Whisk together oil, vinegar, garlic, salt and pepper; add squash, tossing to coat. Thread onto skewers, reserving remaining marinade.

● Grill, covered, on greased grill over medium-high heat, turning occasionally, until tender, 8 to 10 minutes. Transfer to platter.

● Add tomatoes and parsley to reserved marinade; drizzle over squash.

Makes 4 to 6 servings.

PER EACH OF 6 SERVINGS: about 17 cal, trace pro, 7 g total fat (1 g sat. fat), 4 g carb, 1 g fibre, 0 mg chol, 102 mg sodium. % RDI: 2% calcium, 4% iron, 3% vit A, 12% vit C, 8% folate.

Vegetable Packets

The easiest way to cook small or cut-up vegetables on the grill is in a foil packet. You won't have to worry about anything burning or falling through the grate, and you can flavour your favourites as desired. Get started with any of our combinations, then improvise.

● Cut long piece of heavy-duty foil; mound **Vegetables** (right) on 1 side. Drizzle with 1 tbsp/15 mL **butter**, melted, or extra-virgin olive oil. Sprinkle with 1 tbsp/15 mL chopped **fresh herbs** (or ¼ tsp/1 mL dried) and ¼ tsp/1 mL each **salt** and **black pepper**. Seal to form packet.

● Grill, covered, over medium-high heat, turning once, until tender (see Time, right). To serve, shake gently to distribute seasonings. Drizzle with 1 tbsp/15 mL **lemon juice**, if desired.

Makes 4 servings.

VEGETABLES	TIME (MINUTES)
1 lb/500 g asparagus	10
2 lb/1 kg mini new potatoes, halved	18
12 oz/375 g green beans, trimmed, and 1 cup/250 mL sliced mushrooms	12
4 cups/1 L mini-carrots and 1 onion, sliced	15
4 cups/1 L broccoli florets and half sweet red pepper, chopped	9

Grilled Tofu &
Vegetable Antipasto

1 pkg (425 g) **firm tofu**

4 **portobello mushrooms**

4 **green onions**, trimmed

2 **zucchini**, cut in half lengthwise

1 each **sweet red** and **yellow pepper**, quartered

3 tbsp / 45 mL **extra-virgin olive oil**

1 tbsp / 15 mL chopped **fresh basil**

½ tsp / 2 mL each **salt** and **black pepper**

BALSAMIC VINAIGRETTE:

3 tbsp / 45 mL **extra-virgin olive oil**

2 tbsp / 30 mL **balsamic vinegar**

1 clove **garlic**, minced

¼ tsp / 1 mL each **salt** and **black pepper**

● **Balsamic Vinaigrette:** Mix together oil, vinegar, garlic, salt and pepper.

● Drain tofu on paper towels; cut in half lengthwise. Trim stems off mushrooms; place caps in large bowl along with onions, zucchini and red and yellow peppers.

● Whisk together oil, basil, salt and pepper; brush 1 tbsp/15 mL over tofu. Add remainder to vegetables; toss to coat.

● Grill zucchini, red and yellow peppers, green onions and tofu, covered, on greased grill over medium-high heat for 5 minutes. Turn vegetables and tofu; add mushrooms to grill. Grill, covered, turning mushrooms once, until vegetables are tender-crisp and tofu and mushrooms are browned, about 5 minutes.

● Cut tofu into bite-size pieces; place on large platter. Cut zucchini diagonally into ½-inch/1 cm thick slices; add to platter. Thinly slice mushrooms; add to platter. Arrange green onions and red and yellow peppers alongside. Drizzle with Balsamic Vinaigrette.

Makes 4 servings.

PER SERVING: about 320 cal, 11 g pro, 25 g total fat (3 g sat. fat), 17 g carb, 4 g fibre, 0 mg chol, 448 mg sodium. % RDI: 19% calcium, 21% iron, 14% vit A, 163% vit C, 34% folate.

Cider-Glazed Apples & Onion

Grilling fruits and vegetables caramelizes their natural sweetness. Apples and onions are a natural accompaniment to grilled pork.

2 tbsp / 30 mL **cider vinegar**

2 tsp / 10 mL packed **brown sugar**

2 tsp / 10 mL **Dijon mustard**

¼ tsp / 1 mL each **salt** and **black pepper**

2 **apples**, cored and cut into ½-inch/ 1 cm thick slices

1 **sweet onion**, cut into ½-inch/1 cm thick slices

● Whisk together vinegar, sugar, mustard, salt and pepper; brush half over tops of apples and onion.

● Place, mustard side down, on greased grill over medium-high heat; brush with remaining mustard mixture. Grill, covered, turning once, until golden and tender, about 10 minutes.

Makes 4 servings.

PER SERVING: about 91 cal, 1 g pro, 1 g total fat (trace sat. fat), 22 g carb, 3 g fibre, 0 mg chol, 180 mg sodium. % RDI: 3% calcium, 4% iron, 12% vit C, 6% folate.

Grilled Pineapple

Don't worry about coring the pineapple for this recipe — just eat around it. Grilled pineapple is good with highly spiced or tart grills, especially chicken, pork or fish.

2 tbsp / 30 mL **vegetable oil**

¼ tsp / 1 mL each **salt** and **black pepper**

¼ tsp / 1 mL **hot pepper sauce**

1 **pineapple**, peeled and cut into ½-inch/1 cm thick slices

2 tbsp / 30 mL chopped **fresh coriander**

● Mix together oil, salt, pepper and hot pepper sauce; brush half over 1 side of each pineapple slice. Place, oiled side down, on greased grill over medium heat; brush with remaining oil mixture. Grill, covered, turning once, until browned, about 4 minutes.

● Transfer to platter; sprinkle with coriander.

Makes 8 servings.

455

PER SERVING: about 79 cal, trace pro, 3 g total fat (trace sat. fat), 13 g carb, 1 g fibre, 0 mg chol, 66 mg sodium. % RDI: 1% calcium, 3% iron, 20% vit C, 3% folate.

Grilled Mozzarella Skewers with Anchovy Sauce

Fresh mozzarella grilled to a perfect barely oozing consistency between slices of crispy grilled bread — heavenly!

Ten ¼-inch/1 cm thick slices **baguette**

4 balls **bocconcini** cheese, about 4 oz/125 g total, halved

ANCHOVY SAUCE:

2 tbsp / 30 mL **butter**

2 tbsp / 30 mL **olive oil**

2 **anchovy fillets**, finely chopped

1 tbsp / 15 mL finely chopped **fresh parsley**

1 tbsp / 15 mL drained **capers**, finely chopped

2 tsp / 10 mL **lemon juice**

● **Anchovy Sauce:** In small saucepan over medium heat, cook butter, oil, anchovies, parsley, capers and lemon juice until butter is melted, about 2 minutes.

● Alternately thread bread and cheese onto 2 long skewers, beginning and ending with bread.

● Grill over high heat, turning often, until bread is toasted and cheese just begins to melt, 4 to 5 minutes. Transfer to serving plate; drizzle with Anchovy Sauce.

Makes 2 servings.

PER SERVING: about 505 cal, 19 g pro, 40 g total fat (18 g sat. fat), 19 g carb, 1 g fibre, 83 mg chol, 830 mg sodium, 127 mg potassium. % RDI: 38% calcium, 10% iron, 23% vit A, 5% vit C, 15% folate.

Provoleta

Grilled cheese with Chimichurri Sauce is a specialty of Argentine grilling. Provolone comes in large, long cylinders, so have one thick slice cut to order at the cheese counter.

8 oz / 250 g thick slice **provolone cheese**

1 tsp / 5 mL **olive oil**

1 tsp / 5 mL **dried oregano**

CHIMICHURRI SAUCE:

½ cup / 125 mL chopped **fresh parsley**

⅓ cup / 75 mL **olive oil**

2 cloves **garlic**, chopped

2 **shallots**, coarsely chopped

2 tbsp / 30 mL chopped **fresh oregano**

2 tbsp / 30 mL **lemon juice**

2 tbsp / 30 mL **sherry vinegar**

½ tsp / 2 mL each **salt** and **black pepper**

● **Chimichurri Sauce:** In food processor, pulse together parsley, oil, garlic, shallots, oregano, lemon juice, vinegar, salt and pepper until finely chopped.

● Brush cheese all over with oil; sprinkle with oregano. Grill over medium heat, turning once, until cheese is hot, soft and not quite melting, about 4 minutes. Transfer to plate; drizzle with Chimichurri Sauce.

Makes 4 servings.

PER SERVING: about 404 cal, 17 g pro, 36 g total fat (13 g sat. fat), 5 g carb, 1 g fibre, 43 mg chol, 842 mg sodium, 183 mg potassium. % RDI: 46% calcium, 11% iron, 23% vit A, 22% vit C, 10% folate.

Halloumi with Fresh Chilies

Because of its firm texture, salty halloumi cheese stands up to grilling heat. Anointed with fragrant oil and flavourings, it makes a piquant Eastern Mediterranean appetizer.

8 oz / 250 g **halloumi cheese**, cut into eight scant ¼-inch/5 mm thick slices

2 tbsp / 30 mL **olive oil**

1 tbsp / 15 mL thinly sliced **red hot pepper**

1 tsp / 5 mL minced **fresh coriander**

1 tsp / 5 mL minced **fresh mint**

- Grill cheese on greased grill over medium-high heat, turning once, until hot and grill-marked, about 2 minutes.

- Transfer to serving dish. Drizzle with oil; sprinkle with hot pepper, coriander and mint.

Makes 4 servings.

459

PER SERVING: about 269 cal, 13 g pro, 23 g total fat (11 g sat. fat), 2 g carb, trace fibre, 63 mg chol, 751 mg sodium, 10 mg potassium. % RDI: 31% calcium, 1% iron, 21% vit A, 5% vit C.

Grilled Pizza

Grilled Corn Pizza

Grilling pizza is becoming ever more popular. It makes especially good sense when some of the other ingredients are grilled, too, such as the corn and onion here.

1 **cob of corn**

Half **red onion**, thickly sliced

1 to 1⅓ lb / 500 to 680 g **pizza dough**

2 tsp / 10 mL **olive oil**

1½ cups / 375 mL shredded **provolone** or mozzarella **cheese**

2 **plum tomatoes**, about 6 oz/175 g, thinly sliced

PESTO:

½ cup / 125 mL packed **fresh basil leaves**

2 tbsp / 30 mL grated **Parmesan cheese**

¼ tsp / 1 mL **salt**

2 tbsp / 30 mL **olive oil**

1 clove **garlic**, minced

● Husk corn. Grill, covered, on greased grill over medium-high heat, turning occasionally, for 5 minutes. Skewer onion through edges to keep rings intact; add to grill. Grill, covered and turning occasionally, until onion and corn kernels are tender, about 10 minutes. Slice kernels off cob to make ¾ cup/175 mL. Chop onion; set aside corn and onion separately.

● **Pesto:** In food processor, finely chop together basil, Parmesan cheese and salt; with motor running, drizzle oil through feed tube in steady stream until smooth and thickened. Stir in garlic.

● On lightly floured surface, stretch dough to roughly 16- x 12-inch/40 x 30 cm rectangle. Brush with oil. Grill, oiled side down, over medium heat until bubbles form on top and grill marked underneath without charring, 3 to 6 minutes. Turn; grill, covered, just until surface is cooked but not browned, about 1 minute. Remove from grill.

● Spread Pesto over grilled side of crust. Sprinkle with half of the cheese; arrange tomatoes, onion and corn over top. Sprinkle with remaining cheese. Grill, covered, until cheese is melted and bubbly and underside is browned, 3 to 8 minutes.

Makes 8 slices.

Before putting pizza dough down on the grill, make sure your barbecue is fully preheated. If dough forms large bubbles while cooking, pop them to flatten.

PER SLICE: about 294 cal, 12 g pro, 13 g total fat (5 g sat. fat), 35 g carb, 2 g fibre, 19 mg chol, 565 mg sodium. % RDI: 20% calcium, 12% iron, 10% vit A, 9% vit C, 15% folate.

Smoked Salmon Pizza
with Marinated Onion

This fresh and elegant pizza is great to serve for brunch or cut into squares
as an appetizer.

½ cup / 125 mL **sour cream**

2 tbsp / 30 mL chopped **fresh dill**

1 tsp / 5 mL **lemon juice**

Pinch each **salt** and **black pepper**

1 to 1⅓ lb / 500 to 680 g **pizza dough**

2 tsp / 10 mL **olive oil**

7 oz / 200 g thinly sliced **cold-smoked salmon**

2 tsp / 10 mL drained **capers** (optional)

MARINATED ONION:

⅓ cup / 75 mL **white wine vinegar**

1 tbsp / 15 mL **granulated sugar**

½ tsp / 1 mL **salt**

1 large **red onion**, halved and thinly sliced

● **Marinated Onion:** In small saucepan, bring vinegar, ⅓ cup/75 mL water, sugar and salt to boil, stirring until sugar is dissolved. In heatproof bowl, pour over onion; let stand for 30 minutes, stirring occasionally. Cover and refrigerate for at least 4 hours or up to 1 week. Drain before using.

● Mix together sour cream, half of the dill, the lemon juice, salt and pepper; set aside in refrigerator.

● On lightly floured surface, stretch dough to roughly 16- x 12-inch/40 x 30 cm rectangle. Brush with oil. Grill, oiled side down, over medium heat until bubbles form on top and grill marked underneath without charring, 3 to 6 minutes. Turn; grill, covered, until bubbly and underside is browned, 3 to 5 minutes. Remove from grill.

● Spread sour cream mixture over crust; top with salmon, then ½ cup/125 mL drained Marinated Onion (save remainder for another use). Sprinkle with remaining dill, and capers (if using).

Makes 8 slices.

465

PER SLICE: about 221 cal, 9 g pro, 8 g total fat (3 g sat. fat), 28 g carb, 2 g fibre, 12 mg chol, 500 mg sodium, 156 mg potassium. % RDI: 7% calcium, 14% iron, 2% vit A, 2% vit C, 25% folate.

Grilled Vegetable & Feta Pizza

1 **zucchini**, cut lengthwise into 4 slices

5 thick slices (½ inch /1 cm) **eggplant**

Half **sweet red pepper**

3 tbsp / 45 mL **olive oil**

¼ tsp / 1 mL each **salt** and **black pepper**

1 to 1⅓ lb / 500 to 680 g **whole wheat pizza dough**

½ cup / 125 mL **Tomato Pizza Sauce** (below)

1 cup / 250 mL crumbled **feta cheese**

¼ cup / 60 mL coarsely chopped **Kalamata olives**

● Brush zucchini, eggplant and red pepper with 2 tbsp/30 mL of the oil; sprinkle with salt and pepper. Grill, covered, on greased grill over medium-high heat, turning once, until tender, 6 to 10 minutes. Cut into 2-inch/5 cm pieces.

● On lightly floured surface, stretch dough to roughly 16- x 12-inch/40 x 30 cm rectangle. Brush with remaining oil. Grill, oiled side down, over medium heat until bubbles form on top and grill marked underneath without charring, 3 to 6 minutes. Turn; grill, covered, just until surface is cooked but not browned, 1 minute. Remove from grill; reduce heat to medium-low.

● Spread Tomato Pizza Sauce over grilled side of crust; top with zucchini, eggplant and pepper. Sprinkle with feta and olives. Grill, covered, until cheese is melted and bubbly and underside is browned, 3 to 8 minutes.

Makes 8 slices.

Tomato Pizza Sauce

1 can (28 oz/796 mL) **plum tomatoes**

2 tbsp / 30 mL **extra-virgin olive oil**

½ cup / 125 mL finely chopped **onion**

2 cloves **garlic**, minced

½ tsp / 2 mL **dried oregano**

½ tsp / 2 mL **red wine vinegar**

¼ tsp / 1 mL each **salt** and **black pepper**

Pinch **granulated sugar**

● Reserving juice, drain, seed and chop tomatoes. In saucepan, heat oil over medium heat; fry onion, garlic and oregano, stirring occasionally, until onion is translucent, about 4 minutes.

● Add tomatoes and reserved juice, vinegar, salt, pepper and sugar; simmer until thickened, 15 to 20 minutes. Let cool slightly. In food processor, purée until smooth.

Makes 2 cups/500 mL.

PER SLICE: about 260 cal, 9 g pro, 13 g total fat (4 g sat. fat), 33 g carb, 6 g fibre, 17 mg chol, 810 mg sodium, 157 mg potassium. % RDI: 12% calcium, 14% iron, 8% vit A, 28% vit C, 7% folate.

Barbecued Chicken Pizza

1 **boneless skinless chicken breast**

1 tbsp / 15 mL **vegetable oil**

Pinch each **salt** and **black pepper**

2 tbsp / 30 mL **barbecue sauce**

1 to 1⅓ lb / 500 to 680 g **whole wheat pizza dough**

½ cup / 125 mL **Tomato Pizza Sauce** (opposite)

1¼ cups / 300 mL shredded **Cheddar** or Monterey Jack **cheese**

⅓ cup / 75 mL diced **sweet red pepper**

⅓ cup / 75 mL thinly sliced **green onions**

● Brush chicken with 1 tsp/5 mL of the oil; sprinkle with salt and pepper. Grill, covered, on greased grill over medium-high heat, turning once, until no longer pink inside, about 12 minutes. Let cool enough to handle; thinly slice. Toss with barbecue sauce.

● On lightly floured surface, stretch dough to roughly 16- x 12-inch/40 x 30 cm rectangle. Brush with remaining oil. Grill, oiled side down, over medium heat until bubbles form on top and grill marked underneath without charring, 3 to 6 minutes. Turn; grill, covered, just until surface is cooked but not browned, about 1 minute. Remove from grill; reduce heat to medium-low.

● Spread Tomato Pizza Sauce over grilled side of crust; top with half of the cheese. Sprinkle with red pepper, onions and chicken mixture; top with remaining cheese. Grill, covered, until cheese is melted and bubbly and underside is browned, 3 to 8 minutes.

Makes 8 slices.

PER SLICE: about 253 cal, 14 g pro, 11 g total fat (4 g sat. fat), 30 g carb, 5 g fibre, 26 mg chol, 525 mg sodium, 139 mg potassium. % RDI: 15% calcium, 13% iron, 7% vit A, 23% vit C, 4% folate.

Grilled Steak & Gorgonzola Pizza

6 oz / 175 g **beef grilling steak**

¼ tsp / 1 mL each **salt** and **black pepper**

1 small **red onion**, cut into ½-inch/1 cm thick slices

1 tbsp / 15 mL **vegetable oil**

1 to 1⅓ lb / 500 to 680 g **pizza dough**

3 oz / 90 g thinly sliced or crumbled **Gorgonzola cheese**

½ cup / 125 mL packed **arugula leaves**

SUN-DRIED TOMATO PESTO:

¼ cup / 60 mL **dry-packed sun-dried tomatoes**

2 tbsp / 30 mL **pine nuts**

1½ tbsp / 22 mL **tomato paste**

Pinch each **salt** and **black pepper**

2½ tbsp / 37 mL **extra-virgin olive oil**

2 tbsp / 30 mL grated **Parmesan cheese**

Half clove **garlic**, minced

● **Sun-Dried Tomato Pesto:** In heatproof bowl, pour ½ cup/125 mL boiling water over tomatoes; soak until softened, 10 minutes. Reserving 2 tbsp/30 mL soaking liquid, drain. Meanwhile, in dry skillet, toast pine nuts over medium heat, shaking often, until light golden, 3 to 5 minutes. Let cool. In food processor, finely chop together tomatoes, soaking liquid, pine nuts, tomato paste, salt and pepper; with motor running, drizzle oil through feed tube in thin steady stream until smooth and thickened. Pulse in Parmesan cheese and garlic.

● Sprinkle steak with half each of the salt and pepper. Grill, covered, on greased grill over medium-high heat, turning once, until medium-rare, about 8 minutes. Let stand for 5 minutes; slice thinly.

● Meanwhile, brush onion with 1 tsp/5 mL of the oil; sprinkle with remaining salt and pepper. Skewer through edges to keep rings intact. Grill, covered and turning once, until softened, about 5 minutes. Chop coarsely.

● On lightly floured surface, stretch dough to roughly 16- x 12-inch/40 x 30 cm rectangle. Brush with remaining oil. Grill, oiled side down, over medium heat until bubbles form on top and grill marked underneath without charring, 3 to 6 minutes. Turn; grill, covered, just until surface is cooked but not browned, 1 minute. Remove from grill; reduce heat to medium-low.

● Spread pesto over crust; top with onion, steak and cheese. Grill, covered, until cheese is melted and underside is browned, 3 to 8 minutes. Top with arugula.

Makes 8 slices.

PER SLICE: about 321 cal, 12 g pro, 17 g total fat (5 g sat. fat), 30 g carb, 2 g fibre, 22 mg chol, 593 mg sodium, 283 mg potassium. % RDI: 14% calcium, 19% iron, 5% vit A, 3% vit C, 29% folate.

Caprese Pizza with Bacon

6 slices **bacon**, halved

4 oz / 125 g **fresh mozzarella cheese**, drained well

1 to 1⅓ lb / 500 to 680 g **pizza dough**

2 tsp / 10 mL **extra-virgin olive oil**

1 **tomato**, cut into ¼-inch/5 mm thick slices

2 tbsp / 30 mL sliced **fresh basil**

BASIL PESTO:

2 tbsp / 30 mL **pine nuts**

1 cup / 250 mL packed **fresh basil leaves**

Pinch each **salt** and **black pepper**

2½ tbsp / 37 mL **extra-virgin olive oil**

¼ cup / 60 mL grated **Parmesan cheese**

Half clove **garlic**, minced

● **Basil Pesto:** In dry small skillet, toast pine nuts over medium heat, shaking often, until light golden, 3 to 5 minutes. Let cool. In food processor, finely chop together pine nuts, basil, salt and pepper; with motor running, drizzle oil through feed tube in thin steady stream until smooth and thickened. Pulse in Parmesan cheese and garlic.

● In skillet, cook bacon over medium heat until still slightly chewy, about 8 minutes. Drain on paper towel–lined plate. Pat mozzarella dry; cut into ¼-inch/5 mm thick rounds. Drain on separate paper towel–lined plate; pat dry.

● On lightly floured surface, stretch dough to roughly 16- x 12-inch/40 x 30 cm rectangle. Brush with oil. Grill, oiled side down, over medium heat until bubbles form on top and grill marked underneath without charring, 3 to 6 minutes. Turn; grill, covered, just until surface is cooked but not browned, about 1 minute. Remove from grill; reduce heat to medium-low.

● Spread Basil Pesto over grilled side of crust; top with tomato, bacon and cheese. Grill, covered, until cheese is melted and bubbly and underside is browned, 3 to 8 minutes. Sprinkle with basil.

Makes 8 slices.

PER SLICE: about 301 cal, 11 g pro, 17 g total fat (5 g sat. fat), 27 g carb, 2 g fibre, 20 mg chol, 520 mg sodium, 187 mg potassium. % RDI: 17% calcium, 15% iron, 7% vit A, 5% vit C, 25% folate.

Sausage & Grilled Pepper Pizza

This simple grilled pepper sauce can be used as the base for many other kinds of pizza — use your imagination and experiment.

2 **sweet red peppers**

2 **Italian sausages**, about 8 oz/250 g

2 cloves **garlic**, smashed

3 tbsp / 45 mL **extra-virgin olive oil**

½ tsp / 2 mL **salt**

1 to 1⅓ lb / 500 to 680 g **pizza dough**

1 **green hot pepper**, thinly sliced (or half green sweet pepper, chopped)

¾ cup / 175 mL grated **Romano** or other pecorino **cheese**

● Grill peppers and sausages over high heat, turning often, until pepper is charred all over and sausage is firm and almost cooked through. Place peppers in bowl; cover and let cool. Peel and seed peppers. Let sausage cool; slice thinly.

● In food processor, purée together grilled peppers, garlic, 2 tbsp/30 mL of the oil and salt.

● On lightly floured surface, stretch dough to roughly 16- x 12-inch/40 x 30 cm rectangle. Brush with remaining oil. Grill, oiled side down, over medium heat until bubbles form on top and grill marked underneath without charring, 3 to 6 minutes. Turn; grill, covered, just until surface is cooked but not browned, about 1 minute. Remove from grill; reduce heat to medium-low.

● Spread pepper sauce over grilled side of crust; top with sausage, hot pepper and cheese. Grill, covered, until cheese is melted and underside is browned, 3 to 8 minutes.

Makes 8 slices.

PER SLICE: about 428 cal, 15 g pro, 18 g total fat (6 g sat. fat), 52 g carb, 2 g fibre, 30 mg chol, 1,001 mg sodium. % RDI: 14% calcium, 21% iron, 14% vit A, 88% vit C, 17% folate.

Salads & Sides

Tangy Coleslaw

This pleasingly tart coleslaw, made without mayonnaise and with just a touch of oil, is a good accompaniment to most grilled foods.

8 cups / 2 L shredded **cabbage**

1¼ tsp / 6 mL **salt**

1 **sweet red pepper**, thinly sliced

Half **red onion**, thinly sliced

1 tbsp / 15 mL chopped **fresh dill** (or 1 tsp/5 mL dried dillweed)

¼ cup / 60 mL **red wine vinegar**

1 tbsp / 15 mL **granulated sugar**

1 tbsp / 15 mL **vegetable oil**

1 tsp / 5 mL **dry mustard**

¾ tsp / 4 mL **celery seeds**

¼ tsp / 1 mL **black pepper**

● Toss cabbage with 1 tsp/5 mL of the salt. In separate bowl, toss red pepper with remaining salt. Let both stand until cabbage is soft, 1 to 2 hours. Drain cabbage; squeeze out excess moisture. In large bowl, toss together drained cabbage, undrained red pepper, onion and dill.

● Whisk together vinegar, sugar, oil, mustard, celery seeds and pepper; toss with cabbage mixture until coated. Let stand for at least 20 minutes or, refrigerated, up to 4 days.

Makes 8 servings.

PER SERVING: about 55 cal, 1 g pro, 2 g total fat (trace sat. fat), 9 g carb, 2 g fibre, 0 mg chol, 372 mg sodium. % RDI: 4% calcium, 5% iron, 9% vit A, 105% vit C, 22% folate.

Creamy Coleslaw

6 cups / 1.5 L finely shredded **cabbage**

4 **green onions**, thinly sliced

2 stalks **celery**, thinly sliced

1 large **carrot**, finely diced

Half **fennel bulb**, thinly sliced

Half **sweet red pepper**, thinly sliced

⅓ cup / 75 mL **mayonnaise**

⅓ cup / 75 mL **light sour cream**

1 tbsp / 15 mL **Dijon mustard**

1 tbsp / 15 mL **cider vinegar**

2 tsp / 10 mL **granulated sugar**

½ tsp / 2 mL **celery seeds**

½ tsp / 2 mL each **salt** and **black pepper**

● In large bowl, toss together cabbage, green onions, celery, carrot, fennel and red pepper. Mix together mayonnaise, sour cream, mustard, vinegar, sugar, celery seeds, salt and pepper; toss with cabbage mixture until coated. Let stand for at least 20 minutes or, refrigerated, up to 4 days.

Makes 8 servings.

When making coleslaw, for ease of preparation, use a mandoline to slice the hard vegetables paper-thin.

PER SERVING: about 111 cal, 1 g pro, 8 g total fat (2 g sat. fat), 8 g carb, 3 g fibre, 6 mg chol, 258 mg sodium. % RDI: 6% calcium, 5% iron, 46% vit A, 75% vit C, 20% folate.

Indian-Spiced Coleslaw

A nice change from regular coleslaw, this low-fat salad adds a brightly flavoured accent to almost any grilled meat or poultry.

8 cups / 2 L shredded **cabbage**

1 cup / 250 mL finely julienned or shredded **carrots**

½ cup / 125 mL thinly sliced **red onion**

2 **green hot peppers**, seeded and thinly sliced

2 tbsp / 30 mL **peanut** or vegetable **oil**

1 tbsp / 15 mL **black (brown) mustard seeds**

1 tsp / 5 mL **cumin seeds**

½ cup / 125 mL **lemon juice**

2 tbsp / 30 mL **malt vinegar**

½ tsp / 2 mL **salt**

Pinch **granulated sugar**

⅓ cup / 75 mL chopped **fresh coriander**

¼ cup / 60 mL chopped **fresh mint**

● In large bowl, toss together cabbage, carrots, onion and peppers. In small skillet, heat oil over medium heat; fry mustard and cumin seeds until mustard seeds turn grey and begin to pop. Scrape over cabbage mixture; toss well.

● Whisk together lemon juice, vinegar, salt and sugar until sugar is dissolved; toss with cabbage mixture. Let stand for at least 20 minutes or, refrigerated, up to 4 days. Just before serving, toss in coriander and mint.

Makes 8 to 12 servings.

PER EACH OF 12 SERVINGS: about 46 cal, 1 g pro, 3 g total fat (trace sat. fat), 5 g carb, 2 g fibre, 0 mg chol, 114 mg sodium. % RDI: 3% calcium, 6% iron, 13% vit A, 33% vit C, 13% folate.

Left to right: Indian-Spiced
Coleslaw (opposite), Indian
Minced Lamb Kabobs (page 39)

Caribbean Coleslaw

West Indians love coleslaw with their grills; a little pineapple gives it a tropical boost.

8 cups / 2 L shredded **cabbage**

1 tsp / 5 mL **salt**

Half **pineapple**, peeled, cored and cut into thin strips

2 **carrots**, julienned or shredded

1 **sweet red pepper**, thinly sliced

Half **white onion**, thinly sliced

½ cup / 125 mL **mayonnaise**

3 tbsp / 45 mL **cider vinegar** or white vinegar

1 tbsp / 15 mL **granulated sugar**

¼ tsp / 1 mL **black pepper**

Dash **hot pepper sauce**

● Toss cabbage with salt; let stand until soft, 1 to 2 hours. Drain; squeeze out excess liquid. In large bowl, toss together cabbage, pineapple, carrots, pepper and onion.

● Whisk together mayonnaise, vinegar, sugar, pepper and hot pepper sauce; toss with cabbage mixture until coated. Let stand for at least 20 minutes or, refrigerated, up to 4 days. Toss before serving.

Makes 8 to 12 servings.

Photo, page 294

PER EACH OF 12 SERVINGS: about 106 cal, 1 g pro, 8 g total fat (1 g sat. fat), 9 g carb, 2 g fibre, 5 mg chol, 253 mg sodium. % RDI: 3% calcium, 4% iron, 44% vit A, 65% vit C, 14% folate.

Blue Cheese Coleslaw

Blue cheese adds a little mystery to a basic creamy coleslaw.

½ cup / 125 mL light or regular **mayonnaise**

4 tsp / 20 mL **cider vinegar**

2 tsp / 10 mL **granulated sugar**

½ tsp / 2 mL **celery seeds**

½ tsp / 2 mL each **salt** and **black pepper**

8 cups / 2 L shredded **cabbage**

2 cups / 500 mL shredded **carrot**

½ cup / 125 mL thinly sliced **celery**

½ cup / 125 mL thinly sliced **green onions**

¼ cup / 60 mL crumbled **blue cheese**

● In large bowl, whisk together mayonnaise, vinegar, sugar, celery seeds, salt and pepper. Toss gently with cabbage, carrot, celery, green onions and blue cheese until coated. Let stand for at least 20 minutes or, refrigerated, up to 1 day.

Makes 8 to 12 servings.

PER EACH OF 12 SERVINGS: about 65 cal, 1 g pro, 4 g total fat (1 g sat. fat), 7 g carb, 1 g fibre, 5 mg chol, 227 mg sodium. % RDI: 5% calcium, 4% iron, 53% vit A, 30% vit C, 13% folate.

Red Cabbage Coleslaw

10 cups / 2.5 L shredded **red cabbage**

1½ tsp / 7 mL **salt**

Half **red onion**, very thinly sliced

2 large **red apples**, julienned

½ tsp / 2 mL **caraway seeds**

⅓ cup / 75 mL **cider vinegar**

2 tbsp / 30 mL **prepared mustard**

2 tbsp / 30 mL **vegetable oil**

1 tbsp / 15 mL **granulated sugar**

Generous ¼ tsp / 1.5 mL **black pepper**

6 slices crisp cooked **bacon**, crumbled

● Toss cabbage with salt; let stand until soft, about 2 hours. Drain; squeeze out excess moisture. In large bowl, toss together cabbage, onion, apples and caraway seeds.

● Whisk together vinegar, mustard, oil, sugar and pepper; toss with cabbage mixture until coated. Let stand for at least 20 minutes or, refrigerated, up to 4 days. Just before serving, toss in bacon.

Makes 8 servings.

PER SERVING: about 135 cal, 4 g pro, 7 g total fat (1 g sat. fat), 18 g carb, 4 g fibre, 4 mg chol, 345 mg sodium. % RDI: 5% calcium, 6% iron, 1% vit A, 90% vit C, 11% folate.

Creamy Potato Salad

Classic and much-loved by all, creamy potato salad goes with all grilled foods.

2 lb / 1 kg **potatoes**

2 tbsp / 30 mL **cider vinegar**

½ tsp / 2 mL each **salt** and **black pepper**

¾ cup / 175 mL **mayonnaise**

2 tbsp / 30 mL **milk**

1 cup / 250 mL coarsely chopped **celery** (about 2 stalks)

½ cup / 125 mL sliced **green onions** (about 2)

● In pot of boiling salted water, cover and cook unpeeled potatoes until tender, 20 to 30 minutes. Drain; while potatoes are still warm, peel and cut into large bite-size pieces. Pour vinegar over top; sprinkle with salt and pepper. Toss gently until coated. Let cool.

● Whisk mayonnaise with milk. Gently toss together potatoes, mayonnaise mixture, celery and green onions, breaking up potatoes as little as possible. (Refrigerate for up to 1 day.)

Makes 8 servings.

483

PER SERVING: about 459 cal, 4 g pro, 33 g total fat (5 g sat. fat), 39 g carb, 4 g fibre, 16 mg chol, 966 mg sodium, 802 mg potassium. % RDI: 4% calcium, 8% iron, 6% vit A, 43% vit C, 18% folate.

Potato & Leek Salad

Feta cheese and olives are a savoury garnish for this Balkan-style potato salad.

1½ lb / 750 g **new potatoes**

3 **leeks** (white and light green parts only), sliced

1 cup / 250 mL sliced **celery**

¼ cup / 60 mL light or regular **mayonnaise**

2 tbsp / 30 mL chopped **fresh parsley**

2 tbsp / 30 mL **extra-virgin olive oil**

4 tsp / 20 mL **lemon juice**

¼ tsp / 1 mL each **salt** and **black pepper**

¾ cup / 175 mL cubed or crumbled **feta cheese**

½ cup / 125 mL **black olives**

● In pot of boiling salted water, cover and cook unpeeled potatoes until tender, 20 to 30 minutes. With slotted spoon, transfer potatoes to large bowl; let cool. Peel and cut into ¾-inch/2 cm cubes.

● Meanwhile, blanch leeks and celery in same boiling water for 20 seconds; drain. Chill under cold water; drain well. Add to potatoes.

● Whisk together mayonnaise, parsley, oil, lemon juice, salt and pepper; toss with potato mixture until coated. Top with feta cheese and olives.

Makes 8 servings.

485

PER SERVING: about 170 cal, 4 g pro, 9 g total fat (3 g sat. fat), 20 g carb, 3 g fibre, 10 mg chol, 505 mg sodium. % RDI: 8% calcium, 9% iron, 3% vit A, 22% vit C, 12% folate.

Sweet Pea & Potato Salad

*This salad is also delicious made with fresh peas rather than sugar snaps;
use 2 to 3 cups/500 to 750 mL shelled peas.*

4 cups / 1 L **sugar snap peas**

1½ lb / 750 g small **red new potatoes**

1 cup / 250 mL diced **green onions**

½ tsp / 2 mL each **salt** and **black pepper**

2 tbsp / 30 mL **white wine vinegar**

2 tbsp / 30 mL **dry white wine**

2 tsp / 10 mL **Dijon mustard**

1½ cups / 375 mL diced **cucumber**

½ cup / 125 mL diced **radishes**

3 tbsp / 45 mL **vegetable oil**

● Pull strings off both edges of peas. In large saucepan of boiling salted water, blanch until tender-crisp, 2 to 3 minutes. Drain; chill under cold water. Drain; cut each pod crosswise into 3 or 4 pieces. Set aside.

● In pot of boiling salted water, cover and cook unpeeled potatoes until tender, 15 to 20 minutes. While still hot, quarter; transfer to large bowl. Toss in onions, salt and pepper. Mix together vinegar, wine and mustard; toss with potato mixture until coated. Let cool. Toss in peas, cucumber, radishes and oil.

Makes 8 to 10 servings.

PER EACH OF 10 SERVINGS: about 123 cal, 4 g pro, 4 g total fat (1 g sat. fat), 18 g carb, 4 g fibre, 0 mg chol, 363 mg sodium. % RDI: 3% calcium, 10% iron, 5% vit A, 37% vit C, 17% folate.

Roasted Two-Potato Salad

2 lb / 1 kg **yellow-fleshed potatoes**, peeled and cut into 1-inch/2.5 cm cubes

1½ lb / 750 g **sweet potatoes**, peeled and cut into 1-inch/2.5 cm cubes

⅓ cup / 75 mL **extra-virgin olive oil**

½ tsp / 2 mL **dried thyme**

½ tsp / 2 mL each **salt** and **black pepper**

¼ cup / 60 mL chopped **fresh parsley**

2 tbsp / 30 mL **lemon juice**

1 tbsp / 15 mL **Dijon mustard**

½ tsp / 2 mL **hot pepper sauce**

4 **green onions**, sliced

4 slices crisp cooked **bacon** (optional), crumbled

● Toss together potatoes, sweet potatoes, ¼ cup/60 mL of the oil, thyme, salt and pepper.

● Spread potatoes in large roasting pan; roast in 375°F/190°C oven, turning halfway through, until tender and golden, about 40 minutes. Let stand for 5 minutes.

● In large bowl, toss together potatoes, parsley, lemon juice, mustard, hot pepper sauce, green onions, bacon (if using) and remaining oil. (Refrigerate for up to 1 day; bring to room temperature before serving.)

Makes 8 servings.

PER SERVING: about 216 cal, 3 g pro, 9 g total fat (1 g sat. fat), 31 g carb, 4 g fibre, 0 mg chol, 200 mg sodium, 718 mg potassium. % RDI: 4% calcium, 12% iron, 120% vit A, 45% vit C, 9% folate.

Red Potato & Radish Salad

3 lb / 1.5 kg small **red new potatoes**

12 **radishes**, thinly sliced

2 stalks **celery**, sliced

½ cup / 125 mL thinly sliced **red onion**

¼ cup / 60 mL chopped **fresh dill**

½ cup / 125 mL **vegetable oil**

¼ cup / 60 mL **lemon juice**

1 tbsp / 15 mL **grainy** or Dijon **mustard**

½ tsp / 2 mL each **salt** and **black pepper**

¼ tsp / 1 mL **granulated sugar**

● In pot of boiling salted water, cover and cook unpeeled potatoes until tender, about 15 minutes. Drain; let cool.

● Meanwhile, in large bowl, toss together radishes, celery, onion and dill. Cut potatoes into quarters; add to bowl.

● Whisk together oil, lemon juice, mustard, salt, pepper and sugar; gently toss with potato mixture until coated.

Makes 8 servings.

PER SERVING: about 276 cal, 3 g pro, 14 g total fat (1 g sat. fat), 37 g carb, 3 g fibre, 0 mg chol, 524 mg sodium. % RDI: 2% calcium, 10% iron, 40% vit C, 11% folate.

Warm Potato Salad

3 lb / 1.5 kg **potatoes**, peeled and cut into large chunks

⅓ cup / 75 mL **extra-virgin olive oil**

3 tbsp / 45 mL **wine vinegar**

1½ tbsp / 22 mL **Dijon** or brown **mustard**

¾ tsp / 4 mL **salt**

Generous ¼ tsp / 1.5 mL **black pepper**

¾ cup / 175 mL diced **celery**

¾ cup / 175 mL diced **sweet green pepper**

3 tbsp / 45 mL chopped **fresh basil** or parsley

● In pot of boiling salted water, cover and cook potatoes until tender, 10 to 15 minutes. Drain; transfer to large bowl. Let cool for 10 minutes.

● Whisk together oil, vinegar, mustard, salt and pepper; pour over potatoes. Gently toss in celery, green pepper and basil until coated.

Makes 8 servings.

PER SERVING: about 205 cal, 2 g pro, 11 g total fat (2 g sat. fat), 27 g carb, 2 g fibre, 0 mg chol, 563 mg sodium. % RDI: 2% calcium, 5% iron, 2% vit A, 38% vit C, 8% folate.

Baby Potato Salad with Salsa Verde

Using small waxy new potatoes means you can leave them whole for a pretty presentation.

3 lb / 1.5 kg small **new potatoes**

1 cup / 250 mL chopped **fresh parsley**

2 **anchovy fillets**, rinsed (or 1 tsp/5 mL anchovy paste)

¼ cup / 60 mL **extra-virgin olive oil**

4 tsp / 20 mL **wine vinegar**

1 tbsp / 15 mL rinsed drained **capers**

1 clove **garlic**, minced

1 tsp / 5 mL **salt**

½ tsp / 2 mL **black pepper**

● In pot of boiling salted water, cover and cook unpeeled potatoes until tender, about 15 minutes. Drain; place in large bowl. Let cool enough to handle; while still warm, peel potatoes.

● Meanwhile, in blender or food processor, purée together parsley, anchovies, ⅓ cup/75 mL water, oil, vinegar, capers, garlic, salt and pepper; gently toss with warm potatoes until coated. Let cool to room temperature. (Refrigerate for up to 1 day; bring to room temperature before serving.)

Makes 8 servings.

491

PER SERVING: about 176 cal, 3 g pro, 7 g total fat (1 g sat. fat), 27 g carb, 2 g fibre, 0 mg chol, 618 mg sodium. % RDI: 2% calcium, 7% iron, 4% vit A, 40% vit C, 12% folate.

Garlic Bread on the Grill

For a quick, easy and universally popular side, try this buttery garlic bread.

1 **baguette**

⅓ cup / 75 mL **butter**

3 cloves **garlic**, pressed or minced

Pinch **salt**

Scant ½ tsp / 2 mL **smoked** or sweet **paprika**

● Slice baguette crosswise almost but not all the way through at ¾-inch/2 cm intervals; place on heavy-duty foil.

● In small saucepan over low heat, melt butter; stir in garlic and salt. Simmer very gently until garlic infuses butter (do not let garlic brown), 3 to 4 minutes. Stir in paprika; cook for 30 seconds. Brush over both sides of each slice of baguette; brush any remaining butter mixture over top. Seal foil to make packet.

● Grill, covered, over high heat, turning once, until crusty and hot, 10 to 12 minutes.

Makes 6 to 8 servings.

PER EACH OF 8 SERVINGS: about 166 cal, 3 g pro, 9 g total fat (5 g sat. fat), 19 g carb, 1 g fibre, 20 mg chol, 268 mg sodium, 49 mg potassium. % RDI: 3% calcium, 6% iron, 7% vit A, 12% folate.

Baked Beans

Traditional baked beans are a wonderfully satisfying side for any barbecue.

494

1 lb / 500 g **dried navy beans**
(2⅓ cups/575 mL)

⅔ cup / 150 mL **bottled strained tomatoes**

⅓ cup / 75 mL packed **brown sugar**

⅓ cup / 75 mL **cooking** or blackstrap **molasses**

1 tbsp / 15 mL **sodium-reduced soy sauce**

1 tsp / 5 mL **dry mustard**

½ tsp / 2 mL **salt**

1 **sweet onion**, chopped

6 oz / 175 g **slab bacon** or **salt pork**
(or a combination), diced

● Soak beans overnight in enough water to cover well (for quicker prep, see Tip, below); drain. In large saucepan, combine beans with enough water to cover by 2 inches/5 cm; bring to boil. Reduce heat, cover and simmer until tender, 30 to 40 minutes.

● Reserving 2 cups/500 mL of the cooking liquid, drain beans. Place beans and reserved liquid in bean pot or 12- to 16-cup/3 to 4 L casserole; mix in tomatoes, brown sugar, molasses, soy sauce, mustard and salt. Stir in onion, and bacon and/or salt pork.

● Cover and bake in 300°F/150°C oven for 2 hours. Uncover and bake until sauce is thickened and coats beans, about 2 hours.

Makes 8 servings.

If you don't have time to soak your dried beans overnight, boil them for 5 minutes. Remove from heat; cover and let stand for 1 hour. Drain. Continue with recipe.

PER SERVING: about 403 cal, 14 g pro, 13 g total fat (6 g sat. fat), 59 g carb, 10 g fibre, 16 mg chol, 462 mg sodium, 812 mg potassium. % RDI: 13% calcium, 34% iron, 5% vit C, 89% folate.

Spanish-Style Baked Beans

1 lb / 500 g **dried navy** or other white **beans** (2⅓ cups/575 mL)

1 can (28 oz/796 mL) **tomatoes**, drained

1 **bay leaf**

1 sprig **fresh rosemary**

2½ tsp / 12 mL **smoked paprika**

1½ tsp / 7 mL **salt**

⅓ cup / 75 mL **extra-virgin olive oil**

3 cups / 750 mL chopped **Spanish** or sweet **onion**

3 cloves **garlic**, minced

• Soak beans overnight in enough water to cover well (for quicker prep, see Tip, opposite); drain. In large saucepan, combine beans with enough water to cover by 2 inches/5 cm; bring to boil. Reduce heat, cover and simmer until tender, 30 to 40 minutes.

• Reserving 2 cups/500 mL of the cooking liquid, drain beans. Place beans and 1⅓ cups/325 mL of the reserved cooking liquid in large bowl. Seed tomatoes; chop coarsely. Add to bowl along with bay leaf, rosemary, paprika and salt; mix well.

• In skillet, heat oil over medium heat; sauté onion and garlic until onion is soft, about 10 minutes. Scrape into bowl; mix well.

• Scrape bean mixture into bean pot or 12- to 16-cup/ 3 to 4 L casserole. Cover and bake in 400°F/200°C oven until simmering, about 25 minutes. Reduce heat to 300°F/150°C; bake for 3 hours, checking occasionally and adding a little more of the reserved cooking liquid if beans are dry.

Makes 8 servings.

PER SERVING: about 308 cal, 14 g pro, 11 g total fat (2 g sat. fat), 44 g carb, 11 g fibre, 0 mg chol, 525 mg sodium. % RDI: 12% calcium, 29% iron, 8% vit A, 23% vit C, 90% folate.

Spanish-Style Baked Beans
(page 495)

Frijoles Borrachos

These Northern Mexican–style "drunken beans" are also popular in Tex-Mex cooking. Use any leftover beans for refried beans or as a topping for tostadas or nacho chips.

1 lb / 500 g **dried pinto beans** (2⅓ cups/575 mL)

2 **white onions**, chopped

6 slices **bacon**, chopped

4 **jalapeño peppers**, finely chopped

5 cloves **garlic**, minced

1 cup / 250 mL chopped **fresh coriander**

1 cup / 250 mL chopped canned or peeled ripe **tomatoes**

2 cups / 500 mL **dark beer**

1¼ tsp / 6 mL **salt**

● Soak beans overnight in enough water to cover well (for quicker prep, see Tip, page 494); drain. In large saucepan, combine beans, 10 cups/2.5 L water and half of the onions; bring to boil. Reduce heat and simmer over medium heat, adding more water if necessary to keep beans covered, until beans are tender, 1 to 1½ hours.

● In large saucepan or Dutch oven, fry bacon over medium-high heat until fat begins to render, 2 to 3 minutes. Add remaining onions; fry until lightly browned, about 8 minutes. Add jalapeños, garlic and coriander; fry for 2 minutes. Add tomatoes, beans with cooking liquid, beer and salt. Bring to boil; reduce heat to medium and simmer, stirring occasionally, until thickened, 45 to 60 minutes.

Makes 8 servings.

PER SERVING: about 321 cal, 15 g pro, 9 g total fat (5 g sat. fat), 47 g carb, 14 g fibre, 12 mg chol, 522 mg sodium. % RDI: 9% calcium, 32% iron, 3% vit A, 23% vit C, 119% folate.

Roasted Tomato & Olive Pasta Salad

All the sauce ingredients roast together, then get mixed with cooked pasta and mint for an eminently simple and exceptionally tasty Italian-style pasta salad.

4 cups / 1 L **cherry tomatoes**, halved

1 cup / 250 mL halved **green olives**

¾ cup / 175 mL grated **Romano** or other pecorino **cheese**, or Parmesan cheese

⅓ cup / 75 mL **extra-virgin olive oil**

3 cloves **garlic**, sliced

1 tsp / 5 mL **dried oregano**

½ tsp / 2 mL **salt**

½ tsp / 2 mL (approx) **hot pepper flakes**

1 lb / 500 g **short pasta**, such as penne

¼ cup / 60 mL shredded **fresh mint**

2 tbsp / 30 mL **lemon juice**

● In glass baking dish, mix together tomatoes, olives, cheese, oil, garlic, oregano, salt and hot pepper flakes to taste. Bake in 425°F/220°C oven, stirring once after 15 minutes, until tomatoes are roasted and saucy, about 30 minutes.

● Meanwhile, in large pot of boiling salted water, cook pasta according to package instructions until tender but firm. Rinse under cold water; drain. Toss with tomato mixture; let cool. Toss in mint and lemon juice.

Makes 8 servings.

PER SERVING: about 388 cal, 13 g pro, 16 g total fat (4 g sat. fat), 48 g carb, 5 g fibre, 15 mg chol, 738 mg sodium. % RDI: 18% calcium, 21% iron, 10% vit A, 19% vit C, 59% folate.

Cool Wild Rice & Mushrooms

Canada's central northern lakes and marshes provide us with the finest fragrant long-grain wild rice, our country's only native cereal.

2 cups / 500 mL **wild rice**

4 cups / 1 L chopped **mushrooms** (about 10 oz/300 g)

1 small **onion**, chopped

1 stalk **celery**, diced

¼ cup / 60 mL **olive** or vegetable **oil**

3 tbsp / 45 mL **sherry vinegar** or wine vinegar

1 tsp / 5 mL **salt**

¼ tsp / 1 mL **black pepper**

¼ cup / 60 mL chopped **fresh parsley**

¼ cup / 60 mL chopped **fresh chives**

● In saucepan, bring 8 cups/2 L water to boil; add rice and boil gently until tender and many of the grains have burst open, 30 to 40 minutes. Drain; place in large bowl.

● In separate saucepan, stir together mushrooms, onion, celery, oil, vinegar, salt and pepper; bring to boil. Reduce heat to medium; simmer until mushrooms are tender, about 5 minutes. Toss with rice until coated; let cool. Toss in parsley and chives.

Makes 8 servings.

PER SERVING: about 216 cal, 6 g pro, 8 g total fat (2 g sat. fat), 33 g carb, 3 g fibre, 0 mg chol, 297 mg sodium. % RDI: 2% calcium, 11% iron, 3% vit A, 8% vit C, 21% folate.

Baby Bow Tie & Walnut Pasta Salad

Farfalline are tiny bow ties; you can also use orzo (rice-shaped), stelline (stars) or ditalini (tubes). Toasting the pasta adds a nuttiness that complements the walnuts.

1½ cups / 375 mL **farfalline pasta**

1 tbsp / 15 mL **vegetable oil**

Half **onion**, chopped

¾ cup / 175 mL chopped **walnuts**

½ cup / 125 mL chopped **sweet green pepper**

2 tbsp / 30 mL **extra-virgin olive oil**

1 tbsp / 15 mL **lemon juice**

¼ tsp / 1 mL **salt**

Pinch **black pepper**

2 tbsp / 30 mL chopped **fresh coriander**

1 cup / 250 mL **cherry tomatoes**, quartered, or chopped tomatoes

Fresh coriander sprigs

● In dry skillet over medium heat, toast ½ cup/125 mL of the pasta, stirring often, until light brown, about 5 minutes. In saucepan of boiling salted water, cook toasted and remaining pasta according to package instructions until tender but firm. Drain; rinse under cold water. Drain well; place in large bowl.

● In nonstick skillet, heat vegetable oil over medium heat; fry onion, stirring often, just until slightly softened, about 2 minutes. Add walnuts; fry for 2 minutes. Stir in green pepper; fry for 1 minute. Add to pasta; let cool.

● Whisk together olive oil, lemon juice, salt and pepper; add to pasta mixture along with chopped coriander. Toss until coated. Before serving, garnish with tomatoes and coriander sprigs.

Makes 8 servings.

PER SERVING: about 243 cal, 6 g pro, 13 g total fat (1 g sat. fat), 27 g carb, 2 g fibre, 0 mg chol, 157 mg sodium. % RDI: 2% calcium, 8% iron, 2% vit A, 15% vit C, 25% folate.

Tomato & Spelt Salad

Spelt (also known by the Italian name farro*) is a flavourful ancient type of wheat. Look for it in health and bulk food stores. If you wish, substitute whole barley, wheat berries or wild rice for the spelt.*

2 cups / 500 mL **whole spelt**

4 **green onions**, thinly sliced

4 cups / 1 L diced ripe **tomatoes**

4 cups / 1 L loosely packed torn **arugula leaves** or baby arugula

½ cup / 125 mL loosely packed **fresh mint leaves**, torn

2½ tbsp / 37 mL **red wine vinegar**

1 clove **garlic**, minced

1 tsp / 5 mL **salt**

½ tsp / 2 mL **black pepper**

⅓ cup / 75 mL **extra-virgin olive oil**

1½ cups / 375 mL cubed **feta cheese** (optional)

● Rinse spelt in a few changes of cold water. In pot of boiling salted water, cook spelt until tender but firm, 30 to 35 minutes. Drain; chill under cold water. Drain well. In large bowl, combine spelt, green onions, tomatoes, arugula and mint.

● Whisk together vinegar, garlic, salt and pepper; gradually whisk in oil. Toss with spelt mixture until coated; top with feta cheese (if using).

Makes 8 servings.

PER SERVING: about 296 cal, 8 g pro, 12 g total fat (2 g sat. fat), 46 g carb, 10 g fibre, 0 mg chol, 434 mg sodium. % RDI: 15% calcium, 31% iron, 20% vit A, 73% vit C, 61% folate.

Greek Village Salad

This is the true Greek salad, literally called "peasant salad" in Greek, that is served throughout the country. It's a natural fit with almost any barbecued dish. Chop the vegetables fairly coarsely for an authentic result.

Half **red onion**, chopped

1 **English cucumber** or 2 peeled field cucumbers

2 **tomatoes**, chopped

1 **sweet green pepper**, chopped

½ cup / 125 mL **Kalamata olives**

¼ cup / 60 mL **extra-virgin olive oil**

2 tbsp / 30 mL **lemon juice**

2 tbsp / 30 mL **red wine vinegar**

1½ tsp / 7 mL **dried (preferably Greek) oregano**

¼ tsp / 1 mL **salt**

Pinch **black pepper**

5 oz / 150 g **feta cheese**, cubed

● Soak onion in cold water for 20 minutes. Drain; place in serving bowl. Cut cucumber lengthwise into quarters (if using field cucumbers, seed) and chop; add to bowl along with tomatoes, pepper and olives.

● Whisk together olive oil, lemon juice, vinegar, oregano, salt and pepper; toss with cucumber mixture until coated. Top with feta cheese.

Makes 6 to 8 servings.

505

PER EACH OF 8 SERVINGS: about 162 cal, 4 g pro, 14 g total fat (4 g sat. fat), 7 g carb, 2 g fibre, 16 mg chol, 559 mg sodium. % RDI: 10% calcium, 5% iron, 6% vit A, 40% vit C, 11% folate.

Three-Bean Salad

1½ cups / 375 mL **green** and/or **yellow beans**, cut into 2-inch/5 cm pieces

¼ cup / 60 mL **extra-virgin olive oil**

¼ cup / 60 mL **wine vinegar**

1 clove **garlic**, minced

2 tbsp / 30 mL chopped **fresh parsley**

½ tsp / 2 mL **granulated sugar**

½ tsp / 2 mL **salt**

¼ tsp / 1 mL **dried oregano**

¼ tsp / 1 mL **black pepper**

1 can (19 oz/540 mL) **chickpeas**, drained and rinsed

1 can (19 oz/540 mL) **kidney beans**, drained and rinsed

2 **green onions**, thinly sliced

● In saucepan of boiling salted water, blanch green beans until tender-crisp, 3 to 5 minutes. Drain; chill under cold water. Drain well; pat dry on kitchen towel.

● In large bowl, whisk together oil, vinegar, garlic, parsley, sugar, salt, oregano and pepper. Toss with green beans, chickpeas, kidney beans and green onions until coated. (Refrigerate for up to 8 hours.)

Makes 8 servings.

PER SERVING: about 197 cal, 7 g pro, 8 g total fat (1 g sat. fat), 26 g carb, 8 g fibre, 0 mg chol, 505 mg sodium. % RDI: 4% calcium, 13% iron, 2% vit A, 10% vit C, 33% folate.

Marinated Yellow Beans & Mushrooms

You can use green beans instead of yellow ones, but they will not keep their colour as well if you make the salad ahead of time.

1¼ lb / 625 g **yellow wax beans**

2 tbsp / 30 mL **olive oil**

2 cups / 500 mL sliced **cremini** or white **mushrooms**

½ tsp / 2 mL **salt**

3 cloves **garlic**, thinly sliced

1 tsp / 5 mL **dried oregano**

1 tbsp / 15 mL **balsamic vinegar**

1 tbsp / 15 mL **white wine vinegar**

Pinch **black pepper**

● In large pot of boiling salted water, cook beans until tender-crisp and colour deepens, about 3 minutes. Drain; chill under cold water. Drain; place in bowl.

● In large skillet, heat oil over medium-high heat; fry mushrooms and salt until softened and no liquid remains, about 3 minutes. Stir in garlic and oregano; cook for 1 minute. Remove from heat. Stir in balsamic and white wine vinegars, and pepper; toss with beans until coated. Marinate for at least 3 hours or, refrigerated, up to 1 day.

Makes 8 servings.

PER SERVING: about 59 cal, 2 g pro, 4 g total fat (1 g sat. fat), 6 g carb, 2 g fibre, 0 mg chol, 146 mg sodium. % RDI: 3% calcium, 8% iron, 4% vit A, 12% vit C, 10% folate.

Filipino Cucumber Salad

In the Philippines, palm sap vinegar or cane vinegar would replace the rice vinegar in this refreshing salad.

2 **English cucumbers**, or 3 or 4 peeled field cucumbers, thinly sliced

Half **sweet red pepper**, thinly sliced

Half **hot pepper**, thinly sliced

¾ cup / 175 mL **rice vinegar**

½ cup / 125 mL thinly sliced **red onion**

¼ cup / 60 mL **lime juice**

2 tbsp / 30 mL **fish sauce**

2 tbsp / 30 mL finely chopped **fresh coriander** or mint, or 2 tbsp/30 mL each coriander and mint

3 cloves **garlic**, minced

1 tbsp / 15 mL **granulated sugar**

1½ tsp / 7 mL **salt**

¼ tsp / 1 mL **black pepper**

● Toss together cucumbers, sweet and hot peppers, vinegar, onion, lime juice, fish sauce, coriander, garlic, sugar, salt and pepper. Let stand, stirring occasionally, for at least 2 hours or, refrigerated, up to 3 days.

Makes 8 servings.

PER SERVING: about 32 cal, 1 g pro, 0 g total fat (0 g sat. fat), 8 g carb, 1 g fibre, 0 mg chol, 781 mg sodium. % RDI: 2% calcium, 3% iron, 6% vit A, 42% vit C, 9% folate.

Creamy Cucumber Salad

Salting the cucumber helps draw out liquid from it so the dressing doesn't get watered down and the flesh stays crunchy. Soaking the onion makes it milder and crisper.

2 **English cucumbers**, or 3 or 4 peeled field cucumbers, thinly sliced

1 tsp / 5 mL **salt**

1 small **red onion**, thinly sliced

⅔ cup / 150 mL **sour cream**

⅓ cup / 75 mL **lemon juice**

2 tbsp / 30 mL chopped **fresh dill** or mint (or 1 tsp/5 mL dried dillweed or mint)

1½ tsp / 7 mL **granulated sugar**

● Toss cucumber with salt; let stand until soft, about 30 minutes. Handful by handful, squeeze out excess moisture; transfer to large bowl. Meanwhile, in bowl of cold water, soak onion for 30 minutes; drain and add to cucumber.

● Whisk together sour cream, lemon juice, dill and sugar; toss with cucumber mixture until coated. Let stand for 15 minutes before serving.

Makes 8 servings.

PER SERVING: about 64 cal, 1 g pro, 3 g total fat (2 g sat. fat), 8 g carb, 1 g fibre, 9 mg chol, 15 mg sodium. % RDI: 4% calcium, 3% iron, 12% vit A, 17% vit C, 9% folate.

Spiced Carrot Salad

1 lb / 500 g **carrots**

2 cloves **garlic**, pressed or minced

1 **hot pepper**, seeded and cut into fine threads

¼ cup / 60 mL **cider vinegar**

2 tbsp / 30 mL **vegetable oil**

1 tbsp / 15 mL toasted **sesame seeds** (optional)

1½ tsp / 7 mL **granulated sugar**

1 tsp / 5 mL **paprika**

1 tsp / 5 mL **sesame oil**

1 tsp / 5 mL **light soy sauce**

¾ tsp / 4 mL **ground coriander**

½ tsp / 2 mL **salt**

• With vegetable peeler or mandoline, cut carrots lengthwise into thin ribbons. In bowl, toss together carrots, garlic, hot pepper, vinegar, vegetable oil, sesame seeds (if using), sugar, paprika, sesame oil, soy sauce, coriander and salt. Refrigerate, stirring once or twice, for at least 2 hours or up to 3 days.

Makes 8 servings.

513

PER SERVING: about 60 cal, 1 g pro, 4 g total fat (1 g sat. fat), 6 g carb, 2 g fibre, 0 mg chol, 196 mg sodium. % RDI: 2% calcium, 2% iron, 53% vit A, 6% vit C, 5% folate.

Sauces, Marinades & Rubs

Fresh Tomato Salsa

This instant salsa can be enjoyed with fish, burgers or pork chops.

1⅓ cups / 325 mL diced **plum tomatoes**

¼ cup / 60 mL chopped **fresh coriander**

1 tbsp / 15 mL minced seeded **jalapeño pepper**

1 **green onion**, finely chopped

1 tbsp / 15 mL **lime juice** or wine vinegar

1 tbsp / 15 mL **olive** or vegetable **oil**

¼ tsp / 1 mL each **salt** and **black pepper**

- In bowl, stir together tomatoes, coriander, jalapeño, green onion, lime juice, oil, salt and pepper.

Makes about 1½ cups/375 mL.

517

PER ¼ CUP/60 mL: about 27 cal, trace pro, 2 g total fat (trace sat. fat), 2 g carb, trace fibre, 0 mg chol, 99 mg sodium. % RDI: 1% iron, 3% vit A, 13% vit C, 2% folate.

Clockwise from top: Yellow Tomato Salsa (opposite), Grilled Hot Pepper Salsa (page 524), Avocado & Green Tomato Salsa (page 523), Tomato Mint Salsa (page 520)

Yellow Tomato Salsa

Try this attractive, mild-flavoured salsa over grilled chicken or fish.
Of course, it's also good with chips.

1 **sweet yellow pepper**

1 lb / 500 g **yellow tomatoes** (about 5), peeled and seeded

2 cloves **garlic**, minced

¼ cup / 60 mL loosely packed **fresh basil** or coriander

3 tbsp / 45 mL **extra-virgin olive oil**

1 tsp / 5 mL grated **lemon rind**

2 tbsp / 30 mL **lemon juice**

¾ tsp / 4 mL **salt**

¼ tsp / 1 mL **hot pepper sauce**

● Grill pepper over high heat, turning often, until charred all over. Place in bowl; cover and let cool. Peel, seed and coarsely chop. In food processor, pulse together grilled pepper, tomatoes, garlic, basil, oil, lemon rind and juice, salt and hot pepper sauce until chunky.

Makes about 2 cups/500 mL.

To peel and seed tomatoes: Plunge tomatoes into boiling water; boil until skins loosen, about 15 seconds. Drain; chill in cold water and drain again. Peel, core and halve tomatoes. Using small spoon or fingers, scoop or squeeze out seeds.

PER 2 TBSP/30 mL: about 29 cal, 0 g pro, 3 g total fat (0 g sat. fat), 2 g carb, 0 g fibre, 0 mg chol, 114 mg sodium. % RDI: 1% calcium, 1% iron, 23% vit C, 4% folate.

Tomato Mint Salsa

A perfect salsa for grilled lamb, this one also goes well with pork, chicken, liver and seafood.

1 cup / 250 mL chopped **sweet onion**

⅔ cup / 150 mL loosely packed **fresh mint**

⅓ cup / 75 mL chopped **fresh coriander**

2 **jalapeño peppers**, seeded and chopped

1 tsp / 5 mL grated **fresh ginger**

½ tsp / 2 mL **salt**

¼ tsp / 1 mL **black pepper**

Pinch **granulated sugar**

1½ cups / 375 mL coarsely chopped seeded peeled **tomatoes** (see Tip, page 519)

1 tbsp / 15 mL **lemon juice**

● In food processor, pulse together onion, mint, coriander, jalapeños, ginger, salt, pepper and sugar. Pulse in tomatoes and lemon juice until finely chopped.

Makes 2⅓ cups/575 mL.

Photo, page 518

PER 2 TBSP/30 ML: about 7 cal, 0 g pro, 0 g total fat (0 g sat. fat), 2 g carb, 0 g fibre, 0 mg chol, 64 mg sodium. % RDI: 1% calcium, 2% iron, 3% vit A, 10% vit C, 3% folate.

Cherry Tomato Salsa

Instead of the usual condiments, try this fresh-tasting salsa on your next burger, such as our Classy Beef Burgers (page 85). It's great on steak, too.

2 cups / 500 mL halved **cherry tomatoes**

2 tbsp / 30 mL **extra-virgin olive oil**

½ tsp / 2 mL **salt**

3 tbsp / 45 mL finely diced **dill pickle**

2 tbsp / 30 mL minced **red onion**

1 clove **garlic**, minced

2 tsp / 10 mL **red wine vinegar**

½ tsp / 2 mL **dried oregano**

¼ tsp / 1 mL **hot pepper flakes**

¼ tsp / 1 mL **black pepper**

● Spread tomatoes on rimmed baking sheet; drizzle with oil and sprinkle with salt. Roast in 450°F/230°C oven until slightly charred, 15 to 20 minutes. Transfer tomatoes and juices to bowl; mix in pickle, onion, garlic, vinegar, oregano, hot pepper flakes and pepper.

Makes 1 cup/250 mL.

Photo, page 84

PER 2 TBSP/30 mL: about 38 cal, 0 g pro, 4 g total fat (0 g sat. fat), 2 g carb, 0 g fibre, 0 mg chol, 188 mg sodium. % RDI: 1% iron, 2% vit A, 10% vit C, 2% folate.

Smoky Corn Avocado Salsa

4 **cobs of corn**, husked

Half **sweet red pepper**, diced

¼ cup / 60 mL diced **red onion**

2 tbsp / 30 mL chopped **fresh coriander**

1 tbsp / 15 mL **olive** or vegetable **oil**

1 tbsp / 15 mL **lime juice**

¼ tsp / 1 mL each **salt** and **black pepper**

1 **avocado**, peeled, pitted and diced

● Grill corn, covered, on greased grill over medium-high heat, turning occasionally, until grill-marked and tender, 15 to 20 minutes. Let cool; cut off kernels. Toss together corn, red pepper, onion, coriander, oil, lime juice, salt and pepper.

● Gently stir avocado into corn mixture just before serving.

Makes about 4 cups/1 L.

PER 1 TBSP/15 ML: about 15 cal, trace pro, 1 g total fat (trace sat. fat), 2 g carb, trace fibre, 0 mg chol, 11 mg sodium. % RDI: 1% iron, 1% vit A, 3% vit C, 2% folate.

Avocado &
Green Tomato Salsa

When there are lots of green tomatoes available, make this unique and tangy salsa —
it's a natural partner to grilled chicken or shrimp, and nachos, too.

1 **green tomato**, diced

⅓ cup / 75 mL finely diced **sweet onion**

2 tbsp / 30 mL minced **fresh coriander**

1 tbsp / 15 mL **lime juice**

1 **hot pepper**, seeded and minced

½ tsp / 2 mL **salt**

1 **avocado**, peeled, pitted and diced

● Mix together tomato, onion, coriander, lime juice, hot pepper and salt.

● Gently stir in avocado just before serving.

Makes about 2⅓ cups/575 mL.

Photo, page 518

523

PER 2 TBSP/30 mL: about 20 cal, 0 g pro, 2 g total fat (0 g sat. fat), 1 g carb, 1 g fibre, 0 mg chol, 64 mg sodium. % RDI: 1% iron, 2% vit A, 7% vit C, 4% folate.

Grilled Hot Pepper Salsa

This is an all-purpose salsa that's good for fish, red and white meats, and even just for dipping with your favourite chips or crudités. Adjust the heat by using the number of hot peppers that suits your palate. You can use finger chilies or jalapeño peppers.

1 head **garlic** (unpeeled)

4 **shallots** (unpeeled)

2 **tomatoes**

2 to 4 **hot peppers**

2 **anchovies**, minced (or ½ tsp/2 mL salt)

¼ cup / 60 mL minced **fresh coriander** or parsley

2 tbsp / 30 mL **extra-virgin olive oil**

4 tsp / 20 mL **lemon juice**

½ tsp / 2 mL **black pepper**

¼ tsp / 1 mL **salt**

● Grill garlic and shallots over medium-high heat, turning occasionally, until charred all over and tender inside, 20 to 25 minutes. Grill tomatoes and peppers, turning, until charred all over, 4 or 5 minutes; let cool.

● Squeeze garlic cloves into bowl; mash with fork. Peel shallots, tomatoes and peppers; chop finely and add to bowl. Mix in anchovies, coriander, oil, lemon juice, pepper and salt.

Makes 1⅓ cups/325 mL.

Photo, page 518

PER 2 TBSP/30 mL: about 38 cal, 1 g pro, 3 g total fat (0 g sat. fat), 3 g carb, 0 g fibre, 1 mg chol, 85 mg sodium. % RDI: 1% calcium, 2% iron, 4% vit A, 17% vit C, 2% folate.

Why pick up store-bought barbecue sauce when you can just as easily make your own at home? Here are three that you can brush onto food while grilling or use as dips for grilled meats and vegetables.

- Use ½ to 1 cup/125 to 250 mL to taste for 4 servings (1 lb/ 500 g boneless or 2 lb/1 kg bone-in) meat. (Refrigerate in airtight container for up to 1 month.)

Tomato Barbecue Sauce Base

- In saucepan, combine 1⅔ cups/400 mL **bottled strained tomatoes**; 1 can (5½ oz/156 mL) **tomato paste**; 1 **onion**, chopped; 3 cloves **garlic**, minced; ½ cup/ 125 mL **cider vinegar**; ⅓ cup/75 mL packed **brown sugar**; ½ tsp/2 mL each **salt** and **black pepper;** and **ingredients** from one of the variations that follow.
- Bring sauce to boil. Reduce heat to low and simmer, stirring occasionally, until thickened and reduced by one-third, about 1 hour. Let cool. Pour into blender; purée until smooth.

Makes about 2 cups/500 mL.

Fruity Barbecue Sauce

- ⅓ cup/75 mL each chopped pitted **dates** and **raisins**; ¼ cup/60 mL **Dijon mustard**; 2 tbsp/30 mL **fancy molasses**; 2 tsp/10 mL **Worcestershire sauce**; 1 tsp/5 mL grated **orange rind**; and ¼ tsp/1 mL **ground cloves**

East-West Barbecue Sauce

- ¼ cup/60 mL **liquid honey**; 2 tbsp/30 mL **soy sauce**; 1 tbsp/ 15 mL minced **fresh ginger**; and 1 tbsp/15 mL **sesame oil**

Maple Whiskey Barbecue Sauce

- ⅓ cup/75 mL **whiskey**; ¼ cup/60 mL each **maple syrup** and **grainy mustard**; 1 tsp/5 mL **Worcestershire sauce**; and pinch **cinnamon**

Spice Mixes & Rubs

- In small bowl, stir together ingredients for desired spice mix (right).

Makes about ⅓ cup/75 mL.

- For every 4 servings (1 lb/ 500 g boneless or 1½ lb/750 g bone-in meat or poultry, or 1 lb/500 g fish), rub with 2 tbsp/ 30 mL spice mix. Refrigerate for at least 4 hours or up to 1 day.

- For shorter prep time, mix together 4 tsp/20 mL spice mix, 1 tbsp/15 mL vegetable oil and 1 clove garlic, minced, for every 4 servings; brush over food. Let stand for 5 minutes or, refrigerated, up to 8 hours.

- Store dry spice mixes in airtight containers for up to 6 months.

Chili Spice Mix

- 3 tbsp/45 mL **chili powder**; 2 tbsp/30 mL each **paprika** and packed **brown sugar**; 1 tbsp/15 mL **ground cumin**; 1 tsp/5 mL **garlic powder**; and ½ tsp/2 mL each **salt** and **black pepper**

Bombay Spice Mix

- 3 tbsp/45 mL each **ground coriander** and **turmeric**; 2 tsp/10 mL **ground cumin**; 1 tsp/5 mL **salt**; and ½ tsp/ 2 mL each **cayenne pepper** and **dry mustard**

Mediterranean Spice Mix

- 3 tbsp/45 mL **dried rosemary**; 2 tbsp/30 mL each **ground cumin** and **coriander**; 1 tbsp/15 mL **dried oregano**; 2 tsp/10 mL **cinnamon**; and ½ tsp/2 mL **salt**

Cajun Spice Mix

- 3 tbsp/45 mL **dried thyme**; 2 tbsp/30 mL each **paprika** and packed **brown sugar**; 1 tbsp/ 15 mL each **ground cumin**, **dry mustard** and **hot pepper flakes**; and 1 tsp/5 mL **salt**

Mole Spice Rub

- ¼ cup/60 mL **chili powder**; 2 tbsp/30 mL **cocoa powder**; ¾ tsp/4 mL each **salt** and **black pepper**; and ½ tsp/2 mL each **cayenne pepper**, **cinnamon** and **ground allspice**

Middle East Spice Rub

- 3 tbsp/45 mL **sesame seeds**; 2 tbsp/30 mL each grated **lemon rind** and **ground coriander**; 1 tbsp/15 mL **ground cumin**; ¾ tsp/ 4 mL **salt**; and ½ tsp/2 mL **cayenne pepper**

Top to bottom: Chili Spice Mix,
Bombay Spice Mix, Cajun Spice
Mix, Mediterranean Spice Mix

Smoky Barbecue Sauce

This all-purpose barbecue sauce makes a tasty glaze not only on ribs but also on chicken, steak, pork chops and burgers.

1 tbsp / 15 mL **vegetable oil**

1 small **onion**, finely chopped

2 cloves **garlic**, minced

1 tbsp / 15 mL **smoked paprika** (or sweet paprika and ¼ tsp/1 mL liquid smoke)

1 tsp / 5 mL **dry mustard**

¼ tsp / 1 mL **salt**

1 cup / 250 mL **ketchup** or tomato-based chili sauce

½ cup / 125 mL **red wine** or water

2 tbsp / 30 mL packed **brown sugar**

2 tbsp / 30 mL **cider vinegar**

● In saucepan, heat oil over medium heat; fry onion, garlic, paprika, mustard and salt, stirring occasionally, until onion is softened, about 3 minutes.

● Add ketchup, wine, sugar and vinegar; bring to boil. Reduce heat and simmer until thick as ketchup, about 20 minutes.

● In food processor or blender, purée until smooth. (Refrigerate for up to 1 month.)

Makes about 1½ cups/375 mL.

PER 1 TBSP/15 ML: about 26 cal, trace pro, 1 g total fat (0 g sat. fat), 5 g carb, trace fibre, 0 mg chol, 159 mg sodium. % RDI: 1% iron, 3% vit A, 3% vit C, 1% folate.

Hot & Spicy Chipotle Barbecue Sauce

1 tbsp / 15 mL **vegetable oil**

1 **shallot** or small onion, chopped

2 cloves **garlic**, minced

1 tbsp / 15 mL **paprika**

1 tbsp / 15 mL **chili powder**

¼ tsp / 1 mL each **salt** and **black pepper**

1 can (19 oz/540 mL) **tomatoes**

1 can (5½ oz/156 mL) **tomato paste**

⅔ cup / 150 mL **white vinegar**

⅓ cup / 75 mL packed **brown sugar**

2 tbsp / 30 mL **Dijon mustard**

4 **canned chipotle peppers**

2 tbsp / 30 mL **adobo sauce** from canned chipotles

½ cup / 125 mL **fancy molasses**

● In saucepan, heat oil over medium heat; fry shallot, garlic, paprika, chili powder, salt and pepper, stirring occasionally, until shallot is softened, about 5 minutes.

● Add tomatoes, tomato paste, vinegar, sugar and mustard; bring to boil. Reduce heat and simmer, stirring occasionally, until thickened and reduced by about one-third, about 1 hour. Let cool.

● In blender, combine sauce, chipotles and adobo sauce; purée until smooth. Blend in molasses. (Refrigerate for up to 1 month.)

Makes 4 cups/1 L.

PER 1 TBSP/15 mL: about 20 cal, trace pro, trace total fat (0 g sat. fat), 4 g carb, trace fibre, 0 mg chol, 38 mg sodium, 94 mg potassium. % RDI: 1% calcium, 3% iron, 2% vit A, 3% vit C.

Molasses Barbecue Sauce

Add a luscious touch to all your barbecue favourites: during the last few minutes of cooking, brush this sauce over chops, burgers, ribs, poultry or fish.

1 cup / 250 mL **beef stock**

1 cup / 250 mL **tomato-based chili sauce**

½ cup / 125 mL **fancy molasses**

2 tbsp / 30 mL **vinegar**

4 tsp / 20 mL **prepared mustard**

2 tsp / 10 mL **chili powder**

2 tsp / 10 mL **Worcestershire sauce**

1 tsp / 5 mL **celery seeds**, crushed

1 tsp / 5 mL **ground cumin**

½ tsp / 2 mL each **salt** and **black pepper**

● In large saucepan, whisk together stock, chili sauce, molasses, vinegar, mustard, chili powder, Worcestershire sauce, celery seeds, cumin, salt, pepper and ⅔ cup/150 mL water; bring to boil. Reduce heat and simmer until reduced to about 2 cups/500 mL, about 20 minutes. (Refrigerate for up to 2 weeks.)

Makes 2 cups/500 mL.

PER 1 TBSP/15 mL: about 26 cal, 1 g pro, trace total fat (trace sat. fat), 6 g carb, 1 g fibre, 0 mg chol, 190 mg sodium. % RDI: 2% calcium, 3% iron, 1% vit A, 3% vit C, 1% folate.

Grilling Sauces

Teriyaki Sauce

● In saucepan, stir ¾ cup/
175 mL **chicken** or vegetable
stock; ½ cup/125 mL **soy sauce**;
⅓ cup/75 mL **mirin**; 2 tbsp/
30 mL **granulated sugar**; and
3 slices **fresh ginger**. Bring to
boil. Reduce heat; simmer until
reduced by half, 20 minutes.
Whisk 1 tbsp/15 mL **cold water**
with 1 tbsp/15 mL **cornstarch**;
add to pan and cook, stirring,
until thick enough to coat back
of spoon, about 2 minutes.
Discard ginger. Let cool.
(Refrigerate for up to 2 weeks.)

Makes 1 cup/250 mL.

Argentine Chimichurri Verde

● In food processor, finely
chop together 2 cups/500 mL
packed **fresh parsley leaves**;
⅓ cup/75 mL **olive oil**; ¼ cup/
60 mL packed **fresh oregano
leaves**; ¼ cup/60 mL **wine
vinegar**; 1 **jalapeño pepper**,
seeded; 4 cloves **garlic**; and
½ tsp/2 mL each **salt** and
black pepper. (Refrigerate for
up to 1 day.)

Makes 1 cup/250 mL.

Chimichurri Rojo

● Whisk together ½ cup/
125 mL **sherry vinegar** or red
wine vinegar; ¼ cup/60 mL
extra-virgin olive oil; 3 tbsp/
45 mL minced **fresh parsley**;
3 cloves **garlic**, minced; 4 tsp/
20 mL **paprika**; 1 tsp/5 mL
ground cumin; ½ tsp/2 mL
each **salt** and **black pepper**;
and ¼ to ½ tsp/1 to 2 mL
cayenne pepper. (Refrigerate
for up to 1 week.)

Makes about ¾ cup/175 mL.

Korean Barbecue Sauce

● In saucepan, combine 4 cups/
1 L **soy sauce**; 2 cups/500 mL
granulated sugar; 1 cup/
250 mL **sake** or Chinese rice
wine (or combination of both);
1 cup/250 mL **mirin**; 2 **apples**
(unpeeled and uncored), thinly
sliced; 2 **onions**, thinly sliced;
10 cloves **garlic**, thinly sliced;
2-inch/5 cm piece **fresh ginger**,
thinly sliced; and 30 **black
peppercorns**. Bring to boil,
stirring until sugar is dissolved.
Reduce heat to medium-low
and simmer until mixture is
reduced by about one-third,
40 to 50 minutes. Cover; let
stand overnight at room
temperature. Strain.
(Refrigerate for up to 6 months.)

Makes about 6 cups/1.5 L.

Clockwise from top: Tikka
Marinade, Adobo Marinade,
Red Wine Marinade,
Honey Garlic Marinade

Marinades

Marinades usually contain an acidic ingredient, such as vinegar, that helps tenderize as it flavours.

- In small bowl, stir together ingredients for desired marinade (right).

Makes ⅓ to ½ cup/ 75 to 125 mL.

- Use ⅓ cup/75 mL marinade for every 4 servings (1 lb/500 g boneless or 1½ lb/750 g bone-in meat or poultry, or 1 lb/500 g fish).

- Cover and marinate meat or poultry, refrigerated, for at least 4 or up to 12 hours; marinate fish for no more than 30 minutes.

Tikka Marinade

- ⅓ cup/75 mL **plain yogurt**; 1 tbsp/15 mL minced **fresh ginger**; 2 cloves **garlic**, minced; half **jalapeño pepper**, minced; 1 tsp/5 mL each **ground cumin** and **cardamom**; and ½ tsp/ 2 mL each **salt** and **nutmeg**

Honey Garlic Marinade

- ¼ cup/60 mL **cider vinegar**; 2 tbsp/30 mL **liquid honey**; 1 tbsp/15 mL **soy sauce**; and 4 cloves **garlic**, minced

Red Wine Marinade

- ¼ cup/60 mL **dry red wine**; 2 tbsp/30 mL **red wine vinegar**; 1 tbsp/15 mL **olive oil**; 2 cloves **garlic**, minced; 1 **bay leaf**; and ¼ tsp/1 mL each **salt** and **black pepper**

Adobo Marinade

- ¼ cup/60 mL **orange juice**; 1 tsp/5 mL grated **lime rind**; 2 tbsp/30 mL **lime juice**; 2 cloves **garlic**, minced; 1 **jalapeño pepper**, minced; 2 tsp/10 mL **dried oregano**; and 1 tsp/5 mL **ground cumin**

Moroccan Marinade

- 3 tbsp/45 mL **olive oil**; 2 tbsp/ 30 mL each **ground cumin**, **paprika**, **granulated sugar** and **lemon juice**; 2 cloves **garlic**, minced; ½ tsp/2 mL each **salt** and **black pepper**; and ¼ tsp/ 1 mL **cinnamon**

Apple Thyme Marinade

- 2 tbsp/30 mL each **cider vinegar**, **apple juice** and **vegetable oil**; 1 tbsp/15 mL chopped **fresh thyme** (or ½ tsp/2 mL dried); 1 tbsp/ 15 mL **grainy** or Dijon **mustard**; and ½ tsp/2 mL each **salt** and **black pepper**

Lemon Herb Marinade

- ¼ cup/60 mL each **lemon juice** and **extra-virgin olive oil**; 2 tbsp/30 mL chopped **fresh rosemary**, oregano or parsley; 1 tbsp/15 mL **sherry vinegar** or wine vinegar; 2 cloves **garlic**, minced; ½ tsp/2 mL each **salt** and **black pepper**; four 2-inch/ 5 cm strips **lemon rind**; and 2 **bay leaves**, quartered

Flavoured Butters

Flavoured butters are an inspired addition to barbecued meat, poultry or fish. Place round on each portion of hot food to serve, or melt and brush on food while grilling.

- In small bowl, stir ½ cup/ 125 mL **salted butter**, softened, with **ingredients** for desired flavour (right) until smooth. Spoon onto plastic wrap; shape into log and wrap tightly. Or pack into small serving bowl, smoothing top. Refrigerate until firm. (Refrigerate for up to 2 weeks.)

- Slice log into ½-inch/1 cm thick rounds or serve directly from bowl.

Makes about ½ cup/125 mL.

Herb Butter

(all-purpose)
- ¼ cup/60 mL minced **fresh parsley**; 2 tbsp/30 mL minced **fresh chives** or green onion; 1 tbsp/15 mL minced **fresh basil**, dill, tarragon and/or chervil; and pinch **black pepper**

Lime & Chili Butter

(all-purpose)
- 2 tbsp/30 mL minced **fresh coriander**; 1 tsp/5 mL grated **lime rind**; 2 tbsp/30 mL **lime juice**; and 1 tsp/5 mL **chili powder**

Horseradish Butter

(for beef)
- 4 tsp/20 mL **prepared horseradish** and ¼ tsp/1 mL **black pepper**

Anchovy Butter

(for beef, lamb or fish)
- ¼ cup/60 mL minced **green onions**; 4 **anchovy fillets**, drained and mashed (or 2 tsp/ 10 mL anchovy paste); 1 clove **garlic**, minced; and ½ tsp/ 2 mL grated **lemon rind**

Shallot Peppercorn Butter

(for beef and lamb)
- 1 **shallot**, minced, cooked in 1 tsp/5 mL **butter** until softened (let cool); 2 tbsp/ 30 mL **pink peppercorns**, crushed; and 1 tbsp/15 mL **dry red wine**

Caviar Butter

(for fish and steaks)
- 2 tbsp/30 mL each minced **fresh chives** and **red lumpfish** or other **caviar**; and 1 clove **garlic**, minced

Olive Sage Butter

(for poultry, fish and pork)
- ¼ cup/60 mL chopped **Niçoise** or oil-cured **olives**; 2 tbsp/30 mL minced **fresh sage**; and pinch **dried oregano**

Caper Mustard Butter

(for fish)
- 2 tbsp/30 mL each drained **capers** and **Dijon mustard**; ½ tsp/2 mL grated **lemon rind**; and 1 tsp/5 mL **lemon juice**

Clockwise from top: Herb Butter, Lime & Chili Butter, Caviar Butter, Shallot Peppercorn Butter

Acknowledgments

The Canadian Living Barbecue Collection is the collective work of many people. Essential to this project was the initial work of reviewing years and years of magazine recipes with a highly critical eye, then organizing potential recipes to form the backbone of this book. I have Christine Picheca to thank for completing this arduous task. She also helped fill the gaps with a goodly contribution of new recipes and offered advice throughout the development process. She also did an admirable job as food stylist for some of the new photography.

Camilo Costales, a master chef new but not unfamiliar to The Canadian Living Test Kitchen, made a tremendous effort in developing new material, as well as codeveloping recipes with me. He helped enormously in the development and styling of the new photography. Much of the book's authentic Asian flair can be attributed to him directly or to his influence.

This book is as much a thrilling visual experience as it is a useful, creative collection of recipes. For this I give special thanks to the art team of Michael Erb and Chris Bond. Many of the images in this book were created especially for this project, and photographer Felix Wedgwood was exceptional in his contribution. He was always gracious in facing our (sometimes excessive) demands.

If it were left up to me alone, this massive collection of recipes would be an inpenetrable jumble of inconsistencies; the fact that it is not is entirely because of the dedicated and tireless editing of Tina Anson Mine. I appreciated her good humour under duress and her ability to stir me into action. Furthermore, she was the perfect partner to help streamline our recipe language to create the no-nonsense, clear, clean style that appears on these pages.

The devil is in the details, so thanks also go to our copy editor, Rehana Begg, and indexer, Gillian Watts, who polished every phrase until it shone and made it easy for you to find what you're looking for in these pages. I am also grateful to Pat Flynn, who was most efficient and helpful in many of the nitty-gritty aspects of recovering recipes and photography from our archives.

I must also heartily thank the past and present Canadian Living Test Kitchen for their recipes and advice, as well as *Canadian Living* food editor Gabrielle Bright, who always lends me an ear. Our book publisher, Jean Paré, and editor-in-chief, Susan Antonacci, also get a tip of the hat for the encouragement they offered. Thanks also to our magazine publisher, Lynn Chambers.

Last, I am grateful to the staff of *Homemakers* magazine for their patience in putting up with my sometimes overstretched workload. I also must thank them for allowing me to include many of my recipes from *Homemakers*' pages in this volume.

– *Andrew Chase, editor*

Index

545

549

Credits

Recipes

All recipes were developed by Andrew Chase and the Canadian Living and Homemakers test kitchens, except the following.

Camilo Costales: pages 15, 60, 61, 68, 69, 187, 216, 217, 220, 234, 248, 256, 257, 361, 370, 382, 384, 390, 391, 397, 411, 419, 420, 421 and 426.

Christine Picheca: pages 40, 86, 137, 139, 147, 190, 200, 244, 247, 253, 267, 345, 348, 379, 415, 422, 427, 456, 458, 459 and 483.

Photography

Michael Alberstat: pages 125, 148, 174, 258, 403, 484, 502, 508, 527, 532 and 535.

Christopher Campbell: page 269.

Yvonne Duivenvoorden: pages 16, 20, 23, 29, 37, 46, 52, 67, 72, 89, 96, 113, 158, 162, 171, 188, 195, 203, 209, 222, 227, 240, 264, 270, 275, 284, 288, 304, 307, 318, 332, 338, 357, 369, 388, 399, 400, 413, 432, 443, 446, 449, 450, 453, 464, 469 and 507.

Geoff George: page 42.

Donna Griffith: pages 476 and 489.

Kevin Hewitt: pages 26, 32, 49, 55, 59, 64, 84, 92, 118, 121, 161, 177, 192, 198, 206, 212, 291, 294, 312, 315, 335, 365, 366, 372, 375, 404, 435, 479, 496, 499, 511 and 518.

Jim Norton: pages 131 and 380.

Edward Pond: pages 103, 126, 251, 354 and 393.

David Scott: pages 154, 181 and 299.

Seed9: page 5 (portrait).

Michael Visser: page 407.

Felix Wedgwood: pages 12, 77, 80, 106, 134, 141, 144, 150, 167, 168, 185, 186, 191, 218, 230, 235, 236, 246, 276, 280, 322, 326, 331, 343, 344, 349, 350, 360, 385, 396, 410, 417, 418, 423, 424, 428, 457, 460, 472, 492 and 514.

Food styling

Julie Aldis: pages 26, 29, 52, 59, 84, 148, 161, 174, 192, 209, 222, 240, 258, 264, 270, 304, 312, 315, 338, 407, 450, 453, 476, 489, 499 and 518.

Donna Bartolini: pages 16, 20, 23, 46, 125 and 203.

Andrew Chase: pages 12, 80, 131, 134, 141, 144, 150, 218, 235, 236, 276, 280, 322, 331, 343, 350, 360, 380, 385, 388, 399, 400, 403, 413, 417, 418, 428, 460, 472, 484, 492, 502, 508, 514, 527, 532 and 535.

Sue Henderson: page 446.

Christine Picheca: pages 106, 191, 230, 246, 326, 344, 349, 396, 410, 423, 424 and 457.

Lucie Richard: pages 37, 89, 154, 284, 307, 357, 369, 432 and 449.

Claire Stubbs: pages 67, 72, 96, 103, 113, 126, 158, 162, 171, 188, 195, 227, 251, 275, 288, 318, 332, 354, 393, 443, 464, 469 and 507.

Rosemarie Superville: pages 181 and 299.

Nicole Young: pages 32, 42, 49, 55, 64, 77, 92, 118, 121, 167, 168, 185, 186, 198, 206, 212, 291, 294, 335, 365, 366, 372, 375, 404, 435, 479, 496 and 511.

Prop styling

Laura Branson: pages 26, 32, 49, 55, 59, 64, 77, 121, 167, 168, 185, 186, 198, 206, 212, 291, 294, 312, 315, 335, 365, 404, 479, 499 and 511.

Catherine Doherty: pages 12, 42, 80, 96, 106, 131, 134, 141, 144, 150, 188, 191, 218, 230, 235, 236, 246, 276, 280, 288, 322, 326, 331, 343, 344, 349, 350, 360, 380, 385, 396, 410, 417, 418, 423, 424, 428, 457, 460, 464, 469, 472, 492 and 514.

Marc-Philippe Gagné: pages 195 and 318.

Jane Hardin: page 435.

Maggi Jones: pages 158, 240 and 304.

Lara McGraw: pages 125, 258, 527, 532 and 535.

Oksana Slavutych: pages 16, 20, 23, 29, 37, 46, 52, 67, 72, 89, 103, 113, 126, 148, 154, 162, 171, 174, 181, 203, 209, 222, 227, 251, 264, 270, 275, 284, 299, 307, 332, 338, 354, 357, 369, 388, 399, 400, 403, 407, 413, 432, 443, 446, 449, 450, 453, 476, 484, 489, 502, 507 and 508.

Carolyn Souch/Judy Inc.: pages 84, 118, 161, 366, 496 and 518.

Genevieve Wiseman: pages 92, 192 and 393.

Madeleine Wong: pages 372 and 375.